Presented to

Bob Ahrens

on the occasion of
Darling and Hodgson's
fiftieth anniversary

John Hodgson

4. Dec. 1984

A Foundation for the Future

A Foundation for the Future

The Darling and Hodgson Story 1934–1984

Rosemary Hayward and Nancy Stratten

Jonathan Ball Publishers
Johannesburg

All rights reserved. No part of this publication may be
reproduced or transmitted, in any form or by any means,
without permission.

© D&H Industrial Holdings Limited

First published in 1984 by
Jonathan Ball Publishers
P O Box 548
Bergvlei
2012 Johannesburg

ISBN 0 86850 097 6

Design, typesetting and reproduction by Book Productions, Johannesburg
Colour separations by Camsep, Johannesburg
Printed by National Book Printers, Goodwood, Cape

Contents

Foreword	1
D&H Today	4
1890–1934 Bill Hodgson	16
1934–1947 The Early Years	21
1947–1959 A Firm Foundation	29
1959–1963 Development of the Company	48
1963–1973 Years of Growth and Diversification	61
1973–1983 Strength as a Public Company	75
The Construction Story	86
A G Burton	90
Savage and Lovemore	96
Underwater Construction	120
Monahan and Frost	124
Fowler Holdings	127
R H Morris	133
Combrink Construction	137
Stevenson Construction	141
Roadmix	145
Group Five Engineering	147
The Services Story	156
Tanker Services	163
W J Bulk Transport	180
D&H Automotive Services	187
D&H Semi-Bulk	189
Waste-tech	191
The Materials Story	204
Ready Mixed Concrete	211
Mazista	233
Paul's Sand	236
Natal Quarries	242
Embecon	246
D&H Ash Resources	253
The Engineering Story	256
The Coal Story	266
The People Story	274
The Finance Story	283
D&H at a glance	292
Long Service Employees	294
Acknowledgements	297
Selected Index	299

William Alfred Hodgson.

Foreword

> Far better it is to dare mighty things,
> to win glorious triumphs even though
> chequered with failure,
> than to take rank with those poor spirits
> who never enjoy much nor suffer much,
> because they live in the grey twilight
> that knows not victory nor defeat.
>
> *Theodore Roosevelt*

It was thoughts such as these that must have been uppermost in the mind of William Alfred Hodgson during the year of 1934.

From a very small beginning D&H today stands on the threshold of its fiftieth anniversary, and I look back with great humility upon all that has made it possible. At times the future looked bleak and the way through seemed impossible to find, but the sheer joy of tasks successfully completed, ideas tried, tested and succeeding, challenges accepted and turned to good account all combined to provide the momentum so essential to our growth. It was probably in my first years at D&H that I realised that business was fun and through all the succeeding years I have tried to keep it that way and also to make it enjoyable for all those with whom I have worked. When it ceases to be fun then I believe will be the time to move out.

Above everything else it has been the people that have made it all possible, caused it to happen and made it fun. Their loyalty, commitment and dedication through the bad and difficult times as well as the good have enabled the Group to reach the privileged position it enjoys today amongst the major industrial companies in South Africa.

This book has been written to place on record most of the important dates and key developments that have taken place in the growth of the company, but most important of all it has been written around the people, all the people who are and will continue to be D&H. I would like to feel that it represents a tribute to everyone, both past and present members of D&H, who made it all happen.

This book would not be complete without my taking the opportunity to pay special tribute to the five people without whom all this could not have been achieved.

My father, who in 1924 emigrated to South Africa, and in 1934 gave up the opportunity of security and comfort in a good position in a large industrial company for the challenge and unknown problems of establishing a one-man contracting business. The story of what he did is told in the following pages but his most valuable contribution, because of its less tangible nature, will be less apparent. This was the exceptionally high standard he set for himself, and for all who worked for him, in his approach to every aspect of the conduct of his business affairs. It was that imprint that he placed on the business to be an example to all who worked for him and for those who were to follow.

Brian Malcomson, who in 1953 became associated with D&H and shortly thereafter gave up the accounting practice he had just launched, a decision he took with the calm and balanced judgement that has been the hallmark of every decision he has taken for the company since. He has always acted as the counterpoise, taking the contra point of view. It was so easy for the rest of us to get carried away on numerous occasions by our own ideas, but Brian has always been there to point out the pitfalls and possible adverse implications of our plans, fighting tenaciously for his point of view and, at times I am sure,

John Brailsford Hodgson.

feeling very lonely. However, none of us could have wished for greater support and assistance once the decision had been taken to proceed, and the same vigour and tenacity was applied to overcome the very difficulties he had so carefully pointed out to us. His prudent and conscientious care of our finances and subtle contribution to all our decisions have been at the very heart of our development.

Jack Plane, who in 1959 took over as chairman, giving unstintingly of his time, acting as navigator, taking us all through the white waters of the sixties. At a time when all that my father had done could so easily have been lost, he tested our ideas and challenged our actions. He taught us all the value of that essential business element – profit, and that without the establishment of capital there would be no way to finance and put into effect all the opportunities we wished to pursue. He was ever present but never intrusive; he taught us that business was a great game and that first prizes went only to the winners.

Andrew Savage, who retired from the board in 1984 after thirty years, starting with the formation and then the nurturing of Savage and Lovemore to full potential. This story is also well told in the following pages but his intangible and vital contribution must be recorded. His ability to cut incisively through any situation to the very heart of the subject was probably his greatest contribution. It was against the background of his clear direction that we were able to build a major construction company, maintaining the culture so vital to its long-term success alongside more commercial and industrial related activities. Behind his quiet and unassuming exterior we had a very strong and determined colleague with the ability to focus well into the future.

My wife Ruth, who in 1949 took the brave decision to marry a contractor. Only people who are close to or are in construction will fully appreciate the magnitude of those sacrifices made by women who marry men in this industry. These were made by my wife not only willingly but in a manner that made it possible for me to commit myself totally and absolutely to the task ahead. Half-hearted or qualified support, or domestic worries would have destroyed the threads of confidence that wove the very powerful human fabric that was to become the strength that is central to all who have worked at D&H. Her unquestioning support, loyalty, interest and direct involvement in all appropriate aspects of company life have set an example to us all in our dedicated pursuit of what is best for the company.

The original family business is today a 'family of families' in that so many of the additions to D&H over the years were also family businesses and through the very nature of our management philosophy have continued to retain their original attributes. The strength of our group has been the ability to add to and combine those family strengths. This may change, however, but I strongly believe that, just as my father left his stamp on our Group, this underlying culture will remain and be of tremendous value in the future.

The writing of this book involved extensive research as no records or archives had been maintained, particularly in the earlier years. This all had to be done if we were ever going to consider the publication of the D&H story. It is here that I would like to pay further tribute because if it were not for the tenacity of one person this book would not have been written – Rosemary Hayward, my daughter, who had been proposing for a number of years that the story of D&H was worth telling. I gave her an immediate rebuff on the grounds that it would interest very few people. She continued to raise the subject on every appropriate occasion. It was not until 1981 that I asked her to carry out research preparatory to deciding whether a book should or even could be written.

Extensive research was carried out by Rosemary, helped by Cathy Bath, in order to ensure that the history of the company would be correctly portrayed. From the outset I was most anxious that if the story were ever to be written it had to be a people story. The book is therefore based largely on interviews with a wide range of people both inside and outside the Group, after which the story gradually began to fall into place. We are all deeply indebted to those who gave generously of their time to discuss the past, dig into their bottom drawers for photographs, old letterheads and all the many things that have been found to be so valuable in assembling the past. Clearly it was not possible to interview everyone so there will undoubtedly be some gaps in the story. The authors are very conscious of this and apologise for any omissions, but as this book sets out to pay tribute to everyone who has contributed to D&H, whether they are directly mentioned or not, I am sure this will not detract from either its intention or impact.

All the notes and interviews were transcribed, validated and correlated, then coupled to intensive research, providing the base from which to consider a publication. Professional advice was sought and after careful consideration the decision taken to proceed. I believe this publication is another example of the dedication that epitomizes so much of what makes up D&H. I believe also that it does justice to all who have in some way or another made their contribution to a company of which we can all be very proud.

Our thanks go to Rosemary who without question is responsible for this book being published, to Cathy who encouraged her during the first difficult year of interviews and research when there was very little enthusiasm for their project, and to Nancy Stratten who has co-authored the book, accepting responsibility for the script. I will miss our regular sessions with these young ladies, the debating of the format of the book, arguing the facts as we felt we knew them against the research they had done, and in the process learning a great deal about D&H and its people which I never knew and being reminded of many incidents I had long since forgotten. The book provides a fascinating backdrop to the achievements of D&H in this its jubilee year.

J B Hodgson
February 1984

D&H Today

D&H burst into 1984 on a triumphant note with an impact greater than ever experienced in its fifty year history and a stimulating atmosphere of excitement and lively anticipation throughout the Group.

At the end of 1983 D&H's construction division was reversed into Group Five Engineering to create in a single move one of the giants of the South African construction industry, and at the beginning of 1984 the Group entered the cement industry through the acquisition of a 30% stake in Blue Circle Cement. Both transactions were highly significant and strategic moves for the Group and involved dealings on the Johannesburg Stock Exchange which hit the headlines in the press and boosted D&H's public image.

The merger of D&H's interests with Group Five was the culmination of a year-long deepening relationship between the two companies which had started when D&H rescued Group Five from an aggressive takeover bid in late 1982. Both companies are major forces in the construction industry and together they create a powerhouse with an exceptionally strong management team and a comprehensive range of construction activities throughout South Africa. Group Five confidently forecasts a 1984 turnover nearly double that of 1983 with good profits in spite of the state of the South African economy, and through the consolidation of all construction interests in the company D&H anticipates that it will make a significant contribution to Group profits.

The Blue Circle deal was a thrilling step into a completely new field of operations and marked D&H's breakthrough into cement manufacture, which it had been trying to achieve for several years. Although D&H Materials had consolidated its strong position in the aggregate, sand and ready-mixed concrete fields, there was a missing link in the Group's spread of construction materials. D&H saw Blue Circle as an ideal way to close the gap and Blue Circle recognized the reciprocal value for itself through participation in the D&H materials division. Both companies appreciated that the linking of aggregate, sand and concrete with cement has very important implications for their long-term strategy. D&H had spent many long hours discussing ways and means and had initiated negotiations with Blue Circle several times, only to meet with opposition somewhere along the line. Their patience and determination eventually paid dividends and in 1984 everything fell into place and the deal went through with approval and encouragement on all sides. After a short period of speculation about a mystery buyer for Blue Circle shares on the stock market, which tantalized the public's interest, it was announced in mid February that D&H had acquired a significant stake in Blue Circle and at the same time had sold to them 30% of its materials division. This was subsequently increased to 45%.

This transaction is undoubtedly one of the most important ever undertaken by D&H to date because of its many far-reaching implications. The cement industry is closely allied to all construction operations, in particular ready-mixed concrete, and the deal puts the Group in a very powerful position.

D&H also extended their transport facilities in early 1984 with the purchase of two timber-hauling companies, Garocade and Harvester Timbers, in the Highflats/Ixopo region of Natal. These give the services division a strategic base among the vast forestry plantations of the province, creating the potential for moving large quantities of timber from forest to mill.

D&H's philosophy has always been to seize opportunities and then think about financing them and 1984 was no different from other years in this respect. As it was not a good time for borrowing money because of a prohibitive interest rate, D&H turned once more

The D&H board, 1984. Left to right: Hugh Smith, Ted Pavitt, David Bath, Aubrey Welsford, John Hodgson, Tom de Beer, Phil Erasmus, Alex Combrink, Brian Malcomson. Inset: George Clark.

to the stock market for mobilization of funds and in May proceeded with a rights issue, confident that the public would again demonstrate its faith in the Group. The amount of R42 million raised by the issue provided funds for the 1984 acquisitions and also improved the Group's debt equity ratio.

Today D&H is a major industrial holding company in partnership with one of South Africa's major mining houses, Gencor. It stands proudly as a group of locally-based companies which contribute significantly to South Africa's high industrial and economic standards and have participated prominently in the country's development. There has been unprecedented progress and industrial growth in South Africa in the last decade, largely stimulated by the soaring value of gold bringing increased revenue which led to a surge in the country's economic growth. Increasing dependence upon South Africa's own resources led to greater exploitation of local potential. The world energy crisis provoked the establishment of Sasol II and III to provide South Africa with more oil from coal, further hydroelectric power schemes and the first nuclear power-station in this country at Koeberg. More coal fields were opened, and local production of iron and steel was boosted by the construction of a third Iscor at Newcastle. New harbours were built to facilitate export at Richards Bay and Saldanha Bay, and airports were enlarged and improved. Dams were built to conserve South Africa's precious water resources. Factories and office blocks were built. Infrastructure throughout the country was expanded and improved each year. All this development has made South Africa the most industrialized and sophisticated country in Africa and D&H's participation has led to steady growth of the Group's component companies.

These companies are controlled by men of high integrity with intense loyalty to D&H and to the chairman and chief executive, John Hodgson, whose father began the business fifty years ago. John has always encouraged a high degree of independence within the Group, consciously developing a 'family of families' which has created a unique culture and a strong spirit to succeed.

D&H today is a giant organization employing over thirty thousand people, with assets of over R400 million and an annual turnover expected to reach a billion rand in 1984. Its key objectives are to achieve a minimum 30% return both on capital employed and on shareholders' funds. It also aims to achieve an annual compound growth in earnings per share of not less than 25% and a minimum increase in dividends of 20% per annum. These will be achieved by organic growth and by acquisition, and the Group will not be bound by a geographic commitment.

The activities of the Group are co-ordinated from the corporate head office at Hyde Park, Sandton, and are guided by its board of directors which has a strong core of D&H executives supported by the most senior executives at Gencor. At the end of 1983 David Bath and Phil Erasmus joined the board, bringing to it direct representation of the materials and services divisions, and contributing a wider spread of Group executives than before. In 1984 Andrew Savage retired from the board and Tom de Beer, an executive director of Gencor, joined it, adding further strength to the Gencor participation.

The strength of the Group lies in its diversity of operations which have all developed from its historical construction interests. D&H entered its jubilee year as a leader in the fields of construction, materials, transport and waste management, with participation in coal. Through these activities the Group in one way or another touches the life of virtually everyone in South Africa.

CONSTRUCTION is the major contributor to Group profits. Operating under the name of Group Five Engineering, the Group offers a wide range of construction skills

BP head office in Parktown, Johannesburg – Combrink Construction.

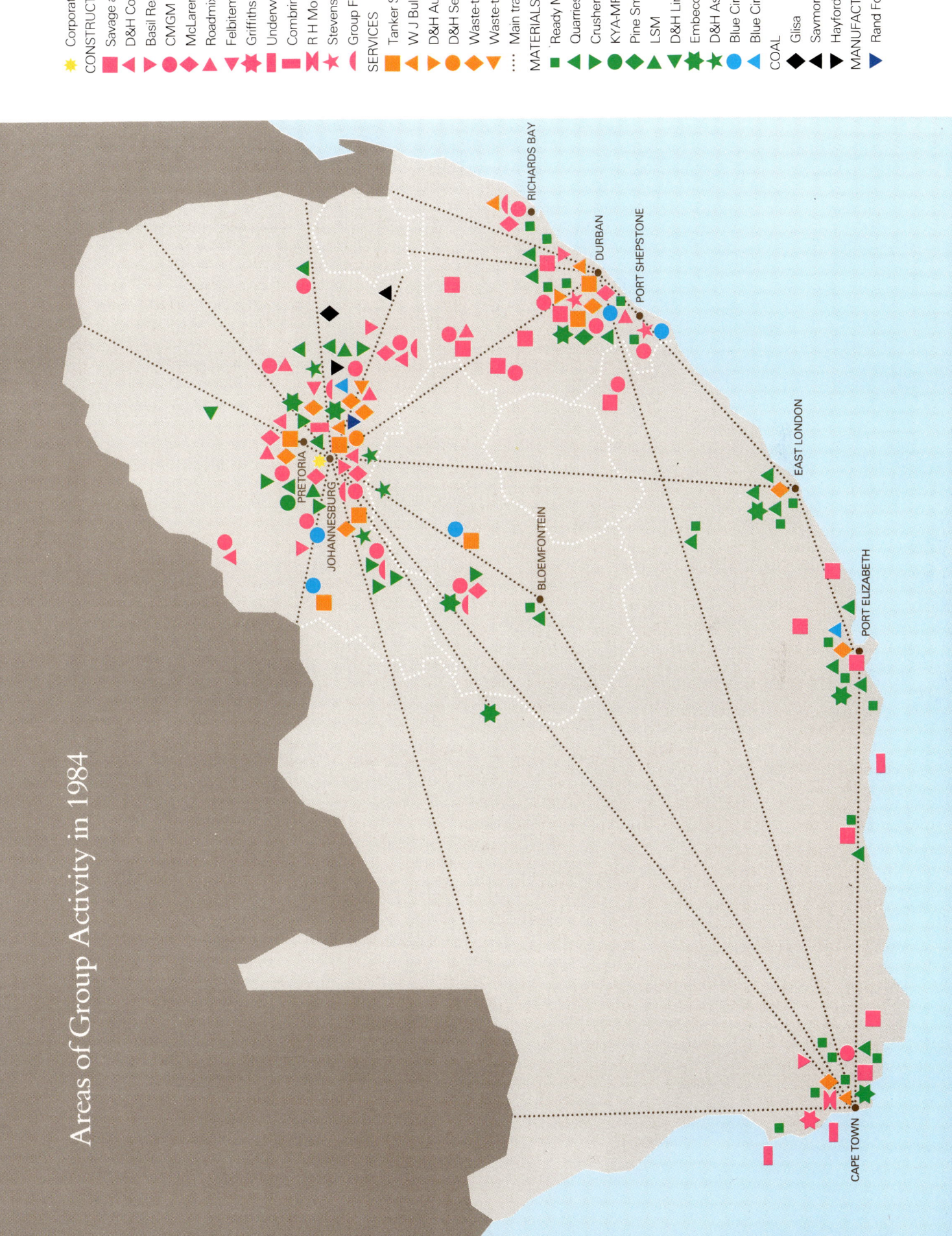
Areas of Group Activity in 1984

Above
Uncle Charlie's interchange, Johannesburg – Basil Read.

Right
Escom head office in Bellville, Cape Town – R H Morris.

Above
The Devland bottling plant and warehouse (Amalgamated Beverage Industries) – Group Five Projects, Basil Read and Normac Building Systems.

Left
Coal silos at Tutuka power-station – CMGM Glybeton.

and services throughout the country with substantial resources and a strong back-up. It is able to undertake major turnkey projects as well as contracts in road building and earthworks, civil engineering and mass concrete, road surfacing and rehabilitation, commercial and industrial building, marine engineering, piling and specialized foundations. These activities are carried out under well known names which include Savage and Lovemore, D&H Construction, Basil Read, CMGM, Roadmix, Felbitem, Griffiths and Inglis, Combrink Construction, R H Morris, Stevenson Construction, Underwater Construction and McLaren and Eger.

Group Five Projects undertakes multi-disciplinary engineering in the fields of mechanical, electrical, and process engineering. This section is seen as an area with great potential for development and expansion.

D&H is a leading supplier of MATERIALS to the construction industry and maintains a strong strategic position with sand and stone reserves for years to come. It has national

Blasting at Clairwood Quarry.

coverage in many fields: ready-mixed concrete, cement, aggregate, sand, mortars, plasters, screeds, gunnites, concrete floor hardners, non-shrink grouts, concrete admixtures and pulverized fuel ash. Operations are carried out under the names of Ready Mixed Concrete, D&H Quarries – with numerous quarries throughout South Africa – Blue Circle, Pine Smyth, Kya-MP, LSM, Embecon, D&H Ash and D&H Lime.

Ready Mixed Concrete on site in Durban.

Mobile crusher at Cookeshaft.

Above
Rooikraal Quarry.

Right
Number 6 kiln at Blue Circle's Lichtenburg plant.

The SERVICES division comprises transport and waste management operations throughout South Africa. A fleet of more than three hundred and fifty tankers transports a wide range of bulk products, including cement and lime, chemicals, fuels and oils, sugar and molasses, timber, casava and sugar-cane, wine, alcohol and beverages, cyanide, fertilizers and also road stabilizers and binders. The vehicles operate under the names Tanker Services and W J Bulk. The division also includes a semi-bulk handling system, and back up for the Group's huge fleet of vehicles in specialist workshops operated by D&H Automotive Services.

Above
Tanker Services operating in Durban harbour.

Left
Loading sugar-cane – W J Bulk.

Above
Hauling timber on a country road in Natal.

Right
The Waste-tech complex at Rietfontein.

D&H Waste Management, under the name of Waste-tech, handles the disposal of dry and liquid waste, both industrial and domestic, including the neutralizing and scientific disposal of toxic wastes, in all major centres of South Africa. It also carries out research into recycling, confident that today's waste will provide the resources of tomorrow. The research division has exciting potential and is likely to show some of the most significant developments within the Group in the future.

The COAL division operates three opencast coal mines, Savmore, Glisa and Hayford. It is one of the larger independent coal producers in South Africa and, in the face of strong competition and adverse market conditions, concentrates on being a low cost producer. It operates under the name of D&H Coal.

For a decade there was also an engineering division which met with misfortune in the early eighties when it moved into the construction of off-shore oil drilling rigs. The adverse impact of this on Group profits led to the decision in 1982 to close the division, and all the engineering operations were disposed of in 1983, except Rand Founders, which specializes in the production of phosphor bronze and ferrous castings.

D&H entered 1984 with confident anticipation. The results of 1983 proved yet again that D&H turns problems into opportunities and transforms adversities into advantages. The year 1982 was disappointing, but 1983 showed a return to the Group's previous profit levels and, in spite of South Africa's flagging economy, results were better than 1981 which was a record year. These profits were soundly based, providing a good springboard for future development.

South Africa is unlikely to see an end to the current recession until at least 1985 but John Hodgson is confident that D&H will continue to grow from its existing strong base, and will participate in the country's upswing when it comes, eager to continue its contribution to the development of South Africa's national infrastructure. D&H is no ordinary company to be judged by ordinary standards. It knows that its greatest asset is its people and treats them accordingly. It does not fear failure, but approaches everything with confidence, aiming always to be a leading profit runner, setting its own standards and emerging a pacemaker. No one knows what the future holds for South Africa, but D&H will be there, strong, active and ready to go …!

Savmore Colliery.

1890–1934
Bill Hodgson

During the nineteenth century the small market town of Stockton-on-Tees on the northeast coast of England grew rapidly as an iron and steel industry developed in that area, utilizing the resources of coal to the north and ironstone to the south of the river. It never became as industrialized as some of the other towns, however, and with its proximity to the open spaces of the Yorkshire moors there were plenty of opportunities for a boy to enjoy his childhood there at the turn of the century.

William Alfred Hodgson was born in Stockton-on-Tees on 19 April 1890, and was brought up by two of his uncles because his parents died when he was still a child. He attended grammar school and later, determined to obtain a professional qualification, he went to night school, teaching himself shorthand to facilitate taking notes. A few years later he qualified as a chemical engineer. In this capacity he joined a large British construction engineering firm, Ashmore, Benson and Peas, based in Stockton-on-Tees, and travelled extensively for them, in England and abroad.

The happy Edwardian days of the early twentieth century were not to last long, however, and travelling abroad became impossible when war broke out between England and Germany in 1914. William joined the Royal Tank Corps and served with them until peace was declared, attaining the rank of major. Back in civilian life, he returned to Ashmore, Benson and Peas and was soon sent by them to South Africa to establish a coal by-product plant at Tweefontein Colliery near Witbank in the Transvaal, for Henderson's Transvaal Estates.

Family history has it that William first came out in 1922 to set up the plant and was then asked to take charge of its operation. In the records of the colliery there is mention of his having arrived in 1924:

> *Mr W A Hodgson came from England to take charge and since the end of the year under review [up to 30 September 1924] he has got the plant under full blast and reports initial prospects as decidedly promising.*

Tweefontein Colliery, which was later taken over by Lonrho SA Limited and continued production for many years, was one of two coal mines which comprised Tweefontein United Collieries. At the beginning of the century these mines were the largest producers of coal in South Africa but much of it was poor quality and unsuitable for ordinary market requirements – hence the board's decision to establish a by-product plant which would utilize this otherwise waste product.

William of course journeyed to South Africa by sea, a voyage of just over two weeks (the Union Castle ships were scheduled to take sixteen days and fifteen hours). He was already a well-travelled man of considerable experience, and he left England a very eligible bachelor in his early thirties. He was good-looking and gregarious by nature, with a charming Yorkshire accent and a great sense of humour, and he participated fully in the social life on board ship. Like many others he fell prey to that almost inevitable occurrence, a shipboard romance, and by the time the ship reached Cape Town an attractive and vivacious fellow passenger, Mabel Victoria Sharland, had persuaded him to marry her! Mabel was an English girl from Southampton and was a year older than William. She had been sent to live in South Africa because of bronchial trouble and was on the ship returning from a visit home to see her mother.

Before the wedding, which took place in Cape Town on 8 September 1924, William went up to Tweefontein to find a house for his bride. He took over two semi-detached

A photograph of Bill, sent to his sister in 1918.

houses and converted them into one, removing all internal doors to allow the air to circulate freely. William had almost a fetish about fresh air and Mabel could remember nights when she had to pin the eiderdown to the bedclothes to combat the wind rushing through the house! It was difficult to change William's mind once he had made a decision and a rigidity of opinion was one of his characteristics. While living at the colliery he always insisted on 'dressing for dinner' each night, he in black tie and Mabel, often reluctantly, in a long dress.

Mabel was never very happy living in the small colliery community. The way of life was a great contrast to the lively social scene of Cape Town to which she was accustomed. Her health had improved considerably in the South African climate and before her marriage she had trained as a milliner in Cape Town, and had been an active member of the amateur theatrical society. However, she made the best of her life at Tweefontein. She and William (or Bill as his friends called him) were a hospitable couple and they entertained frequently in their house and large garden. They were living at the colliery

Tweefontein Colliery management – Bill seated on far left.

when their two children were born: John Brailsford on 26 February 1926, and Diana Mary on 18 September 1928. Mabel wanted to be in Johannesburg for John's birth but at the time the roads were impassable after heavy rains, so she 'hitched' a lift in the engine of one of the coal trains coming up from Witbank and went to stay with friends, Philip and Hilda Lowman, in Parkwood, where John was born.

Bill and Mabel were familiar with Johannesburg as they had numerous friends there whom they visited from time to time. They used to leave John and Diana behind with their Nanny and set off for the city, enduring the wearisome day-long car journey for the satisfaction of being with their city companions. In the winter months they would arrive at the Carlton Hotel covered in dust, and in summer the greatest hazard was crossing the rivers after rain. The local farmers often had to bring their oxen to pull the car through. Sometimes, too, the rain soaked them and their luggage and, because dyes were not colourfast in those days, they would arrive in the big city with streaked and multi-coloured clothing!

In 1928 the South African Iron and Steel Corporation was established, and the directors, under the chairmanship of Dr Hendrik van der Bijl, recommended that a factory for the local manufacture of iron and steel be built near Pretoria. Inevitably at that stage, most of the plant and expertise was brought from overseas. The contract for the coke ovens was placed with an English company, and the blast furnace plant was ordered from Bill Hodgson's old firm, Ashmore, Benson and Peas. In order to reduce the cost of producing steel a by-product plant was established, coming into production in early 1934. The by-products were produced in such large quantities and so comparatively cheaply that the Tweefontein plant was eventually forced to close down. The available Tweefontein Colliery records do not mention the date of closure but Bill always gave this as his reason for leaving his job. He was offered the position of coke oven manager at Iscor, an important job, but he declined, realizing that now, at the age of forty-three, he had the opportunity to fulfil his ambition to be independent and to run his own business. He and his family moved to Johannesburg in 1934 and settled at No 5 Gale Road, in Parktown.

Bill and Mabel at 5 Gale Road, Parktown.

   Perhaps, too, the rapid growth and stimulating atmosphere of Johannesburg attracted him. The city's life has always revolved around gold and when South Africa abandoned the gold standard in 1932 there was a return to prosperity after years of depression. Gold shares soared as the increase in the price of gold made it economical to work even low-grade mines, and there was a tremendous surge in commerce and industry on the Reef, especially in Johannesburg. Old buildings in town were being replaced by new ones, new factories were being built, the suburbs were spreading and people were moving into town to take advantage of the boom.

Mabel and Bill soon became well known for a generosity and hospitality greater than most and among their closest friends were Ernest and Helene Newbury, who used to come over from Pretoria at weekends to play tennis. Mabel loved her home and enjoyed entertaining her friends, and her children remember the warm and busy atmosphere in the house. Never idle herself, she had no patience with those who did not use their lives to the full, and everyone with her was swept up and carried along by her energy and enthusiasm. No one ever saw Mabel inactive; even when sitting and talking her hands were busy, making bead bags and doing tapestry work. Bill's hobby was carpentry and their home was furnished with many items which had been lovingly made by hand, including a magnificent dining-room suite with tapestry seats on all the chairs.

While Mabel was happiest at home, Bill loved to go out. In many ways he always retained an independence echoing his bachelor days, and he enjoyed being 'one of the boys'. He belonged to several clubs and was a staunch member of the New Club, which in those days was in the Aegis Building opposite the Rand Club, and spent many happy afternoons with his friends at the races and on the golf course. His was a straightforward approach to life, due largely no doubt to his English north country upbringing, and he never lost his love for active participation in sport. In later years he enjoyed being a member of the Senior Golfers' Society of the Transvaal.

1934–1947
The Early Years

Bill Hodgson was confident that he could establish a business related to his knowledge of tar and tar products, but he felt a need for some financial expertise. Amongst his friends was Sandy Darling, a well known figure in the motor industry, who agreed to join Bill as a sleeping partner. They each put in a few pounds, Sandy arranged for an overdraft with Barclays Bank to provide working capital, and on 4 December 1934 the partnership of Darling and Hodgson was launched in the business of tarring domestic paths and driveways.

It was a very small beginning with a few black labourers and some wheelbarrows, picks and shovels. Each morning Bill piled everything and everyone into the family car, an old Chev with an extended 'dicky' seat at the back, and set off to work. He could undertake only one job at a time.

Those early days were not easy. Bill was working on a shoestring budget and never knew where the next job was coming from, but the loyalty of his 'boys', amongst them Stanford, Isaac and Hammon, helped to keep things going. Within six months Bill and Sandy parted company by mutual agreement. Bill realized that he could manage adequately on his own and he bought Sandy out in about June 1935, but decided to keep the name of the partnership. He steadily built up a reputation for reliability and honesty, and for several years the jobs were all small and of a domestic nature, although the team sometimes travelled as far as Pretoria and places in the Orange Free State. As time went by and more equipment was needed there was simply not enough room in the old car, and Bill began to hire vehicles. At first he used Proudfoot's horse-drawn wagons for local jobs. These were a slow but dependable means of transport, which were gradually replaced by steam-driven trucks. Jim Mabasa, who started working for 'Boss Hodgson' in 1938, was involved in tarring yards and also waterproofing roofs. The latter was a natural diversification because the roofs were covered with a tar-impregnated felt called Malthoid, which was cut to fit, spread out, nailed firmly in place, and sprayed with a special aluminium paint. Jim was paid 'eighteen bob' a week, which, he said in later years, had been 'all right, was enough, because food was cheaper in those days'.

Some of the larger surfacing jobs were carried out at the big houses owned by the mining magnates in Parktown, amongst them Sir Ernest Oppenheimer and Sir George Albu, and a whole garden layout was completed for Jack Scott in Young Avenue, Upper Houghton. It was on this last contract that Darling and Hodgson's workmen were given a forceful lesson in the practice of contracting. Jack Scott himself was highly experienced in this field and he felt strongly that the work was being carried out in an all too gentlemanly fashion. One day he gathered the men together and lectured them on how to get on with the job in a way that he knew would be profitable. Bill could only be grateful.

He also built a tennis court for Jack Scott. In those days courts were usually sand or gravel but a few years earlier Bill had put a tarmac surface on the court at his home in Gale Road, thus providing what he called the first all-weather tennis court in South Africa. It was so successful that he offered the service to other people, and the first revenue from building tennis courts was recorded as far back as 1937. The tarmac was covered by a thin layer of river sand (Van Ryn Sand brought from the East Rand) which allowed the players to slide as they did on dirt courts. Bill used to mark out the courts himself with remarkable rapidity and accuracy, until in later years he taught Jim how to do it.

Surfacing driveways and backyards was a hot and sticky business and everything was done by hand. In preparation the earth was loosened with picks and shovels and the surface raked smooth and stamped down. The crushed stone was dried out and warmed

Building an all-weather tennis court.

over a fire on long steel plates balanced on bricks, while the tar was heated up nearby in drums. The tar was then mixed in the correct proportions on the sheets – so many gallons of tar to so many wheelbarrows of stone – and several men on each side would mix it thoroughly before shovelling the tar into barrows and then tipping it onto the levelled ground. It was spread out with rakes to a thickness of about one inch and then stamped down and consolidated with hand rollers. Old engine oil, and sometimes wet sacks, were spread on the rollers to prevent the tar sticking.

In 1942 the Hodgson family moved from Gale Road to Parktown North. Their new house at 41 – 13th Avenue, backing down to Buckingham Avenue in Craighall Park, was on two acres of ground, one acre of which was fenced off by Jim and young John (then sixteen years old) to make Darling and Hodgson's first yard. John was always on good terms with his father's workers, and in the holidays used to help his father by going out with him to measure up for quotations. Before the move to Parktown North some of the equipment had been kept between jobs in a garage rented from a householder around the corner from Gale Road in Empire Road, and some in a yard in Norwood belonging to one of Bill's friends, Viv Lyons, who was sympathetic towards anyone trying to establish a one-man business. In 1925, when Viv had started Lyons Transport with just one truck, a one-ton Model T Ford, he could not afford to employ any labour. He used to drive and load the vehicle himself, transporting coal in the early hours of the morning and sand from the Jukskei river later in the day. He built up a fleet of trucks (including the earlier ones which still had solid rubber tyres) and Bill used them for many years to move his equipment from job to job and to deliver materials. Viv's trucks were well known around town because of their catchy slogan – RELY ON LYON ONLY. The two men developed a close relationship and Viv always regarded Bill as 'an upright man with high principles' who took liberties with no one and was scrupulously honest.

Bill purchased most of the stone for his work from Pioneer Crushers which had been formed by the amalgamation of the small stone crushers working the old mine dumps in and around Johannesburg. They were the primary suppliers of stone in the area and their managing director, Joe Forbes, was a great friend of Bill's, often seen with him at the races or on the tennis court. Mannie Kreeve was for many years in charge of Pioneer's sales and deliveries. He sent out the bigger sales in petrol-driven Stewart trucks but for a long time the smaller orders were delivered by horse-drawn scotchcart, each carrying half a yard of stone. Working within a reasonable distance each cart could manage eight loads a day, from 6 am to 5 pm with a break at midday to rest and feed the horse. Mannie always retained a vivid picture of Bill – impeccably dressed and never without a hat.

Above
In the early days Darling and Hodgson used Lyons Transport.

Left
Many hands were needed for road building.

Bill never advertised his business but it grew steadily as his reputation spread by word of mouth. Darling and Hodgson progressed into road building and much of the early work came about through his friend Ernest Newbury, estates manager for SA Townships Mining and Finance Corporation, which owned and developed many suburbs in Johannesburg and Pretoria. The older suburbs (such as Doornfontein, Fordsburg, Belgravia) were already laid out and leased, but the newer ones had yet to be developed and through Ernest Bill had the opportunity to be involved in the development of both Johannesburg and Pretoria. He worked on the opening up of Bryanston; the first bridge built by Darling and Hodgson was just outside the Bryanston Country Club. This has never been replaced, although modern bridge-builders would probably describe it as an elaborate culvert! There was also work on a road which linked the main Nigel-Heidelberg road with a township named Jameson Park. A small bridge on this road was built by Ole Grinaker, who was just establishing his construction company and was a good friend of Bill's. They would often spend fishing weekends together.

Bill was asked to surface the roadway from the gate of the Pretoria Country Club to the clubhouse. This was a fair-sized macadamizing job and Ernest Newbury suggested that Bill should hire a 'puffing Billy' (the name given to a steamroller) from a friend of his, Ken Anderson, who worked for the Fowler Tarspraying Company. This Bill did, on the basis of providing a driver and the fuel and paying £10 a week. The job took about three and a half weeks. Some time afterwards Bill won the contract to surface certain portions of Atterbury Road near the Pretoria Country Club.

From the beginning Darling and Hodgson had an office in town. Bill rented a large room, number 102, in Cullinan Building on the corner of Main and Simmonds Streets in Johannesburg, where the Standard Bank Centre was later built. The building was old-fashioned by modern standards – the wrought-iron railings and tiled floors echoed the clang of the folding metal lift doors, and the passages were dark and dingy. The office itself was large and bright, however, with plenty of light coming through the two big teak-framed bay windows. There was a desk under each window, one for Bill and the other, in later years, occupied by Ben Fletcher, who ran a building business and was happy to share the office rent. There was also a table for the secretary, Mrs Dawson-Squibb.

Cullinan Building.
(Africana Museum, Johannesburg)

Another of Bill's friends, Eric Cade, used to write up the company's books for him in his spare time, and Bill had his own peculiar but remarkably efficient filing system for keeping details of his work. Each job was worked out on a piece of foolscap paper which was folded in half and half again. This long strip was dated in the top left hand corner and all the details were entered on it, usually in pencil. He typed out the quotations himself and they were sent out while the original strips were kept in the office. Nothing that was written on those pieces of paper was ever forgotten!

John was not at home very much. After a year at Parktown Preparatory School, not too far from Gale Road, he was sent to board at Waterkloof Preparatory School in Pretoria and in 1940 he went down to Hilton College in Natal, where he spent three years enjoying all that the school offered. He progressed through school in the C stream, never particularly studious but doing well at sport, especially cricket and tennis. John's schooldays were happy ones and he has retained close links with Hilton. In May 1983, as chairman of the Hilton College Foundation, he officially opened the Old Boys' Club House, a pavilion overlooking the cricket field. Once he had matriculated John left school and joined the army. He spent three years in the Sixth Armoured Division of the Royal Natal Carbineers and he was sent 'up north' to fight in Italy.

Diana's childhood was very different from John's. She contracted polio at an early age and was taught at home for several years before going to school. It was not always easy for Bill and Mabel to pay private school fees, and there was one time when the headmaster of Waterkloof Preparatory School, Mr Ruddles, called John into his study and suggested that he work a little harder for his father's sake, and be more appreciative of the sacrifices being made at home. So, although money matters were never discussed, as was typical of that generation, John and Diana were conscious of the limitations and disadvantages of a one-man business, and John saw the family business as no more than a demanding and unexciting, but necessary, means of making a living, with no future for himself in it. His father had no ambition for anything more but John knew that he needed more challenge, and seeds of ambition were sown when he was young which grew and spurred him on throughout his life.

When war broke out in Europe in 1939 South Africa was inevitably affected and Darling and Hodgson became involved in small defence jobs, doing repair work at Water-

The on-site premix plant soon replaced handmixing.

Dutton and his roofing team.

kloof Air Station and Roberts Heights. There were industrial jobs too, and work for the Public Works Department, especially at schools, including King Edward VII School, Jeppe High, Helpmekaar and Johannesburg Girls High School. With so much more to do Bill decided to employ someone to help him and he took on his first foreman, a man named Bildt, who had a good knowledge of the asphalt business. Jim and Isaac worked under him in the surfacing team. The first step was made towards mechanization with the purchase, in the early war years, of a hand-steered petrol- driven roller, and Bill also employed Dutton to take charge of the roofing team, which included Joseph and Hammon. When it was impossible to import Malthoid because of the war they made do with hessian on the roofs. Just after the war Dutton and his team went down to Welkom, in the Orange Free State, to carry out a big roofing job on the hostels at the Anglo American mines, and a few years later there was a very large roofing contract for D&DH Fraser in Heriotdale. Dutton remained with Darling and Hodgson all his life, and it was he who proudly received the first twenty-one year long service award in the company, a gold watch, which was presented to him by Bill.

Before, during and after the war Bill worked for the Catholic community in conjunction with the architect Brendan Clinch. This included making roads at Marist Brothers in Inanda and Observatory and at Nazareth House in Waterkloof, Pretoria.

There are not many accurate details of the work carried out by Darling and Hodgson that long ago, but Bill was personally involved in everything and he was on the job from 6 am to 6 pm, six days a week, with no holidays other than Christmas Day and Good Friday. It is not surprising that he suffered several minor strokes, which fortunately never incapacitated him seriously.

When John came back from the war he still saw no future for himself in his father's business. For a few weeks he stayed at home and worked in the garden, where he started a vegetable patch, and played some tennis. During this period his sister Diana brought home a friend who made a great impression on John by beating him on the tennis court! John enrolled to study civil engineering at the University of the Witwatersrand. He had never had any intention of going to university but the educational grants offered to demobilized soldiers made it an attractive proposition and he needed time to settle down. Apart from the constant burden of his studies, the days were carefree after the rigours of war and John spent all the time he could playing tennis, for his own pleasure and for the university, with outstanding success. He also played first team league tennis for Wanderers Club for many years.

John, Mabel, Bill and Diana at John's twenty-first birthday party.

At the end of his first year he changed his course to quantity surveying, and continued to play a great deal of tennis. During this year he turned twenty-one and came into a small inheritance from his grandmother. Some of this money was invested in two plots of land, the one residential and some way out of town in Bryanston, the other a half acre in Lower Germiston Road in the developing industrial area of Heriotdale. In his spare time John fenced off the land in Heriotdale with Jim's help, and all the Darling and Hodgson equipment was moved out there. The 'site office' was an old 2 000 gallon water-tank with a hole cut for a doorway. This purchase was the first sign of John's personal interest in the development of the family business.

Some way through his second year a tragic accident occurred which changed John's life abruptly. The strong weedkiller used to destroy the grass bordering the areas which were to be surfaced was bought as a concentrate which Bildt diluted before taking out on the job and at one time it was stored in his pantry in unlabelled sherry bottles. Bildt brought a friend home for a drink on the first day of August 1947 and unfortunately selected one of the bottles containing the weedkiller, with fatal results. It was an appalling disaster which shocked everyone in the business.

The following Monday was the August bank holiday but Bill could never afford to stop work for ordinary holidays, and although he was saddened by the death of his foreman, he had several jobs on hand and badly needed help. He asked his son to step into the breach temporarily, which John gladly did, making his first move into the business on 4 August 1947. By then he had his own car, bought with some of his birthday inheritance. He rarely went into the office in town, but set out early each morning in his blue Plymouth (TJ 70385) to get all the jobs underway, before coming home for breakfast and sorting out the rest of the day with his father. At the end of the day they had further discussions at home over a beer. The first time Mannie Kreeve of Pioneer Crushers saw 'young John' out on the job was when Darling and Hodgson were making the parking area at Houghton golf course, John's young and vigorous appearance making a striking contrast to his father's formal and dignified figure.

Bill was reluctant to interrupt his son's university education, and tried to find another foreman as soon as possible. The calibre of person looking for that sort of job in the postwar years was distressingly poor, however, and John could see that no one was going to give his father the conscientious service that Bildt had done. He had also come to realize that he would never be a real scholar and that getting on with the job and being out and about appealed to him far more than studying. He asked his father if he could join him on a permanent basis and Bill, delighted at the thought of having his son in the business, signed him on – with an immediate increase in salary from £12 to the princely sum of £17/10/00 a month! This was the start of an exceptional father-son partnership, and together they began to make plans for the future. In order to lessen their personal financial vulnerability, Bill and John decided to convert their working partnership into a private company with limited liability, a turning-point in the affairs of the business which created a new structure for future development.

1947–1959
A Firm Foundation

John moved into the office in Cullinan Building and established himself at the big desk across the room from his father. Bill took over the lease of the three adjoining offices (99–101) which for some time had been sub-let by a Mr Blumenthal to Trevor Construction, a British company which was excavating the old Wanderers Stadium to make way for the new railway station (now Park Station), and Darling and Hodgson expanded into the extra space. Bill and John's secretary, Mildred Carmont, sat at the switchboard next to the filing cabinets in a reception office and there was a small room where Mrs van Niekerk did the bookkeeping on a part-time basis. Mr Blumenthal retained the use of a big desk in their office. He cut a dapper figure and each morning was to be seen at the Johannesburg Stock Exchange as a professional 'ticky snatcher', returning to Cullinan Building in the afternoons.

Having joined his father, John was determined to break out of the small-time scene. This was the crossroads in his life: from having little interest in the family business he joined Bill with a burning ambition to transform Darling and Hodgson into a company which would provide financial security for the whole family and succeed in ways of which he could be proud. This ambition was stimulated by the desire to escape the constraints on his parents' lives created by constant debt to the bank. He saw that his father was probably too much of a gentleman in his business transactions, and a hard core of determination grew within him, strengthened by an energy and zest for life inherited from his mother. John was confident that South Africa would prosper and develop rapidly after the war and saw no reason why Darling and Hodgson should not grow with it. Right away he took what was left of his inheritance and bought, on hire purchase, a Dodge tipper truck. John's inheritance money represented the first significant investment in the company and his youthful enthusiasm made a tremendous impact. Bill welcomed the new approach but his natural conservatism would not allow too much to change too soon. He knew, however, that the method of preparing asphalt by hand was both time and labour demanding, and he agreed to import a plant for producing ready-mixed asphalt. A Millar's plant, one of the original types of pugmill, was brought out from England and erected at the Heriotdale yard. It was rather primitive – the stone was carried to the top of the plant in hoppers and the bitumen tipped in by hand, with big paddles doing the mixing – but it was a tremendous advance over the old method. Dar-

Bill and John at work in Cullinan Building.

ling and Hodgson benefited greatly, and other people were eager to buy the premix.

To deal with the business thus generated a new company was established, and in February 1948 Tarmac Industries (Pty) Ltd was incorporated, with Bill and John Hodgson as the only shareholders and directors. The sale of premixed asphalt to various municipalities for surfacing pavements on an annual contract basis created the first regular cash flow that Bill had experienced since he started his own business.

The partnership of Darling and Hodgson was incorporated into a limited liability company on 9 September 1948, and Darling and Hodgson (Pty) Ltd took over all the business from 1 October 1948. Bill was appointed chairman and managing director and John the other director of the company. The minutes of the first board meeting of the company reported:

> *Mr H E Bell was appointed secretary and public officer (at a fee of £15 per month) and Messrs R B Taylor and Hoar were appointed auditors. Messrs W A Morrison, Abel and Somersvine were paid £54 for preparing the Memorandum of Articles of Association and registering the company. The registered office was 102 Cullinan Building, Simmonds Street, Johannesburg and a bank account was opened at the Hollard Street branch of Barclays Bank (DC&O).*

The initial share capital was £5 000, although this was merely a bookkeeping entry as it was represented only by a value placed on goodwill!

The minutes of the meeting held on 22 September 1948 state that John Hodgson's salary was to be £65 per month as from 1 October 1948 – a considerable increase over his starting salary of £17/10/00! With this assured and adequate income John felt that he could afford to get married. During his university years he had become engaged to the charming girl who had beaten him at tennis when he came home from the war and who had increasingly added to his enjoyment of life in all that they did together. Ruth Reid Robson was at college studying for a domestic science and teaching diploma and her friendship with John had grown through partnering him at tennis. They played together for the university and in provincial championships, and the friendship developed steadily into a stronger bond. Ruth's home was in Gill Street, Observatory, and one of the earliest deliveries of premixed asphalt from Tarmac Industries, in the new Dodge truck, was for a job there.

The Millar's pugmill at the Heriotdale yard.

An early delivery of premixed asphalt.

During their engagement John and Ruth started building their home, Sunbury, on the Bryanston plot in Witkoppen Road. They planted trees, softening the bleak veld, and worked together over weekends to prepare the garden. After their marriage on 23 April 1949 they settled down contentedly, laying the foundations of the happy family life which has always been very important to them both. Their three children, Robert, Margaret and Rosemary were born in 1951, 1953 and 1957 respectively. John never wanted the social life that his father so enjoyed, and his home has always been a haven from the demands of his busy business life. He always shared Bill's enthusiasm for tennis, however, and also his love of carpentry; few things have given him deeper pleasure than working with wood.

In 1949 there were not many houses in Bryanston, and John and Ruth's only near neighbour was a man called Jack Plane who became a great personal friend and was to have a far-reaching influence on the development of Darling and Hodgson. He had been brought up in the world of heavy transport in England, and was sent out to South Africa in 1933 by Gardners, the diesel engine manufacturers, as their official service engineer. As the use of diesel engines increased, especially during the war, Jack was kept busy, and after the war he decided to start his own business, J H Plane and Company. He set himself up as the South African agent for Gardner diesel engines and a manufacturer of trailers.

Darling and Hodgson was still a small business, and the financial side was a constant worry. There was a perpetual overdraft at the bank, so Bill and John were very grateful for a helping hand in the form of short-term loans from family and friends. This influx of cash was a great stimulus and the value of the company assets increased five-fold between 1947, when John joined, and 1950. Equipment was bought second-hand, including ex-army lorries and water tankers and two steamrollers from the Johannesburg City Council. Two lorries and an Orenstein and Koppel diesel roller were bought from Aubrey Falkson, an old schoolfriend of John's, who sold reconditioned equipment in Pretoria. A new 933 traxcavator was purchased for one of the first contracts that John worked on, at the Sterkfontein Hospital, where during 1948 and 1949 Darling and Hodgson levelled and macadamized all the roads around the wards and nurses' home and to the staff cottages. Much of the work was still done by hand at this stage.

Gradually larger road contracts were undertaken as municipalities grew and began to put their road construction out to private tender. Darling and Hodgson recorded their first big contracts in 1950 – one to construct Lynnwood Road in Menlo Park, Pretoria, which took a whole year to complete, and another, undertaken at the same time, for

Above
Ex-army water tanker.

Above right
Premixed asphalt for surfacing operations was spread from a seven cubic foot drum in the early days.

making roads for the Johannesburg City Council. The minutes of the second annual general meeting of Darling and Hodgson (Pty) Ltd, held on 29 December 1950, reveal that 'unfortunately, due to various causes including bad weather and difficult ground encountered during excavation, heavy losses were incurred on both jobs'. The following year, however, showed a profit, apparently due to a large amount of roof work, which was always done with a greater percentage profit than road work.

Darling and Hodgson purchased their first grader (second-hand) for the Menlo Park contract, at which time Hattingh was in charge of the premix plant at the Heriotdale yard, and his son Wally was driving the Tarmac Industries truck – the Dodge that John had bought in 1947. Dutton was there and 'old Viljoen' was one of the roller drivers. Arnoldus Venter was employed to operate the grader, with an assistant, Ezekiel, and he remained with Darling and Hodgson until 1963, gradually increasing his knowledge of road building under a number of foremen, among them Daan Lourens, Piet Pelser, Johnny Hall and Jack Stein.

Many miles of the original suburban roads in Johannesburg were made by Darling and Hodgson – in Craighall, Orchards, Oaklands, Linden, Birdhaven, Emmarentia, Westdene, Norwood, Sydenham, Orange Grove – and further afield too, in Springs and Boksburg, and in Soweto. There were two main methods of constructing tarmac roads in those days, differing in the foundations laid down on top of the prepared ground. The first method was very substantial and long wearing, known as Telford Pack. Biggish pieces of mine-dump rocks (sizes ranging from three-quarters of a brick to several bricks) were laid by hand side by side, on end, on the levelled and compacted earth. Smaller pieces were wedged in between and everything was roughly levelled with hammers. Then crushed stone was spread on top and rolled in firmly, several times. Finally, a loamy soil was spread, wetted and rolled over and over again until the entire structure was mechanically locked together. While this provided a road foundation which was immensely durable, it was not an economical method. It was used in the early fifties by Darling and Hodgson for a traffic circle in East London opposite the Nahoon bridge.

The more common foundation was of waterbound macadam, and later tar-penetrated macadam. After the roadway had been shaped and rolled firm, crushed stone of graded size, chiefly two inch, was spread out to a depth of four to eight inches, governed by steel pegs set with a camber board, which had been hammered in across the road. A steamroller then trundled over this, pressing it down firmly. Soil was scattered over the top and the roller went to and fro, from side to centre, so that the camber of the road was never lost. Behind the roller came a line of six to eight men with brooms, moving in unison to the rhythm of their singing, keeping the soil from caking and allowing it to settle down between the stones and lock them together. The surplus was brushed off the surface and everything was cemented together with water. The water cart went first, spraying a flood of water and creating a slurry which the roller spread out, again followed by the men whose overlapping brooms pushed the creamy wave before them. When the

Bill and John visiting the site of a road contract.

surface was dry all the excess soil was brushed off, revealing an attractive compacted mosaic finish.

A tar prime was sprayed over the road by the Fowler Tarspraying Company – the only company with spray tankers at that time – and left to dry for three or four days. Then more tar was sprayed on with a covering of small stones (usually half inch chips) and rolled, then more tar, more stone (quarter inch) and more rolling. This roller was lighter than the first one so that it did not crush the stone, and it dragged a big Z-frame behind it bearing a line of brooms which spread the stone evenly.

Constructing the road from Transkei into Nahoon, East London, using the Telford Pack method.

Darling and Hodgson used to lay four to five hundred feet of macadam base a day, and this had to be kept wet until there was a stretch long enough to bring in a whole tanker of tar for spraying. Fowlers hauled the tar for each job from Iscor in Pretoria which made it uneconomical to use less than a full load. Those early suburban roads had no curbstones; instead there was a premix shoulder on each side, called premix haunching, which prevented washaway.

John travelled extensively supervising the various contracts, and Ruth often lent a helping hand during the early years of their marriage. Many evenings John used to bring home the Tarmac Industries delivery notes and they would work together at the dining-room table after dinner, writing out the invoices. Ruth's smiling face was known to everyone; she sometimes used to take John to work, then go off to collect spare parts for the equipment and deliver them where needed, and on Fridays she prepared the wage packets and delivered those too. It was not unusual for her to get hopelessly lost on her

Right
Some jobs were done by hand.

Far right
An early steamroller.

rounds, but she would arrive eventually and was always warmly welcomed by everyone on the job. Road making was a colourful scene in those days. One day John and Ruth arrived at one of the Linden roads under construction to find the hefty foreman with his jacket off, playing the part of a toreador to the lumbering, steam-snorting, steamroller 'bull', urged on by enthusiastic workmen cheering and waving their shovels and brooms.

It was a sad day when steamrollers became obsolete. It was never easy to find the right men to drive and care for them and even then steamroller drivers were a dying breed. To have a steamroller ready for work at 7 am someone had to start at 4 am to build up a sufficient head of steam. The rollers were too heavy and cumbersome to be driven from job to job and Bill used Hammon's Transport to move them around. It is interesting to note that one of these rollers could run for a whole day on about half a bag of coal, at an approximate cost of two shillings and sixpence!

Bill and his son shared a remarkable working relationship. Although John must have felt a constant restraint from Bill, who never wanted the business to grow bigger than they could manage on their own, there was never any ill-feeling. Gradually Bill ('the old man' as he was inevitably and affectionately called, though never to his face) allowed more and more responsibility to rest on John's shoulders. He even took a month's holiday with Mabel – the first break longer than an extended weekend since 1934. John's desire to prove his capability on his own fell rather flat when it rained so much during Bill's absence, nearly six inches in four weeks, that it was impossible to work.

After a few years Darling and Hodgson (Pty) Ltd acquired the total share capital of Tarmac Industries, and the two were run more efficiently as a joint company, with their combined results making a more impressive contribution to the balance sheets, which had to be shown when tendering for contracts, than their individual operations had ever done. In September 1952 John was left in charge of the company while Bill was away. He looked out of the office window in Cullinan Building one Thursday and, seeing a pall of black smoke in the direction of Heriotdale, remarked: 'It would be terrible if the bitumen tanks at Heriotdale had set alight.' A few seconds later the telephone rang ... The valve between the storage and heating sections of one of the tanks had been left open, the bitumen had overflowed and, before anyone could stem it, had oozed across to the boilers and burst into flame. Most of the flames were soon extinguished but it was impossible to quench the fire burning in the bitumen tanks. Finally the police were summoned to shoot holes in the tanks, thereby releasing the bitumen. The fire was put out, but the yard was left covered in sticky black bitumen which had to be removed during the following few weeks with pick and shovel after sand had been liberally sprinkled over it. There was extensive damage, and Jim, who was the tar supervisor and lived at the yard, lost all his possessions.

At the time it seemed as though the whole business had gone up in flames, and cleaning the yard took several weeks when no work could be done. In fact the incident proved to be a blessing in disguise. While a very favourable insurance settlement paid for a completely new plant, what was left of the old plant was bought from the insurance company for a very modest sum and Bill, with great ingenuity and perseverence, reconstructed and recommissioned it so that Tarmac Industries emerged from the fire with double its original production capacity and a far more modern plant than before. In the same year a steam boiler and steam-heated tanks were installed for heating tar and bitumen, which enabled the plant to produce hot tarmac and hot bitumen macadam. A small workshop was erected for maintenance of equipment with Jack Grady in charge. Jack had the invaluable ability to keep anything working for next to no cost, as well as being able to operate a steamroller if the need arose.

With this expansion and increased turnover Eric Cade could no longer keep the books in his spare time and suggested to Bill that he should employ someone to help with the financial side of the business. R B Taylor of Taylor and Hoar, the company auditors, agreed and he recommended Rod Cross who was just setting up in private practice as an accountant. So in 1952 Rod was engaged to act as secretary for Darling and Hodgson and

The bitumen fire at Heriotdale.

Tarmac Industries, which kept him occupied for two or three afternoons a week. After a few months Rod sent his recently acquired junior partner, Brian Malcomson, over to Darling and Hodgson. This was the beginning of a lasting and rewarding association with the company, and an exceptional friendship between Brian and John which developed over the years.

Brian was educated at Michaelhouse in Natal, and completed his articles with the accounting firm of Robert, Hamilton and Pringle, remaining with them for a couple of years after he had obtained his CA before going to England for about a year. There he enjoyed the life of a young bachelor in London with few responsibilities and with the time and money to travel around and see the sights. He returned to South Africa when his brother died suddenly, and after a few months went into practice in partnership with Rod Cross in Jubilee House, not far from Cullinan Building. That was in 1953, and his first clients were Darling and Hodgson and the owner of a block of flats in Killarney.

At first Brian was accepted as just another pair of hands to help with the work in progress, but when after six months Rod Cross and he decided to go separate ways, Bill and John, who realized that Brian's work was impeccably precise and reliable, asked him to stay with them. Brian also retained his client in Killarney and on the strength of these two commitments he set himself up in an office in Cullinan Building just down the passage from the Hodgsons. His skill was extended beyond immediate company affairs into the administration of the personal finances of some of the employees, including Jack Grady for whom he averted several major disasters. While it was true that Darling and Hodgson could ill afford to lose any of its few employees, the care shown for them was greater than usual and resulted in a very strong loyalty binding everyone into a close team with great spirit.

The Hodgsons' secretary at that time, Shirley Gay, saw Bill as the perfect gentleman in all his dealings with her and other people, John as an energetic, vigorous young man who spoke faster than anyone else she knew, especially when she was trying to write shorthand, and Brian as the man who used to come in and check the petty cash down to the last penny!

Someone had to watch those pennies though, as the company was still struggling. There was a substantial overdraft with Barclays Bank and an unhappy relationship with the bank manager. Sometimes there was just no money to pay out on a Friday, and the previous evening either Bill or John had to go cap in hand to clients to ask for part payment or payment in advance. The cheques would be paid in early on Friday morning and the money taken out later to make up the wage envelopes, a practice which did not please the bank manager.

There came a critical time in 1953 when the company needed money and Barclays Bank was reluctant to increase their loan any further. Bill had a friend, Harry Eastwood, who had worked for the London Assurance Company when Darling and Hodgson was insured with them, and had then moved to Netherlands Insurance, as had Darling and Hodgson. On his suggestion Bill approached the manager of Netherlands Bank, who readily gave the company a loan, with the promise of more if required. Needless to say, the company bank account was changed to Netherlands Bank. Although Harry never admitted it, Bill always believed that it was his personal recommendation that brought about the loan which relieved the nagging financial tension and broke the fetters hindering the company's progress.

Darling and Hodgson survived its early struggling years largely because of Bill's charm and integrity which cemented strong relationships with many people. Harry Eastwood was just one of several men who Bill always said had helped him keep going through difficult times, and there were certain people to whom the company had owed money and who had been prepared to wait, trusting that he would pay as soon as he could. In particular Bill mentioned his gratitude to Joe Forbes and Jimmy Vogt of Pioneer Crushers who supplied stone to Darling and Hodgson from the very beginning and who sometimes allowed as much as nine months' grace. He was always appreciative of the work that came his way through Ernest Newbury, and also as a result of his friendship with Teddy Edward of Escom. The social contact with both these men went back to the Tweefontein days when they were among the many friends who made up the house parties at the Hodgsons' home. Teddy was for many years the contract and construction engineer with the Victoria Falls and Transvaal Power Company (which was taken over in 1948 by the Electricity Supply Commission) and he used to advise Bill of forthcoming tenders.

In the same year that Darling and Hodgson borrowed money from the Netherlands Bank special redeemable shares in the company were issued to John's brother-in-law, Tom Robson, and Jack Plane, and these two men became directors of Darling and Hodgson. They were the first non-executive members of the board and although the financial help was welcome Bill did not approve of bringing 'outsiders' into the business.

The extra capital facilitated expansion and development in many directions and 1953 was a thrilling year for Darling and Hodgson. One purchase in particular was to have a significant influence on the company's future. Bill and John decided that the volume of work being undertaken justified buying a tanker for tar spraying. Up until then they had used sprayers from the Fowler Tarspraying Company for all their work. The idea was no doubt encouraged by the new director, Jack Plane, and the first Darling and Hodgson spray tanker was bought in 1953 from J H Plane and Company. It comprised a Kinney bulk distributor with a capacity of 1 050 gallons, mounted on an Atkinson chassis with a Gardner diesel engine.

The Hodgsons kept the purchase secret until they had tendered for a municipal contract for spraying in Central Avenue in Lower Houghton, from the Wilds through to Oaklands. Fowlers were somewhat surprised by the appearance of competition, especially when the newcomers were awarded the contract – at a cost of an eighth of a penny less per square yard!

Darling and Hodgson's first spray tanker.

As soon as they were running their own tar sprayer Darling and Hodgson began to recommend a tar-penetrated macadam for road building in place of the waterbound macadam base which they had been using. It was a more expensive method, which was beneficial to Darling and Hodgson because they in turn made more money, but was also much quicker, which benefited the customer in most cases. It was used in 1953 to finish off the platforms at the new Park Station, where materials and equipment for the contract, including the spray tanker, had to be brought to the platforms by railway truck. The original surfaces laid by Darling and Hodgson were still in use thirty years later.

For the first time work was undertaken with professional consulting engineers, Scott and De Waal, on a big contract for roads in Linmeyer, and the first professional employee joined the company. Peter Groth was a qualified engineer – someone who could survey and set out roads and really understand plans! There was a contract for the parking area at Wanderers Club and increasing involvement in industrial work. Joseph Nkutha, who had joined the company in 1942 (and was to spend thirty-five years with it) remembered that his first job was 'at African Oxygen's yard when Darling and Hodgson were working there in Germiston', but that was a very small job compared with the work done later at factories such as General Electric, Epic Oil, Premier Milling and Scaw Metals.

The first spraying contract – Central Avenue, Lower Houghton.

Park Station, Johannesburg.

The year 1953 also saw Darling and Hodgson expand their operations to work on contracts further afield. Bill was on holiday in the Eastern Cape when he agreed to construct the main provincial road through Komga. When he got back to the Reef he sent all the necessary equipment down by train and the grader arrived on site with no cab roof because it had been too high to go under the bridges. Bill's daughter Diana was married that year and her father-in-law, Hubert Goetsch, who had retired from working in Johannesburg to live down at Kei Mouth, agreed to keep a supervisory eye on the venture so far away from the Reef. After Komga there was more work at nearby Kei Mouth, laying out the water reticulation scheme. It was on this contract that Peter Groth lost a toe when a pipe fell on his foot.

Darling and Hodgson also moved northwards in 1953 to spray roads in Northern Rhodesia for Cramond Earth Movers, and the following year Darling and Hodgson (Rhodesia) was registered in Lusaka. Work continued there over the next few years, for the Lusaka municipality and for the government on the Choma-Magoi road between Livingstone and Lusaka. Darling and Hodgson (Rhodesia) is still in existence but has not been operative for many years.

All this activity within the company engendered great optimism for the future and for continued expansion. In 1954 another sprayer, S2, was purchased which had a capacity of 1 650 gallons, and the two tankers were kept busy spraying roads for Darling and Hodgson themselves and for customers. The first driver, Tate, did not stay long with Darling and Hodgson and 'Fatty' Strydom took over S1 and began many years of faithful service with the company. His earliest spraying work was done on the roads in Inanda and then in Edenvale, Germiston and Roodepoort. He worked on the contract for the first drive-in cinema on the Pretoria road, soon followed by several more, all of which Darling and Hodgson built – including 'The Stadium' in Malvern, 'Speedy's' on the Heidelberg road and 'Top Star' which is perched on top of a mine dump at Park Central. These were all lucrative contracts.

Fatty became the driver of the second spray tanker, S2, when it was delivered, and S1 was taken over by a new driver, Bill Rowlings. S2's first run was on the South Rand road in Linmeyer. The tankers would pick up tar from Pretoria and Vanderbijlpark before going out to spray, and they also hauled bitumen from Satmar in Boksburg to Tarmac Industries' storage tanks at Brailsford House. Shortly after Bill Rowlings joined he took S1 up to Rhodesia for the spraying contracts there.

The main road through Komga.

Far left
Road construction, Emmarentia dam wall.

Left
Road surfacing, Louis Botha Avenue.

Below
Speedy's drive-in cinema on the Heidelberg road.

Share certificate issued by Darling and Hodgson (Rhodesia).

Peter Groth was soon followed by other engineers in the company. David Hulley joined for a few years during which he concentrated on concrete work, including the big Lynnwood reservoir and all the water reticulation at Spartan Industrial Township. The concrete work did not prove financially successful, however, and Darling and Hodgson did not continue for long in that field. Peter de Neef joined in 1954, working at first on the Cape contracts, and the following year Maurice Burger was employed, a young but competent man. After Komga and Kei Mouth Darling and Hodgson moved their equipment back to the Reef, building roads in Savoy Estates and going up north to Pietersburg. They then returned to East London to construct the new access road to the airport, followed by the road from the north, out of Transkei over the Nahoon river. There was great excitement when Bill bought the company's first new grader just after the Nahoon job; it arrived in East London by sea in a crate, was assembled on the quayside and then driven away to accompanying cheers. A branch office, Darling and Hodgson (Cape), was opened in East London for these contracts.

In 1955 Darling and Hodgson extended their operations into Natal when Peter de Neef moved from the Eastern Cape to Durban for a contract at Umgeni power-station in Pinetown. This was the beginning of Darling and Hodgson's long-standing working association with Escom. Peter remained in Natal for several years, constructing roads in and around Durban, including several contracts in the developing Reservoir Hills area. Darling and Hodgson (Natal) was registered as an operating company in August 1955 but there was no office or yard at first – the equipment was simply moved from site to site and the administration work was done at Brailsford House. The site offices were primitive, at best a tin shack.

As the company developed, it rapidly outgrew its accommodation and, while alternatives were being considered, Brian suggested a move to Germiston. The family of a friend from his schooldays, Mick Wyly, had been living for about ten years in the old manager's house on the Simmer Deep Mine property near Germiston. Mick's father had bought the house and its surrounding four acres from the mine manager and the property had been deproclaimed when the mine had closed down many years before. It was a pleasant place to live but when Mrs Wyly was left on her own after her husband's death, she decided to sell the property. Brian suggested to Bill and John that they should buy it and the idea appealed to them. The house and land were purchased for £4 000 and everything from the office in town and the yard at Heriotdale was transferred there. The Heriotdale property was sold to S&S Woodware which already owned the adjoining property on the north side.

The house was about seventy years old, built of unburnt brick with corrugated iron wall-cladding and roof, a perfect example of the architecture of the early gold mining days. It had an attractive, solid, homely atmosphere and was surrounded by tall old oak trees which lent it a quiet dignity. Darling and Hodgson moved in with the minimum of alteration to its structure or character and Bill and John gave the house the family name of Brailsford. The registered offices of the company were transferred to Brailsford House as from 1 January 1956 and the property itself was put into a new company called Brailsford Investments.

Brian was invited to join Darling and Hodgson in the move to Brailsford House and he accepted on the condition that he could retain some of his own clients whom he did not want to let down, particularly the flat-owner in Killarney. It was not an easy decision to relinquish his own successful accounting practice, but he opted for the challenge and fun of working with the Hodgsons and never regretted it. From the day he joined Darling and Hodgson his efficiency and constant support contributed an inestimable amount to the company's successful development.

The new offices at Brailsford House were big comfortable rooms with high pressed steel ceilings, cool and airy in summer and warmed by crackling fires in winter. Bill and John established their office in the old dining-room – they never wanted separate offices – and Brian settled himself in Mrs Wyly's bedroom, a bright and sunny room. Next to this was the bathroom which was kept for a while because Bill said he might like to bath when he came in dirty from work, but eventually the extra room was needed and the switchboard was installed there. Whenever anyone walked across that little room the floorboards creaked. The switchboard was operated by Grace Richards, a rather special person who added to the pleasant atmosphere of Brailsford House. She was always cheerful and willing to listen to anyone's problems and was especially good with children, although she never had any of her own. The sitting-room was used as the general office where the two typists had their desks, and the little study was converted into a dining-room. Brian spent most of his time at Brailsford House while Bill and John were out and about on the job, but they made a point of getting together each day to partake of Mabel's excellent lunch brought from home by Bill. (There were no cooking facilities at Brailsford House as the kitchen had been converted into a laboratory, where Bill used to do experimental work on rubberized bitumen.) The three men never invited anyone to join them, and sitting around the table they shared ideas and planned the affairs of the company.

The property was quite isolated and those who worked there in the early days recall the lonely road which led to it among the gum trees, the whistling and shunting of the distant trains, and the neighbouring mine dumps which shed sand over everything when the wind blew. Most of the staff came to work by train and were picked up at the station by a small bus provided by the company. The train timetable governed the two sets of working hours at Brailsford House, either 8.15 – 4.15 or 8.45 – 4.45.

The walls of Brailsford House were not strong enough to permit structural alterations but within a few years extensions were made to provide more space, designed by Bill's architect son-in-law, Hubert Goetsch. A wing was built on to one side which included a large wood-panelled room for Bill and John, which is still the main office at Brailsford House. Further extensions were built later to form a cloistered quadrangle effect which maintained the tranquil atmosphere of the old house. There was also another, rather dif-

Brailsford House: early extensions and the steamroller mounted at the side of the building.

ferent, addition which added to the atmosphere of Brailsford House. By the end of the fifties Darling and Hodgson were no longer using steamrollers, but they did keep one of them, preserved for posterity at the company's head office.

Ruth Hodgson was a frequent visitor to Brailsford House and was always willing to help with anything – even wallpapering the offices. She helped maintain the attractive gardens around the house and used to come to plant flowers, bringing her children who played happily around her in the shade of the big trees. There was always a welcome from the men who worked at the yard. Jimmy Cook was the first yard foreman at Brailsford House but the best remembered was Bill Rowlings, who joined the company as a sprayer-driver, but for many years, until he died in 1980, looked after the yard at Germiston. No one ever saw him bare-headed and he was always busy, a real 'Jack of all trades'. The gardens were kept immaculate and beautiful, and each day 'Uncle Bill' used to give a bunch of flowers in turn to the ladies working in the offices. He was one of that rare breed of men who are happy with their lot in life, and those who knew him said that Brailsford House lost some of its soul when he died.

Soon after the move to Germiston a small curbing factory was set up where the vegetable garden had been. This was a small but successful venture with Mack Mashigo in charge. Concrete was mixed and put into steel moulds and about a hundred and fifty curbstones were produced each day. The premix plants for Tarmac Industries were also in the yard. Samuel Mabasa worked on these after the move to Brailsford House and at that time, he remembered, the company was 'making hot mix for Jan Smuts airport and Pretoria North' and 'then worked for the Johannesburg municipality and the Germiston municipality, making tar for the pavements and for the roads'.

A loan from the Transvaal and Delagoa Bay Investment Company Limited in late 1954 enabled Bill to redeem the preference shares held by Tom Robson and Jack Plane. These men resigned from the board and Bill was no doubt pleased that the company was again solely in the hands of the family. However, on 30 June the following year Brian was appointed a director of Darling and Hodgson.

The financial side of the business was a constant worry, and Bill and John were tempted at times to merge with a larger concern. In 1957 there were extensive negotiations with James Thompson who made an offer to acquire the whole of Darling and Hodgson for £125 000 (based on the value of the assets at 30 June 1957 which were estimated at £104 815). The offer never came to fruition. That was the year when Brian acquired the company shares which had belonged to Bill's wife and daughter, thereby gaining an increased personal interest in the business.

By this time Darling and Hodgson had spread itself into five operating companies – Darling and Hodgson (Pty), Tarmac Industries, and three branch companies, Darling and Hodgson (Cape), Darling and Hodgson (Natal) and Darling and Hodgson (Rhodesia). These were all involved in roadmaking and surfacing, but gradually a divergent path became apparent when Darling and Hodgson's two spray tankers began to be in-

Surfacing operations at Brailsford House.

creasingly involved in the haulage of bulk bitumen for clients. In 1954 an oil refinery was built in Durban by the Standard Oil Company of South Africa (Socony – later taken over by Mobil), and as a result bitumen was produced locally in South Africa for the first time and a depot was set up at Isando on the Reef. The Transvaal branch manager of Socony, Switch Cuningham, was a close friend of Bill's. The two men recognized the advantages of bulk transport of Socony's bitumen and came to a verbal gentleman's agreement that Darling and Hodgson would be the pioneers of this operation.

In the beginning the company's two spray tankers, S1 and S2, were used, but when the operation began to prove successful John and his friend Jack Plane together started a new company, Tanker Services, which was registered in December 1959. Gradually a fleet of AEC articulated vehicles, supplied by Jack's business, J H Plane and Company, was built up and S1 and S2 were eventually absorbed into it.

The Tanker Services vehicles at first worked out of the Darling and Hodgson yard in Durban. Darling and Hodgson (Natal) had opened an office in 1958 when Alf Swerdlow joined as the first manager in Natal. The office was in Windleigh House in Winder Street and was shared with African Coal, a company owned by Tom Robson. Within eighteen months a site was acquired for a yard and offices in Point Road near the harbour, and it was there that the tankers were accommodated.

The association with Cramond Earth Movers, which had started in Rhodesia, was continued when, in 1958, Darling and Hodgson embarked on the most exciting and demanding contract that they had ever been awarded. This was a government contract to reconstruct Collondale airport in East London, and was worth over a million rand! It required a work force far greater than the company could provide at the time and a whole

The company's traxcavator at work on the Collondale airport contract.

new group of people was brought in, some to stay only briefly and some to become part of Darling and Hodgson for many years. More equipment was needed as well and John tackled the job with tremendous enthusiasm, seeing it as the challenge he had been waiting for.

There were two phases of the contract: the first comprised an extension to the main runway and the construction of the intersection of the main and the secondary runways, and the second was the construction of the secondary runway and of the coastal road around the airport. Darling and Hodgson were responsible for the sub-surface drainage, the stone layer work surfacing and tarmac, and they subcontracted to Cramond Earth Movers for the initial earth-moving and the layer construction work, and to Grinakers for the concrete work – culverts and hardstanding. The consulting engineers were Hawkins, Hawkins and Osborn, who were affectionately known to most people as H_2O. The first site engineer, Con Roux, was employed after an interview at Brailsford House; he left clutching a bundle of plans and specifications, apprehensive because he had never before tackled such a big and complex project. It was a challenge that he enjoyed, however, and he was recognized by everyone as an excellent engineer and an immensely fair boss.

The rebuilding of the airport was an exciting boost for East London. One day a young man named Buck Adams, whose income had suddenly vanished when fowl cholera devastated his chicken farm, saw reports of the airport development in the local newspaper and decided to try for a job there even though he had no experience at all in the construction industry. His first interview was with Ed Austin, of Cramond Earth Movers, a big volatile man always in khakis and a Rhodesian bush hat, who inspired his workers with his total dedication to the job on hand even when he was shouting and cursing at them! Buck eventually bluffed his way into being offered the job of foreman of the truck drivers by John, which he accepted, thereby plunging into a totally new way of life. He was immediately caught up in the emotional turmoil of the construction community and was increasingly fascinated by the smell of hot bitumen which was to hold him for the rest of his life. On a visit to the airport site, Bill Hodgson spoke prophetic words – 'Young man, once that smell gets into your blood you will never leave construction.'

There was a tremendous team spirit amongst everyone on the Collondale contract, intensified by the battle against the elements – rain and wind as there can only be in East London – and the contracted working hours of 6 am to 6 pm, six days a week, often extended through the nights and over Sundays. Most of the equipment was old and it sometimes seemed as though it spent more time in the workshop than on the job. An old military hangar housed the big workshop where Dick Lattaney struggled to keep everything going for Darling and Hodgson, and a great character, Papa Bianco, reigned supreme over the Cramond machines.

John went down to East London frequently, sometimes by ship from Durban, using the time on board to catch up on his paper work, and sometimes flying down with a friend, Ron Edmiston of Stanley Motors, even though the airport was closed. Con used to light huge bonfires next to the runway to indicate the wind direction so that the plane could land safely. Bill never felt the same enthusiasm for the contract as John did and could see no real reason for undertaking such a mammoth project; he was quite satisfied with a small family business. In fact he visited the airport contract only once because, sadly, in the middle of 1959, he died.

His death was a great shock to everyone because he was not yet seventy and he was a vigorous and active man still doing a full day's work. He felt unwell on 20 July 1959 and was being taken home by Hubert Goetsch when he collapsed in the car. Hubert returned hastily to Brailsford House to summon a doctor, but Bill died as he was carried into his office. His death ended a life which had been lived to its utmost. Those who had worked under him had great love and respect for him, recognizing a true gentleman, and his forceful personality was missed in many spheres. During his life he had laid the foundation of a successful business and had been an example of tenacity of purpose, independence and integrity, heightened by a lively sense of fun, qualities which have guided John throughout his life.

1959–1963
Development of the Company

The father-son working partnership died with Bill and was replaced by a combination of three men. Jack Plane had come back onto the Darling and Hodgson board in 1959 and after Bill's death he was appointed chairman of the company with John as managing director and Brian the third board member and financial director. During Bill's lifetime John's enthusiasm had been held in check by his respect for his father's desire to keep the business small, but now his natural management ability and business acumen expanded readily, tempered gently by Brian's financial wisdom and determined, level-headed approach. Jack was never actively involved in the running of the company but had a very great influence during his years as a director. He was a highly respected and successful business man, and his reputation and dynamism gave Darling and Hodgson a great deal of assistance and backing in their ventures. He was always involved in the diesel vehicle industry and as that grew significantly so did Jack's business. In 1964 his own company, J H Plane and Company, merged with the worldwide Leyland organization to form the Leyland Motor Corporation of South Africa, of which Jack was appointed managing director.

The business and personal relationship between John and Jack had a curious focal point. They had, over the years, developed a unique game of cricket which they used to play together at John's home in Bryanston. It was a one-wicket, 'back-to-the-wall' game played with great enthusiasm and energy by the two men, who claimed that it helped them maintain a remarkable degree of fitness. They also discussed all their business

Scene of great activity in the yard at Brailsford House.

John's secretary keeps in touch.

> **DARLING & HODGSON (PTY.) LTD.**
> CIVIL ENGINEERING CONTRACTORS
>
> DIRECTORS
> J. H. PLANE
> J. B. HODGSON
> B. R. MALCOMSON
>
> SALISBURY
> WINDHOEK
> DURBAN
> EAST LONDON
>
> ESTABLISHED 1935
>
> TELEGRAPHIC ADDRESS "TARPOT"
> TELEPHONES 51-8221/5
> P. O. BOX 688
> BRAILSFORD HOUSE
> JAMES BRIGHT AVENUE
> GERMISTON
> TRANSVAAL
>
> 20th June 1960
>
> Dear Mr. Hodgson,
>
> Herewith copy of letter to Mr. Fulford, the original, of course, left today.
>
> It is unnaturally quiet around here this morning. Already I miss the brightness of people galloping through the office to see you. No more frantic typing, balancing the telephone on the shoulder, yet at the same time answering the inter-com, smiling at some new-comer and getting paper out of the drawer with my foot!!
>
> It is such a beautiful day here today, that I do not even envy you your English Summer. This will remind you that your Engineers can have no excuse for not spraying for the "air" temperature must be well over $60°F$.
>
> Good wishes from all here
>
> *Paula Mitchley*

problems and plans between overs on the cricket pitch. Occasionally other people were allowed to play but they rarely came back for more; it was a hard and rough game. Cricket whites were obligatory. Jack always wore tennis shoes and a peaked cap with his cricket clothes and if he got too hot he would jump into the swimming pool, clothes and all! Both men always looked forward eagerly to their next encounter on the cricket pitch and in 1960 John wrote to Jack just before returning home from a business trip to London: 'I trust that you are not allowing yourself to fall into a state of disrepair and you will be fit enough to proceed with our game of cricket on Saturday.'

The Collondale airport contract continued for a couple of years after Bill died, and was finished in mid 1961. Phase I of the contract had had an important deadline because the airport had to be open for the historic first touch-down of a Viscount (one of those just purchased by South African Airways for their internal service) on 8 December 1959. The runway was ready just in time and the Viscount arrived on schedule, with Ruth Hodgson one of its proud passengers.

Noel Kirsten had replaced Con Roux as site engineer when Con was transferred to Brailsford House at the beginning of 1960 as general manager and a director of Darling and Hodgson (Cape), and in April that year Edward Sunde joined the team. He was a

John and Jack discussing plans between overs.

very capable young man with obvious potential and the contract was brought to its conclusion under his supervision. It was a fitting introduction to a lasting dedication to the contracting interests of Darling and Hodgson. Nowadays a similar contract would probably take half the time to complete, but Darling and Hodgson were working with old equipment and learning by experience all the way. It was a very important contract for them, a turning point in their affairs, because although it was not a financial success, largely because of the adverse weather conditions at the time, it did show John and his senior staff what they could achieve. There was no holding back in the future; it was as if Darling and Hodgson had grown up.

John Hodgson was like a child let loose to explore the world, and Darling and Hodgson's activities burgeoned as never before. It was a time of great opportunity for everyone concerned with road construction as national highways were being planned and gradually built throughout South Africa and many of the old roads were being re-routed and tarred to cater for the ever-increasing traffic they carried. During the fifties government policy had changed from allowing provincial authorities sole responsibility for their major road construction to placing much of the work out to tender by private enterprise. By this time, too, most of the big overseas contracting companies, such as Zanen Contractors and John Laing and Son, were fading from South Africa as they found themselves unequal to the rapidly developing local competition which understood South African conditions so much better than they ever would.

The Natal branch of Darling and Hodgson never moved into national road construction, and concentrated on industrial and township road work instead. It had contracts with the Durban corporation, and built roads for the naval base on Salisbury Island. There was a large contract for roads and water reticulation for the Wentworth railway housing scheme, and more roads were constructed at Reservoir Hills. In 1962 Alf Swerdlow left the company and Peter de Neef, who had been in charge of the very earliest work in Natal in the mid fifties, returned to take charge there. At that stage Tanker Services were operating out of the same premises under Peter – a job which he really enjoyed. The tankers were hauling bitumen from the new oil refinery in Durban for road surfacing, and their operations were quite separate from those of Darling and Hodgson.

Above
Completed runways at Collondale airport.

Left
Completed road system at Reservoir Hills.

In Rhodesia Darling and Hodgson moved their surfacing equipment from north to south and in 1959 they were working with A G Burton, a Kenyan-based construction company, on the road between Bulawayo and Victoria Falls. The Darling and Hodgson operations were supervised at first by Francis Bacon and then by Peter de Neef before he went down to Natal. It was a harsh climate to live in and housing was hard to find. Peter and his wife lived in an old mine house in Wankie and found themselves enjoying a very lively community life there. They spent many happy weekends in the Wankie game reserve or fishing in the Zambezi river – there are always compensations for living in out of the way places. It was so hot that the road surfacing was often done at night, and sometimes in the morning there were snakes and small animals stuck in the tar, which then had to be redone. When the Falls road was finished in June 1962 all the Darling and Hodgson equipment was moved down to South Africa and no more construction work was done by the company in Africa north of the Limpopo.

Darling and Hodgson's association with A G Burton continued, however, and was to become much closer than ever imagined at the time. While working on the Falls road A G Burton had established a South African subsidiary which embarked on the construction of the national road between Willowmore and Aberdeen in the Karoo in 1959. Darling and Hodgson had been subcontracted to the MacNicol Construction Company on the road between Uniondale and Willowmore and continued their surfacing operations for A G Burton over the seventy odd miles beyond Willowmore. They found themselves initially assisting in the base course construction because Burtons were having difficulty in keeping up to schedule, but when Gerry Schoonbee took charge of operations he sorted out the problems and Darling and Hodgson returned to their contracted surfacing operations.

Darling and Hodgson's site manager was Maurice Burger. When he and his wife, Shirley (who had been Bill and John's secretary), moved down to Willowmore it was her first experience of living in a small country town. It was a great adventure and quite a change from city life. Their only fresh water came from a rain tank, and when that was empty water had to be ordered and was delivered by tanker. There was no chance of a weekly hair-set for the ladies in Willowmore – and the men's barber was the local butcher! The people who lived there were friendly, however, and, as Peter de Neef had found in Rhodesia, small communities are far from dull. The Burgers were having a party one hot night when a herd of goats passed their house. The men rushed from the veranda where everyone was sitting and rounded up the goats into the house, where the

Road surfacing in the Cape:

Right
Portable premix plant.

Opposite above
An impressive array of Darling and Hodgson equipment.

Opposite below
Spraying bitumen.

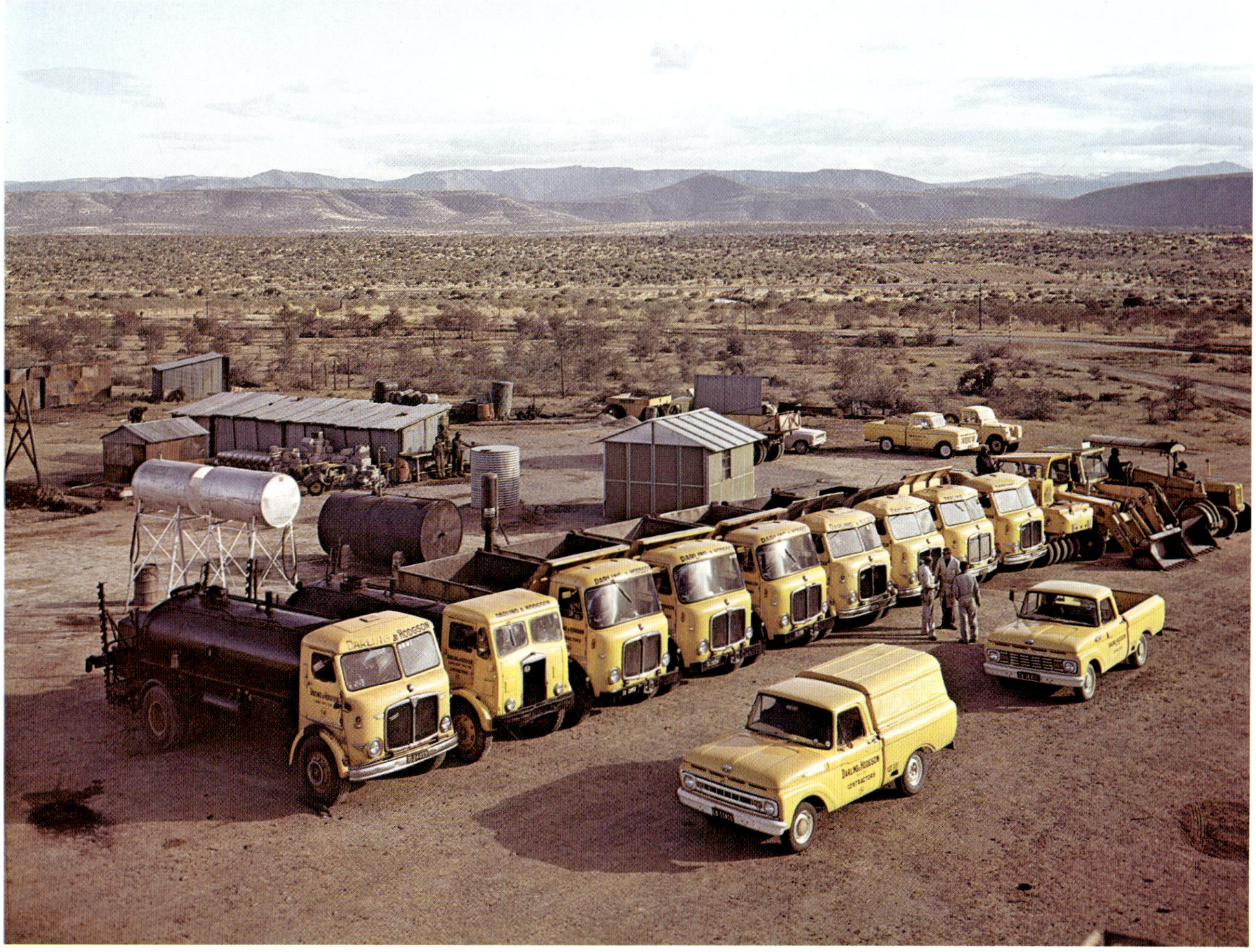

HODGSON
DARLING & HODGSON
T38

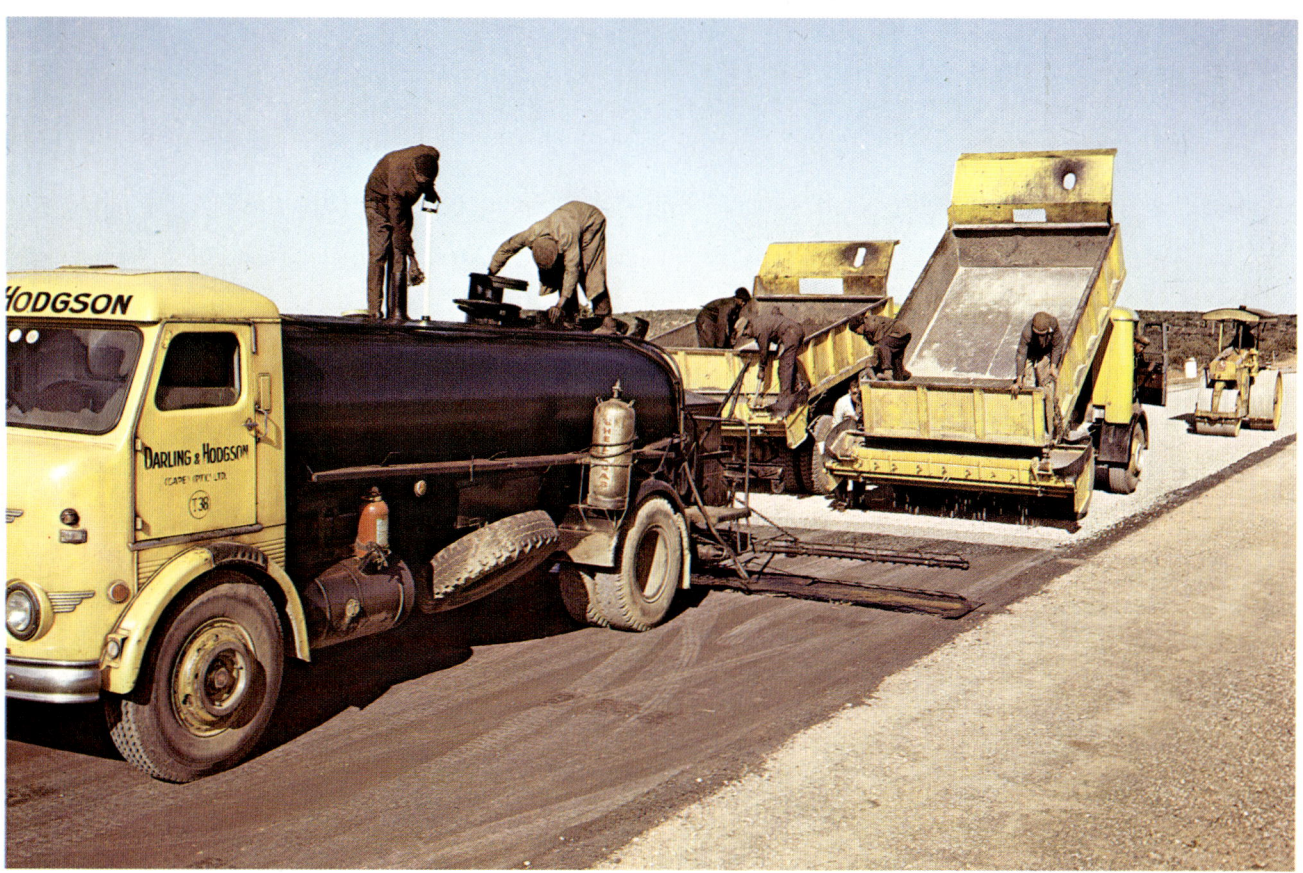

bewildered animals rushed hither and thither before escaping to freedom. There was also a memorable occasion when someone emptied a bottle of gin into the water bottle, from which Maurice unsuspectingly drank deeply, with spectacular results!

After the Willowmore contract A G Burton settled into the Cape with an increasing number of contracts. Darling and Hodgson surfaced all their roads and were moving further afield. During the Collondale airport contract Darling and Hodgson and Cramond Earth Movers had come to a management agreement and in 1959 Cramond moved their headquarters to Brailsford House. This was not really a success, however, and did not last long. Cramond was eventually absorbed partly by Grinakers and partly by LTA, but it was during the shared management period that Darling and Hodgson continued to work with them. They surfaced roads in Swaziland for Usutu Forests at Mhlambanyati, and also extended their operations into South West Africa. In 1959 John Hodgson tendered to the South West Africa Administration for constructing the road from Windhoek to Aris. This tender was accepted and another subsidiary operating company, Darling and Hodgson (South West), was registered on 18 August 1959. The teams gradually moved up to South West Africa from East London, Cramond to construct the road, Darling and Hodgson to surface it and Grinakers to do the concrete work.

The crushed stone for the contract was taken from a quarry near Aris which Darling and Hodgson had bought when they started work on the road. In 1960 Windhoek Crushers (Pty) Ltd was registered and took over the running of the quarry. Buck Adams had been taken from the airport contract and flown up to Windhoek to take charge. He got everything going at the quarry with his usual tough capability and entered into life in South West with great gusto. The pioneering atmosphere suited his personality and he found he was given a refreshingly warm welcome, rather different from the reception normally accorded construction people. Everyone seemed glad to see a new face and Buck participated enthusiastically in the club life of Windhoek, spending many happy hours on the cricket and rugby fields for Wanderers Club.

The site of the quarry was about fifteen miles south of Windhoek. Buck established the plant and offices, which were designed by Hubert Goetsch, and looked around for a good blaster to help him, a search which turned out to be more difficult than he had expected. He eventually applied for a blasting licence himself which was granted surprisingly easily, but he soon realized that the job had to be approached with some delicacy and caution. His first attempt at blasting flung rocks into the air as far away as the hotel in Aris, a good half mile distant! On the other hand Buck commented once that he realized dynamite was reasonably safe after he had 'got his wife to drive a Landrover full of the stuff to Aris over the most terrible deviations and nothing happened'!

Windhoek Crushers.

When the road from Windhoek to Aris was completed John decided to keep the quarry going to supply local contractors, in particular SWA Road Construction, and in 1961 Buck found himself an assistant, Phil Erasmus. Phil had trained as a farmer, specializing in merino sheep, but had found little satisfaction working for the Farmers' Co-operative Wool and Produce Union in South West, where most of the sheep were karakul. He spent as much time as he could playing sport for the Wanderers Club, and it was there that Buck met him. He recognized a kindred spirit and persuaded him to come and work at the quarry as his assistant. Living at the Aris quarry appealed to Phil. It was like being on a farm out in the veld away from city life, and he was happy there, checking stock, driving the trucks, doing the wages, even blasting – a little bit of everything. The quarry was not very busy, however, and within a year Buck was left in charge of operations there and Phil was transferred to Brailsford House where he was appointed assistant to Hubert Goetsch. Hubert was plant manager for Darling and Hodgson and was also in charge of the Tanker Services operations which were just getting underway in the Transvaal. Phil was very much his general factotum.

In the late fifties Darling and Hodgson began a working association with another road construction company, Savage and Lovemore. In 1959 this company was awarded the contract for constructing the road between O'Kiep and Steinkopf near Springbok in the north-western Cape, and Darling and Hodgson were subcontracted to do the surfacing. Edward Sunde was in charge of operations. It was his first experience of working with David Lovemore and they soon developed a healthy respect for each other's ability. The contract will always be remembered because the metric monetary system was made obligatory at that time and, although the contract had been tabled in pounds, shillings and pence, each month everything had to be converted to rands and cents, which created a considerable amount of extra work.

No one who worked on the Springbok contract will ever forget the Namaqualand daisies there. Good rains fell in 1961, bringing relief from the savage heat, and overnight vast carpets of daisies appeared in shades of cream, gold, orange and brown, stretching as far as the eye could see. It was a land of great extremes and the rain also caused floods which washed the railway line away.

After this contract Edward was transferred, in 1962, to Darling and Hodgson's head office at Brailsford House to work with Con Roux. The two men shared responsibility for all of Darling and Hodgson's road construction work. Con took charge of the Reef-based operations while Edward supervised the surfacing activities all around the country which necessitated spending at least two weeks of each month travelling. He drove much faster than present speed limits would allow and often travelled at night to avoid the heat of the day.

The hub of the company was Brailsford House. John travelled extensively, keeping in touch with all the operations around the country, a practice which had a revitalizing effect on everyone in the company, while Brian 'held the fort' at Germiston. Ruth did not often accompany her husband, but her interest in all the company's operations and her calm support of all John's activities were always reassuring.

Just before Bill died, Brian had taken on a young assistant, Trevor Snell, who was appointed the company accountant the following year, to help with the daily routine and to allow Brian to spend more time helping John with all the new operations. Trevor likened Darling and Hodgson at the time of his joining to a steady rock within the mosaic of the Johannesburg business world. During his training as an accountant he had worked in the frenetic atmosphere of the rapidly expanding commercial scene, and recognized with some relief the sound traditional approach of Darling and Hodgson's management. The conservative image belied the forceful and stimulating atmosphere which he found within the company, making work fun for everyone.

One of Trevor's jobs was to help Brian with the wages which had to be brought from Germiston. Brian travelled alone over the lonely roads, and when he was due to go on leave Trevor was horrified by the idea of having to carry so much money on his own. Brian did not see it quite the same way but was eventually persuaded that it would be

Jan Smuts airport.

much safer if the wages were delivered by a security firm.

Trevor saw the resources of Darling and Hodgson being stretched to their absolute limit, and the financial juggling was an exciting challenge. Somehow the system worked and Darling and Hodgson continued to expand its operations. As these were spreading around the country, so there was more work nearer home, in the Transvaal and on the Reef. In 1961 Darling and Hodgson constructed the access road to SAPPI's Ngodwana mill in the Eastern Transvaal, and subsequently roads were built further north at Phalaborwa, the township for the big copper mine on the edge of the Kruger National Park. The SAPPI contract was supervised by Pat Hill, who joined Darling and Hodgson that year, having worked with them in Natal at Reservoir Hills as the consulting engineer. Pat also persuaded John to reopen a 'small works' section of the company which was reminiscent of the early pioneering days. Dutton was the foreman on many of these smaller jobs. He was the oldest employee in the company at that stage – 'a great old man, couldn't change him or hurry him, he went his own way and at his own pace.'

The production of premixed asphalt continued steadily over the years at the Tarmac Industries plants at Brailsford House, supplying both Darling and Hodgson and customers. The service was extended to selling the premix in package form which helped to carry Tarmac Industries through the cold winter months when little surfacing was done. They did a great deal of industrial tarmac work on the Reef and work at Jan Smuts airport, putting in the hardstanding for extensions to the apron in front of the terminal buildings.

In the early sixties Darling and Hodgson were resurfacing roads in Pretoria and Westonaria and constructing roads in the new suburbs of Sandown, Sandhurst, Hyde Park, Bryanston and at Mondeor. They also laid out the parking areas for more drive-in cinemas in Johannesburg and Krugersdorp, and these were under the supervision of Gert Koen who had been with Hawkins, Hawkins and Osborn on the Collondale airport contract and then joined Darling and Hodgson for a few years.

Darling and Hodgson's two spray tankers did stirling work in the surfacing operations. At first they were based at Brailsford House and after picking up tar in Pretoria or Vanderbijlpark they travelled any number of miles to where it was needed. Fatty Strydom once said, 'If I had one penny for every gallon of tar that I hauled I would be a multi-millionaire!' Driving a tanker was a demanding job, with long and indefinite hours, and the drivers used to endure almost unbearable heat in their cabs from a combination of the sun, engine heat and the burners keeping the bitumen hot. Fatty used to pull over and get out to cool off by the roadside, and one day 'the boss', John Hodgson, found him sitting on the grass instead of getting on with the job. Although irate at the time and certainly not appreciating the time wasted, John arranged for a fan to be installed in Fatty's cab – typical of his personal interest in the well-being of all those who worked for him.

Fatty's brother, Koen, was another of the early tanker drivers and had done the spraying at Collondale airport. It was a tremendous shock and sorrow to everyone when he died in a tragic accident at Brailsford House on 18 October 1961. He was doing some welding on his tanker, strictly against all the company rules, because he wanted a leak mended quickly so that he could get out on the job. Unfortunately he had not opened the valve on the tanker and it exploded, killing him instantly and blasting away the side and roof of the workshop.

Fatty was also involved in spraying a specially imported tar which made the ground 'a sort of yellow colour'. It was used at the army's drilling ground in Pretoria, and also in the Kruger National Park where it was hoped that the dirt roads could be sealed without changing their appearance too much. In 1964 the National Transport Commission allocated two million rand to be spent over nine years for tarring roads in the Kruger Park so that visitors would no longer be at the mercy of the heavy summer rains which frequently turned the dirt roads into mud baths, and Darling and Hodgson were awarded some of the earliest work for this project. When Darling and Hodgson's spray tankers were taken into Tanker Services, Fatty also changed companies and continued to work for Tanker Services for several years, eventually retiring for health reasons.

After completing their two contracts in South West Africa and the north-western Cape Darling and Hodgson were involved in the construction of the Windhoek drive-in cinema, but there was no further road construction work for them in those areas. There were many lively round-table gatherings as John discussed possibilities for the future with Andrew Savage and David Lovemore, including an unsuccessful joint tender for the Windhoek airport.

Savage and Lovemore moved their people and equipment back to Port Elizabeth where they had been awarded a contract by the South African Railways at the Deal Party goods yard, and Darling and Hodgson were subcontracted to do the surfacing. It was not a very significant contract, but it was certainly a very useful one because the Railways transported all the equipment from South West for them.

Buck remained at Windhoek Crushers and was instrumental in involving Darling and Hodgson for a brief period in the uncertain world of prospecting. South West Africa was at that time a prospectors' paradise and there were stories to be heard around town that excited anyone who was prepared to listen. Propping up the bar, prospectors used to tell tantalizing tales of fantastic deposits which needed only a little money to get them going. Buck became very involved and used to send all sorts of samples and reports up to Brailsford House, most of which came to nothing. There were even times when the telephone would ring in the middle of the night at John's home with news of an irresistible option just about to expire! There was one particular copper deposit, at a place called Klein Aub, from which Buck sent a sample up to Brailsford House but at the time John was not interested and put it aside.

Meanwhile he had asked Buck to keep an ear open for a good deposit of kyanite, a local stone which was used as a flux in steelmaking and which could be crushed at the quarry when there was no road contract to be supplied with stone. Eventually a prospector turned up with 'a beautiful deposit' – just what was needed – and Buck requested that a geologist be sent up to check it. John turned to a friend with whom he often played tennis, Des Weedon, of G&W Base Minerals. Their geologists were all very busy but they appreciated the urgency of getting an expert to the site before the option expired, and Tony Greville flew up to South West immediately, only to find that the prospector could no longer find his wonderful deposit! It was all rather embarrassing, especially as there was no flight for several days to take Tony back to Johannesburg. In a desperate flash of inspiration John remembered Buck's copper deposit at Klein Aub and asked him to take

The rock sample which led Darling and Hodgson into its close association with Union Corporation.

Tony to see it. The report was so encouraging that the option for prospecting rights was taken up. Further investigations were even more exciting and everyone at Darling and Hodgson was eager to plunge into the mining operation. However, having spent R35 000, which they could ill afford, on the initial investigations there was no way that Darling and Hodgson could continue on their own and John decided to look for assistance.

He went back to Des Weedon who suggested that he approach Union Corporation, a big mining house with plenty of mining experience and 'a good crowd to work with'. The man in charge of exploration administration at Union Corporation was Aidan Buchholz to whom John went with his problem. As a result the Corporation took over the option on the copper deposit, repaying Darling and Hodgson their investment and promising them a ten per cent stake in the mine if it were developed. In fact Union Corporation abandoned the project, though in later years the deposit was mined successfully by other people.

Between the late fifties and mid sixties Darling and Hodgson were involved in the mineral interests of South West Africa and held a share of the prospecting companies Mineral Surveys and H&W Properties, but nothing significant ever came of this.

Buck left South West Africa when the quarry became uneconomical and joined the Darling and Hodgson surfacing team at Loxton in 1964. Windhoek Crushers became a wholly-owned subsidiary of Darling and Hodgson (South West) and was finally sold to SWA Road Construction the same year.

Union Corporation was primarily a gold mining company and in the late fifties they were beginning to realize that gold deposits were not going to last for ever and that there was a need to expand their interests to ensure survival and success in the years to come. They had already initiated the production of paper in South Africa through SAPPI and were seeking ways to broaden their industrial base further. During Aidan's discussions with John he had asked if there had ever been any thought of Darling and Hodgson taking a partner. John firmly rejected the idea at the time, but a seed was sown which soon began to germinate.

In 1962 Darling and Hodgson were riding high. There was a tremendous variety of work based on the Reef and literally hundreds of miles of road around the country, especially in the Cape, had been and were being surfaced by the company in conjunction with A G Burton and Savage and Lovemore, making an important contribution to South Africa's road network. This was the base from which Darling and Hodgson's huge construction division developed, and the foundations of the two other major components of Darling and Hodgson had also been established. The fleet of articulated tankers being built up within Tanker Services was the forerunner of the services division, and even while Tanker Services were getting underway John's fertile mind had been pursuing another original project. He had for some time been intrigued by the concept of delivering ready-mixed concrete in bulk for the building industry, a practice he had seen in other countries, and with the encouragement and support of Robert Horowitz and Jack Plane, in 1961 he had initiated the ready-mixed concrete industry in South Africa. It was expanding rapidly into all the major centres of South Africa, laying the foundation of the materials division. Both Tanker Services and Ready Mixed Concrete operated as part of Darling and Hodgson but John and Jack's initial shareholdings were held in their personal capacities.

Thus in 1962 there was a momentum and enthusiasm bubbling within Darling and Hodgson which could hardly be contained, but to take advantage of it required a great deal of money, far more than a family-based business could ever hope to provide. John went back to Union Corporation where Aidan took him to Ian Wilson, who was in charge of investigating the possibilities of diversification into industry for Union Corporation. John and Brian had spent many anxious hours debating whether they wanted to be tied to a mining house, aware that it could mean the end of their independence and losing control of everything for which they had worked so hard for so many years. Jack was never in favour of the step but John and Brian realized that without financial support Darling and Hodgson could soon be outpaced by competitors and the tremendous potential would be lost. John therefore set out to sell the company to Union Corporation. He put across a convincing picture of how it could grow in a few years into a large and profitable road building and civil construction company. Union Corporation listened and then made investigations into the business and spent a great deal of time with the people in it, sounding out their abilities and the spirit within Darling and Hodgson. They sent Bill Adamson of Unidrilling, which was the Union Corporation subsidiary most closely related to the Darling and Hodgson operations, to report on all the company's activities, and asked Dunlop Heywood to evaluate the assets, which were valued at R250 000. What seemed more important was that the Union Corporation men simply liked what they saw and towards the end of 1962 they offered to put R255 000 into Darling and Hodgson, thereby obtaining a 51% shareholding. John and Brian knew that they did not want to exchange the shackles of the bank for a similar financial hold by Union Corporation and John put his cards on the table before Union Corporation's managing director, Tommy Stratten, and directors Colin Anderson and Whitmore Richards, saying that he would accept the offer providing Union Corporation did not interfere with the running of Darling and Hodgson. The final negotiations were amicable, with a great deal of personal goodwill on both sides, and the deal went through.

The investment was a small one for Union Corporation but within Darling and Hodgson there was a feeling of liberation as the restricting financial fetters fell away. All loans were repaid and all personal bank and insurance guarantees were released. Union Corporation asked John and Jack to relinquish their personally owned shares in Tanker Services and Ready Mixed Concrete, and these companies were brought in with Darling and Hodgson (Pty) as operating companies within Darling and Hodgson Holdings, an arrangement which set the precedent for the future organization of the Darling and Hodgson Group. The new company was registered on 12 February 1963, with a total share capital of R500 000. Union Corporation held 51% of the shares, John Hodgson retained the majority of the remainder, and Brian Malcomson and Jack Plane each had a small stake.

Union Corporation were wise enough to change as little as possible and appointed

Jack as chairman of Darling and Hodgson Holdings, retaining John and Brian in their managing and financial director capacities respectively. The two Union Corporation representatives on the board, Ian Wilson and Bill Partridge, worked closely with these three men and, with sound financial backing for expansion and development, Darling and Hodgson stood poised on the brink of a dynamic future.

1963–1973
Years of Growth and Diversification

The lifeline between Union Corporation and Darling and Hodgson was Ian Wilson, who had been a firm friend and staunch supporter of Darling and Hodgson throughout the negotiations. One of the main problems in his task of taking Union Corporation into industry was that although there was plenty of money available the necessary people were not. In Darling and Hodgson, therefore, he saw the perfect acquisition, comprising a totally new field of operations coupled with competent management, and he was prepared to combine his unshakable loyalty to Union Corporation with inestimable support and encouragement for Darling and Hodgson.

The vicissitudes of the construction industry were completely foreign to Union Corporation and no one other than Ian was really prepared to take much interest in anything outside mining. When the financial men looked at Darling and Hodgson's results they showed no sympathy towards the contributing problems and saw only the absence of the good return on investment which usually accompanied their mining ventures. In fact Darling and Hodgson was in the red for many months and during the first few years with Union Corporation they struggled to keep their heads above water, with borderline profits, as they experienced the growing pains which were inevitable as they broke through into a scene bigger than they had ever known before. They battled to keep control and there was a time when it was difficult to persuade the auditors that the assets of certain subsidiaries exceeded their liabilities! For two years a considerable amount of juggling had to be done before they would issue a clear audit certificate. However, John and Brian talked their way out of that situation and Ian buffered them from Union Corporation for many years. It was true, of course, that Union Corporation's investment in Darling and Hodgson was so comparatively small that the attributable losses appeared small too, but there must have been many occasions when Union Corporation wondered if their acquisition had been a wise one.

Darling and Hodgson returned their banking to Barclays in accordance with Union Corporation policy, but overall they were left very much to run themselves, which was what John and Brian wanted at the time. In retrospect one wonders what would have happened had Union Corporation gathered Darling and Hodgson into a group of industrial companies which were being developed and encouraged with combined resources. They never did provide such an opportunity and their policy of diversification for many years was totally passive.

When they accepted Union Corporation's offer John and Brian decided to forfeit their independence in order to be able to take advantage of all the available opportunities, and to have the resources to plan ahead with confidence on a broader scale than ever before. Within three months they had 'spent' over a million rand, which took everyone a little by surprise but showed significant results. Union Corporation rapidly put the brakes on the lending of any more money but with their strong credit backing Darling and Hodgson were able to borrow from other sources. Before the end of 1963 they procured a loan from Philip Hill (later to become the merchant bank Hill Samuel) which helped to finance all that they had started.

The money was used for development along all three tracks of Darling and Hodgson's operations at the time – road construction, transport and the ready-mixed concrete industry. A large proportion was invested in increasing Darling and Hodgson's stake in the road construction industry. Their work up until then had been predominantly in road surfacing, which was either an inherently small job operation, such as industrial and domestic yards and driveways, or a 'tail-end Charlie' situation as a subcontractor to the large road building concerns, always dependent on others. With resources available to enable them to break out of this position, Darling and Hodgson looked for ways to assure their future in the wider field.

The first opportunity arose early in 1963 when Andrew Savage, of Savage and Lovemore in Port Elizabeth, approached John for financial assistance for a road building contract in South West Africa, where the two companies were already working together. The two men knew each other well, their friendship going back to the war when they had both fought in Italy with the Royal Natal Carbineers, and they understood each other's needs, both of them being at the head of what were essentially family businesses. Andrew saw Darling and Hodgson as potential financial sponsors now that they were part of Union Corporation. With Ian Wilson's support, John persuaded Union Corporation to agree to his helping Andrew in return for a 25% shareholding and positions for himself and a Union Corporation representative (Bill Partridge) on the board of Savage and Lovemore, and also a guarantee that all their surfacing would be done by Darling and Hodgson providing their terms were competitive. All the acquired Savage and Lovemore shares came from Andrew's partner, David Lovemore. It was the first time that Darling and Hodgson had ever become a minority shareholder in another company but it was a decision made with foresight, in the hope that over the years Darling and Hodgson could invest further in Savage and Lovemore, thereby attaining increasing financial control. John was very aware of the vulnerability of a privately owned business. Darling and Hodgson did not interfere at all with the management of the company, and its operations continued unchanged.

This participation in Savage and Lovemore gave Darling and Hodgson only a toehold in the 'big league' operations of road construction, however, and John and Brian were looking for greater involvement. Darling and Hodgson had for several years been working with another contracting company, A G Burton, in Rhodesia and the Cape. This company was experiencing great difficulties in adjusting to the demanding standards of road building in South Africa after the more relaxed atmosphere of Rhodesia, and was running into severe financial problems. John was aware of this and determined to take advantage of the situation. When A G Burton was taken over by the Hunasgeria Tea Company, John flew to London with Ian Wilson to negotiate with them. Darling and Hodgson offered to purchase a 51% shareholding of A G Burton's South African company, and the deal went through in June 1963. Within two years Union Corporation had approved the acquisition of the total shareholding and all of Burton's South African assets were brought into Darling and Hodgson. The deal also brought in men who were to stay and contribute significantly to the development of Darling and Hodgson, among them Gerry Schoonbee, Jim Maguire and Philip Wessels.

These acquisitions gave Darling and Hodgson an important boost and there were changes at managerial level as everyone settled into the new situation. While the negotiations for A G Burton were underway Gerry Schoonbee, who was in charge of their South African operations, had been offered the job of managing director of Savage and Lovemore. It was a very attractive offer and, as at the time the future of A G Burton looked rather uncertain, Gerry accepted the position. He stayed on with Burtons for several months, however, in order to hand his job over to Edward Sunde who was transferred from Darling and Hodgson.

When Edward was transferred to A G Burton his responsibility for all Darling and Hodgson's surfacing contracts was taken over by Gerard Voss. Con Roux remained in charge of all construction activities and was appointed a director and the general manager of Darling and Hodgson (Pty). In order to develop and maintain a successful approach to the financial side of contracting as the company expanded, a planning and estimating department was set up under Pat Hill at Brailsford House, where Hubert Goetsch remained in charge of the entire plant, assisted by Phil Erasmus. Tarmac Industries continued its operations, producing premixed asphalt for Group operations and for customers.

Savage and Lovemore and A G Burton continued their operations independently with their own contracts in the major road construction field, mainly in the Cape, while Dar-

The Heidelberg road on the East Rand.

ling and Hodgson increased their operations in the surfacing field and continued with some road construction. Operations in Rhodesia and South West Africa were gradually closed down while contracts were undertaken in Boksburg and Ruven Township, at Bracken and Leslie mines and at Phalaborwa. Darling and Hodgson had one major highway contract on the Heidelberg road. This gave a great deal of trouble (one report commented that 'certain alterations in drainage design introduced after the commencement of the work, coupled with traffic and service problems, resulted in unforeseen delays') but was eventually completed satisfactorily.

There was no difficulty in finding smaller jobbing contracts which, although they usually gave good returns, supplied no continuity of operation and were never as satisfactory as the bigger contracts. Most of Darling and Hodgson's work was surfacing for A G Burton and Savage and Lovemore on their Cape contracts. Between them these two companies were steadily constructing hundreds of miles of roads in the eastern and western Cape and the Darling and Hodgson surfacing units moved from one contract to another under the overall control of Maurice Burger. They also worked with A G Burton on a contract at Kimberley airport and this unit moved on to Pretoria in January 1964 for surfacing at Wonderboom airport. They did surfacing for other concerns too – for Rand Earthworks at Burgersdorp and for the Natal Provincial Administration on the national road near Pietermaritzburg.

In the early sixties a very exciting project was started in South Africa in a visionary at-

A section of the national road near Pietermaritzburg was surfaced for the NPA.

Blaw-knox paver in operation on the north coast road at Umdloti.

tempt to promote the development of the country. South Africa does not possess many water resources, a significantly limiting factor in its progress. The Government's Department of Water Affairs is constantly seeking ways to use the existing reserves to their best potential, and in 1962 it was officially announced that South Africa's first multi-purpose water resources scheme was to be launched immediately. This was hinged around the great Orange river which flows from high up in the Drakensberg mountains in Lesotho through some of the driest parts of South and South West Africa out to sea on the west coast at Alexander Bay, gathering the water of the Vaal river and other tributaries on the way. The proposed scheme was intended to provide water for irrigation in the Orange river catchment areas and the Fish and Sundays river valleys, and for industrial and domestic use, with several dams planned for the production of hydroelectric power. The first phase was primarily to construct two large dams on the Orange river and a tunnel to take water from one of them into the Sundays and Fish rivers.

The larger of the two dams, to be called the Hendrik Verwoerd dam in honour of South Africa's prime minister at the time, was planned to store the water of the river near Colesberg in the middle of the arid Karoo. The contract for its construction was won by a large consortium comprising Union Corporation and two French civil engineering companies. One of these, Société Dumez, was well experienced in dam building around the world and the other, Les Entreprises de Travaux Publics André Borie, had recently completed the French section of the Mont Blanc tunnel connecting France and Italy through the Alps – an engineering achievement regarded as one of the greatest of all time. Union Corporation had formed a special company to tender with the French and in September 1964, in order to spread their operational base, they asked Darling and Hodgson to take a 20% interest in the new company, Union Corporation Public Works. Pat Hill was transferred to a 'special projects' division of Darling and Hodgson to co-ordinate their participation in the project. The tender was accepted in April 1966, but in fact Darling and Hodgson never participated in the project and by the end of the year had pulled out of the Public Works Company. However, Union Corporation agreed to appoint them as consultants to the company at a fixed annual fee of R5 000, and as a result of this Darling and Hodgson were one of the very few concerns to make any profit from the building of the dam!

When Pat Hill was transferred his place as manager of estimating and planning was taken by Gerard Voss who was in turn replaced as manager of the surfacing division by Peter de Neef. Within a few months Maurice Burger moved up from the Cape to take Peter's place in Natal and Buck Adams, who had returned from South West Africa in 1964 to undertake the Loxton contract, took charge of the Cape surfacing division. The direct responsibility for construction operations within the company was given to Roy Munro, who had been the Transvaal manager for some time, while Con Roux remained general manager. The following year, in 1965, Con left Darling and Hodgson to start his own business, and Peter was promoted to the position of general manager of all construction activities in Darling and Hodgson. Con's business rapidly became a great success, which he partly attributed to the excellent experience he had gained with Darling and Hodgson.

Generally speaking the sixties was not a financially successful period for Darling and Hodgson (Pty) in spite of all their efforts. In 1964 it was the only company within Darling and Hodgson Holdings to have made a loss during the year, and a substantial one at that. One reason for this was that much of their work was surfacing, always an uncertain financial proposition as it is totally dependent upon others and on the weather. Delays in the delivery of materials, break-downs of vehicles, cold and wet weather were all factors which contributed to the poor results. Everyone dreaded the coming of the winter months when there was an ever-decreasing number of hours each day with a temperature high enough to allow operations to continue. Sometimes only a primer could be applied to the base course and the surfacing had to be postponed until the days were warmer.

During 1965 most of Darling and Hodgson's construction work was placed with

A G Burton and a considerable quantity of plant and equipment was sold to them. This helped to redeem some of the working losses.

For some time competition in Natal had kept Darling and Hodgson from expanding to any great degree in that province, but in 1965 an agreement was reached among the different road surfacing companies there, V F J Hall, Limmer and Trinidad and Darling and Hodgson, whereby the major contracts were shared out among them and allocated in a way that allowed efficient and economic handling. In mid 1966 Darling and Hodgson (Pty) and V F J Hall, the chief competitor in Natal, exchanged minority shareholdings, but because of conflicting management policies the association was not a success and the situation was reversed a year later.

In 1967 the rapidly increasing activity within Darling and Hodgson influenced a decision to facilitate management by splitting operations into two divisions. Edward Sunde was placed in charge of all the construction interests, and Peter Langerman, from Ready Mixed Concrete, was made general manager of all the other operations. Edward's place at the head of A G Burton was taken by Johan Schonken, who began to bring their work out of the Cape into the Orange Free State and Transvaal. However, most of their contracts were still in the Cape and they found themselves increasingly in direct competition with Savage and Lovemore, a situation which was detrimental to both companies and quite unnecessary in the light of their relationship through Darling and Hodgson. In November 1968 it was decided to rationalize their operations under the name of Savage and Lovemore. The holding company, Savage Industrial Holdings, in Port Elizabeth, acquired the total shareholding of A G Burton (SA) and also of Darling and Hodgson (Pty) and Tarmac Industries. This brought all the construction activities of Darling and Hodgson Holdings under Savage and Lovemore's management with the result that the other companies all ceased to exist as operating companies and the name Darling and Hodgson was no longer attached directly to any construction activities. However, the amalgamation gave Darling and Hodgson the majority shareholding in a company which had immediately become one of the largest road construction organizations in South Africa – calling to mind John Hodgson's prophetic words to Union Corporation not many years before – with an order book worth R30 million and an anticipated turnover of more than R20 million in the first year. Such a large organization was better equipped than its individual components to take advantage of the opportunities presented to the whole construction industry and opened up exciting opportunities for the people working within it. Operations were directed from Port Elizabeth at first, but before long it became obvious that the senior management should rather be based on the Reef and Gerry Schoonbee moved north from Port Elizabeth to take charge, while Edward went down to the Cape. Offices were initially established for Gerry at Brailsford House but within a short time independent headquarters were set up for Savage and Lovemore.

Surfacing operations continued within Savage and Lovemore but before long they were put into a new company, Limmer Asphalt, owned 50/50 by Limmer UK and Savage and Lovemore Holdings. Savage and Lovemore then sold their share in this company to Limmer UK, and all associations with black top operations dropped out of Darling and Hodgson altogether for the first time since they had started in 1934.

Having reversed their construction interests into Savage and Lovemore, Darling and Hodgson could concentrate more fully on their other activities. The sixties was a period of tremendous development within South Africa and John's irrepressible entrepreneurial talents ensured that Darling and Hodgson exploited many of the available opportunities. Brian was his financial adviser in all ventures and there was a close bond between the two men as they moved together down the track of Darling and Hodgson's development and diversification, building on the years of shared experience. John gathered around him other men with pioneering instincts, men of initiative who were stimulated by challenge, excited by new ideas and willing to take chances and keep going against great odds. They all responded to the infectious enthusiasm and encouragement which flowed from John in all that he did, inspiring an intense personal loyalty. This created a unique working atmosphere and brand of management which was usually highly successful within the company but did not always blend easily with others.

As the scope of operations broadened over the years it was inevitable that Darling and Hodgson should take in partners and when this happened the path was sometimes far from smooth. The partnership with Union Corporation was successful because they never became involved in the management of Darling and Hodgson, allowing them to operate independently. Without the backing and support of this large mining house Darling and Hodgson would never have been able to develop as they did in the sixties. Large sums of money were borrowed from banks over the years, and there were several increases in share capital. In 1968 Union Corporation were allotted the entire rights issue of two hundred thousand shares at R5 per share, thereby providing a million rand towards financing further expansion.

While increasing their investment in the construction industry after joining Union Corporation in 1963, Darling and Hodgson had also put money into accelerating the development programmes of Tanker Services and Ready Mixed Concrete, for whose services there was an ever increasing demand. In January 1964 John, in his capacity as managing director of Tanker Services, said, 'Our company has a great opportunity, particularly at the present time with the big move to mechanization in industry, which cannot be completely successful without the supply of their raw materials in bulk. We must therefore be equipped to provide a service wherever needed.' This was the aim of Tanker Services and, under Hubert Goetsch and Phil Erasmus, a specialized transport fleet was steadily built up, conveying a variety of liquids for the major oil companies, chemical manufacturers, the paint industry and other industries generally. They were to be seen operating in all the provinces of South Africa. In 1968 Tanker Services merged their operations with the South African bulk transport interests of a British transport company, United Transport Holdings, thereby entering into the conveyance of flowable solids, in particular cement. The company thus created, United Tanker Services, owned half by United Bulk Transport and half by Darling and Hodgson Holdings, was not a happy partnership, and the five years of its existence were marked by deteriorating operations and stormy board meetings where the overseas directors seemed to show little sympathy for local problems. Consequently it was with a very real sense of relief that Darling and Hodgson bought out the British interest in 1973.

Ready Mixed Concrete also experienced a period of equal partnership which was not very successful. It had spread its operations into the Cape and Natal and the enthusiasm and perseverance of the men in the industry had managed to convince their potential customers of the convenience and efficiency of ready-mixed concrete, which played an important part in the development of the country as a whole in spheres as diverse as roads, highrise buildings, dams and mines, to name but a few. New plants were opened at regular intervals during the sixties in areas of rapid development.

A rival company, Pioneer Ready Mixed Concrete, was started in Johannesburg not long after Ready Mixed Concrete (SA) had become established and after a few years it became clear that the market was just not big enough for both companies to operate profitably. In order to survive they agreed to merge and in 1965 they divided their operations into clearly defined areas, an arrangement which should have resulted in maximum exploitation of the available market. The two companies operated independently, however, and only combined at board level where it was obvious that they had very different operating objectives. In spite of this the relationship remained in existence for many years.

Ready Mixed Concrete (SA) was created with a number of outside shareholders and in 1968 Darling and Hodgson acquired a proportion of Rand Mines' shareholding in the company. At the same time they acquired a minority interest in Ready Mixed Concrete's major supplier of crushed aggregate, Consolidated Crusher Holdings, and Consolidated Crusher Holdings' holding company which was listed on the Johannesburg Stock Exchange as Trans Atlas Holdings, in which Rand Mines also had a shareholding. In 1970 Darling and Hodgson reduced their interest in Trans Atlas in return for an increase in their Ready Mixed Concrete shareholding, and in 1973 a final exchange of shares resulted in Ready Mixed Concrete (SA) becoming a wholly-owned subsidiary.

The partnerships entered into between Tanker Services and United Bulk Transport, and Ready Mixed Concrete and Pioneer Ready Mixed Concrete were full of problems, but in 1966 Darling and Hodgson embarked on another venture, which was an outstanding success from the very beginning. This was in equal partnership with an American company called Master Builders, a division of the Martin Marietta Corporation of America, which had for many years been manufacturing concrete admixtures, metallic floor hardners and non-shrink grouts. The admixtures had an obvious use within the ready-mixed concrete industry and the new company, Embecon, developed naturally as part of Darling and Hodgson Holdings. Over the years there has been an excellent working relationship with technical knowledge and expertise coming from America and management provided by Darling and Hodgson.

Not long after Embecon had been successfully launched, Darling and Hodgson pioneered an entirely new operation in South Africa when in 1969 they entered into partnership with a British concern to form a new company called Purle Industrial Waste Disposal. For some time there was a very close link with a great deal of technical assistance from Purle in the UK as the new company established itself. It was necessary to educate the South African public and industry to appreciate fully the service offered, but once again Darling and Hodgson was initiating something at an opportune time. Following world-wide interest, South Africa was gradually awakening to the danger of pollution and the man in the street was becoming increasingly aware of his environment. The long-term prospects of a waste disposal service had to be good. Purle enlarged its operations in 1971 when Darling and Hodgson purchased a 51% interest in a rival waste company, Murray Transport Services. The same year saw the link with Britain lessening and Purle soon became a wholly-owned subsidiary.

There was yet another venture into an unknown field in the late sixties when, with an ear ever open to ways of extending their interests in related fields of operation, Darling and Hodgson heard of what seemed like a revolutionary waterproofing agent and concrete protector manufactured in Denmark by Vandex and becoming available in other countries. The franchise was applied for and at the end of 1968, after lengthy discussions in Europe between John and the owner of Vandex, Mrs Pickering, Vandex (SA) was established for marketing all Vandex products, with the sole and exclusive distributing rights in South Africa. Tony Mason was appointed manager of the new company and Jim Reoch sales manager, both transferred from Ready Mixed Concrete. Vandex waterproofing was actively promoted to the construction and mining industries for all kinds of jobs from waterproofing roofs and basements to repairing water tanks and sealing tennis courts. It was used to plug leaking construction joints in the walls of the Spioenkop and Magoebaskloof dams for the Department of Water Affairs, and to waterproof the foundations of the new Cape Town Civic Centre which was being constructed on the Foreshore on land reclaimed from the sea. In the repair field Vandex was the only company in South Africa at the time which could repair leaking structures from the inside.

Before long the services offered were extended to include joint sealers when another franchise agreement was brought into Vandex in respect of Vulkem flexible polymethane sealants from Belgium, and a separate division was set up for these. Sales were extended to all major centres, with a branch company established in Natal and agents in the other provinces.

In spite of the active promotion there was little profit to be had and Darling and Hodgson decided that the operation was not really big enough to be maintained within the Group. At the end of 1971 the agreement between Darling and Hodgson and Vandex International was cancelled and the Danish company opened a subsidiary in South Africa which Jim Reoch took over. All the existing local stock of Vandex products was sold to him, and on this smaller scale the operation prospered.

There comes a time in the development of any company when the pioneering days are

Grain silos at Ogies, Transvaal – treated with Vandex.

over. The excitement and impetuousness of youth have to be left behind and a more mature path followed. As Darling and Hodgson grew and diversified there had to be a change from a situation where everything and everyone revolved around one man to a much broader management base. John had at times displayed almost superhuman energy in his deep involvement in all of Darling and Hodgson's activities, but he realized that it was time for a more professional approach. In 1963 he attended one of the Louis Allen management courses which originated in America and had recently been introduced to South Africa by Ralph Parrott. Many top companies, including Union Corporation, were sending their senior management staff on these courses in order to acquire this discipline, with very positive results. John found the course fascinating and it provided him with a completely new approach to management which he gradually introduced within Darling and Hodgson. He began to build up a group of competent men to form a strong team carrying out decentralized management and in 1972 he attended an executive development programme at Stanford University in America which further stimulated the introduction of his new policy. All the Darling and Hodgson senior managers were sent on the Louis Allen course, which was later established as an in-house programme and became part of every manager's training.

Within a few years the new approach crystallized into the discipline of management by objectives. This basically entailed formulating a plan of objectives against which performance was controlled. Each individual knew what was expected of him and he could observe his own progress in relation to his objectives. It was geared to improving productivity and motivation of employees in a thoroughly professional way and provided a fundamentally similar management within different divisions or companies – a common language as it were – which had a considerable unifying effect.

By the early seventies Darling and Hodgson were well launched into their new style of management and the discipline was showing its strength in the profits which were at last being made. Apart from Savage and Lovemore, there were five divisions within the company, each working towards set objectives under a competent senior executive. There were two non-operating divisions – finance and management services – and three operating divisions. Peter Langerman, who had been with Ready Mixed Concrete since its inception in South Africa, was appointed group manager of the Ready Mixed Concrete division. Transport was under Frank Lever who had joined United Tanker Services in 1971 and the smaller, newer companies, including Purle and Embecon, were grouped together as special services, under Aidan Buchholz. When Aidan left Union Corporation John asked him to join Darling and Hodgson, knowing that his wide general knowledge of industry gleaned during his fifteen years with them would be invaluable, especially as he had already been associated with the activities of Darling and Hodgson for eight years.

These men were part of a small head office staff of twelve which moved in 1970 to new offices. As the company had grown, all the top management of Darling and Hodgson Holdings and its subsidiaries were accommodated at Brailsford House, which represented the heart of Group activities, and although there had been considerable extensions of both ground and office buildings there came a time when there were just too many people for too little accommodation. John and Brian were considering the purchase of more adjoining land and the building of new offices when another possibility attracted them. In 1968 a large block of offices and shops was being built by Roberts Construction on the outskirts of Johannesburg at Hyde Park, following the American trend of developing offices on the perimeter of towns instead of centrally, and Darling and Hodgson successfully applied for a complete wing of office space. Their top management moved across in 1970, expanding gratefully into the spacious offices and appreciating the calm atmosphere which was reminiscent of the early days of Brailsford House and far preferable to the hurly-burly which had developed there as the tanker depots grew and the Embecon factory was established. Brailsford House has never lost its importance to Darling and Hodgson and has continued to be a vital part of the Group, developing over the years into the hub of the transport operations.

The D&H corporate head office is based at Hyde Park Corner, Sandton.

The discipline of management by objectives was made effective throughout Darling and Hodgson, down to the smallest operating companies, through a series of seminars which explained the professional techniques and skills to all the managers. These seminars were run by Ralph Parrott and Ralph Youngworth. Ralph Parrott made a very important contribution to the entire management structure of Darling and Hodgson, and he has maintained a close link with the company, following their progress with interest and offering invaluable advice in his capacity as a business consultant. Ralph Youngworth had been with Embecon since its inception and was transferred to head office as John's personal assistant after a short study course in America. As well as working on the management seminars Ralph helped compile the first policy and procedures manual for Darling and Hodgson which was considered the central core around which to build the Group's interpretation of professional management. An up-dated copy of this manual has been given to each new employee from its inception. This was followed by the drafting of the first formal company business plan which became standard practice each year from then on, providing strength for the company in its anticipation and planning for the future.

Part of the new approach was a decision to boost the Darling and Hodgson image and restore the name which had largely disappeared from the public eye when Darling and Hodgson (Pty) had been absorbed by Savage and Lovemore. Peter Theobold from Walter Kirby was brought in as a public relations consultant in the late sixties to co-ordinate the image of the Group as a strong go-ahead entity, drawing attention to its activities and encouraging the selling of products and services. He worked closely with Hugh Wheeler, one of Union Corporation's 'bright young men', who was seconded to John as his personal assistant for a few years. The Darling and Hodgson logo was designed and later, in 1971, registered as the company's trademark. In 1968 John had considered it important to keep the different companies within the Group in touch with each other's activities and a company newsletter was started. In 1971 the first magazine was distributed, with the stated intention of developing effective internal communications in order to improve productivity, promote team spirit and co-operation within the Group, and to emphasize an integrated Group image. The magazine was sent to each of the 1 200 white and 5 000 black employees of the Group at the time.

Over the years there were changes at Union Corporation which had far-reaching effects. Ian Wilson gained substantial support for his encouragement of Darling and Hodgson for the first time with the appointment in 1969 of John Henderson as assistant managing director of Union Corporation whereby he automatically became a director of the various industrial companies in which Union Corporation had an interest. John had a proven industrial record in Union Corporation through his turning SAPPI into a highly successful venture. A forthright man abounding with energy and with an infectious enthusiasm for life, he came onto the board of Darling and Hodgson in September 1969, replacing Hugh Monro who had been a director since 1966. Before long Ian left South Africa to head up Union Corporation's operations in Australia and his responsibilities for Darling and Hodgson were passed on to Cyril Newnham, a capable young man who had recently been appointed a head office manager of Union Corporation, transferred from his position as managing director of Kimberley Clarke to take charge of a number of industrial interests, reporting to John Henderson. He joined the board of Darling and Hodgson in November 1972. A few months previously another non-mining man from Union Corporation, Hugh Smith, had joined the board, replacing Bill Partridge on his retirement. Hugh has remained a director of Darling and Hodgson, contributing invaluable financial advice over the years.

Cyril, a dedicated accountant concentrating on making Union Corporation's industrial investments more profitable for them, saw Darling and Hodgson as a company with divisions scattered within the range of Union Corporation interests, none of them contributing much to the company. However he recognized the quality of the people in Darling and Hodgson and decided that the best way to make this company effective for the Corporation was to pull it together into a more cohesive force. He suggested that this should be done through going public. He was supported by John Henderson, and when the idea was put to John and Brian they were enthusiastic, appreciating that another financial injection for Darling and Hodgson would allow further exploitation of their potential.

Cyril was the architect of the public listing and set the whole programme in motion. In July 1973 Darling and Hodgson formally applied for a listing on the Johannesburg Stock Exchange. Before that, a restructuring of Darling and Hodgson was effected, mainly by adding a completely new leg to their operations through acquiring a controlling interest in Project Engineering. Union Corporation had for some time owned a major shareholding in Project Engineering which had been involved in the construction of their huge platinum mine near Rustenburg and various other undertakings. Cyril suggested that its acquisition would broaden the spectrum of Darling and Hodgson's operations, thereby presenting a more attractive package. Although it was not entirely supported by John and Brian, the deal went through. Darling and Hodgson purchased the Union Corporation share and also that of one of the minority shareholders, Stan Patterson, giving them a 61% interest. The acquisition heralded the arrival of 'The Three Musketeers' – Dave Verhagen, Barry Lowson and Ivor Yeo – and complemented Darling and Hodgson's other activities. Project Engineering brought with them an order book worth R25 million and immediately made a significant and valuable contribution to Group profits.

Darling and Hodgson also consolidated their existing interests. Ready Mixed Concrete and United Tanker Services became wholly-owned subsidiaries in those first months of 1973. They also increased their shareholding in Savage and Lovemore to 75% and in Murray Transport Services which the following year became 100% owned by Darling and Hodgson.

Cyril Newnham compiled a comprehensive prospectus aimed at selling Darling and

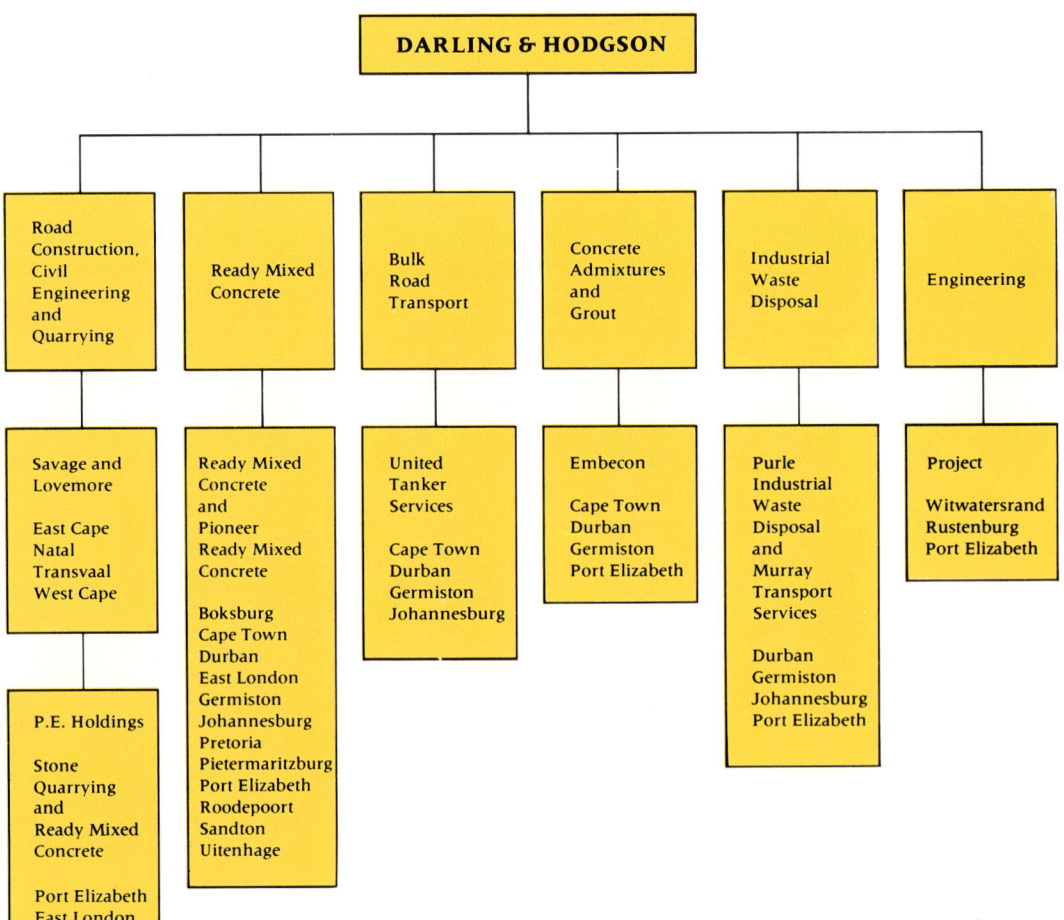

The Darling and Hodgson company structure – 1973.

Share certificate issued for Darling and Hodgson Limited.

Hodgson to the public, which was released on 17 August 1973. It aroused tremendous public interest with a lively response from the financial sector and comment in the press all around the country. One description of the company was 'the dynamic construction giant with a tough financial philosophy, an aggressive approach to recruitment of top personnel and an inward-looking expansion programme which aims for growth in known fields' – a thrilling description for those who had experienced the demands and conflicts as well as the achievements of the previous years.

Looking back it was apparent that the first significant profits had been made in 1970, followed by continued but somewhat erratic progress within the Group for the next couple of years. An optimistic picture was painted for the future and it was forecast that in 1973 the taxed profits would reach R1 800 000 with the major contribution coming from the construction side (33%), followed by the manufacturing operations of Ready Mixed Concrete and Embecon (31%), then the services side comprising bulk transport and industrial waste disposal (22%) and the new engineering operations contributing 14%. The Group financial policy was revealed as one that required that any new division or subsidiary must achieve a 25% return on capital within two to three years or be axed, the same fate applying to any existing company falling below a 25% return for the same period. There was also a policy, which has been retained, that a proportion of senior appointments should be made from outside the Group, thereby bringing in new blood.

In August 1973 Colin Campbell of *The Sunday Times* commented: 'With the South African economy gently gathering steam, with the Government heavily committed to a spending programme on various infrastructure developments, and with the private sector billed to put in significant growth, this road construction/civil engineering/bulk road transport group makes a timely appearance in Hollard Street.' Two million shares were offered through the Standard Merchant Bank to the public by Darling and Hodgson, representing 21% of their share capital. The public responded eagerly, their imagination caught by the vigorous image portrayed, and the shares were three times oversubscribed.

Darling and Hodgson made an unexpected acquisition just before its listing on the Johannesburg Stock Exchange by gaining control of Mazista, a well-known, publicly

John Henderson: chairman 1973–1976.

quoted slate company with extensive national sales and a developing overseas market. The decision to purchase involved considerable burning of midnight oil and the transaction, carried out a few days before Darling and Hodgson went public, was probably one of the most rapid moves ever made by the Group. The purchase price was good at the time and Mazista was seen to fit into the range of Group interests, while contributing to its policy of diversification. It also helped focus attention on the company and was reported as 'backing the suggestion that Darling and Hodgson are moving ahead'.

Unfortunately for Darling and Hodgson, during the period between their application to the Stock Exchange in July and their listing on 19 September, there were riots on the Western Deep Levels mines in the Orange Free State, resulting in fatal shootings, and all share prices plunged. This made the first day of selling Darling and Hodgson's shares somewhat disastrous, ending with a share price below the issue price of 170c. However, the company was successfully launched on the Stock Exchange, listed under the industrial section as 'D&H'. Jack Plane retired from the board after fourteen years as chairman, during which time he had given John a great deal of support and encouragement. John Henderson was appointed chairman of Darling and Hodgson Limited and Tony Croad of Union Corporation also joined the board.

This was a remarkable company in that its successful development had no direct operational links with the mining activities which constitute the lifeblood of South Africa, and the listing under the industrial section was an encouraging recognition of the company's intention to continue to expand beyond its traditional construction activities. 'D&H' was readily adopted by everyone as the name of the new public company which proceeded to enter a decade of growth beyond anyone's imagination.

1973–1983
Strength as a Public Company

The positive public recognition of the company's success with its launching on the Johannesburg Stock Exchange stimulated immediate development and D&H looked to the future with eager anticipation. The increased capital provided for organic growth and the first of the many acquisitions which studded the spectacular growth from 1973 onwards. An executive share scheme was initiated, involving the senior management in a degree of ownership of the company. Brian Malcomson always claimed that he was the first employee to be given this incentive when he acquired shares in D&H in 1957, and heartily endorsed its effectiveness!

Going public enforced an appreciable discipline within the company in that its performance and progress now had to be revealed in comprehensive reports to its shareholders. D&H are justifiably proud of the success story recorded in their annual reports, which are high quality, glossy publications with dramatic illustrations. The lavish production gives them good marketing value, which has been used to positive effect over the years as one of the few ways chosen to promote the Group as a whole rather than the individual companies.

Once on the euphoric path of expansion there was no holding back and within a couple of years further capital was raised through a rights issue to shareholders. Construction continued to be the major contributor to Group profits for a long time but there was a determined move away from dependence on operations so hypersensitive to the economic climate. Hence the major development was in industrial operations, and two main tracks emerged, one into construction materials and the other into transport and waste management, leading naturally out of Ready Mixed Concrete, Tanker Services and Purle Industrial Waste. Engineering activities also grew and extended Group facilities by completing their ability to undertake major turnkey development projects. Acquisitions led to the establishment of a Group engineering division which made a solid contribution to Group profits for many years.

The first step down the materials track was the purchase of Shires Quarry in Natal in 1973 – a significant venture into quarrying. The following year saw the acquisition of Paul's Industrial Investments, D&H's first purchase through a share transaction, which was only possible after going public. This purchase brought into the Group a team of people with refreshing energy and enthusiasm. While primarily a sand-quarrying business, Paul's Industrial Investments had a variety of interests, including a garage. In the same year the Group expanded its franchise business by forming a subsidiary company, Brailscar, to handle a Mack truck and Mazda franchise in the Eastern Cape. This ran successfully for some time, but did not really fit in with Group policy and was gradually closed down.

An important expansion of quarrying interests took place with the purchase of Randmix in 1977. This heralded a period of some turmoil and drama, when Ready Mixed Concrete took over Randmix's ready-mixed concrete operations on the Reef and Pioneer Ready Mixed Concrete took exception to this development. Heated discussions and day and night negotiations led to a complete break with Pioneer, but the success of the reorganized ready-mixed concrete operations was to prove the strife well worthwhile. Randmix also brought to the Group an interest in pulverized fuel ash from power stations which led to the establishment of D&H Ash Resources. Further acquisitions in the quarrying field and widespread extensions of Group ready-mixed concrete operations led to a rationalization of their management on a regional basis within a Group materials division in 1977. This also incorporated Embecon, Mazista and Hucrete,

D&H's brief venture into the manufacture of concrete products and sleepers.

In 1975 Purle Industrial Waste's connection with the United Kingdom was severed, the total equity of Murray Transport Services was acquired and all waste management put into a new company, Waste-tech, which expanded steadily into key areas of South Africa. Transport operations were increased considerably by the acquisition of WJ's Bulk Transport in 1977. The attempted integration of WJ's Bulk and Tanker Services was unsuccessful but after a few months a workable combination was achieved by maintaining their original identities and product lines. Transport also extended into refrigerated trucking and extra-heavy load transport and in 1979 became the major part of a Group services division which included the waste disposal operations.

Meanwhile construction operations had been badly affected by the downturn in the country's economy in the mid seventies and Savage and Lovemore were forced to look for ways to diversify. A logical use of their idle earthmoving equipment and quarrying expertise lay in the field of opencast mining and this led to the establishment in 1978 of a coal subsidiary within Savage and Lovemore. This grew rapidly into a Group division which within two years was contributing to D&H's profits.

Savage and Lovemore also strengthened their base through expansion into specialist skills. In 1977 there was a move into marine construction with the acquisition of 51% of Underwater Construction in the Cape, and 1979 saw the purchase of Monahan and Frost extend the company's skills in concrete operations.

As Group activities expanded successfully John saw the need for assistance in controlling the rapidly developing industrial side which would allow him to concentrate on the role of co-ordinator and minimize Brian's distractions from his financial work. John's attention focused on Peter Loveday as someone who could add a further dimension to the D&H management team and he invited him to join the Group as managing director of all the industrial companies. Peter was educated at Hilton College, and after attaining a B.Com. degree and qualifying as a chartered accountant, he joined Standard Telephones and Cables, the South African subsidiary of the huge American multinational ITT organization, where he was exposed to their tough but effective management philosophy, rising capably to its challenge. This was the experience which he brought to D&H in October 1975. There were four divisional managing directors reporting to Peter – Terry Rolfe, quarrying and building materials, Peter Asher, ready-mixed concrete, Phil Erasmus, transport, and Aidan Buchholz, service and manufacturing.

Peter Loveday saw D&H as a series of small companies operating independently which he felt sure would have greater strength and potential as a group. Within a year he had introduced a new management philosophy which was illustrated in a restructuring of D&H into three divisions: construction (Savage and Lovemore), engineering (Project Engineering) and industrial comprising all other activities. Peter was appointed managing director of the new industrial division.

A central team of senior functional managers, each highly qualified in his own field and assuming strategic responsibility, was established at head office, providing a wide range of specialized skills and expertise throughout the industrial division. Profit centre managers became less involved in day-to-day operations and spent more time planning and organizing. The new system took John away from active participation in all Group operations for the first time, and in order to keep in touch with all that was going on and to maintain communication between the different divisions he initiated executive meetings, the first of which was held on 17 March 1976, attended by John, Brian and Peter. These meetings were held monthly thereafter and the executive committee grew as the company developed, to become the control point of the Group.

John recognized the potential value to the Group of another old-Hiltonian and friend of long standing, Aubrey Welsford, who through his twenty-five years' experience in trust company work had gained considerable knowledge in finance, insurance and real estate matters. When John brought him into the Group in 1976 as director of corporate affairs he added substantial management depth in these fields. It was the same year that John Henderson retired and John Hodgson became chairman and chief executive of the

Group, a positive confirmation of Union Corporation's faith in John's ability. The following year Ted Pavitt, chairman and managing director of Union Corporation, joined the board, further endorsing the Corporation's positive view of D&H.

D&H had been working to a carefully structured business plan for some years, but Peter Loveday refined this to a more sophisticated process, drawing on his experience with ITT. He added new dimensions of control within the Group by taking the business plan down the management line as a control document against which people were accountable. The more disciplined style of management made each company more conscious of belonging to a big organization. Managers were included in discussions of the Group business plans, company objectives were shared and there were broader and more exciting challenges at greater depth. Some people found they could not stay the pace but the majority adapted successfully.

D&H entered a period of very substantial growth in profits. There were several contributory factors. Quite apart from the refined methods of planning and control, many of the investments made in the early seventies (such as quarries) began to contribute to Group profits at that stage, and there were many new acquisitions. When South Africa's economy took an upswing at the end of the seventies D&H were ready to take advantage of this and although the construction operations continued to be the major contributor to Group profits, the industrial companies showed dramatic growth. The Group's achievements were publicly acknowledged when D&H were included in the *Financial Mail's* Top 100 Companies in South Africa for the first time in 1975.

Having achieved such satisfactory and profitable diversification in South Africa into fields related to their traditional activities, D&H aimed for a geographical spread which would balance local operations and possibly develop management in different and more demanding surroundings. When John heard that Steve Sandiford of Embecon was planning to emigrate to the United Kingdom he saw an opportunity to place someone with long-standing loyalty to the Group in a strategic position in Europe. Based in an office in Union Corporation's premises in Gresham Street, London, Steve set out to investigate various possibilities for D&H, including the export of commodities such as Mazista slate and proteas. The overseas subsidiary D&H (Europe) BV was registered in Holland.

At first there seemed few opportunities worth following up. Then John's path once again crossed that of Tony Morgan, who had helped establish Purle Industrial Waste as a D&H subsidiary in the early seventies. Tony had left Purle UK when it was taken over

Above left
John Hodgson: appointed chairman and chief executive in 1976.

Above right
Peter Loveday.

WWM's Vac-All air conveying unit in operation.

by Redland, with a subsequent restraint on his participation in the waste industry. When the restraint was terminated he was approached by George Wimpey Ltd, Britain's largest contracting company, which was considering an entry into waste and Tony suggested that it should join with D&H who could provide the necessary expertise. Aidan Buchholz was appointed managing director of D&H (Europe) and went to the United Kingdom in 1977 to establish a new company, Wimpey Waste Management, which started operations the following year. In the same year that company acquired Powell Duffryn Pollution Control which catapulted it into a really big organization, operating waste disposal and industrial services throughout Britain.

D&H had not been able to finance their share of Wimpey Waste Management from South Africa because of stringent exchange control regulations and they were forced to borrow large sums of money overseas. Unfortunately economic conditions in the United Kingdom deteriorated rapidly and the interest rates soared to an unheard-of twenty per cent and more and Wimpey Waste Management found it an impossible task to meet its financial obligations as well as produce profits. Aware that they were a burden to their partners, standing in the way of expansion and development, D&H in 1980 sold their share of Wimpey Waste Management to Wimpey. The parting was on good terms and close contact was maintained with the United Kingdom company. Aidan opted to stay with the company in the UK and continued for some time as managing director.

Another overseas venture was embarked upon in 1978 when D&H decided together with Wimpey to introduce concrete sleepers to North America. The Group had entered this field with the purchase of Hume Prestressed Concrete (Hucrete) in 1974 and, subsequently, Continental Sleepers. They sold their sleeper operations in South Africa to Grinakers and were granted a licence to sell concrete sleepers in America. In 1979 D&H purchased Loc-pipe and Perma-pipe in Ontario, Canada, planning to use them as local concrete pipe producers and as a launch pad for the sleepers. Laurie Durandt was sent over to head up the operations, while Aubrey Welsford assumed Group responsibility for North America. Canada was unfortunately suffering from an economic depression, and extensive research evaluating the North American market for concrete sleepers was not encouraging. D&H felt that they were again a financial burden to their partners and in 1981 they sold their Canadian interests to Wimpey and withdrew from all international operations pending more favourable conditions. Laurie decided to stay in Canada with Wimpey.

Meanwhile in 1978 Andrew Savage and David Lovemore had retired from their executive positions in Savage and Lovemore, and D&H increased their stake to ninety-six per cent by purchasing the founders' shares. Both men maintained an active participation for some years, and Andrew remained on the D&H board, continuing to contribute to Group affairs even after he became a member of parliament for Walmer in 1981. In 1978 Don Lanigan was brought in to head up the materials division, and a new division, multiproducts, was created under Dudley Pieterse as a home for companies which did not fit elsewhere, such as D&H Flora which exported indigenous flowers from the Cape to Europe. When Don took over the materials division, Peter Asher moved to Natal as director for that region, in particular to develop a close liaison with all government departments.

Towards the end of 1980 Peter Loveday was appointed deputy managing director of D&H, welcomed by John as an able assistant in all Group affairs. In the same year engineering was moved into the industrial division after Dave Verhagen's retirement. Although engineering had contributed well to Group profits until then, this did not continue and substantial losses were recorded in 1980, aggravated by D&H's thrilling but expensive venture into oil rig construction with the formation of Amardah Shipyards in partnership with Murray and Roberts. Don Lanigan was moved to the engineering division in an endeavour to resuscitate it, and his place in the materials division was taken by David Bath. David returned from the UK to take up this position; he had been studying the Sloan Programme at the London Business School for a year, followed by a few months with Wimpey Waste Management.

During 1980 D&H acquired a strategic stake in Grinakers with a view to extending construction activities and entering the electronics field. They were unable to reach agreement with the controlling shareholders, however, and relinquished their shares. The same year D&H acquired the outstanding shares in Savage and Lovemore, which became a wholly-owned subsidiary, thus opening the way for its integration with other Group construction interests.

The following year saw significant changes in construction. The purchase of Fowler Holdings shifted Group contracting resources into new growth areas of commercial building and mass housing and enlarged their road construction operations. Soon after the Fowler/Combrink organization had come into the Group its managing director, Alex Combrink, was appointed managing director of a newly-formed D&H construction division and a director of the main board. Within a short time he had consolidated the old and the new, rationalizing their management within the division and inspiring a common loyalty to the Group. Gerry Schoonbee moved across to D&H Coal for a while but soon retired from all executive responsibilities within the Group. He had contributed a great deal to the progress of D&H throughout his twenty years of dedicated service with Savage and Lovemore.

As the Group expanded, with increasing numbers of employees, John decided to improve communications by re-establishing the Group magazine. Two previous attempts had been discontinued, but in 1975 another series was successfully launched and became known as *D&H News*. This magazine has always provided a platform for the introduction of top executives and their views, and for reports on current operations which make all employees aware of the range of activities throughout the Group. It is essentially people-orientated and records all manner of achievements both in work and leisure environments. The full-time editor travels extensively, necessitating a healthy constitution and a resilient nature, but the reward is a fascinating exposure to all aspects of Group operations. The magazine covers usually depict Group activities, vividly portrayed by Ed-

D&H News.

die Barton, who joined Purle Industrial Waste in its early days but found greater fulfilment in the public relations department where his artistic talent helps promote the Group image in a very positive way.

Public relations and personnel matters became increasingly important within the Group, and the early eighties brought significant developments in these fields. D&H adopted the policy of producing divisional handbooks for all employees, outlining relevant company benefits and policies, and in 1981 the directors approved the establishment of the code of employment practice. At the time D&H had two thousand white and fourteen thousand black employees, a clear indication of the code's vital importance. Apart from the social industrial implications, the code was in some ways a formal recognition of D&H's concern for its staff and at the same time the slogan 'D&H Cares' was adopted as a watchword throughout the company.

Over the years Ralph Parrott had retained close contact with D&H, advising on various matters, and he was the catalyst in the development of D&H's personnel division. On his recommendation Aubrey Welsford, already deeply involved in D&H affairs, was appointed executive director Group personnel and industrial relations in 1981, and later that year a Group industrial relations department was established. Industrial relations rapidly became an integral part of the Group's business strategy and the improved lines of communication between management and labour produced a solid base on which to ride any storms of unrest. The first black D&H manager was appointed to co-ordinate labour relations when Herbert Moloantoa joined the Group with extensive experience in this field. At the beginning of 1983 the Group industrial relations department was disbanded and divided between the construction and industrial divisions, making it easier to work with the two different cultures.

Departments were also established at head office to control corporate affairs and manage strategic planning under Iain Welsh, who had joined D&H as Group accountant for Waste-tech in 1974, and legal administration was put in the hands of Hugh Lane, who had recently joined the Group.

The welcoming reception area of 'The White House'.

The head office had grown considerably since its move from Brailsford House. For several years Margi Hodgson, John's eldest daughter, controlled the reception area with charming efficiency, her warmth and cheerfulness welcoming everyone to D&H. Margi left in September 1979 but the reception desk remained a friendly central communication point, and a vital link with the outside world. In 1983 there were many changes at the Hyde Park offices. As the Group grew the possibility of building new corporate headquarters had been discussed but this had been discarded in favour of adapting and improving the existing facilities. Ruth Hodgson was given the opportunity to participate in a way reminiscent of the Brailsford House days as she helped choose fittings and furniture for a newly designed wing comprising an imposing boardroom and smaller committee room, a dignified dining-room with an adjacent kitchen, and an attractive, welcoming ante-room. No wonder that this area soon became known as 'The White House'!

The new wing added to the facilities which had been established downstairs at Hyde Park in 1982, to provide quiet, congenial surroundings for board meetings and a few other special functions. When the new boardroom on the fifth floor came into use in 1984 the well-equipped downstairs conference centre was made available for training sessions.

As part of the reorganization in 1983 the materials and services divisions moved out to establish their own headquarters, and this facilitated the accommodation of their management teams which had grown significantly as the divisions developed. The reduced coal division was brought into the Hyde Park complex.

John Hodgson has never failed to show his appreciation of those people whose contribution to the Group often goes unnoticed, including the wives who give support at home and the receptionists, the secretaries and the messengers who keep the wheels turning smoothly. When the D&H head office moved from Brailsford House to Hyde Park, Enard Munnik stayed on as John's secretary for a few years until she left just after the company went public in 1973. Her place was taken by Joan Plumb who had been Brian Malcomson's secretary since 1970. Joan soon became invaluable, creating a chan-

The D&H board, 1982. Left to right: Ted Pavitt, Gerry Schoonbee, Alex Combrink, Hugh Smith, John Hodgson, George Clark, Aubrey Welsford, Peter Loveday, Denys la Grange, Brian Malcomson (absent: Andrew Savage).

nel of communication between John and the rest of the company, indeed the rest of the world, carrying out her many duties with elegant and impeccable efficiency.

At the end of 1979 Union Corporation merged with General Mining to create the second largest mining and industrial finance house in South Africa, a significant enterprise by world standards, and D&H was well to the fore among the industrial subsidiaries that the Corporation took into Gencor. These included such companies as SAPPI, Kohlers, Carlton and Union Shipping, all prominent in the South African economy.

D&H continued down the path of success and there was jubilation throughout the Group at the end of 1981 when the year's results were better than ever before. This was the combination of a high level of economic activity in South Africa, especially in the construction and building related fields, and a wide spread of activities which were efficiently geared to exploiting all opportunities to the absolute maximum with well trained and highly motivated staff.

This exhilaration carried D&H triumphantly into 1982, and it was a great disappointment to everyone when at the end of that year Group profits dropped for the first time in fifteen years. They not only dropped, they plummeted by a devastating 48% because of the disastrous results in the engineering division which impacted the profits and the track record of the Group. John publicly acknowledged that 'we have managed the division badly and have paid the price'. The situation was aggravated by the collapse of D&H Coal's export market which had considerably dimmed that division's bright future. There was little despondency, however, as a determined effort was made to rectify the situation. John's comment on the experiences of 1982 was that they would 'serve to get things back into perspective and on track again' – admirably humble words. It was typical of him and of D&H that they had the strength and courage to face up to adversity and see the problems as opportunities in disguise, stimulating increased effort. The Group was trimmed to more streamlined operations and unprofitable activities were sold, including Amardah. Mazista was also sold, somewhat reluctantly because it held a fascination for many people, but it had never fitted satisfactorily into Group activities. Within the services division, Omnibus had outlived its usefulness and it too was sold, and D&H Freight Lines was closed. Meanwhile transport operations had been extended to include semi-bulk handling through the purchase in 1980 of Containerisation Africa – the name was later changed to D&H Semi-Bulk. Although disappointing for the Group as a whole, 1982 was a triumphant year for David Bath and his team when the profits of the materials division peaked above those of construction for the first time – a momentous achievement in the process of decreasing dependence on construction. This

D&H corporate advertisement – 1981.

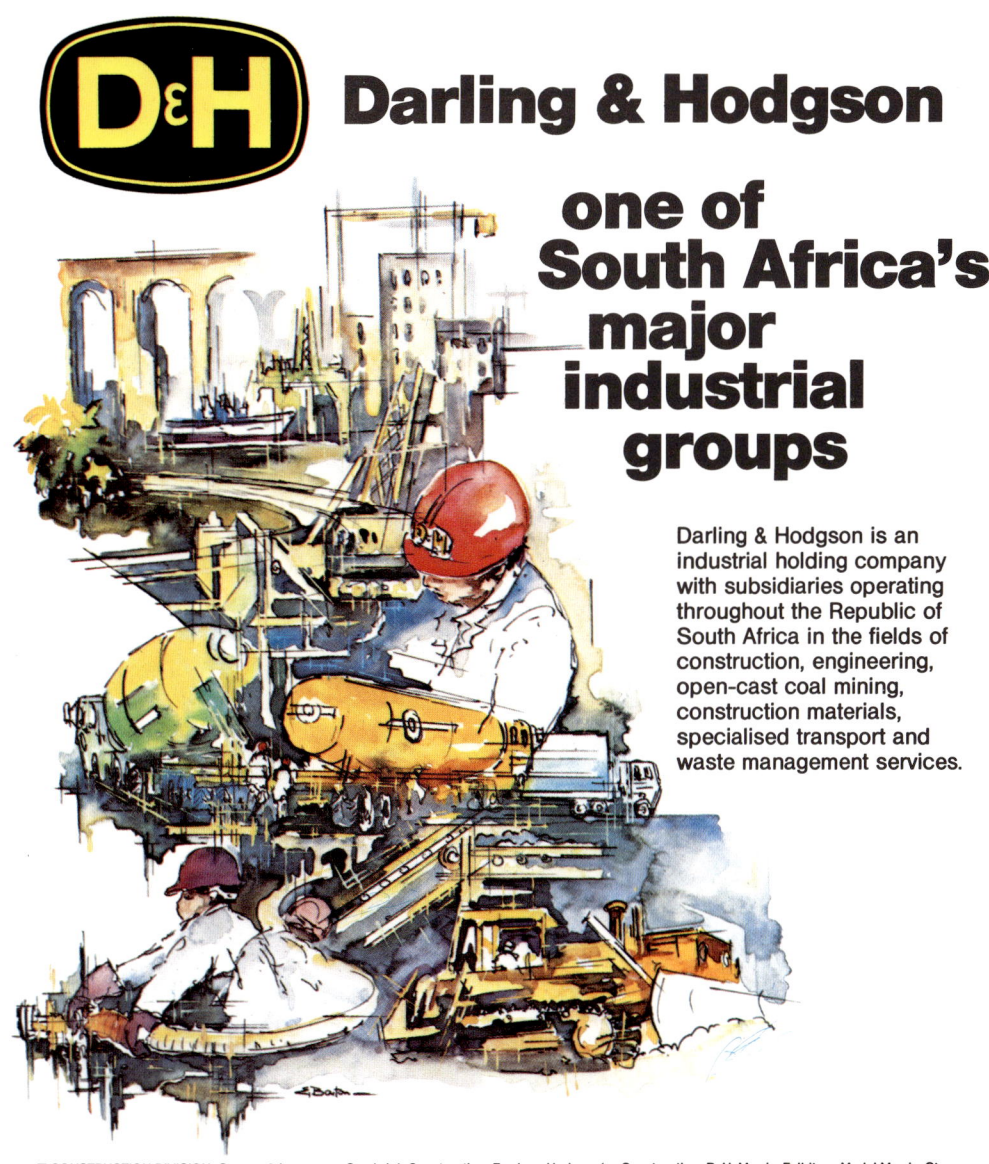

success was partly due to the acquisition of Keir and Cawder, an old well-established company which brought into the Group a wide range of quarrying interests, including a strategic entry into the Orange Free State.

With the subsequent readjustment within the Group, Alex Combrink was appointed joint managing director with Peter Loveday, and Denys la Grange was appointed director of corporate affairs, taking responsibility for five Group functions – property, legal, purchasing, public relations and insurance – as well as administering the corporate head office budget. Denys was no stranger to the Group, having been with Savage and Lovemore since 1966, where he had been deeply involved on the financial side. Another wheel turned a full circle when, nearly thirty years after his first association with D&H, Rod Cross returned to take up the post of manager of Group financial services at head office, a very different scene from Cullinan Building! His particular responsibility was for all aspects of Group tax.

The chairman's executive, 1984. Left to right: Denys la Grange, Aubrey Welsford, Terry Stone, Alex Combrink, Brian Malcomson, John Hodgson, David Bath, Theunis Kotzee, Lloyd Koch, Phil Erasmus.

In the middle of 1983 Peter Loveday left D&H in order to pursue his own interests. He left a Group which had become renowned for its stimulating environment, where management was encouraged to use initiative and creativity, where training was of prime importance on all levels and which attracted employees of the highest calibre. It was a Group that other successful companies were eager to join and to which all its employees were proud to belong. While with the Group Peter had seen the materials and services divisions develop to such a degree that their managing directors were handling as many responsibilities and commitments as John himself had been handling only a few years previously. Peter had watched the 'old timers' Phil Erasmus and David Bath adapt to new systems with confidence and enthusiasm, with impressive results, and when he left the Group these two men became directly responsible to John for services and materials respectively. Comparative newcomer Lloyd Koch had shown a similar aptitude as managing director of the coal division and when Don Lanigan left during 1983 the remaining engineering operations were put into a manufacturing division under Lloyd. At the end of 1983 David and Phil were appointed to the board of D&H, joining the team which was to lead the Group confidently into the future.

Construction swung to the fore again in 1983. Its many facets within D&H were rationalized during the year and its operations enlarged and extended by the acquisition of a majority shareholding of Group Five Engineering. Strict independence of operations was maintained at first, but the Group Five activities dovetailed very neatly with those of D&H Construction and at the end of 1983 it was decided to merge the latter into Group Five, creating an enlarged construction arm.

When Bill Hodgson died in 1959 he had spent twenty-five years building Darling and Hodgson into a successful small family business. After his father's death John, determined to achieve greater things, guided the company into a thrilling period of accelerating growth for the following twenty-five years. He was constantly encouraged and helped beyond measure by his colleague Brian, who has commented on his thirty years with D&H and his deep friendship with John with the words: 'Our rapid progress has been most exhilarating and lots of fun.' These words epitomize the development of D&H and perhaps reflect John's often-voiced opinion that 'when you stop having fun you must stop doing business'.

As its fiftieth year commenced at the end of 1983 D&H looked back over years of contribution to the growth of South Africa and looked to the future with all the facilities and enthusiasm for, to quote John, 'imagineering a greater and better South Africa'.

John, or as he is known to everyone in the Group, 'JBH', is renowned for his opening words – 'I believe …' It is this personal conviction and never-failing optimism in all that he does that has always motivated people and will continue to do so. Rationalization and reorganization within D&H have inevitably taken their toll of the 'family of families', but as long as John continues to lead the Group the loyalty and commitment which he inspires will retain the unique spirit which permeates its countrywide activities in many different spheres.

The Construction Story

After the Second World War there was enormous potential for development in South Africa, a country whose progress was relatively unhampered by the ravages of war. Men of courage and determination took full advantage of this, and in the construction field Basil Read, Andrew and Douglas Roberts, Andrew Savage and David Lovemore, amongst others, built up their own contracting companies. Until the early fifties all major road construction in South Africa was undertaken by the Government and by the provincial authorities and the earliest successful private tenderers were the big overseas firms such as Zanen Contractors and John Laing and Son. Local enterprise developed rapidly, however, and by the early sixties South African companies were well to the fore in road building, and names such as Clifford Harris, Basil Read, Savage and Lovemore and Concor were displayed on sites all around the country.

During this period Darling and Hodgson became well known in suburban road construction on the Reef. They also carried out surfacing subcontracts throughout the country and their subsidiary, Tarmac Industries, produced premixed asphalt for surfacing operations. They won their first million rand contract in 1958 at Collondale airport, East London, which was a significant breakthrough. Bill Hodgson never really wanted the company to expand, however, and it was only after his death in 1959, when John assumed control, that Darling and Hodgson began to move into road construction on a large scale. The significant boost came in 1963 when the company became a subsidiary of Union Corporation, thereby gaining financial backing for their investment in Savage and Lovemore and the South African interests of A G Burton.

These two contracting companies participated fully in the rapidly expanding national road construction programme, and many hundreds of miles of road, especially in the Cape, were built under their names. They operated independently of Darling and Hodgson (Pty) until the end of 1968 when the contracting activities of all three companies were consolidated and rationalized within Savage and Lovemore. The names A G Burton and Darling and Hodgson (Pty) fell away, and Darling and Hodgson increased their stake in Savage and Lovemore to 51%. Apart from participation at board level, however, they allowed Savage and Lovemore to operate independently under Andrew Savage and David Lovemore.

The Savage and Lovemore head office was moved up to the Transvaal and the construction operations were divided into two regional areas, north and south of the Orange river. All surfacing interests were sold and after a settling down period the reorganization showed very positive results.

The early seventies saw an unprecedented boom in road building. Savage and Lovemore were well placed to take advantage of this and were awarded multi-million rand contracts all around the country. Their reputation extended beyond road building with an impressive record in the construction of bridges, railways, building and industrial civil works, dams, reservoirs and canals and airport facilities. While the profit base remained firmly in the Cape, there was an increasing amount of work to be found in the Transvaal and Natal.

A Savage and Lovemore office was established in Natal after the purchase of T G Vorster in 1971, and 1973 saw the acquisition of Seven T Construction which provided a firm foothold in the province. In 1974 W T Rodd Construction was purchased, strengthening the concrete activities in Natal. Savage and Lovemore were well placed to take advantage of the development in the province, especially at Richards Bay and Newcastle.

Darling and Hodgson further increased their stake in Savage and Lovemore to 75% in 1973 when they went public. There was little change in management until 1978, however, when D&H increased their shareholding to 96% and Andrew and David retired from their executive positions although they continued to play a significant role in company affairs for some years.

When the road building boom slumped in the mid seventies Savage and Lovemore found themselves with idle equipment and staff, and they looked for different ways to make use of them. In 1978 they moved into the logical diversification of opencast coal mining, which was soon taken out of Savage and Lovemore and promoted to Group divisional status.

The acquisition of 51% of Underwater Construction in the Cape in 1977 expanded the operating base of Savage and Lovemore into marine work. This continued as a vigorous company, always operating totally independently under Harry Fuchs. Savage and Love-

D&H Construction in Soweto.

more's concrete expertise was extended in 1979 with the purchase of Monahan and Frost, and two years later the Group's construction interests were increased dramatically by the acquisition of Fowler Holdings. This move brought several independently operating companies into the Group under managing director Alex Combrink – Fowler Construction, Combrink Construction, R H Morris and Felbitem. The transaction expanded Savage and Lovemore's historical activities and took Darling and Hodgson for the first time into large-scale industrial building and mass housing. It also brought road surfacing operations to Darling and Hodgson once more – a full circle had been turned.

For some time these companies were all run independently of Savage and Lovemore, which had become a wholly-owned subsidiary of D&H in 1980. At the end of 1981 Gerry Schoonbee, soon to retire for personal reasons, was in favour of the rationalization of all Group construction activities, and the first integration of Savage and Lovemore into Group activities took place with the creation of a Group construction division. Alex Combrink was appointed managing director of this division which incorporated all Fowler Holdings and Savage and Lovemore operations, including Underwater Construction and Monahan and Frost. Alex undertook the formidable task of putting together the different organizations and people, and integrating the fiercely independent Savage and Lovemore into the Group. He was the motivating force behind the emergence of a Group image as operations were streamlined and co-ordinated, mobilizing the various strengths into a cohesive and powerful force. It was a remarkably successful operation, presenting many people with exciting new challenges and opportunities. With the formation in 1982 of the new operating companies of D&H Construction (Transvaal) and D&H Civils the names Fowler Construction, Savage and Lovemore (Transvaal) and Monahan and Frost fell away, although Savage and Lovemore continued strongly in the Cape and Natal, and Combrink Construction and R H Morris continued their traditional operations. The reorganization meant a return of the name Darling and Hodgson to construction operations.

The acquisition by D&H in 1982 of Roadmix and Stevenson Construction brought about a further restructuring of the division, which gave national coverage in the various aspects of construction:

The glass container warehouse for Nampak in Rondebult, Germiston.

Above left
Sandy Jamieson.

Above right
Alex Combrink.

Roads and earthworks
D&H Construction (Transvaal) – comprising the road construction activities of Fowler Construction and Savage and Lovemore (Transvaal) – and Savage and Lovemore (Cape) and (Natal)

Building
Combrink Construction, Stevenson Construction, R H Morris

Asphalt and road rehabilitation
Roadmix – incorporating Fowlers' black top operations – Felbitem

Civil engineering work
D&H Civils – comprising Monahan and Frost and part of Savage and Lovemore (Transvaal)

Marine work
Underwater Construction

This range of activities provided the Group with the resources to tackle major turnkey projects, such as the Nampak factory at Rondebult in Germiston.

In 1983 the major shareholding of another large well-established construction organization was acquired. D&H had for some time recognized that a closer association with Group Five Engineering would be advantageous because of its complementary operations; Group Five's Basil Read was strong in road construction in the Transvaal where D&H was weakest, and D&H's extensive building activities would benefit Group Five. For several months the two groups operated independently and then, echoing the events of 1968, the D&H construction division was reversed into Group Five at the end of 1983, and the D&H companies continued to operate independently under the Group Five banner as from the beginning of 1984.

Thus Group Five, as D&H's construction arm, with Sandy Jamieson as chairman and Alex Combrink as his deputy, became one of the major building and construction companies in South Africa, looking to the future with a confidence supported by increased muscle in competitive tendering and a comprehensive range of activities enabling it to participate in a great variety of projects. Both Group Five and D&H had grown largely through acquisitions over the years, and when the two groups joined forces at the end of 1983 not many of the original road construction companies of the fifties remained which had not come to rest in the D&H fold – no mean success for the company which had been the smallest of them all!

A G Burton

In the mid fifties a long convoy of road building equipment was slowly wending its way down the dusty roads of Africa, reminiscent of a desert camel train, from Kenya to Northern Rhodesia. This was A G Burton, a Kenyan-based construction company, moving south to build the north access road to the Kariba dam which was being constructed on the Zambezi river to provide hydroelectric power for the rapidly developing Federation of Rhodesia and Nyasaland.

An enormous wall was under construction at the Kariba gorge nearly 400 km below the Victoria Falls, and the road from the north was vital to carry an estimated 400 000 tons of cement from a factory near Kafue in Northern Rhodesia. The project was completed in the almost unbelievably short period of five years and the triumphant culmination was the official opening by Her Majesty the Queen Mother on 17 May 1960.

A G Burton's operations were guided by Ben Burton himself, his practical knowledge complemented by the financial expertise of his accountant partner, Terry Hardy. Overall A G Burton made a very handsome profit from this contract which filled Ben and Terry with great joy and confidence. In their euphoria they were prepared to tackle anything and they tendered successfully for three contracts in 1959 in areas unknown to them – in South Africa for the national road between Willowmore and Aberdeen, in Mauritius for part of the first ever double carriageway on the island, and in Southern Rhodesia for part of the road from Bulawayo to the Victoria Falls. They also decided to

Kariba's access road from the north.

open an office in Lusaka and continue contracting in Northern Rhodesia. The Mauritian contract will always be remembered for two things – the huge boulders, so typical of the island, which had to be dealt with as the road was built, and the rain which fell like clockwork at 3 pm every day!

The company was divided into two operating divisions with Ben taking all the work north of the Limpopo and Terry the South African and Mauritian roads. This division was not a success, however, and there was considerable unhappiness throughout the company with no one knowing where his loyalty lay, with the result that all the contracts got into difficulty in one way or another. On the Willowmore road the consulting engineers, Hawkins, Hawkins and Osborn, would not accept the base course that Burtons were laying and this was delaying the surfacing subcontractors, Darling and Hodgson (Pty), to such an extent that eventually Darling and Hodgson were asked to assist, to the annoyance of the Burtons men on the job.

Jim Maguire joined A G Burton on the Willowmore contract in February 1959. The frustrations there arose largely because of very old equipment, most of which had made the long journey down from Kenya. It was only when Gerry Schoonbee joined the company in 1960, from Zanen Contractors in Rhodesia, that the situation stabilized. Gerry's exceptional organizing ability set things moving in the right direction and the contract was finished to everyone's satisfaction.

Willowmore is a tiny town in the middle of the bleak Karoo and it was a great shock to Gerry and Jim's wives when they arrived to join their husbands. They adapted readily to their strange surroundings, however, and even grew accustomed to the brak water and lack of modern toilet facilities. When they eventually left it was with many happy memories, including the helpfulness of the local telephone exchange. Where else but in a country district would the telephone operator tell you where your friends are when there is no reply to your telephone calls, and even listen for your baby crying when you are out if you leave the receiver on the cot?

Philip Wessels also joined A G Burton on the Willowmore contract in 1960, working under Gerry. He then moved to Natal where Burtons had won the contract for the national road between Mooi River and Nottingham Road. This turned out to be a difficult and unprofitable job. The Natal midland mists rolled over them day after day, the ground was too wet to work and the vehicles and machines got stuck time and time again. The site agent was Lyle Thöle, a man born and bred in Natal, but even he could not combat the all-pervasive damp which reduced the linen working plans to limp unmanageable sheets.

Meanwhile the Rhodesian contract was also running into trouble and A G Burton found themselves with considerable financial problems. The contract involved millions of pounds, much of which had been guaranteed by promissory notes from the Federal Government. With the dissolution of the Federation in 1961 people were very wary of the financial situation and did not want Rhodesian money. Burtons found themselves not making their anticipated profits either and were precipitated into an extremely vulnerable situation, as a result of which all Ben Burton's interests were bought out by a company based in London – the Hunasgeria Tea Company.

Darling and Hodgson were subcontracted for the surfacing of the Falls road, and John Hodgson was thus very aware of what was going on. He saw in the situation an opportunity to extend the potential of his own business and take a step into the 'big league' of road construction. A few months previously, with Union Corporation's approval, John had negotiated a 25% stake in Savage and Lovemore, another construction company, but D&H had no control over its operations and the acquisition of A G Burton promised to be much more exciting. John and Ian Wilson of Union Corporation flew to London and negotiated the purchase of 51% of all Burtons' South African interests, by then gathered together under the name of A G Burton (SA), registered in 1960, for the sum of R450 000. This included all the assets from the Rhodesian and Mauritian contracts.

While these negotiations were taking place, Gerry had been offered a job by Savage and Lovemore which was based in Port Elizabeth in the Eastern Cape. They recognized

Road construction operations in the Cape.

his sterling qualities and made him a very attractive offer, including shares in the company, and Gerry, who was understandably feeling a little uncertain of the future of A G Burton, accepted it. He agreed, however, to stay on for several months in order to hand his job over to Edward Sunde, whom John moved from Darling and Hodgson to take charge of Burtons' operations from September 1963. Edward's main headache was the Mooi River contract which was completed satisfactorily but at a substantial loss, which was very discouraging.

In 1963 Roger Cuningham, whose father, Switch, had been a close friend of Bill Hodgson's, joined the Burtons team to take charge of all the concrete work. He also came down from Rhodesia where he had been working for Kilburn Construction. When Roger first applied to Darling and Hodgson he was offered the job of a site agent, which he declined, having spent enough time living 'out in the sticks'. Subsequently he accepted an appointment with A G Burton from which he steadily progressed to a position in the senior ranks of the D&H construction division.

Within a couple of years Darling and Hodgson acquired the total shareholding of A G Burton (SA) from the Hunasgeria Tea Company (whose name had changed to the Consolidated Commercial Company) and a new board of directors was appointed, comprising John Hodgson and Brian Malcomson of Darling and Hodgson, Ian Wilson and Aidan Buchholz from Union Corporation, Edward Sunde and Ken Richardson. Ken had been Burtons' company secretary for many years and in June 1966 his position was taken by Bill Bayliss. The company offices were moved from their old prefabricated military buildings at Rand airport to Brailsford House.

A G Burton continued road construction operations under their own name, with their

Crusher for base course material.

surfacing usually carried out by Darling and Hodgson. Apart from the Mooi River contract and a later one on the road between Mtubatuba and Kwa-Mbonambi, all their early South African contracts were in the Cape, working between Fort Beaufort and Kroomie, Loxton and Carnarvon, Graaff-Reinet and Pearston, and a little later between Victoria West and Loxton and Loxton and Calvinia. The first A G Burton contract to run from start to finish after the Darling and Hodgson takeover was the relocation of eleven miles of national road through the Huis River Pass to Calitzdorp. This was their first mountain road contract and presented many problems. Extensive advance planning paid good dividends, however, and with the benefit of new equipment the pass was completed satisfactorily within two years. There were smaller contracts as well, such as the Loxton municipal dam which made a profit, and a bridge over the Koonap river, unfortunately completed at a loss.

In 1965 A G Burton were awarded a contract for runways at Upington airport. After the mountains of the Huis River Pass the terrain was monotonously flat, and the equipment battled with the hard rock of the Western Cape. The runways were surfaced by D&H and the success of the contract was confirmed when one of the pilots who later landed his aeroplane there remarked that it was one of the smoothest runways in the country.

During 1965 Con Roux left Darling and Hodgson to start his own business and Edward Sunde became responsible for all the road construction contracts. He was based at Brailsford House but spent at least half of each month travelling around to the various contracts, most of the time in the Cape. The following year A G Burton became involved in the building of the Hendrik Verwoerd dam near Colesberg in the Cape as part of the Orange river scheme. They constructed the access road from Steynsburg and the airstrip at Donkerpoort which served as the aerodrome for all those who flew to the dam site. They were also contracted to build a new road from Venterstad to Norvalspont to replace the one that would later be flooded, and the earth saddle dam which was to control the flow of water while the main wall was being built. The latter was not completed by Burtons, who pulled out in October 1968 because of an inadequate and unsuitable sand supply.

The balance between too little work and too much is a delicate one, and through the mid sixties A G Burton often struggled with this problem. In many cases they experienced difficulties arising from over-commitment which led to inadequate equipment and minimal managerial staff on individual contracts, and it was difficult to find enough skilled foremen to cover all the work. As a result many of the contracts ran at a loss and company profits each year were low or non-existent. However, they soldiered on and in 1968 a newspaper report revealed that A G Burton 'has built 233 miles of road' in the Cape Province and 'is currently building a further 121 miles'. Two more contracts underway by then were Sutherland to Matjiesfontein and Postmasburg to Koopmansfontein – names which evoke images of those small communities which were being brought out of isolation as better roads brought them closer to each other and to the rest of the country.

When Edward was appointed a Group manager of Darling and Hodgson in 1967 in charge of all their construction interests, Johan Schonken took his position in A G Burton. Johan was a Transvaler and he looked for contracts nearer home, taking A G Burton out of the Cape and Natal for the first time since they had started operating in South Afri-

Work on the Pretoria Eastern Bypass.

ca. In 1967 they won a contract in the Orange Free State for the road from Bethulie to Goedemoed, and they were jubilant when they were awarded the largest ever road contract at that time in South Africa, for the Pretoria Eastern Bypass. This comprised fourteen miles of motorway, three miles of single carriageway and some twenty-three bridges – tendered at nearly R7,5 million and with a final cost of over R11 million. They were also constructing roads and a railway siding in the western Transvaal at Union Corporation's development of a platinum mine near Rustenburg.

Darling and Hodgson surfaced most of the roads that A G Burton built and also those being constructed by Savage and Lovemore. The two road contracting companies found themselves in increasing competition, however, which was detrimental to both, and in order to improve efficiency and increase profits it was decided to rationalize all D&H construction operations under the name of Savage and Lovemore. This took effect in 1968 and at the time of the merger A G Burton contributed several million rands worth of contracts throughout South Africa. Edward moved down to Port Elizabeth to work with David Lovemore, which proved a very successful combination, and Gerry Schoonbee, as managing director of Savage and Lovemore, assumed responsibility for all contracting work.

On 1 July 1969 A G Burton (SA) was officially changed to Savage and Lovemore (Transvaal) and the name A G Burton disappeared from the Darling and Hodgson Group. Its work continued, however, and most of the staff stayed on. Instead of a division of resources, all were now put together and Savage and Lovemore forged ahead confidently with the new combined strength of the three contracting companies.

Savage and Lovemore

For many years the pioneering aspect of life in South Africa was reflected in the activity of the general merchants. Hard-working men with bold vision made their fortunes through trading – and sometimes lost them again! The larger merchants were based around the coast where their ships brought in goods from other lands, and amongst these was a trading company in Port Elizabeth called Savage and Hill. This company was formed in 1846 and has carried through until the present day, with changes in name and direction, as the backbone of Darling and Hodgson's construction operations.

Savage and Hill became William Savage and Son and their trading activities carried on until the Boer War, when the collapse of ordinary life resulted in their becoming insolvent, along with many other companies. When the war was over and life began to return to normal, it proved impossible to pick up the old threads. The whole world was changing after the turn of the century – communications were improving dramatically, people were travelling, and South Africa was no longer such an unknown place. With the opening up of the Witwatersrand after the discovery of gold, the importance of the coastal cities diminished. The glory of the general merchant had dimmed, and Savage and Son gradually built up a reputation as brokers in the skin and hides business. This continued until the Second World War and it was the business that young Andrew Savage (William Savage's great-grandson) joined in 1946 when he came home from fighting in the war.

Andrew started a transport business under the family name, operating from an office in Paterson Road above the skin and hides store which gave it a characteristic pungent atmosphere! Initially he owned three flat trucks which were used to carry sand and stone for builders. They were all loaded by hand, and the precious shovels were taken home each night lest they were stolen. Gradually the flat trucks were replaced by tip-trucks.

Early days in Port Elizabeth.

The first one was an Albion with a second-hand tip body, which was fitted in the workshops behind the Savage and Son offices. One night when the men were working late to finish the truck Andrew called in on his way home to see how everything was going, and after chatting to the men for a while, he jumped off the truck – straight into a half forty-four gallon drum of old engine oil. Such an incident can only have inspired the organization!

The business grew steadily, soon justifying the purchase of machinery to help load the trucks. This led to the tackling of all kinds of earthmoving jobs, under the name of Savage and Son Excavators, including in the early fifties a reclamation job for Escom in Port Elizabeth, for which the first mechanical shovel was bought, and an irrigation canal in Kirkwood.

Andrew had grown up in Port Elizabeth with a friend, David Lovemore, who had also been in the army during the war. On his return home David started farming and borrowed his uncle's D4 bulldozer to build a dam, on the basis that he would earn the money to pay for the loan of the machine by doing some earthmoving for neighbouring farmers. This fulfilled a need in the neighbourhood and produced more work than David had ever anticipated. The earthmoving contracts were so much more lucrative than farming that by the end of 1948 he was contracting full time, using his uncle's bulldozer and splitting the profits with him. Most of his work involved building dams on farms in the Humansdorp and Steytlerville districts and down the Sundays river valley and his very first contracting job was for Hugh Savage, Andrew's father.

At the beginning of 1950 David was appointed manager of McKiever's earthmoving business and travelled around the country for them gaining considerable experience in this field. Within a year he was back home in order to start his own business, with his father and a friend, P Theophilus, financing the venture. D B Lovemore Earthmoving Contractor started operating with one bulldozer, a second-hand D6 bought as scrap from the Uitenhage municipality for £2 500. David managed to buy another second-hand D6 and then ordered his first new one, on Andrew Savage's advice a D8, which had a three year delay in delivery – giving him time to save up the money to pay for it! The business grew rapidly and David took on his first white employee, Glen Kettlewell, and was able to buy out his two sleeping partners.

Inevitably his success and ambition led to a desire to enter a bigger civil engineering

David Lovemore beside his first brand-new bulldozer.

scene and he turned to his friend Andrew Savage for help and encouragement. Together, in 1954, they tendered for a contract for the South African Railways at Barkly Bridge. There was only one item in the bill of quantities but somehow the inexperienced couple obtained the wrong figure at the end of their calculations. Fortunately the Railways kindly corrected the figure, and awarded them the contract. The two men worked well together, David's intensely practical nature complementing Andrew's management ability. They had not thought of joining up, however, until David had an urge to leave South Africa and see what life would be like in Canada. He asked Andrew if he would supervise his contracting business and look after the books in his absence. Andrew then suggested that the best idea would be for their two companies to amalgamate and he would run the new company while David was away. Savage and Lovemore (Pty) Ltd was created in 1955, David holding 49% of the shares and Savage and Son 51%. The subsequent developments were so fascinating that David gave up his idea of going to Canada and instead became happily absorbed in the activities of Savage and Lovemore.

When the Cape Provincial Administration put out a national road tender to private enterprise for the first time it was awarded to Clifford Harris, and Savage and Lovemore managed to get a subcontract for the earthworks of the north section of the Olifantskop Pass north of Paterson. This was their first participation in a major road construction project and was successfully completed in 1956.

The following year Savage and Lovemore were awarded their first street contract in New Brighton in Port Elizabeth. The drift across the Baakens river from the Walmer side to Newton Park in Port Elizabeth was also constructed by the company. David always regarded this as a tremendous personal achievement because it was his idea to build the drift which cost only £2 500, instead of a much more expensive bridge, and it was still in use twenty years later.

The year 1958 brought a significant breakthrough when Savage and Lovemore's tender as the main contractors for the national road between Merton and Heuningneskloof, south of Kimberley, was accepted by the CPA. It was a brave and somewhat alarming step because neither David nor Andrew had any experience of road building on that scale. However, they employed their first qualified civil engineer, Boyd Wilson, and set about the project with determination and enthusiasm. It was only when Boyd had been signed on that David and Andrew realized that he was not the experienced man they had thought he was – he was the wrong Wilson! Road contracting in South Africa was still in its infancy in those days and none of the local companies was very experienced, so the situation in which Savage and Lovemore found themselves was not as unusual as it would be today.

The first big contract for Savage and Lovemore, which was started in February 1958, was known as the Modder River contract. David lived on site for several months, getting everything underway before leaving to get married and go overseas for a five month honeymoon with his wife Enid. Andrew took charge of the contract immediately after the wedding and he and his wife Twinks have many happy and amusing memories of the months they spent living there. Twinks wrote some very descriptive letters to an aunt. In one she said, 'We have a young engineer called Boyd Wilson, which pleases me because I was becoming quite embarrassed at having to explain so often that neither Andrew nor David were engineers.' The Savages rented a little concrete house on a smallholding which was 'very depressing being cold and dirty and derelict. At £2/10/00 per month one could not expect much more. However, the surroundings are lovely, miles of lucerne, the famous race horse stud belonging to the Oppenheimers, where Tiger Fish was born, peach orchards, cotton fields and every imaginable fruit tree.' Twinks wrote in another letter, 'The children had a very difficult first day at school because they were such a curiosity. Hugh was asked whether Savage and Lovemore was his father'! Living out in the country is a very different experience from being in town and Twinks will always remember the friendly neighbour who used to bale his lucerne at night and call in for coffee at 2 am when she was feeding her baby, Peter. Altogether it was a happy time and the Savages were sad to move back to Port Elizabeth when David and Enid returned.

Geoff Woodland joined Savage and Lovemore on the Modder River contract. He and his wife Gloria had a pineapple farm near Grahamstown in the Eastern Cape, but they had left it because of severe drought and were living with Gloria's father on a farm in the Modder River area. When Savage and Lovemore arrived Geoff applied for work as a carpenter, and was offered the position of foreman/carpenter, which he gladly accepted. He fitted easily into the Savage and Lovemore team and quickly went from strength to strength. His contribution towards the development of the company was immeasurable and he developed his own capabilities at the same time, carrying increasing responsibility as the years went by. His wife Gloria always gave him loyal support, not only making the best of all situations with a rare warmth and understanding, but gaining a strength from all her experiences which she shared with other people.

When the Modder River contract was finished Savage and Lovemore undertook two small road construction jobs, one at Addo and the other at Douglas, before embarking on a CPA contract at the end of 1959 for the road between O'Kiep and Steinkopf in the north-western Cape. This road led from the copper mine up towards South West Africa across wild, desolate country. It was a very happy and successful contract, earning the respect of the CPA and making Savage and Lovemore feel that they had really 'come of age' as road contractors and could tackle anything. They built another small road for the CPA in that area, from Springbok to Carolusberg, and a road for the O'Kiep copper mine from Carolusberg to their mine shaft. The base course was taken from the mine dump and no one had appreciated how much copper was still in the rock until the road showed a surprising green colour – a most valuable road, paved with copper!

Geoff Woodland took the whole Savage and Lovemore team from the Modder River site to Springbok rather like Moses trekking out of Egypt as everything and everyone, literally the whole company, was taken up and moved on. The countryside around Springbok had a bleak grandeur which changed spectacularly when good rains fell in 1961 and the Namaqualand daisies came into bloom forming carpets of unbelievable beauty.

The rain could also have a frightening effect, however, when the rivers changed from dry dust beds into turbulent torrents. As it fell over a large area it concentrated in the river beds and the water would surge down carrying boulders, bushes and debris before it. One time it completely washed away a bridge that Savage and Lovemore were building, and Geoff Woodland was lucky to be alive when he was swept away with it.

Dennis van Niekerk, who joined Savage and Lovemore on the Springbok contract as site accountant in April 1960, was an enthusiastic member of the Savage and Lovemore cricket team which experienced a problem in being near the restricted diamond areas of South West Africa. When they played cricket at Oranjemund the names of the whole team had to be submitted two months in advance for screening, and when the team arrived they played the game and then were hustled out before they had even had a beer with their opponents – very different from what usually happened at their cricket matches!

The Springbok contract took two years to complete and Darling and Hodgson were subcontracted to do the surfacing of the road, under the supervision of Edward Sunde. This was Darling and Hodgson's first introduction to Savage and Lovemore, and they worked together again on Savage and Lovemore's next big contract which was well up in South West Africa, north of Keetmanshoop, on the road from Asab to Mariental.

The terrain there was even bleaker and the contract proved difficult right from its beginning in October 1961. The major problem at first was the lack of water, essential for building a road, and a report of water sources given initially to the prospective contractors proved to be totally false. Savage and Lovemore had to haul water over great distances, at one stage as much as 35 km, which diminished profits considerably. Even when it was available it evaporated as soon as it was sprayed out because of the heat. David turned his practical mind to the problem and invented the 'Lovemore Mixer' which minimized water loss by releasing the water under the surface of the ground – an original design which was written up in one of the civil engineering magazines but which was never put into general use. As so often happens in Africa, when the rains did come at the end of the year there was widespread flooding.

The heat at Mariental was beyond description, and another phenomenon of the area was the tremendous dust storms which reduced visibility to practically nil, stopping all work on the road and restricting everyone's movements, leaving them dehydrated and irritable. Children had to be kept indoors because they could easily get lost. The storms sometimes lasted up to eight hours, the dust infiltrating everywhere so that meals were often reminiscent of beach picnics! Yet another natural hazard was scorpions, and it was only out of loyalty to the company that anybody stayed in the place at all.

Certainly no one was sad to leave Mariental, and it was Savage and Lovemore's first really unsuccessful contract. The worst period came halfway through, and a decision was made then to purchase new equipment, for which money was borrowed for the first time in the company's history, from the United Dominions Corporation. The new equipment boosted morale considerably and the road was finished in 1963.

Although there was another contract offered in South West near Mariental, Andrew and David agreed that nothing would make them tender for it, and they looked for work nearer home in the Cape. They tendered successfully for a contract at Bruintjieshoogte near Somerset East, and then David decided that he would very much like to tender for another between Amospoort and Klaarstroom, south of Beaufort West, which he thought looked very attractive. The company could not run two contracts simultaneously, however, nor did it have the finances to expand sufficiently to do so. Andrew and David put their heads together and cast around for a solution. They knew that Darling and Hodgson did a little road construction work as well as their extensive surfacing operations and they decided to approach John Hodgson. Andrew knew John from their war years together and felt sure that he could approach him as a friend. He suggested that if Darling and Hodgson were to tender for the contracts and supply the money and the people, then Savage and Lovemore could provide the technical expertise because of their greater experience, especially on Cape roads.

John discussed the offer with his financial director and adviser, Brian Malcomson, and they decided that it would be preferable for Darling and Hodgson to buy a share of Savage and Lovemore, thereby providing capital for expansion and at the same time giving themselves a toe in the door for future involvement. This was how, in 1963, Darling and Hodgson acquired 25% of Savage and Lovemore and put their representatives on the board – John himself, and Bill Partridge of Union Corporation.

Andrew was heavily involved in the other aspects of his family business, Savage and Son, in Port Elizabeth – they had interests in transport, quarrying and ready-mixed concrete – and the practical management of Savage and Lovemore fell very much to David. The company was about to take the great step from being a small one-contract concern to becoming a two-contract business with its sights set on still greater achievements, and David felt a need for a qualified and experienced civil engineer with a knowledge of management to steer them forward. In those days the contracting business was still small enough for everyone to know everyone else involved in the field, and Andrew and David set about trying to employ the best possible roads engineer in South Africa. They approached Edward Sunde whom they knew well through their association in Springbok, but he declined the offer, feeling that his loyalties lay too strongly with Darling and Hodgson. They then turned to Gerry Schoonbee of A G Burton, just at the time when Darling and Hodgson were negotiating in London to take over Burtons. Gerry accepted the offer and, after staying some months with Burtons to hand his responsibilities over to Edward Sunde, he went down to Port Elizabeth to become managing director and a shareholder of Savage and Lovemore in January 1964. He took with him a wealth of experience, having lived on contracts since his university days, and his professional approach towards management lifted the company to a new level of sophistication.

By this time the company offices had moved from Paterson Road to Newton Park, where David had bought a large old house. Offices and a yard were established there, in tranquil surroundings, in June 1964, and this was where the company headquarters remained until they moved to Warbler Street, Moregrove, in July 1965. Andrew took with him his special chair which had been in the family since his 1820 settler ancestors arrived in South Africa. An unpretentious man with little concern for material status symbols, Andrew often surprised newcomers to the business with his straightforward and informal approach. When Bunny Lloyd joined Savage and Lovemore in 1966 he had been with the company for about a month when one morning he came face to face in the passage with a man dressed casually in shirt, shorts and veldskoens. When Bunny asked if he could help, the man politely refused the offer and, with a word of thanks, stepped aside to let Bunny pass. Imagine Bunny's embarrassment when a couple of days later he learnt that the man was Andrew Savage!

The Beaufort West contract was very successful and profitable. Those who moved from Mariental to Seekoeigat for the contract in September 1963 went from blazing heat to the chill of snow on the nearby Swartberg mountains, just one of the hazards of a contracting family's life. As so often happens, however, the people already in the area soon changed that bleak first impression into a warmth which carried everyone through the two and a half year contract. The first site agent was Noel Kirsten, who had worked for Darling and Hodgson at Collondale airport, and when Gerry brought him back to Port Elizabeth as chief engineer of the whole company, responsible for the technical direction on all contract sites, his place was taken by Geoff Woodland. Noel was a Border cricketer and a prominent member of the Savage and Lovemore team. While on the Mariental contract, his son Peter, a little boy of six at the time, had played cricket with Glen Kettlewell and the other men there, showing unmistakable talent at an early age. Peter grew up to be a Springbok cricketer, while Noel later retired from the demands of the contracting world to take up the position of groundsman at the Newlands cricket field in Cape Town.

Winter road building scene in the Karoo.

The site agent on the other contract was Jack Breedt, under whose able guidance the construction team completed two sections of road, one over the Bruintjieshoogte Pass between Somerset East and Pearston, and the other between Bedford and Adelaide to the east of Somerset East. This team moved on to another contract on the road between Fort Beaufort and the Koonap river, in 1966, while Geoff took his unit from Seekoeigat to work on the road between Calvinia and Brandvlei. The latter contract was another particularly successful and profitable one.

David had by then moved back to Port Elizabeth to take charge of the company's plant. However, nothing could keep David away from the contracts, which he found stimulating and rewarding even in their worst moments, and before long he had set up a new section of Savage and Lovemore, P E Contracts, which concentrated on local work and saw the successful entry of the company into freeway construction. The first freeway job for the unit was the Albany Road interchange earthworks – a subcontract to Dyckerhoff, Widmann and Thompson – followed by the north-south freeway, and work at the Deal Party railway goods yard, where the subsequent surfacing was done by Darling and Hodgson. P E Contracts was very successful and financially rewarding, apart from a few unfortunate contracts such as the Berry Corner Interchange. That contract lost a lot of money but proved to be an unforgettable experience in the construction of big bridges for everyone concerned!

The maintenance of plant and its effective control was one of the main weaknesses in the early days of Savage and Lovemore, and 'a chronic shortage of really capable men' was reported in mid 1963. In early 1964 Steve Cameron joined the company and made a considerable improvement, and two years later Dick Trickett was employed as plant manager and stayed until his retirement in 1981. Dick came in as a highly capable man with extensive mechanical knowledge combined with a natural sense of economics – very necessary for someone with the entire capital investment of the company in his hands. He was a supremely conscientious worker and claimed that this was inspired by the good team spirit and excellent working atmosphere in Savage and Lovemore.

Another person who was instrumental in improving Savage and Lovemore's growth over the years was Denys la Grange. He joined in July 1966 as the company secretary and quickly developed a professional administrative structure that allowed the engineers to become managers without taking the fun out of their involvement in construction. Andrew once said that Denys was the first man he knew in South Africa who could actually come to terms with inflation! He certainly made sure that Savage and Lovemore took full cognisance of the effects of inflation in their system of costing and continuity.

A successful contract awarded in 1965 was for a series of small roads which were needed by the Post Office Department to give access to their new microwave towers being built on top of hills and mountains in the Cape to improve their communications, first at Cookhouse, Cradock, Newpoort and Olifantskop, and then a series from Albertinia to Sir Lowry's Pass. That was a real challenge. Each road had to be blasted into the steep sides of the mountain, and the weather conditions were consistently bad. Perhaps it made the excellent results all the more rewarding.

Each year saw the introduction of changes in an endeavour to better the company's performance. In 1965 it was decided that the company should do all its own concrete work because subcontractors always seemed to create problems, and in the same year a surfacing unit was transferred from Darling and Hodgson, resulting in a greater all-round capability. New plant was purchased for another freeway construction unit as this was proving a very profitable undertaking, and in 1966 a new company was formed 'to undertake civil engineering contracts of the freeway construction type'. This wholly-owned subsidiary was called Savage and Lovemore Structures and concentrated on the local Port Elizabeth contracts, leaving Savage and Lovemore to undertake the major road contracts elsewhere.

In early 1967 Andrew decided to amalgamate and reorganize his interests in Port Elizabeth by forming a new holding company, Savage Industrial Holdings, which absorbed the entire shareholdings of Savage and Son and Savage and Lovemore, and held 50% of a

Construction of a microwave tower access road at Grabouw, Cape.

company called P E Holdings which had a range of interests. Darling and Hodgson had a 20,4% interest in this new company, and later in the same year Andrew suggested that they increase this still further as Savage and Lovemore needed more capital to enable them to grow beyond their present limits. As Andrew put it in his letter to Darling and Hodgson, 'Our contracting business is firmly established and set to take advantage of the growth in the industry.' He particularly saw the advantages to be gained by expanding Savage and Lovemore into the Transvaal and Natal which were the areas of greatest economic activity and most rapid development. He also knew that Savage and Lovemore would have to grow to be able to resist the increasing competition in the road construction industry.

Andrew was very persuasive: 'We have the framework for the establishment of a construction-orientated firm on a national scale. It has management, profitability and a good reputation. To take advantage of the opportunities it needs capital.' This had a very familiar ring to all those who had been with Darling and Hodgson when it had been in a similar situation only a few years previously. Then Union Corporation had taken a major shareholding and this enabled them to utilize their opportunities. The response was therefore sympathetic. Ian Wilson of Union Corporation believed very strongly that the greatest advantage for both Savage and Lovemore and Darling and Hodgson would come from the complete integration of both groups but at that stage Andrew was adamant that he wanted to undertake the expansion on his own, and it was agreed that Darling and Hodgson would increase their shareholding to 33,5%. John and Andrew agreed that Savage and Lovemore's independence was essential at that stage, but the fact that they became accountable to Darling and Hodgson gave them a basic discipline in running their business which was an important cornerstone for their development.

The first step was to establish Savage and Lovemore (Trans-Natal) in the Transvaal under John van Nus, providing him with an exciting and challenging opportunity. The new company's first contract was for part of the Johannesburg Eastern Bypass, a 7.3 mile section running from Gillooly's Farm to the Pretoria road north of Alexandra township. It was worth over three million rand.

By April 1968 the operations in the Transvaal were being handled by three companies – Savage and Lovemore (Trans-Natal) (purely administrative), Savmore Structures Transvaal (handling concrete work) and Savage and Lovemore (Transvaal) which was a new name given to a recently acquired company, Sable Construction, and which was handling the earthworks and road construction operations.

The first step into Natal came about by chance. Theunis Vorster was well known in the construction industry as a road builder and as the man who had won two of the contracts for clearing the bush for the Kariba dam. These proved very successful and Theunis closed his business and retired to Port Elizabeth where he started up a new contracting company with his son. After working on roads at the Hendrik Verwoerd dam they were awarded a contract in East Griqualand for the road from Kokstad to Matatiele. Unfortunately Theunis Vorster had a heart attack and, aware that his son was not all that enthusiastic about contracting, being more of an academic, he appealed to Savage and Lovemore for expert assistance. Gerry Schoonbee agreed to take over the contract and offered the job of running it to Basil Hancock who was well experienced in road building in Natal after twenty-one years with the Natal Provincial Administration. Theunis Vorster continued to suffer ill-health, however, and Savage and Lovemore purchased his company, thereby opening up their future in Natal. At first all operations reported back to Port Elizabeth.

Meanwhile the Cape operations were also being extended, and in 1968 Savage and Lovemore were awarded a tremendously exciting contract, the first of its kind in South Africa. This was the planning and building of South Africa's first mechanically paved concrete road, which proved to be a great achievement for David Lovemore.

The use of concrete instead of asphalt for road surfaces has always been attractive because of its negligible maintenance costs for at least twenty-five years, by which time most roads need some form of reconstruction. There were a few small stretches of concrete road in South Africa but they had all been constructed manually in small sections, and had never been popular because of the noise created when driving over the wide expansion joints between the slabs. In the mid sixties the South African road authorities were very impressed by the results of tests being carried out in America on the rideability of modern concrete road surfaces and sent some of their engineers to America and also to Europe to investigate their design and construction. Local interest was stimulated by the Portland Cement Institute which organized a national congress on concrete roads, and the CPA decided to invite tenders for a project large enough to test the modern concrete paving and to judge its merits in comparison with the asphalt surface in common use. They chose a 25,7 km stretch of road on the Cape Flats from DF Malan airport to Somerset West, an extension of Settlers Way which is the beginning of the main highway eastwards from Cape Town.

When the news of this tender reached David Lovemore he was very interested in the exciting opportunity to be first in the field in this country. He had read that the most advanced techniques in the world were used in California and in 1967 he spent a month there learning all that he could about modern concrete roads and became good friends with Ron Guntert, who was the designer of the world's most successful machine for constructing concrete roads. This was a slipform paver, which spreads a solid pavement of concrete, providing a surface which endures even the heaviest traffic. Ron subsequently came to South Africa and worked with David and his colleagues, advising them on estimating the cost of the road for tender purposes. Savage and Lovemore put in their tender for R6,5 million, a keenly competitive price, and were jubilant when the contract was awarded to them – for completion within thirty months.

The construction team which had been working at Calvinia under Geoff Woodland was brought down to Cape Town and they set about the construction of the new road without delay. The initial work was conventional road building, earthworks and bridges, and while this was underway preparations were made for the concrete surfacing. In order to bring more knowledge and experience of concrete work into the company, Savage and Lovemore purchased a major shareholding in WJM Construction, specialists in concrete work, but this was a short-lived relationship which was terminated soon after the road was started, leaving Savage and Lovemore with the entire responsibility.

David had arranged for one of the new paving machines to be sent from America, and the Guntert and Zimmerman slipform paver arrived in due course – in a mountain of boxes at Cape Town harbour! Fortunately David had also arranged for an experienced operator to fly out to South Africa to supervise the assembling of the machine and to train the Savage and Lovemore staff. All the equipment, including a fully-automated concrete mixing plant imported from Belgium, was gathered together in time to do a test run for the province on a mile of road just off the freeway. Inevitably all those involved in the project were rather nervous; the slipform paver is a machine which needs very careful and accurate control because there are many things which have to be done simultaneously in order to achieve the desired results. Also once the machine is started

The slipform paver.

there can be no stopping until the end of the day, so a high degree of organization is required. However, the overseas expertise had been passed on well to the paver operators and in the first day the self-set target of a thousand feet was achieved by midday, and even the American trainer/operator was impressed. The paver was then set to work on the construction of the dual carriageway, first laying the cement-treated base layer, at an average rate of 1,5 km per day, and then the concrete surface, at 0,75 km per day.

The thickness of the slab of concrete which is extruded from the paver is controlled by pre-set electronic sensors, and the surface of the Cape Town road was finished by a method which was developed locally, known as 'nail drag', whereby a heavy fringe of nails is dragged over the newly-paved surface to make a series of grooves that provide a surface texture which is rough but not noisy under traffic. The concrete was then given an application of a white curing compound. The quiet ride of the road was helped by the absence of expansion joints. To overcome the problem of expansion and contraction in the new road, contraction joints were sawn into the pavement before it was fully set. The overall high quality of the road and the ease of cutting the contraction joints were attributed to the use of a pozzolith polymer-type admixture which was manufactured under licence in South Africa by Embecon, another company within the Darling and Hodgson Group.

The concrete paving was finished in December 1970, well ahead of schedule, and in November 1971 the Savage and Lovemore minutes reported triumphantly that 'the largest and most profitable contract in the history of the company' was open to traffic. The whole contract was finally completed in August 1972. It was a tremendous success in all respects. Savage and Lovemore's standing as road contractors rose considerably and everyone involved in the contract derived great personal satisfaction from the achievement.

Meanwhile Savage and Lovemore had started another contract between Cathcart and Whittlesea in the Eastern Cape which turned out to be the company's first major financial disaster. It was on these conventional road contracts that Savage and Lovemore found themselves more and more in competition with A G Burton. Since the two companies were associated through Darling and Hodgson it seemed that greater success would be achieved by combining the operations under a single management, and after some months of discussion it was decided to merge A G Burton into Savage and Lovemore along with Darling and Hodgson's contracting activities. At the end of 1968 the total shareholdings of A G Burton (SA), Darling and Hodgson (Pty) and Tarmac Industries were all acquired by Savage Industrial Holdings. At the same time Darling and Hodgson Holdings increased their shareholding in Savage Industrial Holdings to 51%.

Although Andrew was reluctant to lose control of his own company it was obvious that the merger would create an organization which was far more capable of taking maximum advantage of the opportunities afforded by a rapidly expanding economy in South Africa. He also knew that John had experienced a similar situation when Union Corporation took a controlling interest in Darling and Hodgson and, knowing that they had been allowed to go their own way within Union Corporation, he looked to John to allow Savage and Lovemore a similar freedom within Darling and Hodgson. This was indeed the case and the resulting success was beyond anyone's hopes at the time. Darling and Hodgson maintained control through their members on the board of Savage Industrial Holdings (John, Brian and also Ian Wilson of Union Corporation). Andrew jokingly spoke of this as the time when 'the second corporation' became important ('the first corporation' being the United Dominions Corporation who had lent them money during the Mariental contract).

In creating one of the largest road construction companies in South Africa, the merger also provided new and exciting opportunities for the people within the component companies as reorganization took place. The overall management was in the hands of Savage and Lovemore whose new board, still under Andrew's chairmanship, included Edward Sunde from Darling and Hodgson and Johan Schonken from A G Burton. Edward moved down to Port Elizabeth to work as contracts manager with David. Gerry continued as managing director and after some months of trying to run operations from Port Elizabeth he moved up to the Reef at the end of 1969 to establish Savage and Lovemore head offices there. Neither the Savages nor the Lovemores had any desire to leave Port Elizabeth.

Gerry put together an exceptionally competent management team. His natural ability had been strengthened by a visit to Harvard in 1967 to study their 'Program of Management Development' from which he returned full of new ideas and enthusiasm. The organization of the new structure of Savage and Lovemore was an exciting challenge for him, and everyone felt a new stimulation with the promise that 'this expansion and diversification will create interest and opportunities for each member of staff according to his ability and ambitions'.

Gerry's initial reorganization and rationalization of operations early in 1969 started with various changes in company names. Savage Industrial Holdings became Savage and Lovemore Holdings, responsible for major policy recommendations and financial decisions, and operations were divided among regional branches of Savage and Lovemore in the Transvaal, Natal and the Cape. The companies concerned had over R30 million on their order books, mainly in the Cape and Transvaal. Savage and Lovemore themselves were strongest in the Cape, with just one contract in the Transvaal – the Johannesburg Eastern Bypass – and one in Natal at Kokstad.

In spite of the volume of work on hand the financial situation was not very healthy. A G Burton had been running at a loss for several years and not all Savage and Lovemore's contracts were profitable. However, the extra capital from Darling and Hodgson added to the combined resources gave the company a strong base from which to start.

Savage and Lovemore were not very happy about the surfacing operations which came into the new organization with Darling and Hodgson (Pty) and Tarmac Industries, and at the end of 1969 Andrew negotiated with Limmer and Tarmac UK to merge these operations with those of Limmer's South African subsidiary, forming a new company, Limmer Asphalt (Pty) Ltd, owned 50/50 by Limmer UK and Savage and Lovemore Holdings. A very small shareholding was retained by Limmer's Jock Perry who ran the new company with no direct association with Savage and Lovemore. After a time Savage and Lovemore sold their share to Limmer UK and dropped out of surfacing – 'black top operations' – altogether for many years.

When Gerry moved up from Port Elizabeth he was based at first at Brailsford House. In January 1971 the Savage and Lovemore offices were moved to a property at Isando which was not a success – it was always windy and dusty. After a brief stay there the company moved to Elma Park in Edenvale and from there in 1974 to Elandsfontein, which was a large property with a pleasantly rural atmosphere, where a yard was established as well as offices. The Transvaal headquarters have remained there ever since.

The seventies saw unprecedented growth in road construction in South Africa as the Government developed a strategic road network throughout all the provinces and other roads were built to accommodate the rapidly increasing traffic, especially in the vicinity of the larger cities. Savage and Lovemore was growing too and rapidly became the biggest contributor to Group profits. This was maintained even during the economic recession of the latter seventies. Their operations were split into two regions, north and south of the Orange river, the Transvaal, Orange Free State and Natal under Gerry and the Cape under Edward. Although the head office had moved up to the Transvaal when Gerry was transferred to the Reef, the profit base of Savage and Lovemore remained very firmly in the Cape. The southern region fell naturally into two areas – Eastern and Western Cape. In the former Lionel Shemer and later Maarten Taal headed up the PE Contracts unit which constructed the William Moffett freeway in Port Elizabeth, and carried out numerous other small contracts, some as far away as Knysna. A loyal member of Savage and Lovemore was Glen Kettlewell, of the PE Contracts team, who had joined David in his earliest contracting days. Glen has stayed with the company to become one of the Group's very longest serving employees.

Under Geoff Woodland Savage and Lovemore continued to build an impressive

Road interchange in Port Elizabeth.

number of roads in the Western Cape. One contract of which Geoff was particularly proud was the Blue Route, running from the top of Wynberg hill down past Alphen out to Tokai in Constantia. It was not an outstandingly profitable contract but will be remembered as a model for good human relationships and work achievements. This was underway towards the end of the concrete road contract and at the same time as Savage and Lovemore were working on extensions to the runway at DF Malan airport. The latter were completed just in time for the first landing of a jumbo jet on 9 June 1972.

Darling and Hodgson increased their shareholding in Savage and Lovemore to 75% when it went public in 1973 and the annual report of that year summed up Savage and Lovemore's contribution to the Group as 'a proven success on major contracts concerning roads, airports, bridges and a wide range of other projects. It has unparalleled expertise in the construction of concrete roads.'

Contracting is a constant battle against the weather in the Cape, often with little achieved during the rainy months of May to October unless work can be found to prevent men and equipment standing idle. When Savage and Lovemore were working on the Steenbras dam contract in the mountains above Somerset West there was an urgency to finish before the winter rains set in which no one will ever forget. This contract spanned three years, from August 1976 to December 1979. Savage and Lovemore very successfully built an earth dam on the Steenbras river behind the existing concrete reservoir which for many years supplied water for Cape Town. The dam was Phase 1 of a

The completed Steenbras pumped storage scheme.

R40 million project to boost Escom's supply of electricity for the city and reduce the cost. It was the first hydroelectric pumped water storage scheme in South Africa, working on the principle of water dropped from a high level down through a tunnel and surge shaft to turbines at a lower level, producing electricity for peak hour periods. The water is then pumped back in off-peak periods. Having been awarded the contract for the upper storage dam, Savage and Lovemore subcontracted to Murray and Roberts for the lower dam and for the overburden and rock excavation for the power station itself. They worked around the clock to clear the site for the Murray and Roberts team to move in while the weather was dry, tearing the mountain apart with their huge noisy machines. Within a few years the Cape flowers were blooming again on the grassy hillside and the only evidence of the hydroelectric scheme was two tranquil dams and a discreet building housing the power station beside the lower one.

The Steenbras contract will always be remembered for another reason too – among the Savage and Lovemore surveyors was a woman! Elize Wirth came from Germany

Sir Lowry's Pass.

where her presence on site would not have been as unusual as it was in Africa. The men did not give her an easy time at first but her cheerful, straightforward and efficient approach soon earned the respect of her fellow workers. She knew that she had been accepted when a group of her male colleagues told the manager at the local pub that they would all leave if he did not give her a beer along with the rest of them!

Beyond DF Malan airport the national road stretches out, up over Sir Lowry's Pass, and on towards Port Elizabeth. Over a period of time Savage and Lovemore have been awarded contracts all along this route from the airport as far as Riviersonderend and have made handsome profits from them. They have also widened the pass, cantilevering the road out on concrete pillars.

Savage and Lovemore were also involved on the other side of Cape Town in the Du Toits Kloof tunnel project, to shorten the main road to Cape Town from the north, and they moved to something very different from road building when they won the contract for the excavation and embankments of six strategic fuel tanks at Saldanha Bay. This was

The western portal under construction on the Du Toit's Kloof tunnel project.

a most profitable contract in spite of the tender being a great deal lower than any other.

There were several other dam contracts over the years. The Stettynskloof dam contract near Worcester, started in June 1978, was so dogged by bad weather that a witchdoctor was brought to the site, to no avail, but high up in the Langeberg five large storage dams were finished in record time in spite of floods. These dams formed the basis of the Cogmanskloof irrigation scheme which had been planned to supply water to farmers in the heart of the apricot and dried fruit region of the Cape. Floods also hindered the construction of the Elandsjagt dam on the Krom river near Jeffreys Bay. All the preparatory work on the dam, which supplements the water supply of Port Elizabeth and surrounding areas, was washed away and the completion of the initial stages was delayed.

The main offices of Savage and Lovemore (Cape) remained at Newton Park in Port Elizabeth, situated next to Moregrove quarry. In spite of the rocky soil a beautiful garden has been created around them, renowned especially for its roses which are lovingly tended by Pat Thomas. Pat started working as a bookkeeper for Savage and Lovemore when they were still at Paterson Road and willingly continued with the company as a part-time gardener/supervisor after her retirement in 1973. In the mid seventies Bunny Lloyd and Maarten Taal were both appointed directors of Savage and Lovemore (Cape). Bunny had joined in 1966 and remained on the financial side, while Maarten had entered Savage and Lovemore in a fairly junior capacity in 1969 and moved through the ranks from site agent to contracts manager and then to contracts director.

For many years Savage and Lovemore (Western Cape) worked from site offices but in

Examples of Savage and Lovemore's involvement in concrete construction:

Above
The Rietspruit canal system.

Right
The Woodlands reservoir, Durban

1974 a quarry, Dunn's Blue Rock near Somerset West, was purchased in order to secure supplies of stone for Savage and Lovemore's operations. The name was changed to Cape Blue Rock and the farmhouse on the property was extended and offices established there.

Savage and Lovemore undertook a Government contract at Tygerberg as well as road construction from the Milnerton refinery to Moorreesburg and through the rolling wheatlands between Caledon and Bredasdorp. The company was also involved in another pumped storage scheme from 1982 to 1983, for Escom's Palmiet scheme. Beyond Sir Lowry's Pass Savage and Lovemore built access roads to the power station, and to the top dam, Rockview, which was being constructed by the Department of Water Affairs, and also the conduit for the scheme. The road contract was carefully controlled by a resident ecologist who ensured that the fynbos vegetation, peculiar to the Cape and in danger of indiscriminate destruction, was not removed or harmed unnecessarily.

Meanwhile the north region of Savage and Lovemore was developing under Gerry. There was a little work in the Orange Free State (when the Bethulie contract was completed there were others at Aliwal North, begun in 1970, and Trompsburg, 1972) but much more was happening in the Transvaal. Work continued on the Pretoria and Johannesburg Eastern Bypasses and the first concrete road outside the Cape was started in 1970 between Witbank and Middelburg. The slipform paver (the only one in South Africa for many years) was brought up from Cape Town, and after initial problems the contract went well. In the managing director's report of Savage and Lovemore north region, dated September 1973, in which the official opening of the road was announced for October that year, it was reported that 'since O B Rossiter took over, this contract has been a source of pride in our contracting operations in the Transvaal'. In 1974 Johan Schonken left Savage and Lovemore in order to start his own business, and Cecil Rifkind was appointed in his place. Jim Maguire was welcomed back after a few years' absence, to become plant director in the Transvaal.

Among the most memorable contracts of the next few years were the Vereeniging Bypass, at the time the largest contract ever awarded to Savage and Lovemore, and the civil construction of two gigantic jumbo jet hangars at Jan Smuts airport, a multi-million subcontract to L&F Metter, part of the Abercom Group. There was also another concrete road at Grasmere on the stretch between the Vaal river and Johannesburg, and a significant contract was undertaken at a military installation north of Pretoria. Sewerage works were constructed at Bushkoppies just outside Soweto for another contract.

The most spectacular development within the company after 1970 took place in Natal and in 1971 a Savage and Lovemore office was established there and Roger Cuningham was appointed resident director. Basil Hancock had been working for them in Natal since 1968, reporting at first to the Port Elizabeth office and later to the Transvaal. Opportunities were opening up rapidly as Richards Bay developed as an important harbour with all the accompanying growth in infrastructure. Looking back it can be seen how

Far left
Hangars under construction at Jan Smuts airport.

Left
Bushkoppies sewerage works.

Section of the Vereeniging Bypass.

Savage and Lovemore took advantage of this situation and developed into a very strong operation in Natal; a turnover of R1 million in 1971 became R11 million in 1981. The Kokstad contract was finished, as was the Illovo freeway at Amanzimtoti on the south coast, and in September 1971 Savage and Lovemore were awarded a contract for part of the railway line being built to bring coal down from Vryheid to Richards Bay, the section just north of Empangeni.

Jack Breedt was sent from the Cape to be the site agent on this contract and the intense loyalty and devotion which can build up under a good site agent was demonstrated by Alex Gonome who walked from Queenstown to Empangeni to join him. Alex had returned home to Queenstown after working with Jack on contracts in the Eastern Cape, and when his money ran out he decided that he must work again for 'Baas Jack' who he knew had moved to Empangeni. He set off along the road to Natal, his only directions a scrap of paper with the names Durban and Empangeni written indistinctly on it. No one offered him a lift and it was many weeks later that he arrived in Empangeni, only to find that he had to walk for another three days along the railway line to reach the Savage and Lovemore site. He eventually found Jack and, standing before him, his feet swollen from so many miles of walking, he said, with a beaming smile of happiness, 'It is me. I have arrived.' Alex knew that he would be cared for, and he was. Within a few weeks his feet had healed and he was contentedly installed as site watchman for the contract.

There was a great scarcity of white artisans in that area and considerable difficulty in housing those who were available, so Savage and Lovemore decided to train black workers for some of the skilled jobs. Alan Vorster was brought in to carry out the training which was a forerunner of the training programmes that have become of vital importance over the years.

The following year, 1972, brought another large contract, this time for the railway marshalling yard in Newcastle, further north in Natal, and in 1973 Savage and Lovemore (Natal) gained additional momentum through the acquisition of Seven T Construction, the South African operations of Tarmac UK. Roger Cuningham, Basil Hancock, Herman Bauer, the plant manager, and their secretary, Pat Markow, together

The container terminal, Bay Head, Durban.

comprising the total office staff of Savage and Lovemore (Natal), moved into the Seven T head office in Pinetown and took over all their contracts. There were five contracts underway at the time, including a significant amount of work at Richards Bay. A general reorganization of people and operations gradually took place, resulting in the steady, successful growth of Savage and Lovemore in the province over the following years. Roger Cuningham felt that the Pinetown premises were an unnecessary expense for a construction company so after a year they were sold and the offices were moved out to Hammarsdale. There they occupied a small farmhouse and a few caravans before the Natal regional offices were built on an extensive property which created a pleasant country atmosphere. This has been retained over the years, providing an enjoyable working environment.

In 1974 Savage and Lovemore enlarged the concrete section of their operations by purchasing a small company which had been started by Wally Rodd in 1971, specializing in concrete structures. W T Rodd Construction, based in Pietermaritzburg, had built sewerage works for the Greytown municipality and a number of bridges, reservoirs and small factories in Natal. All the people in the company were happily integrated into Savage and Lovemore and made a significant contribution to all the contracts. They were involved in the concrete road which was being constructed by Fowlers between Frere and Estcourt, the first in Natal. The concrete paving was subcontracted to Savage and Lovemore who at first started running it from the Transvaal but soon handed it over to Natal.

The work at Richards Bay included a marshalling yard and a huge multi-purpose storage shed for the Railways, and three contracts concerning the heavy minerals mining project there – for the construction of the smelter, excavating the large dredge pond and building temporary access roads.

Savage and Lovemore (Natal) expanded considerably to carry out these projects and when they were finished there was not enough work available in Natal to accommodate all the staff. Rather than lose them Savage and Lovemore (Natal) chose to work outside the province and in 1977 accepted a contract at Wakkerstroom, just inside the Transvaal. This was for a road high over the Drakensberg mountains linking the northern Natal coal fields and railage points near Volksrust. It had already defeated several contractors, but Savage and Lovemore triumphed over the adversities, enduring bitter cold during the winter months at an altitude which caused the machinery to gasp and cough through lack of power. During this period another company, Wakkerstroom Construction, was absorbed into Savage and Lovemore. Wakkerstroom itself was a tiny place with one small hotel which enjoyed the patronage of the Savage and Lovemore team. Coincidentally, the barman in the pub, Jimmy Cook, had worked for Darling and Hodgson as a steamroller driver and later as a foreman in the early days.

Having taken one step beyond their home ground, Savage and Lovemore (Natal) continued to work in the Transvaal, but there were contracts in Natal, too, some small and some large. The most spectacular was the contract at Ingogo where two railway viaducts now soar high above a valley in the mountains between Newcastle and Volksrust on the route between Durban and Johannesburg.

Contracts followed one after the other all around the country and Savage and Lovemore had become a significant force in road construction by 1978, the year in which Andrew and David decided to retire from their executive positions in the company. They were both unassuming men who had derived tremendous personal satisfaction from the challenge of proving themselves major road builders in South Africa, and who had enthusiastically inspired others to work with them to create this great construction organization within Darling and Hodgson. They had led Savage and Lovemore through its pioneering days and set it on a successful track and they now felt that it was time to pass the reins over to men of a different nature who would maintain what had been established and develop the company further as a contributor to Group profits. They remained actively involved for some years until David relinquished all associations with the Group to become fully involved in farming, and Andrew fulfilled his ambition to en-

Right
Andrew Savage.

Far right
David Lovemore.

The Ingogo railway viaduct.

ter politics when in 1981 he was elected Progressive Federal Party member of parliament for Walmer, Port Elizabeth, although he remained on the Group board until 1984. Darling and Hodgson purchased Andrew and David's shares, increasing their stake to 96%. John became chairman of Savage and Lovemore Holdings, and Edward Sunde took charge of all the Cape operations.

Road building in South Africa was already on the decline and the company was looking around for ways to diversify its operations. An obvious use for idle earthmoving equipment was opencast mining and in 1978 Savage and Lovemore Mining was established, the first step in the development of the D&H coal division. By this time road construction was on the increase again and the following years brought ever-growing profits in spite of escalating costs and the constant shortage of skilled labour. The latter problem led to increased consciousness of the importance of training, and a comprehensive programme covering a broad spectrum of this field was developed. As far back as the early seventies Savage and Lovemore had begun basic skills training under Vic Fraser in the Cape, and when Tony Hibbert joined the company in 1975, with considerable experience in training and personnel work in industry, he established a more formal procedure. Vic continued to work on site, promoting Tony's training procedures with lively humour and his own particular emphasis on safety aspects. He introduced all kinds of slogans which caught the imagination of everyone who saw them, and the increased awareness was remarkably effective in reducing accident rates. He made a considerable impact on all operations in the Cape and his retirement in 1983 was felt throughout the region.

The training programmes were steadily extended to supervisory and managerial levels, and became standard practice throughout the Cape operations of Savage and Lovemore. They were soon introduced to Natal operations with the help of Vinod Ransdayal and eventually to the Transvaal where John de Wet applied his exceptional linguistic abilities to all personnel aspects of Savage and Lovemore's operations. It was difficult to quantify the improvement in results which came from training over the years but it was most definitely there, accompanied by a very rewarding growth of individuals, within themselves and their work. Training has become very closely linked with industrial labour relations in the company.

Training of apprentice mechanics had been taking place in Savage and Lovemore since the early seventies, and in 1980 a special training school was established in Natal, which has been very successful and has helped to overcome the shortage of mechanics in the industry. Savage and Lovemore are proud of their contribution to the concept of training in the construction industry as a whole. They have shared their knowledge and experience at all times and many of the CEITB programmes which have become available were based on theirs. Apart from in-house training, Savage and Lovemore have for several years offered bursaries for university training, and sponsored participation in technicon courses to be followed while working for the company. A high proportion of the technicon students stay with the company after qualifying and their value is indicated by the fact that in 1983 85% of the management of Savage and Lovemore (Cape) had been diploma students. Savage and Lovemore's first sponsored technicon student, Mike Lawson, joined the company on the Bruintjieshoogte contract in 1963 as a learner surveyor and subsequently studied civil engineering at the Port Elizabeth technicon, thereafter making steady progress in the Eastern Cape and contributing significantly to the company. Twenty years later, in early 1983, he attended the ten-week London Business School executive programme which extended his in-depth understanding of general management, and on his return to South Africa he was transferred to Savage and Lovemore (Western Cape) where he was appointed managing director after Geoff Woodland retired at the end of twenty-five years with the company.

In June 1980 Savage and Lovemore became a wholly-owned subsidiary of Darling and Hodgson when the remaining shares held by senior members of the staff were exchanged for D&H shares. It had taken eighteen years for John Hodgson to fulfil his ambition of D&H owning the company. It was a significant step and some of the Savage and Lovemore 'old-timers' felt that the company had lost its independence and would never be the same again. Sadly this was true, but it was inevitable. Savage and Lovemore had grown too much to retain the intimacy and excitement peculiar to the earlier pioneering years and as part of a larger organization it had to develop differently.

From 1977 onwards D&H spread their construction interests as a result of a series of acquisitions which initially retained their individuality within the Group through its philosophy of decentralized management. These included Underwater Construction in 1977 and Monahan and Frost in 1979. In 1981, however, following the purchase of Fowler Holdings, Gerry Schoonbee suggested the rationalization of all Group construction interests within a construction division, which brought Savage and Lovemore under Group management for the first time. Gerry was soon to retire from executive responsibilities to devote his life to the Campus Crusade for Christ ministry, and Alex Combrink was appointed managing director of the new Group division.

Gerry's retirement after twenty years of loyal and effective service to company affairs was another break away from the traditional Savage and Lovemore. Denys la Grange

Far left
Gerry Schoonbee.

Left
Edward Sunde presents the managing director's trophy for safety on site to David McIntosh.

was appointed deputy managing director to Alex and offered great assistance in the merging of old and new through his depth of experience with Savage and Lovemore. In 1983 Denys was transferred to Group head office to head up corporate affairs and was appointed an alternate director to the main board. In 1984 he returned to the construction division as financial director to Underwater Construction in the Cape, together with the responsibility for a Group joint venture with Harry Fuchs of that company for an exciting township development on Milnerton island. As part of the reorganization within the construction division, Tony Hibbert was transferred to the Reef at the beginning of 1983 to standardize training throughout the different operating companies, with the help of Hennie Botha in the field of industrial relations.

The name Savage and Lovemore disappeared in the Transvaal within the new organization and its operations were divided between two new operating companies, D&H Construction and D&H Civils. Savage and Lovemore continued strongly along their own path in the Cape and Natal, with Natal becoming increasingly important. Edward Sunde and Basil Hancock continued as managing directors of their respective regions. Basil had been appointed to this position in Natal at the end of 1981 when Roger Cuningham was transferred to the Transvaal to take responsibility for the northern region of the construction division.

During 1983 Darling and Hodgson acquired a major shareholding in another large construction company, Group Five Engineering, and at the end of the year all Group construction activities were reversed into it. Group Five, as D&H's construction arm, became one of the largest building and construction companies in South Africa into which Savage and Lovemore and its people were inevitably absorbed. Savage and Lovemore's contribution to Group Five was that of a large countrywide construction organization which had developed in just under thirty years from a small contracting team in the Cape.

Underwater Construction

'Anything to do with the sea, we will do' – positive words from the managing director of Underwater Construction, Harry Fuchs, words which epitomize the confident buoyancy of this section of the D&H construction division. Underwater Construction bears a proud reputation of high quality work, finished on schedule, and retains a unique atmosphere of determined enthusiasm reminiscent of the pioneering spirit of D&H in its earlier years.

The company developed from Harry Fuchs' enjoyment of deep sea diving. He and some friends in the early sixties started to hire themselves out as fully-equipped divers, working from a garage in Cape Town and doing small jobs, one of which was laying a

The breakwaters constructed at Koeberg.

Marine construction work at Koeberg.

pipeline across the Langebaan lagoon. In 1966 they formed a company, Underwater Construction and Salvage Company (Pty) Ltd, their logo a diver's helmet, and slowly established themselves in this field. They constructed small fishing harbour slipways, jetties and quays all around the coast of South Africa and South West Africa, and also in Mauritius and the Seychelles.

Much of their work was undertaken for the Fisheries Development Corporation of South Africa, which in 1975 offered Underwater Construction their first major civil engineering contract, to establish a new fishing harbour at Walvis Bay. This was a mighty

Above left
Underwater Construction's dredging barge.

Above right
Harry Fuchs.

leap into a multi-million rand project, and required considerable expansion of people and equipment. Harry rose eagerly to the challenge, however, and successfully completed the construction of the harbour.

Having proved their ability to tackle such a contract, Underwater Construction were confident that they were among the leaders in their specialized field. They were working on a naval contract at Port Elizabeth when they ambitiously put in a tender for the marine construction work at South Africa's first nuclear power station, located on the coast just north of Cape Town at Koeberg, seeing this as a natural progression in their operations. Although Harry had no reservations about his company's ability to execute the work and finance the project, Escom refused to consider them without the surety of a large group's backing. With some reluctance Harry looked for a partner, and found the answer in the D&H Group. John Hodgson was sympathetic, recognizing a situation similar to his own in 1963 when he had needed Union Corporation's backing to allow D&H's potential to be realized but had not wanted to lose his independence. He also recognized the quality and potential of Underwater Construction and, purchasing a 51% shareholding in 1977 through Savage and Lovemore, brought the company into the Group against the background of its philosophy of decentralized management.

Escom readily accepted the newly acquired financial muscle, and Underwater Construction embarked on the first of four major contracts at Koeberg. These turned out to be every bit as exciting as Harry had anticipated, with a few extras thrown in, like the ten metre waves which relentlessly pounded them at times, and the added stimulus of a R45 000 a day time penalty! There were inevitably many 'firsts' in such an original project, which increased the ever-present risk of failure, but Underwater Construction triumphed over all adversities and finished their contracts on time. It was a great achievement, and a financial success beyond their dreams.

When the work at Koeberg was nearing completion Underwater Construction were asked to construct a tidal pool at Strandfontein in False Bay, designed to extend beach amenities. This was completed in time for the holiday season of Christmas 1980. The following year brought contracts as far apart as Cape Town, Walvis Bay, Saldanha Bay, Mossel Bay and Durban. One was for dredging Home Bay at Zeekoeivlei, and dredging and enlarging Princess Vlei for the Cape Town City Council. This led to Underwater Construction purchasing the largest demountable dredger in use by a South African company.

The tidal pool at Strandfontein, False Bay.

Underwater Construction's head office is in Cape Town, but each project is run on site by an engineer who is involved with the contract from the design and tender stage right through to completion. The standards of efficiency in all respects throughout the company are high and their immaculate workshops handle all maintenance and repair work, and as much manufacturing of equipment as is possible.

Harry Fuchs' philosophy is one of strong individuality and motivation within his company, leading to a great deal of personal self-discipline. The result is a close team of highly motivated people who are proud to belong to the D&H Group and contribute significantly to its profits, while fiercely maintaining their independence.

Monahan and Frost

Most small construction companies reach the stage where they must either stop expanding their business or find a 'big brother' to provide more capital. The lure of bigger and more exciting contracts is great at this time and the more succcessful the company, the more likely it is to broaden its horizons by joining forces with someone else. This was the case with Monahan and Frost when it came into the D&H Group in 1979.

Peter Monahan and Arthur (inevitably 'Jack') Frost had established an excellent record in the concrete structure field since they started their company in January 1959, based in Peter's house in Linksfield, Johannesburg. Their first contracts were for crushing plants for Amcor, one near Pretoria and the other near Postmasburg in the Cape. However, they soon established an ongoing relationship with Escom, building electricity distribution stations throughout South Africa. The first was in 1962, at Penge just north of Lydenburg, and a total of thirty-two stations were constructed over the next few years. There were other contracts, too, such as the Minute Maid factory at Letaba – the company claimed that this factory had the best cold rooms in the country!

As Escom's major distribution programme neared completion and there were no more stations to be built, Peter and Jack turned their interests to Escom's power-station chimneys. They had both worked for Lewis Construction on a power-station contract and thus had some knowledge in this field, and the company successfully completed one chimney at Hendrina, two at Arnot and another two at Kriel. They also constructed Escom's first multi-flue chimney, designed for Duvha power-station. It was to be the tallest chimney in Southern Africa – 300 metres – and presented a formidable challenge. Conventional building methods just did not work, and eventually Monahan and Frost devised a new method, which they called 'jackform', working all hours to finish the contract on time. It was considerably more expensive than anticipated, and when the Matla

The Duvha chimney.

Kriel power-station – Monahan and Frost constructed two tall chimneys and four massive cooling towers.

chimney went out to tender Monahan and Frost put in a realistically high price which was not accepted. They watched with interest when the chimney had to be demolished soon after its completion!

Having established such an excellent working relationship with Escom, it followed that Monahan and Frost should be asked to tender for the construction of cooling towers. This was in 1972 and the apprehension and doubts expressed by Peter and Jack were overcome by the enthusiasm and confidence of Arthur Hills who had joined the company. Four cooling towers were successfully built at Kriel, followed by four at Sasol II and four more at Sasol III.

The company offices soon moved from Peter's home to Lawson's Corner in Braamfontein and a yard was established in Wynberg. In 1968 the offices moved out to Wynberg too. As more exciting and prominent contracts came their way, Monahan and Frost began to attract well-qualified and enthusiastic young men who formed a team of high repute, quickly recognized as specialists in concrete structures. When Peter and Jack began to put out feelers for financial backing necessary to maintain their rate of development they received several offers from larger construction firms which were eager to acquire the company's expertise. These included Savage and Lovemore, whose offer was accepted. Peter was an old friend of the managing director, Gerry Schoonbee, and was glad of the opportunity to join up with people whom he knew and liked. Monahan and Frost thus became a wholly-owned subsidiary in 1979.

The company retained its operating identity and, with confidence inspired by its new backing, tendered for the Armscor factory in Pretoria. This involved a new rapid method of construction with precast concrete slabs and an enthusiasm developed for trying new things that other companies considered too difficult, an attitude which proved both successful and profitable. Monahan and Frost also accepted a R2 million subcontract for the construction of bridges and culverts for Moolman Brothers at the huge Bapsfontein railways marshalling yard.

The company continued to operate from Wynberg until 1981 when it moved to the Savage and Lovemore offices at Elandsfontein. The following year, after rationalization of Group construction activities, Monahan and Frost's operations were merged with the civil engineering work of Savage and Lovemore (Transvaal) in a new company, D&H Civils, of which Peter Monahan became technical director until his retirement later in the year. The name Monahan and Frost fell away. In 1983 D&H acquired a majority shareholding in Group Five Engineering, and in the middle of that year D&H Civils also ceased to exist, absorbed into Group Five's CMGM with all existing contracts, including the initial construction of the new chimney at SAPPI's Ngodwana mill in the Eastern Transvaal.

Fowler Holdings

When Fowler Holdings was acquired by D&H in March 1981 it boosted Group construction turnover and profits significantly, making 1981 an outstanding year. It continued to operate independently, following D&H's traditional policy of decentralized management, and contributed its own 'family of families'. At the time it comprised Fowler Construction, Combrink Construction, R H Morris and a 50% shareholding in Felbitem.

Fowlers were the pioneers of tar spraying in South Africa. Their operations commenced in Cape Town in 1922 when Thomas Fishwick and Philip Lowman arrived in South Africa from England to demonstrate the use of a steamroller manufactured by John Fowler of Leeds. It was the very latest model which boasted several improvements over the old ones, including a tar spraying attachment. A steam coil from the boiler heated tar in a tank at the back of the roller and a spray bar was attached for distribution of the tar over the road surface. Stone chips were scattered by hand from a box at the back of the footplate or distributed from a two-wheeled gritter drawn behind the roller. The tar used at that time was all imported from Europe.

The roller was used successfully in municipal road construction and after a short time Thomas and Philip decided to purchase the roller and launch their own tar spraying service. The Cape climate with its wet winters was not conducive to spraying throughout the year and the two men decided to buy a second roller and establish themselves on the Witwatersrand. Wolton Gray came out from England to drive the new roller and the Fowler Tarspraying Company was registered in 1924 with these three men as the main initial shareholders.

The company rapidly established an excellent reputation as the only tar sprayers on the Reef and they found themselves in constant demand. Instead of using imported bitumen, Thomas, Philip and Wolton obtained a local product from Tweefontein Colliery near

Buitengracht Street, Cape Town, 1922 – the first tar spraying contract carried out by Fowlers.

Surfacing Jan Smuts Avenue, Johannesburg, 1934.

Witbank, where Bill Hodgson was running the by-product plant. The three men struck up a lasting friendship with Bill and were among the large number of visitors who used to stay with the Hodgsons. Bill and Mabel also visited their friends in Johannesburg and when Mabel wanted her first child to be born in the city she stayed with Philip and Hilda Lowman. John was born in their home in Flint Road, Parkwood in 1926.

These friendships continued when the Hodgsons came to live in Johannesburg, and a close link developed between Fowlers and Darling and Hodgson. Bill always spoke with admiration of the way in which Fowlers had grown. As their contracts grew bigger so the smaller jobs were passed on to Bill, and when Darling and Hodgson moved into road construction in the early fifties all their spraying operations were carried out by Fowlers.

In 1928 Thomas decided to try his luck in establishing a similar business in Australia and, having sold his shares in the company to Philip, he left South Africa. Within a few years Philip had sold most of his shares to Wolton and he left the company in 1932 to join the Johannesburg City Council as a regional engineer. He was appointed assistant manager of Rand airport and soon became manager, a position which he held until he retired in 1961. He sold the remainder of his shares in Fowlers to Wolton in 1935. The company had increased its assets considerably by then and was using more sophisticated surfacing methods.

When Iscor came on-stream in the early thirties it recognized Fowlers as an effective means of marketing its by-product tar and acquired the company from Wolton in 1936. Wolton then turned his talents to starting another company, this time under his own name, while Fowlers continued to develop as part of Iscor. The three men who had worked for Wolton continued to run the company – Syd Berry as general manager, Tom Berry as plant manager and Bob Adam in charge of spraying operations.

Fowlers were to reign supreme in South Africa in the tar spraying field for many years until 1953 when Darling and Hodgson moved into direct competition with them with the purchase of their first spray tanker, soon followed by a second. The two companies were rivals from then on. In 1954 Mobil established South Africa's first oil refinery in Durban, and locally produced bitumen was used by both companies.

Through constructing Iscor's internal road system Fowlers graduated to operating in the open market. They built part of the Lower Main Reef road on the Witwatersrand in the thirties, major roads in Rhodesia and in Waterkloof, Pretoria, amongst others, in the fifties, and in the sixties one of their major contracts was the William Nicol highway on the outskirts of Johannesburg, from Hyde Park to Bryanston. They were also involved in other large projects such as the access roads and parking areas of the new Jan Smuts airport.

In the late sixties an oil pipeline was built from Durban to the Reef and in 1969 the Natref oil refinery was established at Sasolburg by the Sasol and Total oil companies. This considerably reduced the profitability of transporting bitumen from the coast and at the end of 1971 Fowlers decided to join forces with the oil companies and put all their bulk haulage and tar spraying assets into Fowler Tarspraying Company, owned 50% by themselves and 50% by Sasol/Total. The new company held the rights to market and distribute bitumen from the Natref refinery and tar from Sasol and Iscor. Thereafter Fowler Construction concentrated on its road construction activities. It also entered into the bitumen emulsion business in 1970 in a joint venture with a French company, Jean Levebre, the acknowledged specialists in the emulsion field. The company formed was Felbitem.

In the same year Fowler Holdings became a subsidiary of Iscor's investment company, Metkor Holdings, which in 1973 applied for a listing of the company, as Fowler Construction Limited, on the Johannesburg Stock Exchange. It was intended to be the first of a whole succession of Iscor subsidiaries to be shared with the public. Initially the prospects seemed good, with after-tax profits soaring for several years. The managing director, Bill Venter, freed from the limitations of Government ownership, thrust Fowlers into a period of diversification. In September 1973 Fowlers moved into mechanical erection work with the acquisition of 50% of Sofam (Pty) Ltd (the remaining 50% held by Montalev (SA)) and in 1974 there were two acquisitions, a well-established Cape Town based building company, R H Morris, and a large railway track-laying and component manufacturer, Racec Construction. At the end of the year Fowler Holdings was created to facilitate management of the widespread Group activities. Racec continued successfully within Fowlers but, sadly, R H Morris was a different story.

There was little building experience within Fowlers, nor really any understanding of the business, and several of the contracts undertaken by R H Morris around the country were unprofitable. These significantly affected Fowlers' profits and aggravated their own difficulties. The company had been awarded the largest single road contract to date in South Africa, worth R33 million, for the national road between Estcourt and Frere in Natal. This road had been designed for conventional surfacing and later changed to concrete paving because of the world oil crisis. Consequently there were many problems with the contract which commenced in January 1975 and these, together with R H Morris's unsatisfactory contracts, gave Fowlers several years of bad results.

When Bill Venter was killed in an accident the subsequent management was unable to maintain the quality of performance, and in 1978 the company was taken off the Johannesburg Stock Exchange with Metkor purchasing the minority shareholding. Metkor then persuaded Alex Combrink to take over the management of Fowlers in exchange for a participation in Fowler Holdings, which purchased Alex's own company, Combrink Construction. Fowlers' associated companies were not included in this transaction.

Alex moved into Fowlers' head office at Kempton Park, next to the soaring cooling towers of Kelvin power-station, in August 1978. A big man with a powerful personality, he soon made his presence known throughout the company. There was little dramatic change in management but positive guidance put everyone on the right track once more. R H Morris was quickly re-established in its traditional home, Cape Town, where its historical reputation was good, and Combrink Construction and Fowlers settled down in the Transvaal, all three working together to become a happy and successful team. The top management comprised Alex Combrink as managing director, Theunis Kotzee as financial director and Garth Kelly, who joined the company as commercial director.

Mike Watson continued in charge of Fowler Construction and he pulled it around to an impressive success in a remarkably short time. In 1979 two major contracts were awarded to the company. One of these was part of the Government's plan to link Pretoria with Mabopane, where most of the city's black commuters live. There was strong

Fowlers' headquarters in Kempton Park.

The Mabopane contract.

opposition from environmentalists at the prospect of forcing a way through the beautiful Magaliesberg mountain range, and Fowlers accepted the challenge of constructing a cutting which would blend in perfectly with its surroundings with the minimum of disturbance. It was a mighty project, producing within thirty-six months a poort which would have taken nature many thousands of years to create. Twenty-six different species of grasses and natural vegetation were lifted before the bulldozers started moving earth, to be kept alive and replanted on the side of the cutting in the original topsoil. The natural beauty was then enhanced by the planting of hundreds of indigenous trees.

Fowlers were also working in Mabopane itself, constructing part of the internal road system, and at the same time there was a team working on a large-scale maintenance contract on 100 km of the N4 between Pretoria and Witbank, using over 4,5 million litres of bitumen in a twenty-two month resealing process.

Some time after Alex had been appointed managing director of Fowler Holdings, a quirk of fate led him to be seated beside John Hodgson at a seminar at the Landdrost Hotel. Conversation led to discussions which resulted in D&H purchasing 100% of Fowler Holdings in March 1981. This brought Fowler Construction, Combrink Construction, R H Morris and Felbitem into the D&H Group.

Felbitem was successfully manufacturing and marketing bitumen emulsion and slurry seals for road making in its factory on the Fowler property in Kempton Park. The Jean Levebre 50% shareholding had been passed on to Basil Read of Group Five through a series of acquisitions and was then sold to Tosas, the combined Sasol/Total oil company, thereby establishing a close link with a major bitumen producer and giving Felbitem considerable strength. Fowlers retained responsibility for management of Felbitem. Ironically the other 50% which remained with Fowlers came into Group Five through its merger with D&H Construction.

Felbitem in operation.

John Hodgson was appointed chairman of Fowler Holdings and Alex Combrink joined the D&H board. At first the Fowler companies and Savage and Lovemore operated independently under their managing directors Alex Combrink and Gerry Schoonbee. Before the end of 1981, however, a new Group construction division was created, based at the Fowlers' offices in Kempton Park with Alex as managing director.

The acquisition of Fowlers brought black top operations back to D&H after fourteen years, and in 1982 the Group acquired further surfacing interests with the purchase of Roadmix. In the subsequent rationalization Fowlers' surfacing operations were put into Roadmix and their road construction operations were merged with those of Savage and Lovemore (Transvaal) so that the name Fowlers was withdrawn from the construction scene. Felbitem continued to operate under its own name. Alex was faced with the formidable task of streamlining and co-ordinating the activities of companies which fiercely guarded their own independence, but he did this very competently, successfully evoking a Group identity within the division and mobilizing the various strengths into a cohesive and powerful force.

R H Morris

D&H acquired the oldest building firm founded in South Africa when R H Morris came into the Group in 1981 through the acquisition of Fowler Holdings. In 1878 two young men in Cape Town became partners in a small building firm. When one of them left after a few years the other, Richard Henry Morris, continued operating on his own and before the turn of the century he had established an impressive reputation, his work including the major part of the Standard Bank of British South Africa's gracious building in Adderley Street and several commissions for the eminent architect Sir Herbert Baker. Among these were the rebuilding of Groote Schuur after a disastrous fire in 1887 and the City Club in Queen Victoria Street.

Over the years Richard was joined by Frank William Lardner and Arthur Plint, and in 1919 these three men were the first directors of the newly registered company of R H Morris Ltd. The firm also became renowned for the manufacture of high quality furniture for churches, schools and offices (their telegraphic address was 'Desks') and this carried them strongly through the vicissitudes of the building industry over the years.

Just before the outbreak of the Second World War a civil engineering department was set up, which developed into a large organization in its own right. It carried out extensive work for various municipalities in establishing sewerage and storm water drainage schemes. During the war the company made a vital contribution to the Allied war effort as a member of a joint contracting syndicate which constructed the largest graving dock in the southern hemisphere.

By 1950 both Frank and Richard had died (Arthur had left some years previously), but the firm continued to develop, constructing high-rise buildings such as Thibault House and Zeeland House, and establishing a long-standing working relationship with the University of Cape Town. Their paths had crossed for the first time last century when

Standard Bank, Adderley Street, Cape Town.

The Robert Leslie Building at the University of Cape Town.

R H Morris built the imposing edifice Strubenholm, which now houses UCT's College of Music, and since 1965, when the firm began work on the Beattie Building, it has seldom been without work at the university. The striking Baxter Theatre and concert hall and the Robert Leslie Building, both winners of architectural awards, are prominent examples of its participation in the seventies.

Stellenbosch University's Conservatoire of Music showed that R H Morris did not confine their activities to the UCT campus, and beyond the academic sphere there were contracts for the Cape Provincial Administration such as the Tygerberg Hospital in Parowvallei and the colossal CPA offices which straddle Wale Street in Cape Town.

Behind this impressive list recording the success of R H Morris lay the frailties typical of a construction company and the agony of financial uncertainty. In the early seventies R H Morris was bought by Fowler Holdings, a Metkor-owned road construction company, and an extensive expansion programme was introduced. The head office of R H Morris was moved to Johannesburg and an area office opened in Durban, which resulted in most of the senior management resigning because they were not prepared to leave Cape Town, and the company plunged into misfortune.

It was at this stage in 1978 that Metkor asked Alex Combrink to take over the management of Fowler Holdings, and he was appointed chairman of R H Morris. Alex closed down R H Morris's national operations and returned the head office and all activities to

Cape Town where the firm was traditionally held in high repute, restoring a large degree of their former independence. In 1980 Peter Read was appointed managing director and he achieved great success in putting the company back on its feet.

R H Morris had entered into an interesting and successful partnership in 1977 with a local Cape Town firm, Model Development (Pty) Ltd. The company Model Morris spanned the colour line so prominent in South Africa and was established to undertake mass housing construction at Mitchell's Plain. The direct management of Model Morris lay with Model Development and within a few years they had built over six thousand houses, all finished to a very strict standard of acceptable quality.

In 1981 Fowler Holdings was brought into the D&H Group, and R H Morris became the Cape constituent of the building section of the D&H construction division. In this capacity they continued to undertake many projects, including the new Medical Amenities Building and the Jagger Linear Library at UCT, a meat processing plant for Kanhym in Montague Gardens in Milnerton, a large Cash 'n Carry store for Metro in Lansdowne, and the Standard Bank in Bellville.

The Baxter Theatre.

The most prominent contract begun in 1983 was the new regional headquarters for Escom in Bellville. This R32 million project was one of the largest in the Western Cape for many years. It was not an easy contract as the basement had to be constructed below the existing water table and extensive de-watering was carried out for R H Morris by Underwater Construction. The team on this site was the proud winner of the 1983 BIFSA regional and national safety and loss control awards.

In spite of the unsettled years and many management changes between 1974 and 1978 R H Morris retained its individuality right through to the eighties, spanning more than a century in the building industry. The strong team spirit of the early days was restored by Peter Read and his team, and the combination of its traditional reputation and the strong support of a successful national group gave everyone in the company confidence in the future.

Combrink Construction

When Alex Combrink left Roberts Construction after twenty-one years to start his own company from scratch, his staff gave him a farewell party. He still has two champagne corks from the occasion, reminding him of the comment made with reference to their different sizes – 'They do the same job.'

Today Combrink Construction is an impressive company in its own right, and as part of D&H's construction operations the small champagne cork has grown almost beyond recognition. In the early seventies, however, when the new company was establishing itself, it was Alex's confidence in its ability to carry out contracts as well as any of the big companies that kept it going.

Combrink Construction was established at Hyde Park Corner, Sandton in February 1970, in the offices now occupied by John Hodgson and not far from the Darling and Hodgson head office at that time. Alex was soon joined by Peter Slabbert, an old friend who had worked with him at Roberts Construction, Ian Lundie and Theunis Kotzee. These men were all shareholders, as was MGM for a couple of years. The office staff comprised Alex's wife Fay, and Lyn Tulloch who had been his secretary at Roberts Construction for many years. Theunis was Alex's right-hand man and he made an outstanding contribution to the early development of the company. Alex had made a decision to employ only the most highly qualified people in the conviction that his company would soon be able to accommodate them, so although Theunis was an accountant he spent some months doing little more than bookkeeping. He also turned his hand to anything that needed to be done as willingly and efficiently as he tackled his professional work. The company operated with the minimum number of people who all managed to work together extremely competently and happily.

After a few weeks of wondering whether there would ever be any work, the first contract was awarded to the company. This was for extensions to Bakers' factory in Isando.

The Johannesburg Hospital.

The job was done well, and over the following years Combrink Construction completed four further contracts for Bakers, just one example of several long-standing associations with prominent clients which the company has established. It is justifiably proud of its repeat orders.

Before long Combrink triumphantly landed a big fish – a R3 million contract for the Trust Bank in Kempton Park. The first company crane was purchased for this building, not without accompanying hazards. One of the few accidents Alex remembers today is the crane bucket crashing through a window in a nearby block of flats – an embarrassing situation!

The company grew rapidly into one of the most dynamic building construction companies in South Africa, concentrating on the Witwatersrand area. In July 1972 it became part of the consortium which built the new Johannesburg Hospital on the Parktown ridge, a mammoth concrete edifice which some consider is no contribution to the aesthetic beauty of Johannesburg but which provides the most modern amenities for the sick. Visible from far and wide its construction was exceedingly controversial.

At the beginning of the contract in September 1972 Combrink Construction moved their offices to Randburg, to the Bouhof building (which they had recently built). They remained there until December 1978 and during that time were responsible for the building of Barlow Park – head offices of the Barlow Rand Group – Nestlé House and other industrial projects and commercial head offices.

In 1978 Alex was asked to become managing director of Metkor's ailing subsidiary, Fowler Holdings, in return for a substantial interest in Fowlers, which in turn purchased 100% of Combrink Construction. Subsequent operations were managed from the Fowlers' headquarters in Kempton Park and in January 1979 the head offices of Combrink Construction were moved there as well.

It was an exciting move for Alex, but a little sad on the personal side. Fay was 'made redundant' and the family business atmosphere was lost forever. Soon there were no more Christmas tree and end-of-year parties at the Combrinks' home, events which had been highlights in the company for many years.

Barlow Park, Sandton.

Alex maintained his reputation for being highly demanding but scrupulously fair. He competently reorganized all activities within Fowlers, and Combrink Construction continued its operations in the Transvaal, alongside R H Morris's building activities in the Cape and all of Fowlers' road construction. Alex was frequently seen on site maintaining close contact with all that was going on, and the atmosphere within the company was vibrant.

Having readily grown accustomed to the demands of this step in his career, Alex was prepared for the next challenge. In 1981 D&H entered into negotiations which led to the purchase of the entire shareholding of Fowler Holdings and the amalgamation of all its operations with those of Savage and Lovemore within a Group construction division, of which Alex was appointed managing director.

Combrink Construction retained its operating identity and carried out the Group building operations in the Transvaal, maintaining an excellent reputation for well-executed work. Contracts included extensions to the Rosebank Hotel, the new corporate head office buildings for Barlows' Caterpillar tractor division in Ormonde, and for Group Five Engineering in Rivonia. There were further contracts for Pretoria Portland Cement and for Air Products, as well as extensive additions to the Toyota complex. Combrink Construction is very proud of the excellent on-going working relationship that has been established with both Barlows and the Wesco group of companies owned by Albert Wessels, which includes Toyota. The company also built a wholesale storage warehouse and office block in Germiston for Beacon Sweets, a contract which was finished well ahead of schedule.

One of the most exciting and attractive contracts was for a new glass container warehouse at Rondebult, Germiston. Nampak's requirements were a single responsibility undertaking with a guaranteed completion date, plus quality and quantity performance standards. Combrink Construction accepted the challenge. The contract included major earth and road works as well as civil and building construction, and other Group companies were brought in to work together to fulfil all the requirements.

Alex is a staunch believer in an informal style of management and this attitude has paid

Pretoria Portland Cement, Parktown, Johannesburg.

Toyota complex, Sandton.

good dividends. The effectiveness of his philosophy is reflected in an outstanding record of long-term employees, both black and white. It was their loyalty which created the close-knit team spirit throughout the company, which has taken it from strength to strength over the years – people like Gert Skolz and Jannie Scheepers who served their apprenticeship under Alex and worked their way up to become supervisors of major contracts in the early eighties. Jannie was general foreman on the Pretoria Portland Cement contract, and he commented at the time that he had been working with Alex for so long that 'I call him Uncle'!

In 1983 D&H acquired a majority shareholding in Group Five Engineering, and at the end of the year reversed its construction division into this large and well-established company. Sandy Jamieson continued as chairman of Group Five and Alex was appointed deputy chairman. In the resulting rationalization and reorganization Combrink Construction very firmly maintained its independence while constituting the Transvaal section of the Group's building division within Group Five.

Stevenson Construction

Bob Stevenson's life is the classic success story of someone with little academic education who made his way to the top through determination and exceptional personal qualities of leadership and skill. Having started his working life in Durban as an apprentice carpenter, he worked his way through the ranks until he was appointed resident engineer for James Thompson in Natal – no mean achievement for a man without a civil engineering degree. After a stint in Cape Town with a large building company under judicial management, a valuable financial experience, he returned to Durban and joined Ready Mixed Concrete (Natal) as their first sales manager, where he applied himself energetically to the challenge of introducing a totally new concept to the building industry.

It was a trip to America in 1967 to study ready-mixed concrete operations and building trends that made Bob aware of the potential in the South African construction field, and within a year he had left Ready Mixed Concrete to set up his own business in partnership with Ronnie Spring. Spring and Stevenson Building and Civil Engineering Contractors (Pty) Ltd began in 1968 with an initial capital of R2 000 and some land in Greyville purchased with an overdraft. Within fourteen years it had grown from a turnover of under R400 000 a year to over R30 million.

In the beginning Bob assumed the roles of foreman, contracts manager and building surveyor, and set about estimating, measuring and tendering for work in the Durban area. The company soon made an impact on the local building scene, their contracts including the large Sanlam shopping complex at Umbilo and the KWB warehouse. After a while they moved their offices to Umgeni Road in Durban.

In 1971 Ronnie left the firm and the name was changed to R L Stevenson Construction. Bob was optimistic about the future – 'I think we must be among the top four unquoted construction firms in Natal. There is no reason why we cannot improve on that.'

Bob Stevenson on site.

Umlaas canal pipe bridge.

Prophetic words – Stevenson Construction never looked back and over the next ten years amassed an impressive list of contracts in the construction of hospitals, factories, schools, institutes, shopping centres, apartment blocks, railway stations and bridges.

While always ready to undertake the more lucrative private and industrial contracts, Bob maintained a close involvement with government and provincial work which stood him in good stead during the economic depression of the mid seventies. He once remarked that a slump in the private building sector always solved his labour problems!

Alongside their own development, Stevenson Construction also grew through acquisition. The year 1973 saw their first expansion outside Durban with the takeover of Mann and Garstang in Port Shepstone which took the company into the developing south coast. Under the new name of Stevenson Construction (South Coast) they built an extension to the Port Shepstone hospital, the new Margate post office, and continued to maintain a strong presence in the area. In 1980 they picked up over R4 million worth of work there, including the Checkers shopping centre in Margate.

Stevenson Construction acquired the century old Natal firm of Blakey and Hope in 1977. The firm specialized in kitchen equipment but had retained the manufacture of an earlier product, crutches; there was one particular employee of forty-one years' standing whose job had always been to turn the crutch handles on a lathe.

In 1979 one of Durban's oldest building firms, J&J Smith, was saved from the jaws of the liquidators by Bob Stevenson. Its operations continued independently within Stevenson Construction, swelling the turnover considerably.

At the end of 1980 the company's name was changed to Stevenson Construction and all its diverse operations were brought under one roof the following year with a move to splendid new premises in Old Main Road, Pinetown. These comprised offices, showrooms and a factory.

The phenomenal growth of Bob's company was not merely fortuitous, but was the result of determination, expertise and hard work all along the line – with a guarantee of attention to detail and contracts finished on time. There has always been a high degree of efficiency within Stevenson Construction, with Bob insisting on immaculate conditions even on construction sites, and pleasant offices with the female staff attractively dressed in smart blue uniforms. He has also become a well-known figure in the building industry as a whole, serving on the Durban Master Builders Association in 1978 and 1979, and

Construction of the Berea Road station, Durban.

The Wentworth Hospital redevelopment scheme.

holding the office of president of the Building Industries Federation of South Africa from 1979 to 1980.

Bob had been friends with Alex Combrink for a long time and, in January 1982, this led Stevenson Construction into the Group. The D&H construction division had been looking for an entry into the building industry in Natal in order to extend their national coverage in that field, and Bob's company fitted their requirements perfectly. Its healthy reputation and order book were an immediate success and it also contributed a fine team of people with considerable strength in top and middle management.

The D&H philosophy of decentralized management was a major influence on Bob's acceptance of the offer of total acquisition, and apart from three D&H members being appointed to the board and the attractive opportunities arising from involvement in such a strong organization, there were no changes within the company. Stevenson Construction continued to play a conspicuous role in the development of Natal, proudly constituting a reliable and eminently successful section of the Group construction division.

Roadmix

With the establishment of Tarmac Industries in 1948, Darling and Hodgson pioneered the commercial production of premixed asphalt in South Africa and it was only in the late sixties that they pulled out of surfacing operations altogether to concentrate on road building. Another construction company, C and J Reid, at about the same time decided to move into black top operations and benefit from the big contracts which were accompanying the increasing construction of freeways on the Reef. They acquired Roadmix in 1966 and ran it as a surfacing division under Roy Munro until 1972 when it again became independent, rapidly developing into a leader in the field of premixed asphalt for surfacing and maintaining roads. Roy had worked for Darling and Hodgson until 1965 when he had left to start his own company and another member of the Roadmix team, Gert Koen, had also been with Darling and Hodgson for some time in the early road building days.

Roadmix established its head office and a permanent plant in Boksburg North, and another plant near Pretoria. From these plants they worked over distances within which the premix could be kept hot, while jobs further afield necessitated the setting up of mobile plants for the duration of the contract. This they did as far afield as the Eastern Cape and the Caprivi Strip for highway resurfacing but most of their work was maintenance of roads for various municipalities.

There was another company which had been in the surfacing business since the early twenties and had never relinquished its activities in the bitumen field. This was Fowlers, which was acquired by D&H in 1981. When Roadmix joined the Group the following year subsequent rationalization saw the amalgamation of the black top operations of Fowlers with Roadmix within the asphalt and road rehabilitation section of the construction division. Events had turned a full circle and D&H were restored to their traditional work. The field was larger now, though, and in many ways more sophisticated. Ma-

Road paving operations.

Premix plant at Port Shepstone, Natal.

chines had taken over the work that used to be carried out by hand.

Mike Watson was moved from Fowler Construction to head up the new Roadmix company, and Manie Nel went with him to join the strong and close-knit team which still included Gert Koen. There was an exceptionally large number of long-serving employees and at a long service award ceremony in July 1983 a total of three hundred and fifty-three years of service was divided amongst twenty-eight members of staff!

In April 1983 Roadmix extended their operating area with the purchase of Griffiths and Inglis, a well established Cape Town company, and at the end of that year there were eleven mixing plants distributed throughout South Africa. The company had acquired its own crushing equipment as well so that where necessary it could produce its own aggregate material. Work was carried out over a widespread area and the huge crowd which flocked to see the last race of the 1983 World Grand Prix series at Kyalami watched the cars racing on a track which had very recently been resurfaced by Roadmix.

There is a lively research and development department in the company, headed by Les Davidson, which constantly strives for improvements to give Roadmix an edge over its competitors. A uniquely South African rubberized bitumen has been developed which incorporates scrap rubber and is designed to improve the quality and service life of the road surface. Roadmix have placed several rubber bitumen products on the South African market, including Flexiseal and Flexispray for sealing work and Flexiphalt for overlay work.

This innovative approach epitomizes the company's awareness of the future demands and responsibilities of road maintenance, the need for which can only grow as the authorities cut back on capital expenditure on road building, while the ever-increasing traffic constantly takes its toll of all road surfaces.

Group Five Engineering

One of the dramas enacted on the Johannesburg Stock Exchange in 1982 was the story of Group Five Engineering and the way it came into the D&H fold. Group Five was a successful company with a widespread shareholding and plenty of cash in the bank, making it vulnerable to possible takeover, and in October of that year their shares began to move on the stock market. The buyer was identified as Magnum Holdings, a group of investment companies, and although Magnum's chief executive laughed at the suggestion that they were bidding for control the directors of Group Five felt very uneasy, particularly as it was common knowledge that Magnum desperately needed financial support.

During this period Sandy Jamieson attended a charity race meeting in Germiston where he met John Hodgson and Alex Combrink. This led to a meeting between Group Five and D&H executives within a few days, which resulted in a statement from Group Five that D&H had acquired 20% of its equity. John's public comment was 'We are protecting our friends', and the crisis appeared to be over. Within a few weeks, however, the Stock Exchange was all agog with the collapse of Magnum. When their shares were put on the market by the liquidators, D&H, with the full agreement of the Group Five board, bought their 30% shareholding in Group Five and moved into a majority situation.

Group Five's initial reaction was one of apprehension. They did not want to be taken over by anybody, but D&H's management philosophy of non-interference once again won the day, and the result was a happy and constructive association. D&H put three members on the board – John Hodgson, Brian Malcomson and Lloyd Koch – and the companies within Group Five continued to operate independently as they had done since the group began. Soon after Group Five became a Group subsidiary Fred Law retired as chairman and his place was taken on 1 March 1983 by Sandy Jamieson who had been deputy chairman.

The name Group Five has always been somewhat misleading. The original amalgamation comprised only two main companies – CMGM and Basil Read – and at the time there was considerable discussion about a suitable name. Group Two was thought to sound too much like a pop group, and the choice of Group Five confidently gave them room to manoeuvre! When Group Five became a public company in 1974 the prospectus described five companies: McLaren and Eger, CMGM, Peter Clogg Construction, MGC Engineering and Basil Read. These companies were operating in three fields, namely road and industrial construction, civil engineering, piling and specialized foundations.

The largest component of Group Five was the CMGM Group, which originated as MGM just after the war when three young men left Roberts Construction to work together under their own names, Morgan, Gunning and Mitchell. In its early years the company was responsible for a number of major construction schemes, including the Stanger hydroelectric project, the Grootgedagt dam at Vryheid, sewer reticulation schemes at Stilfontein, Buffelsfontein and Welkom and extensions to Amcor steelworks at Newcastle. In 1959 MGM was taken over by Stuart Dawson and Gus Johansson and it broadened its scope over the years until it ranked among the top few civils companies in South Africa.

In 1971 MGM became part of a consortium which tendered for the third Iscor steelworks which were to be established at Newcastle in northern Natal. One of the other companies in the consortium was Peter Clogg Construction which had been started in 1969 by Peter Clogg, Mike Lupton-Smith and Dries Prinsloo. Roberts Construction,

Iscor's No 3 steelworks, Newcastle, Natal – CMGM.

for whom they had all worked, took a minority share in the company and they were soon joined by Fred Law who had been a director of Roberts. Peter Clogg Construction started working in the Vaal triangle area and expanded very rapidly as far afield as Pietersburg where they built a water purification plant, to northern Natal for a bridge across the Sand river at Utrecht, and up to Hotazel in the northern Cape for a mine development. On the Reef, Peter Clogg Construction built an effluent plant, a boiler plant and an ethylene tank for Sasolburg, worked on the Natref refinery, restacked four of the cooling towers at the Vanderbijlpark steelworks and, among a number of other civil contracts, began to move into steelworks with extensions to Highveld Steel and Ferro Alloys.

When the new Iscor steelworks was announced Peter Clogg Construction were determined to tender for the work and, realizing that such a major project would require greater resources and expertise, they formed a consortium with MGM and Gillis-Mason Construction in early 1971. This company, MGM, Gillis-Mason and Clogg (Pty) Ltd was awarded the contract.

In October that year Peter Clogg Construction merged with MGM to form CMGM, and during the Newcastle contract this company bought out Gillis-Mason's share in the consortium which became known as MGC Engineering. This constituted one of the largest construction companies in South Africa at the time. The satisfactory completion of the enormous contract was a breakthrough for CMGM from which they never looked back.

The success of the contract precipitated the decision for CMGM to go public and open the way to financial strength for future development. In order to create an even stronger body, CMGM purchased McLaren and Eger, which became a wholly-owned subsidiary in 1972, and after the decision to merge with Basil Read, Group Five Engineering was formed.

McLaren and Eger was the oldest component of the Group. It was a company which

Herkules piles awaiting installation at SAPPI's Ngodwana mill – McLaren and Eger.

had been started in 1928 by J W 'Mac' McLaren and Fred Eger. Both these men had come to South Africa with considerable experience in civil engineering and marine construction, which guided them into such early successes as the launching of the Green Point outfall sewer and the construction of the Steenbras river bridge – the longest arch span in the country at the time. Other pre-war contracts included three bridges over the Orange river, the intake and purification works at Vereeniging for the Rand Water Board and the cooling water intake and foundations for the Dock Road power-station in Cape Town. After the war, during which McLaren and Eger were involved in the construction of the Sturrock graving dock in Cape Town and various coastal defence works, the company's emphasis changed and it moved steadily to the forefront of the piling and foundation industry in South Africa.

Basil Read, the final component of Group Five Engineering, was a name well known throughout South Africa. Basil qualified as a civil engineer at the University of Cape Town before joining up to fight in the war. On his return home he joined Wolton Gray in the Transvaal, a relatively small road and earthworks company which was sold within a few years to W and C French. Basil continued as managing director of French and Wolton Gray until 1951 and the following year he set up his own company, plunging confidently into the high risk business of contracting. He soon landed his first big contract, for the J B M Hertzog airport at Bloemfontein, which was awarded to him in association with the Cape company Triamic. All profits made by the company were always ploughed back, enabling it to expand rapidly in the industry. Basil Read made a lasting name for themselves in the design and construction of the Kyalami racetrack which was rated as one of the best circuits in Grand Prix racing, and the mid sixties and seventies saw a great variety of work, from multi-million rand highways to contracts like the Malalane sugar mill and the Rosslyn factory for SA Breweries.

Sandy Jamieson joined Basil Read in the mid fifties, having worked for the South African Railways and James Thompson since leaving university. He became a shareholder and director of the company in 1960 and was appointed managing director in 1966. Basil was experiencing increasing bad health and in 1971 Sandy and his fellow directors bought him out. When Basil died in 1974 Sandy became chairman and chief executive of the company.

This was the situation just after Group Five went public. The company's first chairman was Stuart Dawson of CMGM, with two joint deputy chairmen, Basil Read and Ian McLaren (Mac's son, who had entered the business as soon as he had qualified as a civil engineer). Basil died a couple of months later, leaving Ian as deputy chairman, to become chairman in 1977. Ian's deputy chairmen were Fred Law and Sandy Jamieson, both of whom were to become chairman in the future. The first Group Five board comprised Stuart Dawson, Basil Read, Ian McLaren, Sandy Jamieson, Fred Law, Peter Clogg and Peter Tucker (financial director of McLaren and Eger). At first there were no corporate headquarters and board meetings rotated among the different companies. In early 1978 Group Five decided to rent offices from Gough Cooper in Randburg but before long they had bought land in Rivonia where they built elegant offices far from the turmoil of Johannesburg but within easy access of all major businesses. These were built by Combrink Construction.

Within the group each company expanded. McLaren and Eger completed the foundations for six of the nine power-stations commissioned by Escom in the following years and in association with Dura Foundation they installed the forty thousand piles required for the Sasol II and III plants. Major foundation contracts were undertaken for Iscor at the Pretoria works, SAPPI at the Ngodwana paper mill in the Eastern Transvaal, a new cement works for Pretoria Portland Cement at Dwaalboom, the new Vaal colliery

Construction of cooling towers at Tutuka power-station – High Structures.

for Letaba power-station near Maccouvlei and a new sugar mill for Huletts at Felixton. During much of the time Roy Heddon was chairman of McLaren and Eger. He had joined the company in 1950 and was appointed chairman in early 1976 when Ian stepped down. When Roy retired as chairman in early 1984 he was acknowledged as having contributed more to the development of foundation techniques in the Republic than anyone else in his time.

CMGM were also involved at Ngodwana, carrying out much of the civils work there and taking over D&H Civils' construction of the high chimney. They also built what was the largest coal storage silo in Africa at Tavistock near Ogies, and what is still the largest grain silo complex in Africa, at Lilongwe in Malawi. More recent projects included a sewerage outfall tunnel at Bushkoppies on the edge of Soweto, a diamond plant at Jwaneng in Botswana and most of the civil engineering work at Tutuka power-station for Escom. Subsidiary companies developed for specialist services: CMGM Glybeton (mainly silos and chimneys), CMGM Building (low cost accommodation), Normac Building Systems (industrial roofing) and High Structures, the last named a company owned jointly by CMGM and Gillis-Mason which built the cooling towers at Matla, Arnot and Grootvlei power-stations, followed by six more at Tutuka, near Standerton, with a contract for a further six at the new Kendal power- station.

Basil Read expanded considerably after 1974, and various acquisitions were made, notably Reef Levebre and Triamic, the old Cape company with whom Basil Read had worked in the fifties, and also C and J Reid. Turnover increased dramatically with contracts including multi-million rand road and freeway systems, industrial projects for many clients, such as AE&CI and Escom, and various defence projects. As the supply of

Construction of terminal buildings at Mmabatho international airport in Bophutatswana – Basil Read.

Baddeleyite leach plant at Phalaborwa – Group Five Projects.

road contracts dwindled the Basil Read group decentralized to some extent into a number of specialist and regional operating companies. Later contracts included the building of Uncle Charlie's interchange on the edge of Johannesburg and the new Mmabatho international airport in Bophutatswana.

Some years after the formation of Group Five Engineering it was decided to move into project engineering, and a subsidiary company, Group Five Projects, was started in January 1978 under Syd van der Walt, a former director of Roberts Construction responsible for engineering, management, mechanical, electrical and instruments, construction and their inspection authority companies. It began with a modest staff of three, who were careful to take on only what they could handle without stretching their resources and they soon established themselves with a reputation for high quality work. There were contracts for the fire-fighting system at Saldanha, refrigeration plants at Vaal Reefs and Elandsrand and a coal-washing plant at Welgedacht. Before long project management was added to their repertoire, undertaking a baddeleyite leach plant at Phalaborwa for the Phosphate Development Corporation (Foskor). This was a turnkey project, as

The Group Five board, 1984. Left to right: Bob McCue, Brian Malcomson, Neil Douglas, John Hodgson, Sandy Jamieson, Syd van der Walt, Lloyd Koch, Peter Clogg (absent: Alex Combrink).

was the cryolite recovery plant for Alusaf's Richigate project at Richards Bay. Another project was a totally integrated in-house turnkey development for a warehouse and Coca-Cola factory at Devland near Johannesburg for the Amalgamated Beverage Industries, with other Group Five companies handling the earthworks, civils and building work. Another interesting development saw the company involved in the construction of factories, initially seven in Rosslyn and three in Brits, for the Small Business Development Corporation.

Syd van der Walt built up an outstanding team in Group Five Projects and, encouraged by the success of this division, Group Five decided to diversify further. Within a few years they had developed an industrial division through the acquisition of several companies: Reliable Production Company, which supplied a wide range of industrial fasteners from its factory in Electron; Gassecure, general precision engineers; Merrol Fire Protection Engineering; Servitek, a group of companies with high expertise in the field of electronics and communications with nationwide spread, which supplied and installed all the new OCR postal automation equipment at the Jeppe Street post office in Johannesburg and other centres, and all the VOR beacons on the main air routes in South Africa. Servitek established offices in Boksburg, where it also handles much of its own research and development. Group Five Projects became a wholly-owned subsidiary in September 1982.

Although Group Five's entry to the Group was precipitated by the Magnum episode, D&H had for some years recognized the advantage of a closer association of the two groups, appreciating that their activities would satisfy mutual needs. The strong executive team of Group Five, headed up by Peter Clogg and Syd van der Walt under Sandy Jamieson, was retained but the influence of D&H was soon felt. Group Five developed a new disciplined unity which gave it even greater strength and this was reflected in increased profits.

Ways were considered of how best to rationalize the construction activities of the two groups, and at the end of 1983 the decision was made to reverse the entire D&H construction division into Group Five, to be effective from January 1984. Following the merger, D&H's interest in the ordinary share capital of Group Five increased from 50,7% to 65,5%. For some time D&H's construction components all retained their operating identities and continued to develop alongside the Group Five companies. Together they constituted one of the major building and construction companies in South Africa, with a formidable strength and exciting potential for everyone involved. Sandy Jamieson continued as chairman of the new Group Five, Alex Combrink was appointed deputy chairman, and Neil Douglas, who had joined Group Five as financial director in October 1980, assumed responsibility for the financial operations of the new company. With the other members of the executive board these men led Group Five into 1984, confident of the capabilities of the comprehensive range of activities within their company.

The Services Story

The services division of Darling and Hodgson comprises transport and waste management operations, semi-bulk materials handling and specialized service facilities.

Transport was D&H's first diversification beyond the field of road construction, and developed from the company's involvement in haulage of bulk bitumen in South Africa. Bill and John had the courage and foresight to break with tradition and pioneer the change from transporting bitumen in drums to bulk haulage by tanker. The success of the operations led to the establishment of Tanker Services by John and his colleague Jack Plane at the end of 1959, not long after Bill's death. This new company gradually built up a fleet of tankers and was soon handling all of Socony's and most of Shell/BP's bulk bitumen distribution around the country, based in Natal and the Transvaal.

Tanker Services moved beyond hauling bitumen in 1962 with the acquisition of the Socony fleet of vehicles which carried liquid sulphur, oxidized asphalt, solvents, furnace oil, toluol, paraffin and various grades of lubricating oil. In 1963 Tanker Services became a subsidiary of Darling and Hodgson when the latter joined Union Corporation, and strong financial backing encouraged them to enter a period of rapid development into the haulage of all kinds of bulk liquids. They made a tremendous impression on the South African transport industry and operations spread to the Cape with branch offices in Cape Town and Port Elizabeth.

In 1964 John Hodgson gave a neat summary of Tanker Services' achievements to date: 'The last three years have seen rapid development in the bulk transportation of liquids and flowable solids by road tankers. The aptness of this move into a new field can be gauged by considering the saving effected by industry in eliminating containers such as drums, cans, bottles, bags. The one-off loading, filling and emptying of these represent time and labour that can be saved.' His words highlighted the widening recognition of the rewarding advantages of bulk transport.

Over the following years Tanker Services introduced many technical innovations to the industry in South Africa. In 1964 they launched the first liquid petroleum gas tanker and two years later the first stainless steel tankers. The latter established the concept of the multi-purpose tanker, easy to clean and able to carry a range of different commodities. In the sixties chassis-less tankers were put into use, which significantly increased the payload of each vehicle through decreased body weight.

There were other bulk haulage companies in South Africa, and at the end of 1967 Tanker Services merged with United Bulk Transport, comprising Stag Bulk Transports and Thorntons Bulk Transport, part of the British company United Transport. These two companies specialized in powders, and a combination of complementary operations made the new company, United Tanker Services, the largest privately operated bulk fleet in South Africa. The merger expanded D&H Transport's operations heavily into the haulage of cement, sugar and cyanide.

The potential of United Tanker Services was great, but sadly the partnership was not a success and in 1973, just before D&H went public, the overseas partners were bought out and the name reverted to Tanker Services. It became a wholly-owned subsidiary except in the Cape, where Jowells Transport retained an interest and management control until 1978 when Darling and Hodgson sold out altogether and Tanker Services ceased to operate in the Western Cape. In the Eastern Cape D&H had a direct investment in mobile tankers through their 50% interest in P E Holdings.

Phil Erasmus was appointed managing director of the enlarged Tanker Services in 1973. He had been with the company since its earliest days and had an in-depth knowledge of all operations. In his capable hands the company was reorganized and expanded over the following years and started to make a significant contribution to Group profits.

In 1975 D&H made the first of a series of acquisitions which were to broaden their transport activities and considerably accelerate profit growth. The purchase of 60% of Omnibus, a company based in Alberton, took the Group into extra-heavy transport and abnormal loads, and gave them the opportunity to benefit from the major capital works underway in South Africa, in particular Sasol II and III at Secunda. Omnibus's owner, Arthur Webster, had seen a new area of opportunity in the development of heavy industry and the expansion of the chemical and energy sectors, which would in time produce a need for the transport of extraordinarily large and bulky loads with which the South African Railways could not cope. He had equipped himself to satisfy this need, and Darling and Hodgson saw in his company an attractive way to extend their operations.

Omnibus continued to operate autonomously under Arthur Webster for several years, and carried out a number of contracts with enormous vehicles which made a great impression on everyone who saw them. It was difficult to forget the sight (and inconvenience) of a vehicle which was sixty-nine metres long, nearly six and a half metres high and over eight metres wide – that was a huge BOF furnace ladle being transported from the Reef to Highveld Steel and was the widest suspended load that had ever been transported in South Africa to date. One of them left an overwhelming impression of wheels, wheels and more wheels as three huge Kenworth Brutes towed two Commetto bogies bearing an enormous carbonyl stripper tower from an Elandsfontein engineering company to Sasol III. The overall length was 104,6 metres and it was followed by another equally long load pulled by three Mack loaders transporting a stainless steel ammonia fractionater. An interesting example of team work was demonstrated by the three drivers – radio contact enabled them to change gears in unison with perfect co-ordination and smoke appeared simultaneously from the exhausts as the drivers changed down, moving forward as if they were one unit. Not only did the transporting require a high degree of professional skill, but there was a great deal of preparation to be done before the vehicles commenced their slow journey. Each route had to be planned in great

Omnibus on the road to Sasol III.

Apples being loaded into a D&H Freight Lines vehicle.

detail and checked for overhead wires, bridges and other hazards. Permission and permits had to be obtained all along the way.

Paul Norris was transferred from Tanker Services to work with Arthur Webster, who after a while moved into Darling and Hodgson's head office at Hyde Park. Arthur did not fit happily into the corporate scene, however, and in 1978 he sold his shareholding in Omnibus to Darling and Hodgson. The demand for Omnibus's specialized service gradually dwindled, largely because the South African Railways adapted to deal with abnormal loads, and Darling and Hodgson finally sold the company in 1982.

The acquisition of 1976 was a specialized fleet of refrigerated trucks. It all began when John Hodgson was chatting to Peter Barlow in the pub of a hotel in St Moritz, Switzerland, one skiing holiday, and Peter remarked on the problem of moving fruit from his farm in the Cape to the markets. This made John ponder on the advantages of moving into refrigerated transport and led to the purchase of Zweiamic Transport, with six refrigerated vehicles operating out of a depot in Philippi in the Cape. The company was renamed Refrigerated Transport and started ferrying fruit, mainly apples, from the Cape to the Reef, and eggs in the opposite direction. At the end of 1979 the name was changed to D&H Freight Lines and the company began to haul products other than cold commodities, offering to 'carry anything, any time, any place'. They took delivery of their first multi-cargo trailer which had four compartments with individual temperature controls, each able to carry a different product, varying as widely as Easter eggs, beer in cans and frozen fish. D&H Freight Lines ran as an independent operation and moved mainly between Durban, Johannesburg and Cape Town on long hauls. It operated successfully but not very profitably and it was eventually closed down in 1983.

Owning refrigerated trucks led D&H into an interesting diversification when they undertook to transport freshly-cut proteas from the Cape across the dry Karoo to Jan Smuts airport on the Reef from where they would be flown to Europe. The initial success of this venture so fired the imagination of the transport executives that they decided to go into protea handling in a big way and a new company, D&H Flora, was formed to purchase, pack and export South African indigenous dried flowers as well as the proteas. A farm was purchased at Villiersdorp in the Western Cape where the flowers were grown, and offices, packing sheds and cold storage facilities were quickly established. Flowers were soon arriving in Europe within forty-eight hours of having been packed in the Cape. The farm was found to have a KWV wine quota, which was an enjoyable bonus for some members of D&H! D&H Flora eventually proved to be an unprofitable venture, mainly because the cartel in Europe made it very difficult to penetrate the market. The company was closed down in 1980 and its assets sold.

A major and outstandingly successful acquisition was made in 1977, with the purchase of W J's Bulk Transport, which instantly launched Group transport interests into a bigger and broader field of operation. Permits from the Road Transportation Board allowing the haulage of specific products are the lifeblood of any transport company and W J's held a wide range of these, which made the company an exciting addition to the transport division. W J's had always worked with clean chemicals and foodstuffs, especially glucose, which complemented Tanker Services' work and released them from the limitations of refinery and road-related products. The amalgamation of operations and people was not without problems, but within a few years a successful organization emerged, both names being retained and each company as a general rule hauling its traditional products. Jans van Vuuren continued his capable management of all W J's activities.

Another transport-orientated company had been started in the Group in 1969 with the establishment of a waste disposal service. Purle Industrial Waste Disposal (later to become Waste-tech) pioneered an entirely new industry in South Africa over the following years. In 1979, when there was a major restructuring of the whole Group, all transport and waste management activities were put together, with the intention of improving performance through a number of common functions, in a newly created services division under Phil Erasmus. Phil in turn reported to Peter Loveday, managing director of the Group industrial section.

The small management group of the services division included Phil Erasmus, Len Hall and Peter de Beer. Len joined the Group in 1976 as the transport accountant and has remained with D&H, making an unobtrusive and invaluable contribution to the financial well-being of the services division throughout its development. Peter was manager of the technical side of the division. His expertise contributed to Tanker Services' progress for many years and helped place the company in its prominent position amongst the leaders in transport. While in Natal he introduced electrical tanker heating of bitumen – a significant improvement since the lighter equipment allowed more bitumen to be hauled. He and his highly-motivated team helped increase flexibility through developing compartmentalized tankers and a highly sophisticated washing system on a par with any in the world. They also initiated the production of specialized vehicles – 'horses for courses' – over the years, and effected improvement of payloads in many ways, such as the introduction of trailer tankers, referred to as 'pups' in the transport industry.

Big vehicles require a great deal of mechanical maintenance and repair, and with the intention of minimizing the time used for these, a central specialized service facility was established in Natal in 1976 under Peter de Beer. As this facility developed, its operations were put into a new company, D&H Automotive Services, whose workshops were made available to any Group company. Increased profits and prolonged auto life soon demonstrated the enhanced efficiency of expertly serviced vehicles.

The efficiency and maximum utilization of the transport fleet improved dramatically over the years through computerization. The first computer was installed at Tanker Services (Natal) in 1978, and another in Germiston the following year. Their programmes

The operations control tower at the Jacobs terminal, Durban.

rapidly revolutionized all aspects of operations and management. Radio communication remained vitally important and the control room of each region has always been the nerve centre of operations.

When Tanker Services and W J's had settled down together and operations were running successfully, D&H looked towards further broadening of their transport activities. In 1980 they acquired a 60% share of Containerisation Africa. The name was changed to D&H Semi-Bulk Systems, which described its unique and dynamic concept of handling materials. Within two years the total equity was acquired and the company was firmly established as an independent operation within the services division.

Another interesting development in 1980 was announced thus in the D&H magazine: 'To D&H on 24 October 1980, a Mercedes Benz luxury coach.' This was the brainchild of W J's' Jans van Vuuren. His idea of running a Group coach for internal and external public relations activities within Darling and Hodgson was enthusiastically received and so the *D&H Explorer* was born, to be available for hire, at a fixed rate per day, by any

Group company for the purpose of improving relationships with clients while introducing them to Group operations in a most enjoyable way. The coach's full-time driver, Neville van Aswegan, had been with W J's Bulk Transport for some time and was specially chosen for the job by Jans. The coach was garaged and maintained by W J's Bulk, and although its operations and booking were at first carried out by the Group public relations department at head office, before long responsibility for all its activities was given to W J's. There was one particularly hair-raising experience aboard the *D&H Explorer* when Neville was driving a coachload of important guests through the Kruger National Park. They were on a narrow road where it was impossible to turn when suddenly an elephant appeared walking determinedly towards them. Neville stopped the coach but could not reverse as there were cars behind him. He was wondering how well the fibreglass body would withstand the elephant when fortunately the animal changed course and moved off the road.

The *D&H Explorer* was a great success and within two years it was replaced by an even more luxurious coach with added facilities to accommodate business conferences and board meetings. Neville drove the new coach, the *D&H Enterprise*, and the passengers' comfort was ensured by the presence of a D&H hostess on each trip. During 1983 it made three major tours based in Cape Town, Johannesburg and Durban, during which a captive and appreciative audience of D&H key shareholders, prominent South African businessmen and investors, were shown a comprehensive range of D&H activities. The success of these trips proved the worth of this original marketing tool, and similar tours are planned for the future.

By 1983 strong management teams were active in all the operating companies of D&H Transport, and depots had been established in the key areas of South Africa. Tanker Services' two major transport terminals were at Brailsford House, Germiston, and Jacobs, Durban, and there were also depots at Lichtenberg, Hennenman, Vanderbijlpark and Pretoria. W J's continued to share the Germiston terminal and retained their depot at Mobeni in Natal. In 1983 another depot was opened at Mtubatuba and in the same year W J's moved from Muldersvlei in the Cape to Stickland, an ultra-modern terminal which provided a base for all D&H transport activities in the Western Cape and was an indication of Group intentions to maintain and increase their operations in the region.

D&H Transport have always had a reputation for friendliness and hospitality. For many years they have had a cricket side challenging other teams both within and outside

Above left
Phil Erasmus.

Above right
Neville van Aswegen and the D&H Enterprise.

Theoretical and practical training go hand in hand.

the Group – with varying degrees of success on the field but always great enjoyment after the match! For some time there has been an annual fishing trip organized by W J's for its customers, usually to the Zululand coast, and Jans has built up a great reputation as host and organizer. There was a particularly successful trip to Kosi Bay in 1980 which Jans reported as 'a unique experience', a comment with which everyone agreed. Jans will never forget one night when the men heard hippo very close to their anchored boat and then, in the pitch darkness, to Jans' speechless horror, one of the hippos heaved itself into the boat – only to be revealed as Peter de Beer enjoying a midnight swim!

This good spirit was continued within the division with the establishment of recreation areas at the depots where everyone was encouraged to join in the fun. W J's Natal manager, John Todd, was determined to establish such a facility for his staff and, overcoming all obstacles with determination and enthusiasm, he set up the J B Hodgson Recreation Centre in a large warehouse at Mobeni. It was officially opened by John Hodgson in March 1980 and has been used for award ceremonies, parties and end of year gatherings as well as everyday enjoyment for 'the banana boys'. Tanker Services set up their recreation facilities in the Tank Inn at Jacobs, while in the Transvaal one of the old staff houses at the Germiston depot was converted by W J's to a recreation club in 1980.

Phil Erasmus has always been very proud of the fact that many of the key managers in transport have come up through the ranks, as he did himself. He has also made an appreciable contribution to the development of the heavy transport industry in South Africa. When the Professional Hauliers Association was formed in early 1975 by eight of the local transport companies, to represent and co-ordinate the industry's views, Phil was appointed the first chairman. His genial personality has always supported his philosophy that 'business is people' and the success of D&H's transport companies has been influenced considerably by his introduction of training at every level. This has given individuals confidence and benefited the whole organization. When asked whether at the start of Tanker Services anyone had envisaged how big it could grow, Phil replied: 'John Hodgson knew it; he could see over the hill even at that stage.' It was John's enthusiasm and encouragement that gave Phil the determination to succeed and achieve so much, and after some years of reporting to Peter Loveday, he enjoyed working directly with John again when Peter left in 1983.

The services division has operated for many years with a high degree of encouragement through incentives. There are annual awards in each company with respect to good and safe driving, with the ultimate recognition of the 'driver of the year', and workshop efficiency, all of which serve to further individual enthusiasm and promote a good team spirit.

By 1983 D&H Services were running a fleet of more than three hundred and fifty specialized vehicles covering a distance of about thirty million kilometres a year – twice around the earth's circumference each day, or three return trips to the moon every month! That was merely the skeleton of a vibrant 'people' organization which penetrated all corners of South Africa, co-ordinated by Phil Erasmus from the headquarters of the services division in Fernpark, Randburg.

Tanker Services

Darling and Hodgson pioneered the transport of bulk bitumen in South Africa and developed it through Tanker Services. The bitumen used in South Africa was all imported until 1954 when the Standard Oil Company of South Africa established the country's first oil refinery in Durban. This subsidiary of the Standard Oil Company of New York, Socony (eventually taken over by Mobil), began to market a local bitumen as a by-product of refining crude oil from the Middle East. This was viewed with great suspicion at first, until extensive tests carried out all over the country by a special section of the CSIR indicated that there was no significant difference in its behaviour compared even with the high quality naturally-occurring bitumen from Trinidad. In 1961 an embargo on exporting bitumen to South Africa opened up the market to the new product.

The imported bitumen had always been transported to site in drums and heated up in tar-pots, a messy procedure which resulted in a wastage of up to twenty per cent. The local production offered the possibility of bulk delivery and heating which was more economical and time-saving. Socony's Transvaal sales manager at the time was Switch Cuningham, a good friend of Bill Hodgson, who knew that Darling and Hodgson were operating two spray tankers. The two men agreed that these tankers should be used to initiate the bulk haulage of bitumen from the new refinery to customers. This proved highly successful, and the gentleman's agreement between Bill and John of Darling and Hodgson, and Switch and his colleague John Little of Socony led to the establishment of Tanker Services, registered on 10 December 1959. This new company built up a fleet of tankers, at first handling bitumen but later expanding its operations to other bulk liquids as well.

Bill died just before the company was formed, and the initial shareholders were John and his friend Jack Plane. It was a project wholeheartedly supported by Jack because his primary business interests lay in the manufacture of diesel trucks and trailers, and he was therefore intensely interested in promoting anything that would increase this market. The initial Tanker Services vehicles all had AEC chassis from J H Plane and Company with tankers built by their subsidiary, Trailer Manufacturing Company.

Darling and Hodgson's spray tankers S1 and S2 continued to operate independently while the Tanker Services fleet developed. It was based initially in the Darling and Hodgson (Natal) yard in Point Road under the local Darling and Hodgson manager, Alf Swerdlow. The first vehicle was a big articulated tanker used to spray roads for the Natal Provincial Administration, using hot bitumen straight from the Socony refinery. The brand new tanker with a 1 800 gallon Etnyre distributor was delivered late the day before the first contract was started and there was no time to check it before filling up at the refinery and driving down to Port Shepstone. A crowd of interested spectators had gathered to watch, but alas the jets on the sprayer did not work properly and too little bitumen was released. It was decided to respray the road at a later date. About eight months later Alf received a telephone call from Brian Malcomson, the financial director of Tanker Services, asking what had happened about the respraying. To everyone's amazement the engineer in charge of the road said that the job was 'perfect', and Alf never knew whether it was a case of 'under calibration' or 'over specification'! It was certainly an example of Brian's meticulous checking of every job that was undertaken.

A second tanker was soon purchased and for the first six months work was carried out only for the NPA, spraying roads. Within a year, however, John had negotiated with Socony for 100% of all the road haulage, spraying and railcar business of their bituminous products, and with Shell for most of their bitumen work in South Africa. More

Fatty Strydom with the first articulated bitumen tanker at Brailsford House.

tankers were purchased and Tanker Services began to make their presence known on the roads. The vehicles all had vivid yellow cabs with 'Tanker Services' inscribed in large black letters. There was one occasion when their name was inadvertently well advertised: a vehicle jack-knifed in heavy rain on the main Durban road, causing a tremendous build-up of delayed traffic which was reported on the front page of the next day's newspaper with a large photograph of the offending tanker, clearly marked Tanker Services!

There were many hazards in those pioneering days. Setting out early one chilly morning on an important spraying contract, Alf was beside the driver in the cab and Solomon on the seat at the back of the tanker, keeping an eye on the burners which were keeping the bitumen hot. As the tanker was travelling along the road it was overtaken by a truck with someone in the back waving frantically and looking curiously like Solomon. Eventually both the tanker and the truck pulled off the road and there indeed was a dishevelled and bruised Solomon who, it transpired, had huddled too close to the burners on the tanker to try to keep warm and had been overcome by the fumes. He had fallen off onto the road, and a passing truck had picked him up.

Tanker Services' first year showed disastrous financial results and the future in Natal seemed unpromising, so operations were started in the Transvaal. At the end of 1961 only one of the four vehicles in the Tanker Services fleet was still in Natal; the others were based at Brailsford House, working for both Socony and Shell in conjunction with Satmar. The third tanker (TS3) gave endless trouble; it rarely completed a journey without breaking down and spent a distressing amount of time off the road in the workshops of J H Plane and Company. TS4 was just the opposite, 'seldom off the road for anything but preventive maintenance'. The tankers covered many miles, and the haul between Durban and Johannesburg was a long and weary journey over the narrow, winding road, with heavy units often hindering progress. The AEC vehicles frequently had trouble in getting over Van Reenen's Pass because their engines lost power rapidly with increasing altitude, and they were forced to take an alternative route.

The volume of work in the Transvaal increased rapidly. Tanker Services ran an advertisement which summed up the service offered:

Filling a tanker at Socony.

Bulk bitumen – on site
　　　　　　　on tap
　　　　　　　on time
You spray – we spray – either way call Tanker Services

It also pointed out that the method of bulk transport had no equal in saving of time and handling labour at both ends of the journey, not to mention the convenience with no mess, no drums, no fuss.

An increasing number of municipal authorities and contractors on the Reef began to use this service. The provincial roads department of the Orange Free State began to make use of it as well and the bitumen was railed to Warden station where it was pumped out into a heating unit and then into the sprayers. Tanker Services took over a Cleaver and Brookes railcar heater from Socony for this and for other contracts where the distance involved made bulk railage more economical than road transport.

The Tanker Services fleet in the Transvaal was managed by Hubert Goetsch, the Darling and Hodgson plant manager. Hubert was Bill Hodgson's son-in-law, who had joined the company the year before Bill died. He was an enterprising man, a qualified architect who had also studied business administration in America. He married Diana in 1953, and in 1958 was working as a car salesman when Bill asked him to join the rapidly expanding family business where his architectural knowledge was put to good use over the years. All the extensions to Brailsford House were designed by him as well as the various office blocks for Darling and Hodgson around the country, starting at the Aris quarry in South West Africa. He spent many years with the company in various capacities, making a loyal and valuable contribution, and he was an integral part of the early years of Tanker Services.

At the beginning of 1962 T H Frith, from Putco, was appointed to the board of Tanker Services and became chairman in place of Jack. That year S1 and S2 were brought into the Tanker Services fleet to simplify administration and at the end of the year the centre of operations swung back to Natal when Tanker Services took over from Socony a fleet

Early road spraying operations in the Transvaal.

of vehicles comprising three truck tractors and five trailers for transporting liquid sulphur, oxidized asphalt and solvents, including furnace oil, toluol, paraffin and various grades of lubricating oil. They were thus extending their hauling capabilities beyond tar and bitumen for the first time, and the sudden increase in the number of vehicles necessitated a much bigger depot. Land was purchased in Jacobs, and Tanker Services erected their own offices and workshops there and moved away from their dependence on Darling and Hodgson.

The Jacobs depot was established by Peter de Neef who had been appointed manager of Darling and Hodgson (Natal) when Alf left in 1962. During Peter's first couple of years in Natal incredibly rapid expansion took place into hauling all kinds of bulk liquids and it was impossible to buy tankers fast enough. It was a tremendously exciting time, made possible financially by Tanker Services becoming a subsidiary of Darling and Hodgson when the latter joined Union Corporation in 1963. Two Union Corporation representatives, Ian Wilson and Bill Partridge, joined the company board but there was no management interference, and John, as managing director, seized every opportunity that came his way and infected everyone with his own enthusiasm.

In 1964 land adjoining the Jacobs yard was purchased to enlarge the depot and the management of Tanker Services in Natal was separated completely from Darling and Hodgson. When Peter de Neef was promoted to Darling and Hodgson's head office in July 1964, he was replaced by two men. The new Darling and Hodgson manager was D H Wakelin, and all the Tanker Services work was taken over by Phil Erasmus. Phil was an enthusiastic young man who had joined Darling and Hodgson in South West Africa in 1961, and in 1962 had been sent to Brailsford House to work under Hubert Goetsch. Phil did a 'little bit of everything' at first, but, as the operations of Tanker Services grew, he became more involved in that side of the business and in early 1964 was appointed Transvaal manager, while Hubert was made general manager of Tanker Services. Within a few months Phil was transferred to Natal. This was a great challenge to which he eagerly responded and under his capable management the Natal depot gradu-

Tanker Services soon became established in Cape Town and Port Elizabeth.

ally grew into the hub of Tanker Services activities and became the nursery of all new systems. It has produced many of the top people in the Darling and Hodgson services division today. Phil's place at Brailsford House was taken by Stan Booth, who worked enthusiastically with Hubert in the Transvaal.

Tanker Services extended their operating base into the Cape in 1964 in order to be ready to offer their services to the Caltex refinery due to open in Cape Town in early 1966. Tanker Services (Cape) was established in partnership with Clifford Harris (60%

Tanker Services and 40% Clifford Harris) on a site in Parow. Buck Adams came from the Darling and Hodgson (Cape) surfacing division to head up the Cape operations, which included hauling molten sulphur to African Explosives in Somerset West, as well as regular bitumen work. The first bitumen contract was for the Worcester municipality who were pleased to be able to save their ratepayers the cost of extensive road repairs by using Tanker Services to reseal the existing surfaces.

Tanker Services (Cape) in turn took up a 37,5% interest in Tanker Services (EP) which was established at Woolhope in Port Elizabeth. The other 63,5% was held by P E Holdings which had for some years controlled bulk cement delivery from E P Cement in the Port Elizabeth area and environs through a subsidiary company, E P Bulk Cement Transport. All their tankers were transferred to the new Tanker Services company, which also took delivery of a new tanker built for bulk transport and distribution of bitumen for the entire Eastern Cape under contract for Mobil and Shell.

In 1964 the press reported that 'a far-reaching innovation in bulk road-transportation was ushered onto the South African economic scene when Tanker Services recently took delivery of their first liquid petroleum gas tanker'. This was an immediate success and more followed. The LPG tankers were commissioned and built in the Transvaal by the Trailer Manufacturing Company (which was eventually sold to Henred Fruehauf Trailers) but were used in Natal where this fuel was in constant demand.

In order to keep operations up to date, in 1965 Hubert Goetsch travelled to America to investigate the latest methods of fleet control and management, and many of his findings and resulting recommendations were gradually introduced to Tanker Services. In particular more emphasis was placed on the design of different tankers, resulting in much greater efficiency. The following year Hubert was made a director of Tanker Services when Bill Partridge resigned.

Tanker Services introduced another technical innovation in the latter sixties when they began to use chassis-less tankers. These were new to South Africa, manufactured by Jack Plane's Trailer Manufacturing Company, and the lighter vehicles made it possible to carry much larger volumes, thereby increasing the payload.

South Africa's first liquid petroleum gas tanker, 1964.

Off-loading a consignment of chemicals in Durban harbour.

In Natal Tanker Services became increasingly involved in harbour work. In 1964 a contract was awarded to them for delivery to factories of all the fish oil which came via African Coasters from the Cape to Durban, and another operation was connected with the refuelling of the African Coaster ships. These used to fill up partially at the Island View fuel depot in order to avoid the overfilling and leaking into the harbour (and the consequent fine from the harbour authorities) which all too often resulted from the pressure-feeding, by postponing the final topping-up until they were being loaded at Maydon Wharf. There Tanker Services would pump in the necessary fuel with quiet efficiency and no wastage.

In early 1966 John made the amusing but pertinent comment that all Tanker Services' largest profits had been made at critical times when they had been able to respond to emergencies at short notice, and these times had conveniently arrived once each year! At the time they were hauling fuel up to the Rhodesian border after the United Kingdom sanctions, applied because of UDI, had cut off all oil supplies. He also quoted railway crises which had resulted in requests to move more bitumen from Durban to Satmar, and problems in the Cape which had resulted in extensive transport of wine in bulk for the Stellenbosch Farmers' Winery. He made the point that ready availability was of paramount importance, and announced the purchase of a stainless steel tanker which would widen their service area to 'clean products' such as fruit juice, edible oils and kaffir beer – all of which he felt had great potential. This was the first of a fleet of multi-purpose tankers which could be washed out easily and filled with a different product. A further improvement took place with the division of tankers into sections which provided even greater versatility. Backing up all the operations was John's determined intention of obtaining as much as possible of the bitumen transport throughout the country, and he had on-going negotiations with all the major oil companies to achieve this aim. There was only one competitor in the field at that time – Fowler Tarspraying Company.

In 1967 Tanker Services bought out a small transport business, Palframans, which carried goods out of Durban harbour for clearing agents. It gave Tanker Services a general goods harbour carrier licence which they were later able to trade with the Railways for an exclusive bulk permit which made them a member of the Harbour Carriers' Association with limitless access to the harbour area without payment of the usual fee. This was of inestimable value in the Tanker Services operations of off-loading shipments of bulk commodities and transporting them to their respective depots in Durban.

A further harbour carrier licence was acquired by taking a share in a small company called Crawley Motors which transported bagged sugar from Huletts' Rossborough refinery to various factories, and to the docks where Grindrods loaded it onto their ships for transport around the coast. The operations were run very efficiently by Tony Everitt. The movement of bagged sugar never fitted the Tanker Services bulk operations, however, and in 1970 Tanker Services sold out to Grindrods who also had an interest in Crawley Motors.

Tanker Services underwent a great upheaval at the end of 1967. At that time all the bulk cement deliveries in the Witwatersrand and Durban areas were carried out by another large tanker company, Stag Bulk Transports, which was owned by a British company, United Transport, and which, with Thornton's Bulk Transport, comprised United Bulk Transport in South Africa. The Anglo American Corporation of South Africa had a 40% interest in the company. In 1966 Tanker Services tendered for a road stabilization contract for the Orange Free State Provincial Administration and were awarded it. This entailed hauling cement to the north-eastern Free State and spreading it mechanically over the road surface – a contract which had until then been carried out by Thorntons. Tanker Services built special cement trailers for the contract and Thorntons were aghast at the encroachment upon their traditional territory. A bitter confrontation was looming when John decided that joining forces was perhaps the answer to the problem. After negotiations with United Transport in London, in particular with Charles Boyd-White, and the local management headed by John Swait, Tanker Services and United Bulk Transport agreed in 1967 to merge operations. Each company had thoroughly investigated the other's assets, and there was one embarrassing incident when Phil Erasmus was very abrupt with a stranger whom he found wandering around the Jacobs yard, only to find that he was a senior member of United Transport, Joe Buckingham, visiting Tanker Services!

Two new companies were registered: United Tanker Holdings, half owned by United Bulk Transport and half by Darling and Hodgson, which in turn owned all the shares of the new operating company, United Tanker Services. The complementary operations of Tanker Services (specialists in hauling liquids) and Stag and Thornton's (who had concentrated on flowable solids) created the largest privately-operated bulk fleet in South Africa, with seemingly vast potential covering the haulage of an extensive range of materials from bitumen, furnace oils and tar to the more sophisticated petroleum-based solvents, from cement to cyanide, from wine to sugar, and many others. Operations were based in the Transvaal, Natal, the Cape and Swaziland and ranged throughout South Africa. Swaziland United Transport were responsible for the delivery of petroleum products for all the major oil companies there; they remained an autonomous subsidiary until they were sold in 1971. A separate agreement was made in the Cape where Jowell's Transport was a partner of United Transport, and did not wish to sell out.

The merger became effective from 1 January 1968 and the combined fleet began to operate under a new logo, which comprised a bar with the name United Tanker Services superimposed on a red circle representing a wheel. Phil Erasmus remained manager in Natal and was soon joined by Des Bell as administrative manager, while a United Transport man, Jim Beaumont, recently from the United Kingdom, was made general man-

An impressive array of vehicles at the Jacobs depot in Durban.

ager of the new company. After a while Tony Alty was appointed as the Transvaal manager, nominated by Chris Griffiths, the Anglo American representative on the board of United Tanker Services.

At the end of the first month of combined operations Jim Beaumont reported that 'the merger has not interfered with the current day to day operation of the fleets, thereby establishing continuity of customer contact and service throughout this difficult transient period', words which sounded optimistic and encouraging. In fact, however, the merger was the beginning of an unhappy and unprofitable partnership. The United Bulk Transport fleet did not match Tanker Services in standards of maintenance and efficiency of operations, and when they were brought into the Tanker Services depots in Durban and Germiston they created an almost impossible situation. There was physical overcrowding of both people and vehicles which resulted in a situation epitomized in a somewhat desperate cry from Phil Erasmus in Natal in January 1969 when stating that after the merger 'the branch grew from a small closely-knit team to a mass-production undertaking'.

The traditional hauling and spraying of bitumen throughout the country continued as a very significant part of United Tanker Services' operations and one that the public readily associated with them. All the tankers were controlled by radio on a country-wide basis from Brailsford House; when one had delivered its load it would be sent to the nearest depot to reload rather than necessarily returning to base, thereby enabling maximum use to be made of each vehicle.

A new venture which came into United Tanker Services with Stag was a contract for hauling bulk raw sugar from the Umzimkulu Sugar Mill near Port Shepstone to the sugar terminal at Maydon Wharf in Durban. It was Phil who got the scheme really working. Specially designed trailers were found to be necessary but the first attempt was a disaster – the vehicle overturned on a corner – and Phil placed an order with Barens Shipbuilding and Engineering Company for the construction of a new design of articulated tanker which soon became a familiar sight on the south coast road. The dual-

UTS specialized tankers outside the Durban sugar terminal, 1971.

coupled bulk sugar trailer-sets, looking rather like early versions of a submarine, were pulled very noisily at high speed by Diamond T tractors, each vehicle making two round trips in twenty-four hours throughout the week. The local community was not at all happy with the situation and a letter written to the newspaper in 1969 bitterly referred to the tankers as 'an unearthly curse' and expressed concern about 'the abnormal wear and tear taking place on the road'. The contract continued until December 1979, however, and was instrumental in the efficient delivery of many thousands of tons of sugar to the harbour terminal.

Stan Booth was appointed manager of the United Tanker Services operations in Cape Town, which included Jowell's Transport's extensive cement haulage from the Cape Portland Cement factories at De Hoek and Riebeek-Wes. Bitumen was hauled great distances up to the north-western Cape and South West Africa and into Botswana; there was one driver who used to balance matches between his finger tips to ensure that he did not fall asleep on long journeys! Wine was carried for various co-operatives and wineries, and a powerful mixture called cola punch was hauled from the Distillers' Corporation in Cape Town to Wadeville (the return load was gin concentrate for Gilbeys). Early one morning one of these tankers collided with a banana truck near Beaufort West, and both compartments of the tanker were punctured; one spurted like a fountain and the other drained rapidly to form a lake. In spite of a police guard, many people enjoyed free alcohol that day; they came from far and wide, eagerly scooping up the liquid, and by that evening the scene was littered with bodies!

In the Cape depot at Epping the worst oil fire with which the Cape Town fire brigade had ever had to contend broke out one night in early June 1971. Bitumen caught alight when it was being transferred from a leaking tanker, and when the tanker tyres burst because of the intense heat the trailer rolled over, spilling out bitumen which carried the fire across to a stockpile of tyres. The flames and smoke could be seen from all over Cape Town, and the firemen battled to extinguish the fire with foam. Miraculously it was under control by 3 am, and Stan was very proud of the fact that although many thousands of rands worth of damage was done the operations at the depot were hardly affected.

The fleet had rapidly outgrown the facilities at Epping, and development of a larger depot was already underway at Philippi. After the fire construction was speeded up and United Tanker Services (Cape) moved there within a few months. Stan stayed on until 1972 and when he left Dave Pieters was appointed manager in his place.

In the Transvaal the largest single and most profitable contract was the Stag agreement with the Cement Producers Association of South Africa, and another important contract was with Cyanamid for hauling flake cyanide in bulk from Witbank to the gold mines in the Transvaal and Orange Free State, where it was used in the reduction process, making possible the recovery of at least 98% of the crushed gold.

In spite of the variety and quantity of bulk hauling that was undertaken, the overall situation in United Tanker Services went from bad to worse. The various managers struggled to keep things on an even keel but in May 1969 a critical stage was reached when it was apparent that there had been a steady deterioration of profits over the seventeen months of the company's existence. Phil had stayed at the helm in Natal, but the Transvaal branch had experienced several managers under Jim Beaumont – Tony Alty, Eduardo Garcia, and Lawrence Till. Lawrence had only just settled into the job when he died in a tragic accident at his home. He had been held in high esteem and was greatly respected by all those who knew him.

In the middle of 1969 a new managing director of United Tanker Services was appointed in an attempt to set it in the right direction. Frank Lever brought with him over forty years of experience in transport. He had spent the previous four years in Zambia with United Transport, coping with the many transport problems which resulted from the sanctions against Rhodesia after UDI. In 1969 he was planning to take extended leave, but instead he came to United Tanker Services!

He made an expert and thorough review of the situation and set about creating order and enthusiasm in all sections of the company. Within the new organization Natal operations remained unchanged but United Tanker Services (Transvaal) was split into two separate divisions, 'liquids' under Tony Serrano and 'solids' under Manie Wiese.

The cement tankers were moved to a separate solids depot at Crown Mines, the site of the Group's original ready-mixed concrete plant. It was felt that greater control and efficiency would follow and in fact all three companies showed significant improvement over the following months. While placing high priority on the human element, Frank also improved the quality of the tanker fleets and the workshop facilities, building up a new image employees could be proud of and attracting the eye of customers. Soon the projected profits were being achieved.

The solids division made good use of the old Ready Mixed Concrete facilities at Crown Mines. The leaning control tower was occupied with some apprehension as it looked as though it would topple any moment, but it remained firm, and the old laboratory building was used for offices until a new prefabricated block was built.

John's son Robert spent several happy years at the Crown depot. He had joined United Tanker Services as a trainee manager after leaving school and serving a short apprenticeship with the Leyland Motor Corporation. He spent a year with United Transport in the UK and was then appointed operations manager at Crown where he stayed until he left Tanker Services in 1975 to work on various special projects within D&H.

Frank Lever stayed with United Tanker Services for three and a half years, retiring at the beginning of 1973. In his last report he thanked everyone for their help and co-operation, in particular John Hodgson who, as chairman of United Tanker Services, had been at all times the epitome of support and assistance as well as a vital personal inspiration. He also mentioned Brian as a constant source of valuable financial guidance and help who was always available to advise on even the most insignificant matters.

Both John and Brian were very aware of the operating problems of United Tanker Services and had derived little satisfaction from the company's patchy performance since the merger. When the opportunity arose in 1973 to bring the relationship to an end, at the time when Darling and Hodgson were going public, John made a successful offer to the

Tanker and pup trailer clearly showing the Tanker Services logo.

overseas partners to buy out their share and the company came into the Darling and Hodgson Group as a wholly-owned subsidiary. The name United Tanker Services reverted to Tanker Services, except in the Cape where the 'United' was retained because Jowell's Transport did not want to relinquish their shareholding, and, in John's words at the time, 'everyone began looking forward to further acceleration of the progress of this company'.

Phil Erasmus was appointed managing director of Tanker Services and came up from Natal to head office towards the end of 1973 with the task of consolidating the company's progress down the right track. He was encouraged by the prevailing mood in the transport industry in the early seventies, which was one of positive optimism. The industry had experienced phenomenal growth in the sixties as an offshoot of the considerable industrial development in South Africa and there seemed no reason why the demand should not continue. Even the worldwide oil crisis could not detract too much from the advantage of road over rail transport in flexibility, and the continuing improved quality of roads and vehicles resulted in a comparatively low increase in the cost of road transport.

The Tanker Services vehicles were soon travelling under their own logo again, and within a year extensive reorganization had taken place. Phil's feeling was that although 'United' had been lost as a name, unity had been gained in all other respects.

The Cape was not involved in the reorganization and operations there continued largely unchanged. In 1978 all Tanker Services' interests in the Western Cape were sold to Jowell's Transport and they have not operated there since then. In the Eastern Cape

Tanker Services continued as part of P E Holdings, which was reorganized under the name of Quarryman in 1980.

In Natal Dudley Pieterse from Ready Mixed Concrete (East Rand) was appointed manager when Phil was transferred, and the following year Derrick West took his place. There was much activity in this profit centre and in 1975 Tanker Services (Natal) triumphantly clocked one million kilometres on the road in the month of July, the first time that this had been achieved through one terminal in the company – a significant achievement. This was partly due to increased sugar haulage resulting from excellent cane production in the mid seventies. In August 1975 Derrick commented, 'this is the highest kilometre operation in the Group'.

Tanker Services continued their bulk contract with Durban Cement in Natal. Some years previously Phil had split the United Tanker Services contract in two, one for hauling packaged material and the other for bulk haulage. After 1973 Tanker Services retained only the latter. They operated out of the factory premises with Hannes Engelbrecht as senior controller for the outlet. Hannes had joined Thornton's Transport in 1955 and came into United Tanker Services in 1967. He was renowned as a keen sportsman as well as for his many hours behind the wheel of a tanker.

From the middle of that year Tanker Services were also involved in transporting transformer oil for Kuhne and Nagel from Durban to Cabora Bassa, on the Zambezi river in Moçambique, where one of the world's largest underground hydroelectric powerstations was being built. This was designed to make economic development possible in the lower Zambezi valley and for several years once a week a tanker set off from Durban to cover the four and a half thousand kilometres there and back, normally taking seven days. Strains of Scottish music floating from the cab of the tanker revealed the ancestry of the driver, Jock Mundell, who revelled in the strenuous drive. The route wound through the beautiful African countryside, in the early days through Rhodesia and later, when the war had started, through Komatipoort and on to Tete.

Amongst other contracts Tanker Services were hauling molasses from Umzimkulu to Durban harbour and maize pellets for export from Epic Oil's mill in Pietermaritzburg. They rapidly outgrew their office accommodation, and the operation staff members were housed in caravans for a while until in 1976, with expansive sighs of relief, they moved into new offices at the Jacobs' depot. In the mid seventies a depot was established in Ladysmith, filling the need for a stopping place between Johannesburg and Durban.

In the Transvaal a series of management changes took place over the next few years, and gradually closer co-operation was established among the operating companies in the Transvaal and Natal. There was a steady improvement in the liquids division, and tanker traffic between the two provinces increased significantly. Paul Norris was appointed manager of the solids division with probably the most formidable of all tasks within the new Tanker Services. The division had been created to handle cement and slagment, and for several years had held a contract with the Cement Marketing Organization, whereby they did all the marketing of cement and Tanker Services delivered for them. Unfortunately Tanker Services did not do a very efficient job and the contract was lost just before Paul was transferred to the Crown depot, which meant that they had to deal directly with the cement users and contend with vigorous competition. The Tanker Services vehicles were mostly old and breakdowns were frustratingly frequent, which all contributed to a poor market image. Paul concentrated on improving the fleet and the image, gaining an increasing number of satisfied customers. The division went from strength to strength.

Solids depots were established in strategic places over the years. In early 1974 one was opened at Hennenman in the Orange Free State, conveniently close to the cement factories of Anglo Alpha and White's Cement; there was also great potential in the area resulting from increased activity in the gold mining industry. Cement was supplied to local consumers in the Virginia/Welkom area and delivered to the Orange Free State Provincial Administration for road stabilization. The depot operated under Abie van Wyk, from Tanker Services (Natal). He was a man of great character, who had been with Dar-

Spreading lime for the stabilization of roads.

ling and Hodgson as a foreman for six years before moving to Tanker Services in 1966.

Another depot was started in Pretoria, an important potential growth area. In early 1976 two tankers worked out of the Waste-tech premises, and their major customer at first was Pioneer Ready Mixed Concrete. The following year there was a contract for spreading lime for stabilization on the new double highway being built by Murray and Roberts between Warmbaths and Pienaar River. This was not a pleasant job, as there always seemed to be a wind blowing which swirled the cement up into the air, forming a fine film on the face which gave a painful burning sensation.

Two more strategically placed cement depots were established in the late seventies. A contract to deliver cement to the Hoedspruit air base had been so successful that Tanker Services decided in 1978 to establish a permanent base in Phalaborwa, near the Fedmis factory, to meet the continuing lime and cement needs of the area. In 1979 another depot was opened at Lichtenburg, near the new cement factory, to cater for deliveries in the far western Transvaal, the West Rand gold fields and the Vanderbijlpark area, as well as for developments in Bophutatswana, especially near Rustenburg.

Phil Erasmus has always maintained that one of the main reasons for the success of Tanker Services has been the training at every level within the company. He was the first person to appreciate the need for compulsory and standard training for the tanker drivers. There had always been some degree of on the job training but a visit to America in 1971 convinced Phil that this was not enough. In the same year he asked Graham Dick to start a small training school at the Jacobs depot, and the success of this school led to another being established at Germiston under Vic Callegari. Graham compiled the first Tanker Services drivers' training manual, which he readily confessed was originally 'cribbed' from various overseas manuals but was updated and changed to deal comprehensively with the South African environment. His dedication to driver training resulted in his promotion to manager of the training department which has grown steadily in strength and effectiveness over the years.

The benefit of the drivers' training was excitingly and clearly demonstrated to everyone when in 1976 a driver from Tanker Services (Natal) won a nationwide competition, Truck Roadeo. Theogarajan Govender (known as Dan II) was a clear leader in the field – South Africa's first ever 'truck driver of the year'. His prize was a trip to the United States – further than Dan had ever dreamt he would travel. He won the same national

Delivering cement to a road contract.

award in 1979, and several other Tanker Services drivers have done well regionally over the years. Tanker Services soon introduced their own 'driver of the year' awards, which are distributed each year at a grand party attended by the men and their wives. The awards for defensive and safe driving soon became an immense incentive, with the drivers ever conscious of the fact that considerate driving brings rewards. The quality and efficiency of driving steadily increased with a corresponding decrease in the accident rate. Phil also travelled to America in 1976 and reckoned at the time that Tanker Services would fit in as thirteenth in the list of top trucking companies there, which reflected an amazing achievement.

With their traditional operations well established, Darling and Hodgson began to diversify their transport interests and from 1975 onwards a new company was acquired each year: Omnibus, Zweiamic Transport (later changed to Refrigerated Transport and then to D&H Freight Lines) and W J's Bulk Transport. The last was a major step with far-reaching effects. The W J's fleet had always worked with clean chemicals and food

Award winners in the National Road Safety Council's 'driver of the year' competition, 1981: Robin Chanderpol and Dan II with driver trainer Steve Hirst.

products, in particular glucose, and the company's acquisition gave Tanker Services an immediate boost through its range of transport permits for these commodities, which opened new fields of opportunity.

The operations of Tanker Services and W J's Bulk were restructured within the Group transport division, of which Phil Erasmus was managing director, and Paul Norris was given the task of absorbing W J's Bulk into Tanker Services, which was not easy. The W J's team did not want to lose its independence, and amongst other problems was the difficulty of accommodating the fleets and their drivers within the new organization. W J's' tankers were immaculate in appearance and each of their drivers, all of whom were white, was responsible for one vehicle of which he was intensely proud. Tanker Services' drivers, on the other hand, had for many years been selected purely on merit and were not attached to any one of the tankers, many of which carried bitumen and cement and could never present the same clean image as W J's. It was an unhappy period and the rationalization of operations was obviously not going to prove successful.

In 1979 the two companies reverted to their traditional products. Paul Norris was appointed manager of Tanker Services (Natal) and Jans van Vuuren of W J's was appointed general manager in the Transvaal. The controversial 'dirty' black bitumen work was firmly put back into Tanker Services, which was otherwise mostly solids, and W J's retained their cleaner, mainly liquid products. Tanker Services moved their cement operations from Crown back to Germiston, to where W J's had moved from Boksburg. Derrick West was transferred to the Transvaal and appointed managing director of D&H Transport within a new Group services division, comprising transport and waste management, of which Phil was managing director. The new operating companies settled down to consolidate their activities and increase their markets, and the reorganization was a success.

Tanker Services had ceased bitumen spraying operations some time previously. It had become uneconomic because vehicles often had to wait for suitable air temperatures (and where there are no wheels turning there is no money) and the extra weight of spraying equipment meant that less bitumen could be hauled. It also required specialized operators and Tanker Services decided to concentrate on bitumen haulage and leave the spraying to the contractor.

Dirkie Strydom had been one of the specialist bitumen distributor operators in Natal,

Transporting a Mini-bulk silo.

having joined Tanker Services as a driver in 1969 after fourteen years with D&H as a sprayer driver. He was appointed wash bay supervisor at Jacobs in 1974 and in 1979 was promoted to take charge of depot maintenance. Under him the yard and workshops were kept in immaculate condition and he also took great pride in the garden which brightened the working environment. Dirkie continued in this position until 1982 when he retired from Tanker Services to maintain the equipment on John Hodgson's farm in the Seven Oaks district of Natal.

By the end of 1983 D&H had consolidated all its transport activities into the operating company, D&H Services. Paul Norris continued as manager of Tanker Services (Natal) at the terminal in Jacobs, and Des Johannsen ran Tanker Services (Transvaal) from the Germiston terminal. Both men reported to Phil at the services division head office in Randburg. Jans van Vuuren ran W J's country-wide operations independently from Germiston. There were four other Tanker Services depots in operation: Pretoria, Hennenman, Lichtenburg and Vanderbijlpark. The last named had been established in 1980 to serve Iscor and Natref and nearby chemical companies, transporting coal, tar, fuel, bituminous products and purified sodium phosphate.

Natal maintained its reputation for innovative ideas in 1983 with a totally new concept of cement transportation called Mini-bulk. This was launched as a practical solution to the problem of providing an on-site cement supply which relied on neither sacks nor bulk deliveries. Mini-bulk provides a highly portable ten ton bin, the equivalent of two hundred 50 kg sacks of cement, which is completely sealed and totally waterproof, and is delivered on site where it can be kept locked with a padlock. The bin decants one full bag of cement at a time and has brought a new dimension to the handling of the product, offering many advantages including economy and reduced labour.

Mini-bulk is just one example of the determination of D&H Services to keep ahead of its competitors. Tanker Services has secured a sizeable market coverage in South Africa, but its policy is always to strive to move beyond satisfying present demands, and this will carry it strongly into the future.

W J Bulk Transport

Most men at some stage in their careers have a yearning to be self-employed and opportunities to realize this arise in many different ways. When Wilhelm van der Spek was working for a transport company in the early sixties the opportunity arose to transport bulk glucose from the Reef to East London. Wilhelm could not find anyone willing to join him in this venture, so he decided to go it alone. He registered his own company, W J's Bulk Transport, in August 1965, and applied for a glucose permit. While waiting for the permit to be issued Wilhelm acquired an old and dilapidated truck which he loaded with scrap aluminium and took from the Reef down to Pietermaritzburg. He travelled down the back roads to avoid inspection as the truck was unroadworthy and besides he had no permit for transporting the aluminium!

Wilhelm then acquired an aluminium permit and embarked on a long-standing commitment to Alcan which was extended to Reef deliveries as well when Alcan opened new premises in Alberton. At first Wilhelm did the Natal runs himself. He used to find a place to sleep at the market by persuading someone to let him make himself 'a little hokkie among the vegetables'.

During this period Wilhelm asked a friend with whom he had worked in the past to join him, and Jans van Vuuren came into W J's Bulk Transport on 15 May 1967, just before the glucose permit came through. This was the first country-wide glucose permit ever awarded and allowed unrestricted delivery of the product from South Africa's leading manufacturer, African Products Manufacturing Company, which owned two factories, one in Germiston and the other in Bellville in the Cape. Wilhelm purchased six

W J tanker at African Products.

stainless steel tankers, insulated with fibreglass to insure that the temperature of the hot glucose did not drop by more than four degrees in twenty-four hours, and W J's started delivering to factories for the manufacture of sweets, beer and many other commodities. The very first delivery was to the Wilcox sweet factory in King William's Town on 6 July 1967.

At that stage W J's Bulk Transport had no premises of their own, but in 1970 a workshop and wash bay were erected on a five acre site purchased in Dunswart, Boksburg, and permanent headquarters were established there.

Wilhelm had an amazing ability to acquire haulage permits, and the range of products that the company handled grew rapidly. It comprised foodstuffs and chemicals, and Wilhelm pursued his policy of operating the cleanest and most efficient tanker fleet in South Africa. Depots were soon opened in Cape Town and Durban and the immaculate vehicles, resplendent with gleaming stainless steel offset by attractive blue, became well known on the roads between the Reef and these cities.

One of W J's first drivers was Ginger Frederickson. He and a small group of friends, which included Robbie Horn, formed the nucleus of the loyal W J's driving team and set the high standards which have continued to be a strong characteristic of the company. Ginger and Robbie have remained with the company for many years, proud of their long service and their continuing contribution to W J's. In the early days of heavy transport in the Republic there was a wonderful camaraderie among all the drivers, who grew to know one another as they inevitably met somewhere along the road over the years. No one ever failed to help someone in trouble and there were many occasions for 'a little barney and a beanfeast'.

Washing vehicles at the Germiston depot.

W J tanker refuelling at night.

    The W J's drivers always travelled with a lorry-mate who helped maintain the impeccable appearance of the huge tankers, sometimes even to the extent of dusting and polishing the driver's shoes before he climbed into his cab! Each driver was responsible for his own vehicle and a fierce sense of pride developed, giving rise to healthy competition between individuals. Wilhelm van der Spek was well liked and respected by all those who worked for him. He always had a welcoming handshake for the drivers at the end of their long journeys and never lost the personal touch in his working relationships.

    It was Ginger who established W J's in Cape Town. For the first few months he supervised operations from his tanker, which was home and office, but when the appointed manager proved unsatisfactory, Ginger took his place and remained in charge for many years. The Muldersvlei depot was established and steady development took place, mainly supplying glucose to sweet factories. The glucose tankers were sometimes stopped by the traffic police for inspection, which could be a disaster, because once opened up the temperature dropped and the contents solidified and changed colour!

A resplendent W J tanker with its pup trailer, travelling along the highway overlooking the Paarl valley in the Cape.

As with Tanker Services, W J's earliest vehicles were Leylands, but they were soon replaced by more powerful Volvos. These were the first tankers to have self-contained cabs with a bed and a heater, making the driver's life much more comfortable. The first load of Whitbreads beer to the new Grabouw bottling plant was hauled with one of the brand new Volvos. A few years later the new vehicles were Mercedes trucks which introduced the modern, luxurious cab with bed, heater (and cooling fan), radio and tape-deck – nearly all the home comforts.

John Todd came to join W J's in Durban in 1976 through selling Mercedes trucks to them. The company operated out of a site in Prospecton and worked with a wide range of commodities, including solvents, glycols and oils. The tankers travelled all over the country, even up to Rhodesia on regular runs in particular delivering glue.

Because of the large number of transport permits which W J's had amassed over the years, the company was a very desirable acquisition and John Hodgson made several unsuccessful approaches to Wilhelm during the seventies. In 1977, however, Wilhelm agreed to sell, and W J's Bulk Transport became a wholly-owned subsidiary of D&H. It was an exceptionally successful transaction for D&H who were to recoup the purchase price within two years as a result of W J's' acceleration in operations and profits.

Wilhelm himself was no longer involved with the company but Jans van Vuuren stayed on. He and the other W J's employees appreciated the advantages of working for a big Group which could provide better staff benefits and more potential for development. The future of W J's was inexorably drawn into that of Tanker Services as the operations of the two companies were merged. It was not an easy period. W J's was a small, very

The ultra-modern wash bay at Stickland.

personal company and its staff had been together for a long time. They did not want to be spread out within a bigger organization and strongly resisted losing their identity, to the extent that when there was a Tanker Services planning weekend 'away from it all' in Swaziland in mid 1977, where the future of the D&H transport operations was under discussion, including the co-ordination of W J's' entry into Tanker Services, the message was clearly stated on the T-shirts of some of the men, in the words, 'Independence for W J's'.

The fight for independence bore fruit and after a somewhat traumatic settling down period, W J's emerged operating under their own name and colours once more and carrying most of their traditional products. Jans remained in charge of their operations, which expanded rapidly within the Group, thriving under the more sophisticated management. The Transvaal depot was moved from Dunswart to join Tanker Services at Germiston and share the facilities there. In Natal a new depot was opened at Mobeni in 1979 after two years of rather cramped accommodation in two caravans at the Tanker Services' Jacobs site, and when W J's were awarded a contract in 1983 for hauling casava, the cultivation of which was a new venture by Anglo American in Zululand, a small depot was opened in Mtubatuba. This depot was later used for sugar-cane and timber haulage operations in Zululand as well.

The Cape depot at Muldersvlei operated until 1983 when a new ultra-modern transport terminal was opened for W J's at Stikland. Its design was of an exceptionally high standard after years of research into all the variables which could have an effect, and experience gained in its design and construction guided the rebuilding of the main transport terminal in Germiston. While eager to use the new facilities, the W J's team, under

Above
Hauling timber.

Left
Specialized vehicles are used for transporting casava from the fields in Zululand.

Above left
In 1981 John Hodgson presented Hugh Brooks with three awards: 'national driver of the year', 'Durban depot driver of the year' and 'senior depot driver'. John Todd looks on.

Above right
Jans van Vuuren with 'Mannetjies' Beets who holds W J's 'driver of the year' trophy, 1979. Vic Callegari in the background.

depot manager Lawrence Blundell, moved with some regrets. The depot in Muldersvlei, affectionately known as 'The Farm', had a relaxed, countrified atmosphere full of character, and one of the questions asked when the transfer was announced was 'what's to become of the geese?' These geese had lived on the property for years and had become part of the depot's everyday life, as had the chickens which laid eggs behind the curtains and under the desks.

Lawrence had been manager of Muldersvlei since 1981, having moved down to the Cape as depot superintendent the previous year. It was a great change from the Germiston terminal, set amongst the mine dumps of the East Rand, where he had been working since he joined the company as a controller in 1979.

W J's has been a vital component of the services division from the time of its acquisition and Jans van Vuuren's contribution has been a significant one. He became known throughout the division as 'Mr W J Bulk'! The increasingly nationwide operations of W J's have maintained their high standards within the Group under his guidance as general manager. In 1982 John Todd was transferred from Natal to the Reef as operations manager for the whole company. His position as depot manager of Mobeni was filled by Paul Botha who was based in Germiston while Mobeni's daily operations were run by a depot supervisor.

W J's present several annual awards which encourage a keen spirit within the company. These are based on a range of criteria such as safe and expert driving, cleanliness of vehicles, accident record, workshop efficiency and customer relations, all of which promote a good image of the company. The best image of all, however, is the splendid sight of the immaculate W J's tankers roaring along the highways of South Africa, making a significant and powerful contribution to the heavy transport industry in the country.

D&H Automotive Services

Big vehicles require a great deal of mechanical maintenance and repair, and the most profitable way to run a transport company is to minimize the time the vehicles are not in use. With this in mind the D&H transport division introduced a new approach to vehicle maintenance in 1976 with the intention of improving the standard of all the equipment and increasing the economic life of their vehicles. Peter de Beer was given the task of establishing a central specialized service facility in Natal, under the name Central Services. At first this centre was not readily supported, largely because the individual profit centres were used to operating on a decentralized basis in all respects. Its use was not enforced, however, and when the advantages became apparent, especially in the reduction of costs, Central Services was accepted and became increasingly popular.

Within two years a larger and more sophisticated workshop complex was opened in New Germany. The Central Services team moved across there and the name was changed to D&H Automotive Services. The official opening by the Secretary for Transport, Mr A B Eksteen, took place on 7 September 1978, when the spotless facilities of the R1 million truck maintenance and diagnostic centre provided a wonderful example of progress in D&H.

At the opening of the new complex John Hodgson stated that the mechanical condition of vehicles had a strong influence on the performance of their drivers, and he was proud that the D&H transport accident costs per kilometre that year were the same as those in 1970, even though the costs of repairs had trebled. This was a clear indication, he

The workshops at New Germany.

Above left
Overhauling one of the Tanker Services fleet.

Above right
Tyre recapping.

said, that the D&H Automotive Services facility contributed significantly to safe driving as well as having economic benefits.

The new workshops were among the most modern in South Africa and were staffed by highly skilled mechanics. Vehicles were sent there for major overhauls during which each one was reconditioned, repainted and generally restored as near as possible to its original state. It was difficult to tell the difference between a vehicle that had just been through this special M-service and a new one, and the life of each vehicle was extended by three years or more. It also became standard practice for new vehicles to go to D&H Automotive Services to be equipped for their purpose within the Group, to a standard specification for each company. The vehicles were then returned every two years for their M-service. The specialized service with its accompanying benefits has been extended throughout the Group and to some extent beyond it so that the facilities are used to their fullest extent. D&H has steadily developed a policy of purchasing Mercedes vehicles which has helped to standardize operations.

In 1979 Peter de Beer was transferred to the Group head office where he retained responsibility for D&H Automotive Services. The workshops were put under the capable management of Trevor Barlow, an appointment following fifteen years with Tanker Services in Natal. He perpetuated the high standards established from the beginning in D&H Automotive Services, maintaining that 'our aim is to give good service to the Group', and succeeding admirably. The following year another Tanker Services old-timer, Des Bell, joined the company, bringing twelve years of experience in the administration of Tanker Services (Natal) to the position of administrative manager of D&H Automotive Services. Des stayed with the company until he retired in 1982.

When the new complex was built in 1978 provision was made for a tyre recapping plant to be installed at a later date when anticipated increased volumes would justify the expense. This came about in 1983 when the plant was brought into operation, both for economic reasons and so that the quality of the recapped tyres could be maintained at a high standard through monitoring by the D&H services computer. The plant was officially opened by Dennis Rowe of Durban Cement, who had become a good friend of D&H over the years of close association between the two companies.

This added to the level of sophistication at the D&H Automotive Services facility in Natal, which by 1983 had become an integral and valuable part of the Group services division, and of the transport industry as a whole through its contribution to safe driving in South Africa.

D&H Semi-Bulk

'If something can go into a packet or drum, it can go into a flo-bin or liqua-bin.' This was said of the flo-bin system, which had been developed in America and used in Europe for many years, when in 1968 Messrs Janks and Bishop of Containerisation Africa in the Cape obtained an operating licence for it in South Africa. In 1978 Mike Proudfoot joined them, the business started moving and within a short time profits were good and the future looked bright. Mike's partners had by then reached the age of retirement however, and Mike looked around for a good organization for the business to fit into, where the system would be properly marketed. Darling and Hodgson seemed to fit the bill and Mike approached them. In July 1980 the Group acquired a 60% share in the company, seeing it as a valuable extension to its existing transport operations.

The name Containerisation Africa was changed to D&H Semi-Bulk Systems, a good description of the unique and dynamic flo-bin concept which included the semi-bulk transport, storage, handling and dispensing of products. It added a new dimension to D&H's transport activities and provided an invaluable service for concerns which were not equipped to handle bulk deliveries but wanted to move away from packages and manual handling. A flo-bin can replace up to forty 50 kg bags of powders or granules and a liqua-bin up to ten 210 litre drums of liquid. Both can be used for transporting and for storage, and the acquisition by D&H Semi-Bulk Systems of a national road permit lessened the dependence on rail for the former. Products handled included detergent, oils, paints, pigments, bleach, cement, carbon black and foodstuffs.

Mike Proudfoot continued to run the company, which operated independently within the services division. He was assisted by Sally Bayley, who had been with the company for some time and carried the distinction of being one of the few female managers in D&H's industrial companies.

D&H Semi-Bulk vehicle transporting flo-bins.

D&H purchased the remaining 40% of the company in 1981 and the word 'systems' was dropped from the name of the company as it was absorbed into the transport division. The following year a new distribution terminal was opened at Alrode on the Reef in the former D&H Structural Engineering building. Mike left the company that year and Ken Sibson became manager until 1983 when Tony Arnot was appointed. Tony moved into the position with enthusiasm, confident that D&H Semi-Bulk's flo-bin system is the answer to many of tomorrow's product-handling problems.

Waste-tech

Life creates waste and there is no getting away from it! Disposing of it is a problem that grows greater daily. As the population of the world increases so does the need to prevent all kinds of pollution, and as the resources of the world become depleted the need to recycle waste becomes vital. The raw materials of tomorrow lie in the waste of today, and D&H's waste management division has accepted the challenge of turning waste to commercial advantage.

One Sunday early in 1969 two sailing boats collided on Cinderella dam in Boksburg. It was not a serious accident and the two skippers met amicably over a beer at the end of the day. One of them was a visitor from England, Tony Morgan, who revealed that he worked for a company in the United Kingdom which was interested in introducing professional waste management to South Africa. The other was Hubert Goetsch, John Hodgson's brother-in-law and at the time manager of the Darling and Hodgson transport fleet, who suggested that Tony should talk to John before approaching anyone else.

Tony described the professional handling of waste as an attractively profitable procedure, and it appealed to John as an opportunity to establish another innovative growth industry in South Africa and give Darling and Hodgson a broader operating base. John knew that there was little sophistication in waste disposal anywhere in South Africa. Even in Johannesburg it was 1972 before professional staff were appointed in the municipal cleansing branch, and there was a distressing tendency to dump waste indiscriminately with little or no thought of subsequent pollution. With the intention of providing a service in this field, therefore, Purle Industrial Waste Disposal (SA) was registered in August 1969, 85% owned by Darling and Hodgson's transport holding company, United Tanker Holdings, and 15% by Purle Brothers in the United Kingdom.

For the first year all Purle's administration was carried out by United Tanker Services while the new operations were being established, and it was only in 1971 that Purle broke away from Darling and Hodgson Transport and became a Group subsidiary in full control of its own operations. The offices and depot remained at Brailsford House.

Purle (SA) paid a royalty to the UK company in exchange for technical expertise, and the first manager, Joe Southey, went to England for several months' training before the launching of Purle's services in South Africa. Initial operations were carried out by two skip loaders which delivered containers to any premises for the collection of dry waste, replacing them when full and disposing of the rubbish. A tanker for liquids disposal soon joined the fleet, and shortly thereafter an interesting vehicle arrived from the United Kingdom. It was a front-end loading compactor, the first ever seen in South Africa, which lifted the container on two prongs over the driver's cab and tipped the contents into the compacting unit on the truck. The compacting of the waste speeded up operations considerably.

Although Purle's clean and efficient solution to the problem of waste disposal had instant appeal, customers' enthusiasm waned rapidly at the suggestion of paying for 'just removing rubbish' and the early months were filled with uncertainty. Before Purle had started operating, a competitor had already taken some of their potential customers. Two young men, Rob Blackwood-Murray and Peter Foyn, were running Murray Transport Services and had moved very effectively into the dry waste market. They were fortunate to be awarded the contract for removing rubble from the demolition of buildings to make way for the Carlton Centre in down-town Johannesburg. Because of this Purle decided to concentrate at first on long-term contracts with industry and they steadily built up a list of regular customers. Their bright orange vehicles bore the com-

Above
The Dumpmaster front-end loading compactor.

Right
Purle's skip loaders.

pany's distinctive trademarks which became well known around town – the sludge gulper and the rubbish gobbler.

The first driver was Rodney Roscoe, soon joined by Caspar Rademeyer from Tanker Services and Sydney Moodley. The first rounds included the Colgate and Lever Brothers factories, Epic Oil in Isando, Haggie Rand in Germiston, Plascon Paint in Springs and Gillettes in Krugersdorp. There was a big cleaning job at the Atlas Aircraft Corporation as well. In 1970 Caspar took a sludge gulper to the Rand Show and operated there for two weeks. They were a very special attraction and one day a child, looking at the curly-tailed elephant on the side of the tanker, asked, 'Is there a pig inside drinking that up?'! The time spent at the showgrounds was a successful advertisement for Purle and from then on the tankers were in ever-increasing demand. They usually carried unpleasant liquids, and Sydney nearly asphyxiated a traffic policeman one day when he drew up beside him at a robot with a tanker full of sulphuric acid from Afrox. The acid was also dangerous to load – just a few drops of water would make it boil and spit.

At first the Johannesburg city engineering department refused permission for Purle to operate within the municipal area, resenting the competition and referring to them angrily as 'pirate operators', but most of the East Rand municipalities within Purle's operating area made their dumping sites available for dry waste, and Rand Mines offered the use of a site for the Johannesburg area. The Germiston City Council allowed them to use its liquid disposal site.

Joe Southey did not stay long with Purle and in June 1970 Ian Hattingh was appointed manager. At the same time Teddy Sykes was appointed technical manager, having been transferred from Embecon. Teddy was the first to admit that he knew very little about waste disposal and he and Ian were greatly assisted by Purle UK's technical director Peter Newman, marketing director Stan Higham and Tony Morgan, who were all instrumen-

A sludge gulping tanker in operation.

tal in getting operations underway in South Africa. Purle was pioneering each step and gradually introducing the necessary technical expertise to the country.

In November 1970 Aidan Buchholz was appointed managing director of Purle and the company began to increase its operations in the treatment and disposal of liquid waste. This service seemed to have the greatest potential of all Purle's activities and included the disposal of toxic waste, which required the approval of the Department of Water Affairs. The initial application met with an unexpected and very firm rejection in terms of the Government's 1956 Water Act and there followed many unprofitable months of expensive scientific research and organization before the site and system were finally accepted.

Although fired with enthusiasm and determination the men with Purle had little technical knowledge of any aspect of waste management, and in later years they looked back and marvelled at their getting the company off the ground at all, quite apart from doing so successfully. The first visit made by Aidan, Ian and Teddy to the Department of Water Affairs included a long discussion with the Department's Mr Legge, during which he frequently talked about 'TDS' and on the way back to the office afterwards the three Purle men all confessed that they had absolutely no idea what he had been talking about! ('TDS' stands for 'Totally Dissolved Solids' which are the main hazard of liquid waste disposal because they can leak from the waste site into surrounding underground water and do untold, and unexpected, harm by contaminating the aquaflow.)

Technical expertise was soon introduced to the South African company with the appointment in 1971 of a new technical manager. Mike Jones was a chemist who had worked in the UK with effluent treatment and regulation at power-stations. He soon established a procedure which had never been seen before in South Africa, although it was well known in America and Europe. This was a scientifically planned co-disposal of solid and liquid wastes – the best way of getting rid of all but the most noxious material. To put it very simply, all liquids were treated in a way that rendered them harmless before being co-disposed with solid waste in such proportions that the liquids were totally absorbed. It was a breakthrough in South Africa, the culmination of a pioneering struggle, which was recognized with due praise at the official opening of the Purle Pollution Abatement Centre at Rietfontein in November 1973, two years after its operational beginning. John Hodgson emphasized the safety and control features at Rietfontein in comparison with most waste disposal sites, and Mr R J Laburn, chief engineer of the Rand Water Board, congratulated Purle on their solution to the industrial waste problem, especially important in a land of limited water supplies. He pointed out that for the first time South Africa had a credible alternative to the closure of factories because of pollution.

John and Purle management had the foresight to anticipate the need to provide for future waste disposal sites and in January 1972 a company, Purle Landfill (Pty) Ltd, was formed. Brickor had a 50% shareholding and a proportion of the profits in return for guaranteeing the availability of their existing and future quarry sites to Purle. This company was involved only in landfill work using the co-disposal of liquid and solid wastes.

All this coincided with South Africa's increasing environmental awareness, following the pattern of much of the Western world, and Purle's image was boosted in 1972 with a visit from Derek Irlam, an executive director of Purle UK, who spoke to government departments, municipalities and industrialists about the British regulations concerning poisonous waste. He also explained the 'PPP' principle which was being adopted throughout the world – Producer Pays for Pollution – and the South African Minister of Water Affairs agreed that pollution abatement costs should be an integral part of the production cost of any product causing pollution.

Meanwhile Murray Transport Services had been expanding their dry waste operations, and in April 1971 Darling and Hodgson decided to join forces with them and purchased a 51% interest in the company. After this, Murray Transport Services doubled their profits within two years.

The two companies worked independently for some time, each servicing specific areas, but in 1972 they moved together to a depot in Crucible Road, Heriotdale and in mid 1973 Darling and Hodgson increased their shareholding in Murray Transport Services to 90% and operations were combined. Murray Transport Services' rear-end loading compactors were used to replace Purle's Dumpmaster, for which it was increasingly difficult to obtain spare parts. Its repair defeated even the workshop manager, Ollie Magnusson, who was renowned for his ability to keep vehicles on the road with minimum cost and maximum safety. His magic touch was sorely missed when he was promoted to operations manager in July 1978, and Waste-tech was sad to lose him to W J's Bulk Transport at the end of 1980.

As Purle developed on the Reef they also expanded their operations into other main centres of South Africa. In 1971 Teddy Sykes was transferred to Natal to establish operations there with the help of Ric Nevill in charge of sales, Harold de Beer in the workshops and Edith Campbell in the office. The four of them adopted the name 'The Hut Club' because they were based in huts at the Tanker Services yard at Jacobs. The huts were always either too hot or too cold, and the wind blew dust and ash everywhere unless it had rained, when it became very muddy. The lack of human comforts fitted the pioneering atmosphere, however, and the early days were characterized by a close team spirit and a readiness to tackle anything.

Natal is a conservative province, traditionally slow to accept new ideas, and the early months were predictably unprofitable. The big breakthrough came in 1972 when the Durban municipality decided to incinerate its rubbish, and increased its charges considerably to cover their costs – from nothing to R5 per ton! Purle (Natal) saw the opportunity to offer their services at a lower price, and took it. At the same time the Howard College project was just beginning – one of the highlights of their achievements. For some time builders' rubble from the development taking place in Durban had been dumped in an area near the University of Natal where there were several unused valleys, and Teddy Sykes decided to try to obtain permission for Purle to use the same site for industrial waste. He explained his scheme for an extensive landfill, which would eventually provide a large area of level land with good potential, to the university authorities. They approved the idea, the agreement was signed on 22 February 1973 and the project started on 13 August that year. The project continued for eight years and was completed in May 1981, providing a site for extensive playing fields.

By the end of 1974 there had been such dynamic growth in Natal that the construction

Compacting machine in action at the Howard College landfill site.

of Purle's own depot at Prospecton was justified. In that year Purle contracted to remove waste from Safmarine ships in Durban harbour, and by the end of May 1975 they had moved nine thousand cubic metres. The company expanded further in 1977 with the acquisition of a local competitor, Southern Waste, which had developed a solid industrial waste collection service out of a scrap metal business.

Purle started slowly in the Eastern Cape. At first P E Holdings was the majority shareholder but by the end of 1971 the manager, Steve Fox, was reporting to Ian Hattingh, and in 1974, when Winston Odendaal took charge of the region, Purle's activities increased dramatically. The depot was at Deal Party and in June 1974 Purle took over the New Brighton disposal site when they were awarded a contract for the disposal of refuse from the township. A pollution abatement centre was opened at Aloes and a depot was opened in East London when Waste-tech was awarded a domestic refuse contract by the Beacon Bay municipality. Winston continued as manager of the Eastern Cape operations until 1977 when he was transferred to D&H Flora.

Operations started in Pretoria in 1973 (one of the earliest contracts was with the Chrysler company) and a hold was established in the dry waste disposal industry in Cape Town through Murray Transport Services' interest in Wasteaway. Various transactions resulted in this company and another waste disposal operation, Rubbish Removers, becoming subsidiaries of Purle (Cape) in 1973. This in turn was 50% owned by Murray and Stewart, who took over direct management control for many years. The other 50% was shared by Purle (SA) and Trencor.

The energetic persistence of everyone in Purle eventually paid dividends when in 1973 the company made its first contribution to Group profits. The following year Purle attained the greatest percentage increase growth within the Group and D&H felt confident

Waste-tech tanker releasing liquid onto dry solid waste for co-disposal.

enough to break away from the UK company altogether. Purle became a wholly-owned Group subsidiary, a decision encouraged by the fact that Purle UK had been taken over by Redland and was no longer interested in the South African company. The remaining equity of Murray Transport Services was also acquired that year and early the following year, in March 1975, a new company was formed with a new name, Waste-tech. Aidan Buchholz continued as managing director and Ian Hattingh as company manager. A new co-ordinated image was presented, of strong technical leadership in all aspects of waste control and management. It was still a small company with a management team initially involved in all aspects of its operations. Iain Welsh, who had joined the Group as an accountant the previous year, took more than just a financial interest and he and Eddie Barton, who was appointed sales manager of the Witwatersrand area in August 1975, played an active part in promoting Waste-tech. New company colours of blue and white were chosen to depict cleanliness and operations were carried out with great enthusiasm. The backbone of the work was industrial, but there were some municipal contracts for domestic and garden refuse and much was learnt by experience in all fields.

Within a short time the liquids operations were split off into a separate division based at Rietfontein, where operations became increasingly sophisticated and technical. Realizing that a highly-qualified scientist was essential to guide the company into the future, Aidan Buchholz invited Peter Scott, a chemist with a doctorate in chemical engineering, to join Waste-tech in June 1976. Peter set about consolidating and refining the system that Mike Jones had initiated, spending several years formulating standard procedures for the co-disposal of waste to be used at all Waste-tech sites. When Peter first went to Rietfontein the facilities were still rather primitive. Mike's laboratory and the office were in an old building where the rain came through cracks in the roof and one wall of the laboratory would fall out when anyone leant against it!

A comprehensive and modern laboratory and new offices were later built and officially opened in 1981. By then the sophisticated process was well established; liquid wastes were tested in the laboratory and accordingly rendered harmless in the neutralizing plant. The inorganic sludge separated out was disposed with dry waste and the liquid pumped to adjoining plastic-lined dams where it was evaporated through spraying. Really poisonous and untreatable wastes were encapsulated in concrete blocks and buried.

The laboratory at Rietfontein.

Above left
Tanker offloading liquid waste into the treatment plant.

Above right
Overhead spray evaporation ponds with the treatment plant in the background.

The co-disposal site developed at Rietfontein was a huge hole where typical landfill procedure was followed. Trucks deposited dry waste at the bottom while tankers released liquid waste for co-disposal, and a monster machine trundled to and fro over the waste material, ripping it up, spreading it out, and compacting it to a fraction of its original volume. Often there was a lone figure watching, not a mere spectator but a Waste-tech salesman guaranteeing that his customer's waste was totally destroyed and not someone else's free gain. At the end of each day the waste was completely covered by a layer of soil, thus eliminating the risk of smell, vermin and flies. This allowed Waste-tech to use disposal sites near habitation, and the scientifically controlled procedure often made possible the reclamation of otherwise unproductive land, as had been the case in the Howard College project.

During the seventies Waste-tech's expertise spread beyond the boundaries of South Africa, with a consulting mission to Argentina to advise on waste disposal and the short-lived participation in Wimpey Waste Management in the United Kingdom. In 1977 the company was given Group status as the waste management division which two years later joined D&H Transport to create a new D&H services division under the head office management of Phil Erasmus. Aidan was transferred to the UK and appointed managing director of Wimpey Waste Management, and Ian took over as managing director of the waste management division which encompassed all waste technology and operations. These were extended in 1979 to include industrial cleaning operations after the acquisition of a 51% share in Hydrochem.

Hydrochem had been started in 1969 by Paul Potgieter, Tony Holness and Digby Jennings, with several other enthusiastic and dedicated young men, who together formed Natal Underwater Maintenance with the intention of cleaning ships' hulls under water. Opposition from South African Railways and Harbours diverted their operations into industrial cleaning and the company changed its name to Hydrochem, with the philosophy of 'doing anything, providing it is possible and profitable'. One contract was for high pressure water cleaning the exterior of the new Carlton Hotel when the building operations were finished, but most of their work was for industry, for such companies as Shell, Sasol, AE&CI and the sugar companies in Natal. They moved successfully into chemical cleaning and into inert entry and catalyst handling, which required life support equipment. Hydrochem's efficient services considerably reduced industries' downtimes, and the demand was large enough to justify the establishment of depots at Secunda and Sasolburg, apart from their head office at Vereeniging.

A project in the United Kingdom took Paul Potgieter to England to work with Wimpey Waste Management and the success of the combined operations led Aidan Buchholz to suggest that Paul should stay on and establish a specialized cleaning service for that company. Hydrochem's operations came into the Group at about this time, retaining

Above left
A member of the Hydrochem team equipped for cleaning the interior of tanks.

Above right
Hydro-jetting by Hydrochem at a petro-chemical plant.

their own identity very firmly at first. Before long, however, D&H had increased its shareholding to 100% and, in mid 1981, acquired the total shareholding of one of Hydrochem's competitors, Chemintal, a company specializing in sophisticated chemical cleaning services complementing Hydrochem's operations. The two companies were merged to create D&H Industrial Services, all under one roof at Alrode with Teddy Sykes as general manager.

After rationalization of the two companies' operations only the really successful product lines were retained – industrial cleaning, high pressure water and chemical cleaning – which operated at Sasol, Escom, Iscor and AE&CI. The future seemed uncertain, however, and in 1983 the division was reduced in size. High pressure water cleaning services and industrial vacuuming were taken over by Waste-tech and incorporated into the Transvaal region.

At the end of the seventies Waste-tech started to undertake original research to lead it into an exciting and rewarding future of extracting resources and energy from waste. Peter Scott led this research and in 1983 was appointed manager of all Waste-tech recycling operations, based at Nuffield, Springs. Investigations have been made into the sterilization of sewage sludge and chicken litter for use as a fertilizer and cattle feed. The sterilizing is carried out in an electron accelerator. The irradiating beam in this giant machine is also used to sterilize medical disposables and to improve the heat-resisting properties of plastic insulation on cables. Waste-tech has also developed a protein precipitant to reclaim dissolved protein and fat oil from organic waste at abattoirs and food processing plants for use as a protein concentrate in animal foods. Widespread use of this could save South Africa millions of rands worth of foreign exchange. Not all research is done at Nuffield, however, and a new way has been developed of neutralizing acid oil sludges from the oil re-refining industry with pulverized fuel ash from power-stations to produce a very effective inert filler and cover material. A permanent plant for this was established at Badenhorst near Boksburg. Methods have also been developed for recovering minerals from various effluents, and experiments carried out on the production of methane from waste. In the Cape furnace fuel is being extracted from waste oil.

Waste-tech finally established its national coverage by moving strongly into Cape Town in 1983 when Wasteaway became a wholly-owned Group subsidiary and changed its name to Waste-tech. Ian Bewick was appointed manager, operating from the offices in Parow. The Western Cape work was primarily domestic; Waste-tech was responsible for the complete refuse removal services in Pinelands, Kraaifontein and Fish Hoek and

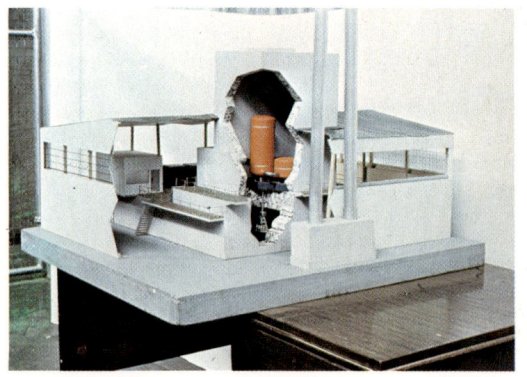

Right
A model of the electron accelerator.

Far right
The heat resisting properties of plastic insulation on cables are improved by reeling the cables under the irradiating beam of the electron accelerator.

for the final disposal in Somerset West. Waste-tech trucks were seen servicing the larger supermarkets, and a unique service was offered whereby a stationary compactor was installed which needed emptying at only fairly lengthy intervals. This was done in many public places ranging from the University of Cape Town to Cavendish Square shopping centre. In 1983 Waste-tech was running the largest waste removal operation in the Cape out of two depots at Parow and Vissershok. The operations at Vissershok, the site of the Cape branch's landfill site, gave Waste-tech its third pollution abatement centre.

Operations in other regions remained primarily industrial, although there was a constant endeavour to increase municipal work. In Natal, municipal contracts were obtained for the removal of garden and environmental litter from Durban parks and domestic refuse from Yellow Wood Park. The Howard College project had established Waste-tech's credibility and reputation as leaders in land reclamation through sanitary landfill, however, and there was considerable development in this direction under Ray Lombard, who joined the company as Natal's technical manager in 1979. Further projects were started at Umlazi and Ntuzuma for the Kwa-Zulu government, and in 1981 the Westville municipality awarded Waste-tech the tender to take over their existing refuse site and raise the levels over a six year period to provide sports fields for the community. Ray was also responsible for the pioneering of co-disposal techniques for liquid waste on these sites. With Natal's 1000 mm annual rainfall this necessitated techniques somewhat different from those in the often parched Transvaal, and the leachate recycling system pioneered at Umlazi proved comparable with anything of its kind in Europe or the United States.

By the early eighties the only members of the original Hut Club who were left in Waste-tech (Natal) were Edith Campbell and Ric Nevill. Ric had taken over the management of the region in 1979 and maintained the traditional lively and innovative atmosphere. In 1983 Waste-tech (Natal) was investigating the use of a synthetic material for intermediate landfill cover, and had reintroduced front-end loading compactors which were effective in attracting attention to the company's operations.

The Eastern Cape, under manager Mike Winter since 1978, continued to be largely dependent on the motor industry, and in 1983 moved to a new modern depot close to the Aloes landfill site and pollution abatement centre.

In 1981 Geoff Wood was appointed manager of the Transvaal region, and since then more depots have been established at Springs, Vanderbijlpark and Rietfontein to service the East Rand, Vaal Triangle, and eastern Johannesburg and Sandton respectively. In 1982 the Heriotdale depot was moved to Crown Mines, the site of the original Ready Mixed Concrete plant and later a Tanker Services depot, set among the mine dumps with the towering skyline of Johannesburg in the near distance. In 1983 each of these depots had a fleet of trucks operating within a 10 km radius.

The drivers of these vehicles have always been very important people and comprehensive training programmes were established within Waste-tech in keeping with Group policy, as well as an incentive scheme of awards for good driving made on an annual basis.

Waste-tech has initiated another yearly event in providing a welcome oasis at the

Waste-tech's domestic refuse collection service in operation at Yellow Wood Park, Durban.

34 km mark of the Johannesburg Stock Exchange marathon each year. The runners' spirits can only rise when they see the cheerful faces of those manning the gaily decorated Waste-tech tables and partake of the refreshment offered as they pass by. It has become a grand family day with husbands, wives and children all helping to keep the waterhole running smoothly, and it seems remarkably appropriate for the company to participate in a function which is so clearly linked with a healthy approach to life.

By 1983, fourteen years after Purle had begun operations, Waste-tech was supplying a highly sophisticated service comprising the handling, treatment and disposal of waste. It also offered a consulting service for on-site treatment of industrial effluent. With regard to municipal work, Waste-tech had made the decision to assist rather than compete which led in 1983 to the company supplying six rear-end loaders and drivers to the Johannesburg municipality, to operate for a five year period under the Johannesburg municipal colours of brown and cream. This was a major breakthrough, providing steady work which helped smooth out the valleys in the waste collection business.

When Ian left the Group in 1981 his place as managing director of Waste Management was taken by David Shephard. David had come into D&H through the acquisition of Randmix and from there had moved to spend three happy years in Embecon. He came into waste with great confidence in the future, aware of an increasing trend towards the use of private enterprise in the public sector as costs escalated, an increasing need for pollution control in industry, and excited by the revolutionary research. David's head office team included David Smith who has contributed a great deal to the waste management division during his years as financial manager.

Waste-tech continues to move forward, making a significant contribution to Group activities and always retaining much of the enthusiasm and liveliness of its early days. Those concerned with industrial and domestic waste disposal proudly call themselves 'garbologists' and work under the banner 'Garbage is Beautiful'. Alongside the garbologists securing access to the waste stream of South Africa, the Waste-tech boffins are using their technological expertise to ensure that D&H leads the way into exploitation of waste as raw materials of the future. Together these have made Waste-tech an area of great potential within the Group.

structed for Rand Mines on the corner of Fox and Sauer Streets in Johannesburg. No doubt John persuaded his partners that it would be showing a regrettable lack of faith if ready-mixed concrete were not used. Unfortunately technical problems were experienced on this particular job and the consulting engineers condemned the quality of the concrete column foundations in the basement. Suddenly the whole future of RMC was at stake! The Corner House building was already conspicuously well above ground level and if any demolition were necessary because the concrete foundations were not strong enough it would be difficult to persuade anyone ever to use ready-mixed concrete again. All turned out well, however. Sample cores were taken to be tested at the PCI, where a young technician, David Bath, proved that the concrete was in fact up to standard. David has always felt that his work must have impressed Peter Langerman because very soon after that he was asked to join RMC and take charge of the laboratory at Crown Mines.

It was an easy transfer. The PCI's policy was to promote concrete technology in any way and the director, Dr Sandy Fulton, was very happy to see one of his young technicians move into the ready-mixed concrete industry. David took over the laboratory in February 1964 and his quiet efficiency immediately lessened the load on Peter's shoulders. The growing technical knowledge within the company resulted in an increasingly superior product which gradually became an integral part of the construction industry.

Although large orders were the most satisfactory, RMC were always ready to help with smaller jobs and were quite willing to deliver small quantities. They even put out a

Ready-mixed concrete for the home owner.

The Materials Story

When the first Ready Mixed Concrete trucks began to rumble around the streets of Johannesburg in 1961 no one had any idea that this new venture was going to be the base from which a large materials division of Darling and Hodgson would grow and which, in twenty years' time, would become a major contributor to Group profits.

John Hodgson and Jack Plane, with friends in the stone-crushing business, pioneered the ready-mixed concrete industry in South Africa. They formed a company, Ready Mixed Concrete (SA) (Pty) Ltd, in Johannesburg in 1961, asking Rand Mines to join them as partners and provide finance for rapid expansion into the Cape and Natal. In 1963 John and Jack sold their shares to Darling and Hodgson when it took Union Corporation as a major partner. This transaction provided capital for still further expansion, and plants were established in key areas with accompanying recognition of ready-mixed concrete as a valuable building material in the construction industry. Rival operations which appeared at intervals were mostly taken over by RMC (SA), and a partnership was formed with Pioneer Ready Mixed Concrete, the largest competitor on the Reef, which had a significant influence on their future development.

Darling and Hodgson's interest in ready-mixed concrete led to the establishment of Embecon in 1966. This company is a 50/50 partnership with Master Builders, a division of the Martin Marietta Corporation of America, and it manufactures and markets in South Africa the wide range of Master Builders' products for improving concrete.

In 1973 Darling and Hodgson made the decision to go public. At the time the company was still primarily dependent on road construction, but an objective had been set that within the following decade this should comprise only a third of company operations, which opened the way for tremendous development in other activities. The success of the ready-mixed concrete operations pointed clearly down a construction materials track. Existing sand and stone suppliers were becoming absorbed by larger concerns, often associated with competitors, and it was strategically opportune for D&H to remedy this vulnerable situation by securing their own supply of raw materials and also to move into a positive situation in the commercial quarrying and stone-crushing arena. RMC has its own story within Darling and Hodgson and integration backwards into raw materials created a powerful force which has held its own over the years in a fiercely competitive field.

Within a year D&H acquired a rock quarry in Natal and sand quarries in the Transvaal with the purchase of Shires Quarry in 1973 and Paul's Industrial Investments in 1974. A different kind of quarrying operation was acquired with the purchase of Mazista Slate in 1973.

Paul's Industrial Investments brought with it a wide range of activities in addition to its extensive sand quarrying operations. Many of these did not suit the D&H objectives and were gradually sold. One subsidiary which was kept has made its mark in the building trade. This is LSM – Lime Sand Mortar – which manufactures specialized ready-mixed mortars.

In 1974 D&H moved into prestressed concrete with the acquisition of Hume Prestressed Concrete Products (Pty) Ltd. This company manufactured concrete sleepers, interlocking road stones and a range of pre-stressed concrete products, including Spiroll hollow core building slabs, at the Alrode factory near Johannesburg. The name was changed to Hucrcte and all product lines were phased out except the production of sleepers. These were being manufactured in a pre-cast, post-tensioned, instantly demoulded process under licence to Dyckerhoff and Widmann in West Germany for a

Concrete sleepers and Slimline pipes – Hucrete.

large contract with the South African Railways. In one year the monthly production improved from 36 500 to just over 55 000, largely through improved working conditions and a streamlining of the manufacturing process.

A second sleeper-manufacturing company, Continental Sleepers, which held the same Dividag patent, was purchased and merged with Hucrete. In 1977 the company was manufacturing 42% of the sleeper requirements of the South African Railways, providing a product which had a long life, was resistant to distortion and weathering and had excellent electrical insulation resistance, amongst other attractive properties. Unfortunately, however, this process was superseded by improved technology developed by Grinakers which was more cost effective and caused a significant decrease in Hucrete's market share, in particular the loss of the Railways contract. In an attempt to improve the situation a new line was developed producing Slimline glassfibre reinforced concrete pipes which seemed to have a promising future. Overall, however, the prospects became increasingly unfavourable and in late 1979 Hucrete was sold.

D&H's expansion into concrete activities created a need for specialist technical 'know-how' in concrete technology and concrete products design and manufacturing fields. The Group's foremost concrete technologist, Walter Barker, was transferred from Embecon to the head office at Hyde Park in November 1974, thereby mobilizing his considerable experience and skills to the benefit of overall Group interests in the materials field.

Successful long-term strategy was identified in the production of basic construction materials. Positive development took place down this track, largely through acquisitions, over the next ten years, while the ready-mixed concrete operations showed a steady improvement and an ever-increasing geographic spread. The Group's stone-crushing activities accelerated in 1976 when Darling and Hodgson acquired the sole rights to work the rock from mine dumps in the Evander area. When the building of Sasol II commenced at Secunda in the south-eastern Transvaal it created a great demand for construction materials and D&H formed a company, Evander Crushers, with the Union Corporation gold mines in the area as minority shareholders. It rapidly became a valuable contributor to the Group's quarrying operations. Evander Crushers steadily worked through an enormous mine dump at Winkelhaak and their crusher plant was then moved to Kinross.

Evander Crushers, Mazista, Hucrete, Shires Quarry and Paul's Sand were all gathered together within the Group, separate from the ready-mixed concrete operations, under Terry Rolfe, former managing director of Paul's Industrial Investments. Terry soon left the Group to further his experience in other fields, however, and a D&H sand and quar-

Evander Crushers.

ries division was formed incorporating these companies under managing director Peter Asher, the man who had managed Ready Mixed Concrete (Natal) from its inception.

In 1977 this small division grew dramatically with the acquisition of Randmix which, while of great significance to the operations of Ready Mixed Concrete, was purchased primarily for its quarrying and stone-crushing interests including options over Clairwood Quarry in Durban, some unworked quarry land near Bapsfontein, and a quarry near Newcastle in Natal, as well as a range of crushing plants in the Transvaal, including East Rand Crushers, Cookeshaft Crushers and Mooiplaas Crushers in Pretoria. Randmix also brought to Darling and Hodgson the rights to use the pulverized fuel ash produced at the Escom power-stations which led to the establishment of D&H Ash Resources as a fully-fledged company within the Group.

In 1975 Peter Loveday joined D&H and was appointed managing director of all industrial companies within the Group. Two years later he introduced the idea of combining quarrying and ready-mixed concrete operations in a materials division under Peter Smith, the former managing director of Randmix, operating from head office. This was the manufacturing side of the industrial division. Peter Asher remained at the head of the quarrying section and all the ready-mixed concrete operations within D&H were put under Bryan Johnson, who ran this section from Cape Town. Hucrete, Mazista and Evander Crushers were put together under Laurie Durandt.

The year 1978 was a difficult one for the quarries section. Problems in merging Paul's

Drilling in preparation for blasting at Clairwood Quarry.

Industrial Investments and Randmix resulted in several managerial changes and many resignations. The unhappy atmosphere was aggravated by a serious economic recession in South Africa, and competition on the Reef resulted in drastic price cutting, causing stress within the industry. However, in 1979 the economy picked up and the staff position stabilized; prices increased and trade performances improved. One by one the D&H quarries pulled their operations out of the red and the section announced its first profits at the end of 1979.

A newcomer, Don Lanigan, was appointed managing director of the materials division in 1978. Don was an American who had come to South Africa eight years previously for Standard Telephones and Cables, where he had worked with Peter Loveday. Under his guidance a keen team spirit and favourable company image gradually built up, and 1980 saw a considerable upswing and consolidation of the quarrying operations. Meanwhile Embecon and SAFIC Resources, the latter soon to be changed to D&H Ash Resources, had been brought into the materials division as well. Laurie Durandt had been transferred to Canada to head up D&H's operations there, and Peter Asher spent some time as managing director of D&H ash and concrete products before moving back to Natal as regional Group director in January 1980.

At the end of 1980 David Bath was appointed managing director of the materials division when Don moved to the engineering division. David had developed a deep understanding of the business as he rose through the ranks of Ready Mixed Concrete on the

Cape Blue Rock Quarry.

Reef and in Natal, acquiring managerial skills which were strengthened through studying the Sloan Programme at the London Business School. The division continued its progress under his capable leadership and in 1982 for the first time it headed the construction division in its contribution to Group profits. This was a triumphant fulfilment of the strategy set in 1973 to balance construction with the other Group activities which had been introduced in the previous decade.

Success was achieved through organic growth and through significant acquisitions which gave the D&H materials division a comprehensive national coverage and assured long-term quarry reserves. In 1981 Cape Blue Rock Quarry near Somerset West in the Cape was transferred from Savage and Lovemore, which had been responsible for its development since they acquired it in 1974. The quarry had been started as Dunn's Blue Rock Quarry in 1958, and was purchased from Mr Dunn by Savage and Lovemore to provide material for their contracts in the Western Cape. They appointed a new manager, Alan Pluck, in February 1976 and modernized the plant. Over the years the quarry was extended by purchasing neighbouring farms and property towards Sir Lowry's Pass. There were further improvements after its transfer to the materials division, including new offices and workshops. It is the Group's only quarrying interest in the Western Cape, and has an economic life expectancy of approximately twenty years.

D&H had been involved in sand supplies in Natal for a long time but in 1980 they established substantial control over sand supplies in the greater Durban area by acquiring a 50% interest, in partnership with Peter Kernick, in a company called Pine Smyth, which recovered and processed natural sand from rivers and pits. In 1982 the farm Rooikraal near Boksburg was purchased and a hard-rock quarry established there, with immense reserves of high-quality dolomite and dolorite and a predicted working life of about a hundred years. The East Rand is predicted to remain a major growth area, and Rooikraal is strategically placed to meet the needs of all the municipalities and major consumers there. It is a large quarry with the most up-to-date equipment and materials handling facilities. Also in 1982 Brits Crushers and Mooinooi Crushers were acquired, close to major Bophutatswana and western Pretoria infrastructure developments, and Umzimkulu Quarry on Natal's south coast. In 1983 D&H established quarrying operations in the Nelspruit area with the purchase of M&S Crushers.

An important boost was given to the materials division by the takeover of Keir and Cawder. This long-established company had for some time been regarded as an acqui-

Clayville Quarry.

sition target as it seemed to provide the ideal way to extend reserves and expand the market spread. John Hodgson had approached the owners several times to no avail, but at the end of 1982 the Stirling family agreed to sell and by early 1983 D&H had the total equity. The most significant aspects of the acquisition were the Olive Hill quarry in Bloemfontein and crushing operations on the Far West Rand gold mines. These took D&H Materials into quarrying in the Orange Free State for the first time. Keir and Cawder also owned Crofthead Quarry in Swaziland, Brockley Quarry near Durban, a virgin quarry site near Vereeniging and a high quality agricultural lime quarry (Immerpan) near Potgietersrus in the Northern Transvaal. The company's integration into Darling and Hodgson took place smoothly.

The acquisition of Keir and Cawder provoked the reorganization of the historical provincial structure of the division. In 1983 concrete and quarrying operations were brought together in five regional profit centres. The regional general managers all reported to David Bath, who moved his offices from Hyde Park to Sandton City during the year. When Peter Loveday left D&H in mid 1983 David reported directly to John Hodgson, which he found very stimulating. The new structure resulted in greater fulfilment of mutual needs within the division, and the ready-mixed concrete operations helped stabilize the cyclical quarry results. The historical D&H Quarries section became the northern region based at Honeydew under Ross Heron and included Immerpan under the new name D&H Lime. The central region comprised the Keir and Cawder quarrying and crushing operations in the Orange Free State and was run from Bloemfontein by Elmor Leo. Ready-mixed concrete operations were introduced to this region for the first time and established in the Olive Hill quarry. The eastern (including Swaziland) and south-western regions continued to be primarily ready-mixed concrete operations under Graham Hardy in Durban and Bryan Johnson in Cape Town.

The south-eastern Region carried out its quarrying and ready-mixed concrete operations under the name of Quarryman, a company held in equal partnership by D&H and Murray and Roberts. The managing director of Quarryman was Brian Spiers who had pioneered Ready Mixed Concrete's operations in the Eastern Cape.

The reorganized materials division included Embecon and D&H Ash Resources, run as 'national businesses' with central administration and country-wide distribution. Mazista was included on the same basis until it was sold in 1983.

Quarrying is inevitably an operation which desecrates the landscape, and the world-

Right
David Bath.

Far right
Crusher at Rooikraal Quarry.

wide trend of environmental preservation has spurred D&H into a commitment to land rehabilitation. While recognizing this as a social obligation, D&H sees it also as a means of extending the profitability of the land it owns. Extensive long-term plans have been developed for the use of the land at Shires Quarry and D&H's Honeydew property as attractive townships and recreational areas. These are but two examples of D&H's awareness of its environmental responsibility.

For the materials division 1983 did not live up to its optimistic projections. However, David Bath wisely used it as a year of consolidation during which people were settled into well-motivated teams within the reorganized division, continuing to produce a high standard of technical work. At the end of 1983 David was confidently forecasting a steady increase in revenue and profits for the years ahead, with significant long-term achievement.

Ready Mixed Concrete

It all began in 1960, over a shared box of sandwiches, when John Hodgson was invited to lunch by the man who owned Consolidated Stone Crushers, from whom Darling and Hodgson bought some of their stone. Robert Horowitz was an enterprising man who, in remarkably few years, had made his way from working as a butcher's blockman to a position of considerable wealth with extensive business investments. In 1960 he was looking for a way to expand his stone-crushing interests into the premixed concrete field and he turned naturally to the man who had pioneered the commercial availability of another premixed product in South Africa. John Hodgson's Tarmac Industries had introduced premixed asphalt to the South African market in 1948 and it was still a highly successful part of Darling and Hodgson's operations.

The ready-mixed concrete industry comprises the manufacture of concrete according to definitive specifications at a central plant, with delivery to sites in special trucks with rotating drums from which the concrete is placed where it is needed. There had been an attempt to establish such an operation in Johannesburg some twelve years previously but it had been shortlived, and all investigations by overseas companies had indicated that the building industry was too well based on the use of cheap labour to make it a viable proposition. However, John was attracted by the idea of establishing another new product on the South African scene and his close friend and business associate, Jack Plane, was also enthusiastic. (No doubt all the possibilities were thrashed out between them on the cricket field!) Jack was always stimulated by the vision of a great future for diesel transport in South Africa, in which he readily included the specialized vehicles which would be necessary for this new industry. The three men were an ideal combination to initiate it – Robert was offering financial backing and one of the essential raw materials, Jack was in the all-important field of transport and John provided the necessary frontline management and enthusiasm.

John and one of Robert's partners, Mark Greenberg, an astute and perceptive businessman, flew to London in December 1960 to make a full survey of the industry in the United Kingdom, where the use of ready-mixed concrete was widespread. It had been established there in the early fifties by a large Australian company, Ready Mixed Concrete Limited.

The two men travelled extensively around Britain and parts of the Continent, their letters home revealing some longing to escape from the relentless grey skies and rain of Europe and return to the sunny warmth of Africa. They completed a very worthwhile visit and John wrote in his subsequent report that 'it was an undoubted success in every respect, and we feel quite certain that the subject has been covered from every angle'. They met with exceptional helpfulness and generosity in the provision of information wherever they went, and received a positive impression of the success of the ready-mixed concrete industry and its on-going expansion. The general opinion of everyone in the industry was that this was the process of the future in the construction industry, and it would be foolish to miss out on the opportunity of starting it in South Africa.

Inspired by the atmosphere within the industry, John and Mark Greenberg set about choosing and ordering equipment. The final choice was for batching equipment (the basic plant) and mixer units from Wingets of Rochester. They were strongly advised to use AEC chassis, which tied in well with Jack Plane's business in South Africa (J H Plane and Company was the local supplier of AEC trucks) and Wingets were persuaded to give Jack their agency as well. Eight mixer units were ordered, six of the smaller size (4 cubic yards) and two of the larger size (6 cubic yards), to be mounted on AEC Monarch and Marshall chassis respectively.

Before leaving South Africa for England, John had insisted that their new company be registered under the name 'Ready Mixed Concrete' so that 'everybody who talks about ready-mixed concrete will actually advertise our name'. This was initially rejected on the grounds that the words described a process, but with the addition of the initials 'SA' it was recognized as a company name and Ready Mixed Concrete (SA) (Pty) Ltd was registered just after John's return from the United Kingdom, on 28 December 1960. The South African colours were appropriately chosen for the truckmixers and the very distinctive logo designed by Peter Theobald of Walter Kirby and approved as the company's registered trademark on 3 August 1961. The concept of the Ready Mixed Concrete rotating drum was cleverly portrayed by green lines curving around a golden circle.

The company's registered offices were at Brailsford House and the first shareholders were John Hodgson and Jack Plane, with Robert Horowitz and his three partners in Consolidated Crusher Holdings, Mark Greenberg, Solomon Broude and Isaac Horowitz. These men constituted the initial board of directors, with the addition of Brian Malcomson from Darling and Hodgson as secretary and public officer and J M Beveridge, from J H Plane and Company. Jack was appointed chairman and John managing director.

Ready Mixed Concrete soon needed financial support for their highly capital intensive venture, and John approached Corner House Investments, part of the huge Rand Mines organization which had significant interests in cement production in South Africa. In June 1961 Corner House took a 20% shareholding in RMC (SA) and appointed C de G Watermeyer to the board. The remaining 80% belonged to Bulk Concrete, a holding company owned by RMC's original shareholders. In June of the same year Ralph Blakeway of Rand Mines was appointed to the board. He had been involved in negotiations with the cement companies from the very beginning and continued to maintain this important liaison, making a very significant contribution to the establishment of the ready-mixed concrete industry in South Africa.

There were not many people in South Africa who knew anything about this industry, and individuals were brought into the company largely through personal associations within the concrete industry as a whole, in particular from the Portland Cement Institute, which specialized in cement and concrete technology. It was vitally important to find someone who had some knowledge of the industry for the position of general manager, and Con Roux, manager of Darling and Hodgson's construction operations at the time, recommended an old friend who was the Natal regional manager of the PCI. Peter Langerman was a civil engineer who had studied cement and concrete technology in England, where he had become interested in the concept of ready-mixed concrete. He gladly accepted John's invitation to join the new company, starting on 16 March 1961, full of enthusiasm for the new project.

He gathered around him a group of men who were all dedicated to the innovative philosophy of ready-mixed concrete. It was a great leap into the unknown, and those involved pressed on with an almost blind faith and little professionalism in their approach. They were action men with considerable energy and enthusiasm, prepared to turn their hands to any aspect of the job, and there was a pioneering atmosphere in all that they did.

The first plant was erected on a site at Crown Mines not far from the centre of Johannesburg, in close proximity to a supply of stone from Crown Crushers. It took some time to assemble everything and in the meantime a pilot plant was erected on the Hume Pipe Company property adjoining Brailsford House to provide ready-mixed concrete for testing the first truckmixers. It was a slow and rather antiquated plant but it remained in use for several years because it was convenient for the East Rand market. It provided the ready-mixed concrete for the demonstration delivery to one of Robert Horowitz's building sites in town at the much publicized launching of the new company in June 1961.

The Crown plant was commissioned in August that year with just four truckmixers

Above
The first truckmixers.

Left
The first RMC plant, Crown Mines.

213

working out of the depot. The first driver to be employed by Peter Langerman was Gerry Labuschagne, who joined before the trucks were commissioned and helped to set up the Crown plant. He was then made senior driver, with a reputation of keeping everyone well in line. Always a leader, he was at the head of the first strike when the drivers demanded more money and permission to join the Drivers' Union. Peter Langerman coped remarkably well with the situation which was rapidly defused when he said that they were welcome to join the Union, and the company would willingly pay Union rates, which he knew were fifteen per cent lower than their existing wages! The strike died a natural death.

Production at the Crown plant was soon put under a new company, Ready Mixed Concrete (Reef), which was registered on 13 August 1961, and Ready Mixed Concrete (SA) became solely a holding company. The official opening of the plant took place the following year on 24 January 1962. It was conducted by Dr H J van Eck, head of the Industrial Development Corporation, who said in his speech that Ready Mixed Concrete was a courageous pioneer in a field which was hardly known in South Africa, but which was firmly established in many overseas countries. He quoted that in 1961 there were 3 647 ready-mixed concrete producers in the United States of America, consuming 52% of that country's total cement production. He also remarked on the admirable courage of the men who had gone ahead with their plans in spite of a slackening off in the building and construction industry in South Africa at the time.

For some time Peter Langerman was the only person in RMC with an extensive knowledge of concrete technology, and he was responsible for the technical side as well as launching the business, a task which he tackled with great zeal. He made an arrangement with the PCI whereby all RMC's sampling and testing work was carried out by them until a laboratory was established at the Crown site. Initially Peter was helped in the laboratory by Joseph Lehlabi.

It is difficult now to appreciate the resistance to the concept of ready-mixed concrete which RMC experienced at first, and the effort which was made to put the product across as a working proposition, especially in the conservative building industry. The specifying authorities and consulting engineers were also highly suspicious of it. They all knew concrete as a material which was mixed on site and used almost instantly and many let it be known that they thought that only idiots would attempt to mix concrete several hours before it was used, not to mention the stupidity of driving it around the countryside! To overcome the opposition a comprehensive programme of educating potential customers was initiated, acknowledging that most people could make good concrete but stressing that it was not easy to make consistently good concrete. RMC, using sophisticated equipment, guaranteed consistent proportions of all raw materials and offered a total flexibility of volume, something which had never been possible before. The heavy responsibility of the quality of the concrete no longer rested on the builder but on those who were qualified to interpret and implement concrete specifications. The use of ready-mixed concrete was advocated in all jobs for economy of use and efficient service to the purchaser; it was obvious that no equipment would be needed on site, nor was there any need for storage or danger of material loss, nor would there be hours of wasted labour when no site mixing was being done. Delivery when needed would avoid bottlenecks which delay building programmes, and the builder was assured of a predetermined accurate cost per unit of concrete, which minimized estimating errors.

The men promoting ready-mixed concrete were convinced of its advantages but the concept was slow to catch on and sales were low at first. Everyone played Sherlock Holmes in the early days, investigating any demolition site or hole in the ground, any sign of building, in the hope of finding the right people to convince that they should use ready-mixed concrete. One day Robert Horowitz invited John to share his sandwiches once more, and to listen to another suggestion. He had seen the truckmixers standing idle in the Crown yard, waiting for orders which did not come, and he advised John to get the vehicles out in the public eye and arouse curiosity – get the truckmixers loaded up with a cubic yard of stone and have them driven around town with the mixers turning noisily to give the impression that ready-mixed concrete was in great demand! When anyone requested a delivery he was to be told that the order books were full, which would make the product even more desirable. The suggestion was put into practice for two weeks, and the agony of refusing orders that were so badly needed was more than recompensed when the demand for ready-mixed concrete increased steadily and the business was set firmly on a forward course.

Most of the early orders came from the smaller building contractors. Peter Langerman knew many of the builders personally and managed to persuade some of them, including John Barrow and Archie Gibb, to use ready-mixed concrete. In those early days Peter had an assistant, John Crow, who had worked for Ready Mixed Concrete in England. He maintained an extremely important relationship with the builders, explaining how ready-mixed concrete should be used and helping with the initial operations. His expert knowledge helped to break down the builders' resistance, and his contribution to the sales side of RMC was invaluable. Someone else who made a great contribution in those early days was Jim Reoch who had been taken on as a site and service man but was made manager of the Crown plant in 1962 when Peter was made general manager operating from Brailsford House. In those days feverish activity followed the receipt of an order: a call was hastily made on the old crank-handle telephone to get the concrete mix underway, and a handwritten delivery note was rushed out to the driver who then set off for the site – very different from modern control methods.

The first big order was from Frankipile SA for building operations at Windsor Gardens and further orders followed from other contractors, including Roberts Construction. RMC were grateful for all orders – even the all too frequent very last minute ones which came in only when all else had failed on the construction site. It was not unknown in the early months for most of the deliveries to be done after 3 pm. There was a gradual penetration into the civil engineering scene, and at the end of the first year of production John said, 'It is my belief that we are further ahead at this stage than I, for one, felt to be possible.' The end of 1962 saw a steady increase in the number of large orders and brought in for the first time a significant number of unsolicited enquiries about ready-mixed concrete.

In 1962 RMC was asked to provide concrete for the New Corner House being con-

Delivery and placing of concrete on an early contract in Johannesburg.

structed for Rand Mines on the corner of Fox and Sauer Streets in Johannesburg. No doubt John persuaded his partners that it would be showing a regrettable lack of faith if ready-mixed concrete were not used. Unfortunately technical problems were experienced on this particular job and the consulting engineers condemned the quality of the concrete column foundations in the basement. Suddenly the whole future of RMC was at stake! The Corner House building was already conspicuously well above ground level and if any demolition were necessary because the concrete foundations were not strong enough it would be difficult to persuade anyone ever to use ready-mixed concrete again. All turned out well, however. Sample cores were taken to be tested at the PCI, where a young technician, David Bath, proved that the concrete was in fact up to standard. David has always felt that his work must have impressed Peter Langerman because very soon after that he was asked to join RMC and take charge of the laboratory at Crown Mines.

It was an easy transfer. The PCI's policy was to promote concrete technology in any way and the director, Dr Sandy Fulton, was very happy to see one of his young technicians move into the ready-mixed concrete industry. David took over the laboratory in February 1964 and his quiet efficiency immediately lessened the load on Peter's shoulders. The growing technical knowledge within the company resulted in an increasingly superior product which gradually became an integral part of the construction industry.

Although large orders were the most satisfactory, RMC were always ready to help with smaller jobs and were quite willing to deliver small quantities. They even put out a

Ready-mixed concrete for the home owner.

guide for the home owner with do-it-yourself, step-by-step instructions, first pointing out that 'to mix two cubic metres of concrete yourself requires five tonnes of sand, stone, cement and water (and that is a lot to mix with a shovel)' and 'ready-mixed concrete is delivered ready for laying where and when you want it'. An amusing story is told about a load of concrete delivered to a home one day where the housewife instructed the driver – 'Please drop it at the front gate. It's a surprise for my husband who is going to concrete a path at the weekend.' Fortunately the driver did not discharge. The short life of ready-mixed concrete is a very real hazard and another story is told of a truck which broke down in a township where the concrete had to be dumped because it had been in the drum too long. News of the free concrete spread rapidly and five cubic yards of concrete disappeared as if by magic, some in wheelbarrows, some in cans (one of which a woman tried to carry on her head – with little success) and some even in an enamel chamber pot towed with a piece of rope by a small child!

RMC soon decided to move into the fast-developing East Rand and secure their position there. On 5 December 1962 Ready Mixed Concrete (East Rand) was registered and a plant was erected in Boksburg, starting production in September 1963 with Keith Robertson as manager. Gerry Labuschagne was sent over from the Crown plant to help establish the plant, and was appointed production manager. The Hume plant in Germiston was closed in 1964 as RMC (East Rand) were meeting the need in the area. Another plant was later established in Springs but remained in operation for only a short time.

As RMC operations became established on the Reef, Robert Horowitz's opposition, Pioneer Crushers, became increasingly apprehensive of his involvement and in 1962 they started their own ready-mixed concrete company in association with the cement producing companies Pretoria Portland Cement, Anglo Alpha Cement and Whites Cement (the last mentioned later became Blue Circle Cement). Ian Glauber was appointed manager of this company and a plant was erected on a site in Stafford, Eloff Street Extension. A distinctly unpleasant atmosphere developed as both companies strove to capture a market which as yet was minimal for even one to supply. Pioneer opened a plant in Minaar Street, Pretoria in 1964 while RMC were debating whether to go there, and another near the gasworks close to the centre of Johannesburg in 1965, establishing their position in prime areas.

By this time RMC had spread its operations into other parts of the country. John and his fellow directors were determined to move into key areas before any competition appeared, and even before operations were started on the Reef negotiations were underway in Port Elizabeth and Cape Town. John set out to establish strategic associations such as the one that RMC had with Consolidated Crusher Holdings, which would safeguard the supply of basic raw materials.

He had a friend, Andrew Savage, in Port Elizabeth who ran a family business with quarrying interests, and Ready Mixed Concrete (PE) was established in April 1961 in partnership with Savage and Son. The new company was based in the Savage and Son offices, with Andrew as chairman and first managing director, and the plant was set up in the quarry owned by Savage and Woodward Quarries. Andrew's business also dealt in hides and skins, and no one who worked in those offices ever forgot the pungent smell which floated up from the store below.

Brian Spiers, who was appointed manager in Port Elizabeth, was an engineer but had been working for the PCI for some time. Keen to return to the commercial world, he had accepted a position with Pioneer Ready Mixed Concrete in Australia and was preparing to leave South Africa with his wife when Andrew, whom he had known for some time, suggested that he take charge of establishing RMC (PE).

Brian accepted the offer and took up the position of manager on 1 December 1961 when the Port Elizabeth plant at Moregrove went into production. In early 1962 Savage and Son's quarrying interests were merged with Fraser Quarries, owned by Murray and Stewart of Cape Town, to form PE Holdings, of which Brian was appointed managing director. The shares of RMC (PE) were held 62,5% by PE Holdings and 37,5% by RMC (SA), and the Eastern Province Cement Company was a preference shareholder. Alto-

An early contract in Port Elizabeth: a factory floor for the Ford Motor Company, 1962.

gether the company was in a secure and healthy position.

The Eastern Cape went through a period of very rapid development in the sixties and early seventies and RMC (PE) out-performed the rest of the company in the first five years of RMC's existence. This indicated clearly the effectiveness of integrating quarrying and ready-mixed concrete operations, although it was some time before it was applied throughout the company.

Expansion into the Western Cape was largely financed by an increase in Rand Mines' interest in RMC. In Cape Town John turned to Murray and Stewart who had an interest in quarrying and who, as well known contractors, could help in the speedy establishment and recognition of the new industry. When Ready Mixed Concrete (Cape) was registered on 18 April 1961 Murray and Stewart held 33,3% of the shares and they have continued to do so. Funds were also provided by National Portland Cement Company (controlled by Pretoria Portland Cement) in Hout Street in Cape Town, and the chairman of this company, Edwin Keegan, was appointed the first chairman of Ready Mixed Concrete (Cape).

The Cape Town operations were managed by Bryan Johnson who had worked for Ready Mixed Concrete in the UK for several years, and in April 1956 had been sent out to investigate the possibility of setting up the industry in South Africa in partnership with Roberts Construction. The scheme was postponed, however, owing to the very low labour rates prevailing in Johannesburg at that time. Bryan married a South African girl and settled in this country, working for AE&CI at Modderfontein. When he heard about RMC's operations he decided to return to the ready-mixed concrete industry and joined the company on 18 September 1961. He was at first destined for Port Elizabeth but when Brian Spiers was appointed there Bryan took up the challenge of Cape Town instead.

RMC (Cape) started off in the happy position of having some substantial orders before they even started production. These had been negotiated by Peter Langerman and it was because of them that the considerable outlay of money to erect another plant was thought to be worthwhile. One of the orders was with Christiani and Nielsen on their contract for Part I of the Black River Parkway project. When this project was started before the RMC plant was in production, two truckmixers were sent down from the Reef to convey concrete, free of charge, from Christiani and Nielsen's contract at the Tygerberg reservoir so that the order was not lost. The project's first supply of concrete from RMC was delivered on 15 December 1961. R H Morris then gave the new company a large order of 8 000 cubic yards of ready-mixed concrete for their Langa contract. The civil engineering contractors gave it a favourable reception, but it was much more difficult to persuade the Cape Town builders to accept it – even the offer of a free load was refused!

The first plant in Cape Town was erected at Paarden Eiland, next to premises belonging to the Total Oil Company. The site was purchased in March 1961 and when Bryan saw it for the first time in October, there was little there – 'just green grass and yellow daisies' growing on the sea sand. Vehicles frequently used to get stuck in the sand, in spite of the ash which was put down to improve the surface. These delays could be very frustrating as the first truckmixers were used to their absolute maximum to meet all the orders. They started work each day at 4 o'clock in the morning and were often still on the road at 10 o'clock at night. The RMC (Cape) offices moved to Paarden Eiland from town in June 1962.

The Cape company developed successfully with a remarkably happy team spirit, which has been maintained over the years. It has always had a reputation for excellent staff relationships, creating a situation where many individuals have been able to realize their potential. Bryan was assisted by Frank Sokolic, who joined in 1965 as company secretary, and from the beginning by Frank Hansen, who was very actively involved in everything until an accident in 1974 restricted him to office work. The maintenance of plant and truckmixers was the responsibility of Dick Lattaney who came to RMC from Darling and Hodgson's Collondale contract in East London. Dick had a very able assistant, Setembiso Mafusini, who had joined Darling and Hodgson at the same time as Dick and moved with him to RMC. They made a very effective combination in the workshop. The first drivers for RMC (Cape) were 'Pottie' Potgieter and Elias van Rhyn. The first uniform for the drivers comprised overalls, berets and compulsory ties – it was a great concession when the drivers were allowed to go open-necked in summer! Bryan had a reputation of being a hard taskmaster, but it was rarely resented because he was always ready to turn his own hand to anything to get it done. On an occasion when one of the plants had no water, Elias, Bryan and two labourers set about digging trenches for a water pipe with a pick and shovel which they each used in turn. At the end of the day Bryan drove the truck back to the plant because Elias's hands were covered in blisters.

Johannesburg has always been South Africa's city of high-rise buildings but it was inevitable that they would appear in Cape Town as well, and their construction created a great demand for ready-mixed concrete. There was one much publicized contract at the end of 1967 for Mobil House in Hans Strydom Street where the concrete core was erected using a unique building technique known as a slide, which continued around the clock without ceasing for three weeks, using 4 000 cubic yards of ready-mixed concrete. To provide concrete for development in the city a plant was erected at Woodstock, on land belonging to the Railways. The intention initially was to work from there while the Paarden Eiland plant was being enlarged, but it turned out to be a long stay which came to an end only in 1980. Other plants were commissioned, one in 1964 at Bellville to provide for orders in the northern areas, and another in 1969 at Wetton. The latter was a modern plant, incorporating ideas which Bryan had brought back from a visit to Australia the previous year. That visit also resulted in RMC importing Australian Fowler Rex truckmixers. Mounted on International chassis, these replaced the Winget and Rapier truckmixers on the AEC chassis which had not kept abreast of new technology.

In the late sixties LTA began building a new shopping centre, Cavendish Square, in Claremont, Cape Town. They established a ready-mixed concrete plant on site, operated by a company called Pumpmix, owned at first by LTA, later in partnership with Darling and Hodgson. This company had developed the technique of pumping concrete

Delivering ready-mixed concrete to a Savage and Lovemore bridge contract near Somerset West, 1969.

and when RMC bought out Pumpmix in 1971 they took over its operations in the Cape and the Transvaal. When Cavendish Square was completed in 1972 the ready-mixed concrete plant was moved to a strategic position at Epping. Pumping soon became an integral part of RMC operations throughout the country because, although it is an expensive procedure caused by the abrasive nature of concrete creating exceptionally high maintenance costs, it extends the use of ready-mixed concrete significantly.

Ready Mixed Concrete (Natal) was registered on 15 May 1962 as a wholly-owned subsidiary of RMC (SA) some time before operations started. At one stage a plant was planned for the site of Coedmore Quarries where the new Durban Cement Company factory was to be built in 1963, but RMC then picked up the option held by Anglo Alpha Cement on the Thesens' depot at Maydon Wharf, when Thesens moved down to Knysna in the Cape. This was a more desirable position, with easy access to the harbour, the city, expressway projects and building developments in the central and South Beach and Marine Parade areas. It had the added advantage of a railway siding on site.

The plant erected at Maydon Wharf went into production in January 1964, four months before cement became available from the Durban Cement Company's factory. For those few months the cement had to be debagged, a messy and time-consuming job, and all the staff were very glad when bulk delivery from the factory commenced and facilitated operations.

While Peter Langerman was in Durban with the PCI he had worked indirectly with a man called Peter Asher, who had been at Hilton College with John, and his name came up when a manager was needed for the Natal company. Peter Asher, who was a civil engineer with Sayle and Rossaak, reinforced concrete engineers, knew little about the ready-mixed concrete industry and, as he himself confessed, 'didn't know what a ready-mixed concrete truck looked like.' However, he recognized a challenging opportunity coupled with strong personal support from both John and Peter, and readily accepted the job offered to him, joining RMC in September 1963. Gerry Labuschagne was appointed the first production manager, bringing with him the valuable experience gained from helping to establish the Crown and Boksburg plants. Because there was no telephone at first, and all communications were through their home, Peter's wife found herself helping as well, sorting out applications for drivers and accountants. Peter quickly settled into his new job, becoming so familiar with the truckmixers that he could sit in his office and recognize who was driving each truck by the way the gears were changed! He kept a close eye on operations, maintaining high standards – though one day a hapless individual was nearly fired for wearing overalls that were too white and clean!

The company was developed by a group of men, most of whom were destined to stay together for many years as a lively team. The first truckmixers were brought down from Crown by Len Holtman, who joined RMC (Natal) as a mechanic at the end of 1963. Noel Young, who came into contact with RMC in 1964, when he was sent to Maydon Wharf to drain the pits for the bins being installed, had within a few months joined the company as a dispatcher and from then on there was never a dull moment in Natal! The financial side was capably organized by Geoff Maynard, who gave valuable assistance to Peter for a number of years.

The initial reaction to ready-mixed concrete in Natal was not very favourable, and early orders were almost entirely dependent on personal contacts. Peter had been living in Natal for many years and he had on his staff, as technical sales manager, Bob Stevenson, who had spent many years in the construction industry. Both men liked to be out on the job which always made a favourable impression. One job in the early days was for Standard Building whom they had managed to persuade to try ready-mixed concrete on a construction site in the centre of Durban. The first delivery was scheduled for 5 am, and Standard Building's managing director was very impressed to find both Peter and Bob

Reconstruction of the Peter Pan playground, Durban, 1964.

there before him when he arrived to watch the pour. That incident sold many more cubic yards of concrete to the company!

The first concrete pour in Natal was for Federated Developments on a block of flats in Musgrave Road, followed by work for many of the large contracting companies. In the beginning all the mix designs were done by Peter Langerman up on the Reef but before long the Natal team was self-sufficient and the industry began to spread within the province. Inevitably the expansion followed the growth pattern of Natal at the time. Two of the most rapidly developing industrial areas were Pinetown and New Germany, and a plant was erected in Pinetown next to the drive-in cinema in 1965 under the supervision of Rod Phillipson. The following year another plant was erected at Isipingo, to provide concrete for the development on the south coast. Its first contract was for the canals which were to drain the flats for the big Prospecton township.

By 1965 RMC was thus firmly established in key areas of South Africa – the Reef, Port Elizabeth, Cape Town and Durban – and had built up a fleet of over a hundred truck-mixers. The initial resistance to the new concept of ready-mixed concrete was breaking down too and the industry was beginning to face the future with confidence. The development had been facilitated by RMC moving closer to Darling and Hodgson in 1963 when John and Jack sold their private shareholdings in RMC to them at the time when they became part of Union Corporation, a move which provided strong financial backing.

In 1964 a new and exciting venture came about through a personal friendship between John and Bill Metter. RMC (SA) joined up with L&F Metter to form Cranemix Plant Hire, a company which hired out cranes to place large volumes of concrete over a large area in a short time. They soon became popular with builders for all kinds of operations. The use of cranes accelerated building operations and facilitated a much quicker turn-around of RMC truckmixers. However, the rapid acceptance of cranes fulfilled the main objective of participating in Cranemix, and in 1968 RMC sold their interest in the company to their partners, having disposed of all the cranes that were on hire to the contractors using them.

The commissioning of RMC's first mobile plant took place in Pietermaritzburg in

Jack Plane handing over the keys of RMC's 100th truckmixer to John Hodgson, December 1964.

1965. The concept of the mobile plant offered greater versatility to the ready-mixed concrete industry, extending its use beyond the normal limited radius from fixed plants into rural projects throughout the country. It also provided a means of testing the potential of an area before investing in the expense of a permanent plant. The mobile plant was moved up to the Reef in 1966 and established at Vanderbijlpark, under Jim Reoch, who recognized an opportunity to use slagment from local Iscor steelworks in the production of ready-mixed concrete. It was an idea which could have been successful, but the available market was not large enough to support the plant and it was closed down in 1968. That was the year when RMC (East Rand) moved in to take advantage of one of the most rapidly developing areas of South Africa by transferring the Crown plant to Spartan, strategically placed to serve Isando, Kempton Park, Buccleuch and Bedfordview.

RMC was the pioneer of the industry in South Africa but on the Reef Pioneer Ready Mixed Concrete was a very strong competitor. The market was not large enough to accommodate two ready-mixed concrete operations and, realizing that neither would survive on its own, in 1965 the rival companies decided to merge. Pioneer's holding company was Parem Enterprises, comprising the cement producers and Pioneer Crushers, and half of their interest in Pioneer Concrete was sold to RMC (SA). RMC acquired a reciprocal 50%. The merger did not include operations in the Cape Province, and RMC retained responsibility for all of Natal and the East Rand, while Pioneer managed the operations in Johannesburg and Pretoria. The two companies maintained their individuality very strongly, a situation accentuated by their different coloured trucks and separate depots.

The partnership with Pioneer continued for many years, but it was a stormy relationship all the way, largely owing to the two companies having different objectives. RMC always felt that Pioneer was too greatly influenced by the cement-producing companies whose main concern was to sell more cement. The two ran as separate companies and combined at board level where there was a constant divergence of policy.

In Natal RMC absorbed their rival operations with two acquisitions during the sixties. A small company called Supermix was operating an efficient automated plant at Chatsworth and good quality truckmixers. When it got into difficulties in 1964 RMC took the company over and instantly increased their fleet from four to twelve! In 1965 SA Crushers started a ready-mixed concrete business called Rapidmix which RMC absorbed two years later.

The Natal company made another acquisition in the mid sixties, this time on the human side. When Pioneer and Ready Mixed Concrete merged David Bath was asked to go across to Pioneer as they had a shortage of technical people. He declined the offer and was about to be transferred to the East Rand when technical problems in Natal arose and he was sent there to assist. Peter Asher invited him to stay and David and his family moved to Natal, where they settled happily. David fitted readily into the efficient and successful Natal team which has always been a winner, with a tremendous dedication of purpose. In early 1973 he was appointed technical manager.

Another popular member of the Natal team was Peter Randles, who had joined RMC in 1966 as manager of the Pietermaritzburg area and was later promoted to sales manager for Natal. He was well known and liked for his buoyant optimism and easy wit, and his flair for promoting company relations. He will always be remembered for his amusing 'Book of Hodge' which was the local RMC magazine.

Rand Mines retained their 50% interest in RMC (SA) until 1968 when Darling and Hodgson first acquired a proportion of the Rand Mines shareholding and RMC became a subsidiary. A series of negotiations increased D&H's shareholding until RMC became a wholly-owned subsidiary just before D&H went public in 1973. In the same year the three senior managers, Peter Langerman, Peter Asher and Bryan Johnson, were all made directors of RMC (SA) which involved them more deeply in planning the future of the company within the D&H Group. Peter Langerman was appointed managing director, a position he held until the following year when he handed over his responsibilities to Peter Asher. Peter ran the company from Natal, while Peter Langerman took charge of a new division comprising Group interests in building materials until he left D&H in July 1974.

The rapid development of D&H as a public company included further organic growth of RMC. The industry moved into the Orange Free State in 1975 with the establishment of a plant at St Helena gold mine near Welkom and there was a steady increase in Group quarrying and stone-crushing interests, which were initiated in order to protect supplies of sand and aggregate for RMC operations. In 1977 an Australian company, Randmix, was purchased for its quarrying activities. It also had five ready-mixed concrete operations on the Reef, which offered significant competition to Pioneer Ready Mixed Concrete. This caused considerable friction between the partners, and led to the termination of the partnership. In spite of this unhappy relationship Ian Glauber established a lasting friendship with John Hodgson and has remained on good terms with RMC in subsequent years. Randmix's ready-mixed concrete operations were sold to Pioneer, who took over all operations on the Reef and in the Orange Free State and relinquished their shareholding in Natal. Darling and Hodgson retained the quarry and stone-crushing

The Roadhouse plant.

operations of Randmix, which provided the nucleus of their further development in this field, leading to the establishment of long-term reserves of raw materials.

RMC operations remained under separate management from quarrying for some time. In 1977 the Group was divided into two divisions, construction and industrial, and a materials division was created within the latter to control ready-mixed concrete, quarrying and stone-crushing operations. Bryan Johnson was appointed managing director of RMC throughout the Republic and Eddie Meyer became manager of the Cape operations. Bill Hooper joined Bryan Johnson in Cape Town as Group accountant for RMC (SA), transferred from Paul's Sand in the Transvaal. The following year a newcomer to the Group, Don Lanigan, was appointed managing director of a materials division within which regional managers became responsible for both ready-mixed concrete and quarrying activities in their areas for the first time. Bryan relinquished his position as managing director of RMC (SA) to take charge of the wider materials field in the Cape.

Meanwhile steady growth had taken place in Natal where David Bath was appointed

Delivering ready-mixed concrete to a Savage and Lovemore contract at Richards Bay.

manager of the coastal region in 1974 and, a year later, of RMC (Natal), moving out of the technical world to shoulder the responsibilities of management which broadened his horizons considerably. The Roadhouse plant was commissioned in 1973 on the bank of the Umgeni river to supply the northern areas of Durban, and in 1974 RMC (Zululand) was established under Des Cole with the Alton plant at Richards Bay. This was growing at an incredible pace as the new harbour and industrial area developed. Another plant was set up that year at Esikhaweni where a large township was being built near Richards Bay.

In 1977 the White Road plant, which had operated for a while on a temporary site secured on a month's notice from the Durban City Council in the early seventies, was moved to Tongaat to provide for the growing community attracted by the sugar industry. The Esikhaweni plant was moved to Empangeni the following year, where it became known as Ninians.

In 1978 David readily accepted the extra responsibility of quarrying in Natal, recognizing the advantages that would follow the amalgamation of operations. Bill Hooper

The RMC plant in Clairwood Quarry.

was appointed financial manager of the region, and he and David established a good relationship from the start, based in no small degree on their shared passion for long-distance running. The following year David went to London to study the Sloan Programme at the London Business School and Graham Hardy succeeded him in Natal. Graham was an old-Hiltonian and had been a D&H bursary student, graduating from the University of the Witwatersrand as a civil engineer at the end of 1973. Initially Graham had worked for Hucrete in the Transvaal and then for RMC in the Cape before his appointment in Natal. During that year Peter Randles' good humour and cheerfulness were lost to the Group when he died in November; he was missed by all who knew him.

In December 1978 the Maydon Wharf plant was closed down and replaced by a new plant in Clairwood Quarry which had come into the Group the previous year, and the property was sold in 1979. Plants were also established at Phoenix, the growing Indian industrial and residential area among the rolling hills of green sugar-cane just north of Durban, and at Port Shepstone and Park Rynie to exploit the building boom on the south

RMC (Cape) supplied concrete for the Exhibition Hall in Cape Town.

coast which had started when the Holiday Inn casino was sited in Transkei just south of Port Edward. A cement factory opened at Sumuma to provide for this and other developments. By 1983 Graham had gathered around him a close team which included many old-timers who had become managers – Len Holtman in maintenance, Noel Young in operations, Rod Phillipson in marketing, and Bill Hooper in finance. Des Erikson (another runner) was technical manager in Natal until he was promoted to head office in 1981. This position was filled by Peter Steyn from Embecon. Two brothers, Willie and Tommy Edwards, were the production managers in Pietermaritzburg and Zululand; they had both joined RMC in the mid sixties as drivers, with a third brother who did not stay with the company for long.

There was comparable growth in the Western Cape, with expansion into developing areas. Plants were established at Saldanha Bay, in 1974 in Murray and Stewart's new quarry Vredenberg and a second one in 1977, and in Somerset West. In 1975 a plant at Bellville South was taken over from Ritemix and operated under that name until it became an RMC plant in June the following year. Another plant was established near Cape Town in the same year at Atlantis, where industries were being established with accompanying residential growth, and at Mitchell's Plain to provide for a mass housing scheme on the Cape Flats. The Cape's first mobile plant was established for a period at the De Hoek cement factory in 1978 and two years later a modern plant was opened at Paarden Eiland, which had been only an administration and workshops centre for some years while the Woodstock plant was in operation. The latter was closed down in 1980 when the lease terminated. Several members of the original Cape team enjoyed the challenge of

The RMC plant at Mitchell's Plain, Cape.

The Hugo river viaduct was built with ready-mixed concrete, using the incremental launching method of construction.

this rapid expansion. Bryan, as managing director, was the driving force, and Frank Sokolic, who had been financial manager for some years and in 1978 was appointed a director of RMC (Cape), was also there, as was Geoff Jordaan, the production manager, who had spent several years with the company as a driver before assuming managerial responsibilities.

By 1983 there were eleven plants in operation, from Grabouw to the east of Cape Town, to Paarl in the north, and at Montague Gardens. The Paarl plant supplied one of the most beautiful construction sites in the country – the Hugo river viaduct, carrying the N1 between Klein Drakenstein and the future Du Toit's Kloof tunnel. In 1982 a central despatch office was established at Paarden Eiland from where all the plants were controlled by means of sophisticated systems and radio communications which considerably improved efficiency. This system proved highly successful in an area where all the plants were within a short distance of each other. In 1983 the marketing division of RMC (Cape) was moved temporarily to Salt River while new offices were built for it at Paarden Eiland.

Over the years pumping had become increasingly significant in RMC operations in the Cape, and had spread to the rest of the company. Pumps place concrete far more quickly than wheelbarrows and also increase the accessibility of many building sites. By 1983 an average of twenty per cent of all company operations were using ready-mixed concrete pumped with their own pumps.

At the time the sales manager was Bernard Jelley, who had joined RMC fourteen years earlier as assistant to Bryan Johnson with considerable experience of the industry in the United Kingdom. At first in charge of the laboratory, he soon became technical manager and later was appointed sales manager. He carried out extensive research into the use of

Coastal work in the Cape.

pulverized fuel ash as a cement substitute in concrete, and at the end of 1983 was appointed manager of resource development, a position which held great scope.

The Eastern Cape retained independent management under Brian Spiers. Operations grew as the area prospered and plants operated in Umtata, Butterworth, East London, King William's Town, Uitenhage and George, as well as in Port Elizabeth. After the mid seventies the boom in the area faded and industry suffered a severe set-back, but in the late seventies operations were established in Transkei and Ciskei to meet the needs of these developing areas. In 1978 PE Holdings rationalized the management of its component activities under the name of Quarryman: quarry products, ready-mixed concrete operations and transport were combined within three regions – Port Elizabeth, East London and George. RMC retained their Cape partners Murray and Roberts in Quarryman. In 1982 Quarryman was awarded the national productivity award for strengthening its operations effectively to accommodate the economic recession of the past few years. The general manager of the Port Elizabeth area of Quarryman, Bernard Pakes, had been with the Group in various capacities before his appointment as marketing manager of PE Holdings.

At the end of 1980 Don Lanigan was transferred to the Group engineering division and David Bath returned from London to take up the position of managing director of materials. At the end of David's second year as managing director, the profits of the materials division exceeded those of the construction division for the first time, through a series of acquisitions and worthy effort in every profit centre.

The materials division made a significant acquisition in 1983 with the purchase of Kier

Mobile quality control unit on a road contract in Natal.

and Cawder which considerably increased the Group's quarrying reserves. A ready-mixed concrete plant was established in their Olive Hill Quarry in Bloemfontein. David decided to restructure the division into five geographical regions. In each region the different product lines inevitably became increasingly interdependent and the new organization provided mutual strength as ready-mixed concrete and quarrying operations ran in tandem to serve the same market.

Each of the five regions established a central laboratory which maintained close quality control over all company products. Mobile laboratories in the field contributed further to this vital aspect of production, and in 1983 RMC took a significant step towards satisfying the needs of the future with the establishment for the first time of a temporary fully equipped and staffed laboratory on site. This was done to facilitate the fast track building methods used in the construction of Amlife Towers at 362 West Street in Durban by providing the contractors with concrete strength reports at the site. The modern trend towards such methods can only be to the advantage of the ready-mixed concrete industry.

Above left
Moregrove plant, Port Elizabeth: the original plant on the right and the more recently commissioned one on the left.

Above right
Ready-mixed concrete from top to bottom at 362 West Street, Durban.

In line with the rest of the Group, comprehensive training has become important at all levels within RMC. From the early days driver training has included a basic knowledge of concrete technology as well as an understanding of all aspects of the trucks and mixers, and to ensure that their drivers are important representatives of the company, RMC have always schooled them in customer relations as well. Over the years training has been extended to all employees, from basic skills to managerial expertise, including industrial relations. In all regions employees are encouraged, with financial assistance, to further their education by studying outside the Group, in particular the City and Guilds concrete technology correspondence course from London.

The successful implementation of training methods imbued RMC with confidence that they would continue to satisfy their customers, sensitive to the possibility of changing demands, with the ability to adapt, and follow a path of success into the future.

Mazista

'In what might go down as being one of the most rapid moves ever made by the Group and during which a great deal of midnight oil was burned, control has been gained of Mazista Limited, a public quoted company listed under the Industrial Building section of the Johannesburg Stock Exchange.' This is how Mazista was introduced in a company news-sheet circulated to D&H employees on 14 September 1973. The acquisition was said to be in line with the Group's overall policy of diversification, and was made just as D&H itself was going public, adding to the excitement and buoyant atmosphere within the Group at this time.

Mazista had been running at a loss for some time but, knowing that the quarry was the largest of its kind in the world and that the slate was of a very high quality, D&H were confident that they could turn the situation around. They also saw that Mazista's production of lightweight blocks and custom masonry could be useful in the prevailing shortage of bricks at the time. Within a couple of years the initial purchase of 65,3% of the registered shareholding was increased to 100% and the absence of outside shareholders facilitated the integration of Mazista with other Group activities.

When D&H acquired Mazista the slate quarry had been in existence for over forty-five years. The property is in the western Transvaal between Swartruggens and Koster, covering over 2 000 hectares. The Elands river runs through the land, most of the way in a deep gorge, the steep cliffs on either side revealing the immense reserves of slate under the surface of the ground. There is evidence of past quarrying going back to the last century when the local farmers took what they needed for their own purposes, but the first commercial exploitation only began after the farm Klipbankfontein was purchased in 1927 by the founders of Mazista, Messrs Schmidt and Bernstein.

The name Mazista is said to have come about as a result of a local tribe having been massacred in the middle of the last century by Mzilikazi, one of Chaka's generals. The mother of the tribal chief, whose name was Zista, was the only survivor, and she remained in the area living on one of the Boer farms. She was known as 'the mother of Zista' – in Afrikaans, 'die ma van Zista', which became Mazista over the years. Don Cronje, one of the first employees, joined D&H with Mazista in 1973 and remained with the company long enough before retiring to be awarded a forty-five year long-service award. He could remember the early days when there were just two quarrymen and a few black labourers, and all the transporting was done by donkeys. Amongst other old-timers was Beattie Sharpe who during her forty years with Mazista had worked her way up from 'a pipsqueak shorthand typist' to the sales side of the business where she was renowned for her friendly voice on the telephone.

The Depression years in the thirties were a bad period for the quarry and there were some months when there was no pay. Better times came, however, and after the war experienced slaters were brought from overseas, the community at the quarry gradually grew larger and the Mazista village developed. It was an isolated community which had to be self-sufficient, and the village catered for all the needs of the people who worked there and their families, with church, school, clinic, post office, shop and a clubhouse with sports facilities. Not unexpectedly, all these buildings were roofed in the local slate. This close community epitomized the extended family concept of D&H, John Hodgson's 'family of families'.

Soon after D&H took over Mazista in 1973 Paul's Sand was acquired, and a degree of rationalization resulted in Mazista's marketing and transport administration being integrated with that of Paul's at Honeydew. A very positive sales campaign was started,

Cutting slate in the quarry.

with particular emphasis on exporting, in the knowledge that the colours and variations in texture of Mazista slate were found nowhere else in the world. An R800 000 expansion programme was started at the quarry covering the three product centres which catered for roofing, flooring or slabs. There were successes on the local market including the largest contract in Mazista's history for the roofing of the Mmabatho Sun hotel in Bophutatswana. The entire roof was completed in the record time of twelve weeks at a rate equivalent to one house per day instead of the normal one per week – an incredible achievement. Slate was used in the homes of many of the Bophutatswana ministers and also the new civic centre in Rustenburg. D&H demonstrated their loyalty by decorating their reception areas in both the Hyde Park head office and Tanker Services (Natal) with slate. The enthusiasm aroused for Mazista products was revealed in the enticing words of a sales pamphlet produced for the retail trade: 'Slate is imprisoned colour. Forged in the richest of ochres, red, blue and greens that nature first created four hundred million years ago. Slate is forever.' This led to other less traditional uses for slate, such as swimming pool surrounds, shower cubicles and kitchens, and a range of slate coffee tables.

There was an early improvement in the company's profits and everyone involved with Mazista found it a fascinating business. Unfortunately the good results were not maintained. Delays in delivery of new machinery held up the expansion programme and there were problems in finding enough labour to increase production. Sales were affected by the recession in the building industry in South Africa in the mid seventies. In an attempt to improve the situation the division of Mazista which made building blocks was sold and in 1980 it was decided to turn away from mechanization at the quarry in order to reduce the tremendous wastage of material. The extraction operations and subsequent handling of the great slabs of slate were returned to the human hand which works more delicately than a powerful machine. It was a move back to using basic tools such as hammers, chisels, crowbars and guillotines, which were forged in Mazista's own blacksmith's shop, and a return to the old days as the area resounded with the sound of metal on slate. The result was a considerably increased yield. A new promotional centre was opened in Blairgowrie near Johannesburg – 'The house that slate built' – for local sales, and the export market, absorbing sixty-five to seventy per cent of production, stretched far afield, most successfully to Australia and even further to New Zealand and Japan as well as Europe and America. In 1980 the Mazista head office was established at Honeydew on property belonging to Paul's Sand, based in an old house which was revamped to

Mmabatho Sun: an illustration of the extensive use of roofing slate.

demonstrate a variety of slate applications and further promote sales.

By 1981 Mazista was making a contribution to the overall success of the Group materials division and had been awarded several significant contracts including the extensive roofing of the Barclays Centre for Management Study in Sandton. It had, however, been one of the division's biggest headaches for several years, and many people felt that too much energy was expended for too little return. The Group had also grown too large to deal with such a specialized product line, and it was therefore decided to part company. In April 1983 Mazista was sold to National Acceptances Limited. One of the foremost conditions of the sale was that it should be in the best interests of the management and employees, the majority of whom stayed with Mazista. No doubt for as long as the beauty of natural slate is appreciated the quarry will continue to echo with the sounds of activity.

Paul's Sand

Sand being shovelled or pumped out of the Jukskei river on the outskirts of Johannesburg was a common sight until the early fifties when the sand was no longer readily accessible. Amongst those involved was a small business which was later to become a vital part of Darling and Hodgson.

Before and during the war a small sand-washing plant was operated on the banks of the river behind Alexandra Township by Adelmo Ansermino. After the war the plant was sold to Otello Nucci who also ran a small transport business. With the help of one of Adelmo's sons-in-law, Aldo de Luca, Otello operated a fleet of five trucks from a small corrugated iron shed beside the river at 42, 3rd Street, Kew, transporting sand, stone, garden materials and occasionally rubbish. Over the years the emphasis moved from transport to sand and in 1955 a quarry was established in Lombardy, just a few kilometres from the office, with a plant which for those days was large and sophisticated. The company established for these operations was called Paul's Sand.

When Otello left to further his interest in transport Aldo formed a partnership with Gordon Frew, a young man who had for some years been writing up the books for Paul's Sand in his spare time. In 1957 they established a remarkable working relationship based on complete mutual faith and trust. Gordon ran the accounting, financial and administrative side of the business with clear-thinking efficiency and Aldo concentrated capably on the practical aspects with a good degree of common sense. They were joined in 1959 by Rose Baiocchi, one of Adelmo Ansermino's daughters, who worked in the office with Lucas the clerk, a loyal and trusted employee who was to remain with the company for many years. Rose used to type out the quotes – there was one for D F Corlett for delivered river sand at 7/6 a yard and Darling and Hodgson used to take the odd delivery for Tarmac Industries.

It soon became obvious that larger deposits of sand were needed, and Gordon and Aldo also felt a need for a permanent base owned by themselves because the Lombardy property was only leased on a yearly renewable basis. In 1959 they purchased 120 morgen in Honeydew, about 19 kilometres north of Johannesburg. This was an enormous commitment and proved to be the turning-point in the history of Paul's Sand. The property was farmland, and for the next year a great deal of money was spent, for no return, and much energy expended in developing infrastructure, offices and plant. Honeydew seemed desperately dry in comparison with Lombardy, and top priority was given to building a dam on the new property – the first of many. Because of the limited water supply there had to be a recycling process for washing the sand and this involved the establishment of slimes dams. Aldo had learnt through bitter experience about the problems of slimes control, and he made sure that the dams were well built and efficiently controlled. He also designed and built the first sand-washing plant on the property which was to continue operations steadily for over twenty years with only slight modifications.

It was a small business, but the staff were loyal and dedicated and a reputation for excellent service was soon established. Paul's Sand became well known as suppliers of fine aggregate materials on the Witwatersrand, willing to deliver at any time of day or night. The first big customer for sand was Parkview Golf Course, while the biggest client was Ready Mixed Concrete operating from Crown Mines. When Peter Langerman telephoned for sand everyone jumped! There were no salesmen at first and all the selling and marketing was done by telephone; the only advertising was on the trucks or by word of mouth.

A Kya-MP truck and Rose Baiocchi with some of the company's longest serving employees.

It soon seemed desirable to enlarge their market coverage, and during the sixties other small sand quarries were purchased. The first was Maraisburg Sand, situated only a few kilometres from Paul's Sand, which had hindered Paul's initial progress because they were already popular amongst potential customers. The others were Rand Sand, Chloorkop, the Houtkoppen plant near Randburg, which was used to supply sand to Randmix who had become a major customer, and Sewefontein, which produced a very fine sand of exceptionally high quality. These quarries all operated independently with central management control and regular visits from Aldo de Luca.

A number of transport companies were also acquired during this period, small companies with only a few trucks and few customers, which had fallen on bad times. These included Strick's Cartage, Belgravia Cartage, Booysen's Transport, Kya Sand and MP Sand Suppliers. The last two were put together to form Kya-MP as a subsidiary of Paul's Sand. Kya-MP absorbed all the other companies, gathering together the conglomeration of vehicles under new colours of green and white. It was never acknowledged that the new company, of which Rose Baiocchi took sole charge, was associated with Paul's Sand and it operated outwardly as opposition. Rose ran Kya-MP independently within the Paul's Group and her warm nature combined with an astute business sense soon developed it into an exceptionally efficient and successful business.

During the sixties there was a natural expansion into a wider field of activities. In 1966 Paul's extended their service to builders by investing in a building materials company, Ranch Building Materials, out of which developed an associated joinery shop. These were established in a new shopping centre, constructed at a cost of over R200 000, at the crossroads in Honeydew, providing shops, a post office, banks and an estate agency in a very strategic position. Two garages, Meteor Motors and Honeydew Motors, were also developed and, in anticipation of an increased desire for 'country living' amongst those who work in Johannesburg, 140 acres were set aside for property and development. Two small industries were purchased to make use of the clay which accumulated as a by-product of sand washing, and their factories were moved to Honeydew. These were Belmont Tiles, which manufactured high quality roof tiles, and Figula, a pottery company, in 1966 and 1970 respectively. Figula's attractive handmade domestic pottery was designed by Pieter Grobbelaar, who moved to Honeydew from a small studio in Panorama.

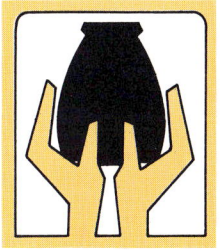

During this period of expansion Terry Rolfe joined Paul's as managing director, taking overall charge of the many different operations. Having qualified as an accountant and gained experience overseas, Terry did not want to be immersed in a large corporation and he found a happy niche working with Gordon and Aldo. In 1970 Bill Hooper joined the company to take charge of administration and finance, rapidly establishing a good friendship and working relationship with Terry which created a strong administrative team.

Another acquisition was a ready-mixed mortar business called LSM (Lime Sand Mortar); the entire plant was moved from Roodepoort to Honeydew at the end of 1970. Ed-

Above
The LSM plant at Honeydew.

Right
Pieter Grobbelaar and Albert Moleta in the Figula factory.

die Meyer took charge and set about convincing the building industry that his products were invaluable. He could quote the ancient structures of the Colosseum and Hadrian's Wall, amongst others, as confirmation of the successful use of lime in construction! Eddie laid firm foundations for future development before leaving LSM in 1977 to take charge of Ready Mixed Concrete (Cape).

Paul's established an excellent profit growth record, increasing three-fold between 1970 and 1974. This made the company very attractive to D&H who had been considering it as a source of continued supply for their ready-mixed concrete operations on the Witwatersrand where there was an overall shortage of exploitable natural aggregate. In 1974 they acquired a 91,3% interest in the entire Paul's Group, excluding Meteor Motors but including a team of refreshingly enthusiastic people. Amongst the employees were

D&H Quarries, Honeydew, 1983.

nine men who in 1976 received D&H twenty-one year long-service awards, with a combined length of service of two hundred and twenty-three years! The remaining shareholding reflected the interest retained by the company management which continued with Terry Rolfe at the helm, though Gordon Frew and Aldo de Luca left at that stage. The following year the building industry slumped dramatically, severely affecting Paul's building supply business, and D&H decided to sell it in 1976. The shopping complex and garage were continued for some time, with an interesting diversion into car dealership, at first General Motors and later Ford. This proved very successful and the service was extended to include Impala Caravans.

None of these operations reflected the traditional D&H image, however, and they were sold within a few years. Belmont Tiles ceased production soon after D&H took over and Figula was sold at the end of 1979.

D&H's other quarrying interests were at first integrated with those of Paul's under Terry, and when he left in 1976 to broaden his experience in other fields, a D&H sand and quarries division was created under Peter Asher, incorporating Paul's Sand, Evander Crushers, Shires Quarry, Mazista and Hucrete. At the same time Paul Nucci was appointed manager of the Paul's group of companies – a proud occasion for the son of one of the founders of the business. Bill Hooper, who had continued as administrative manager when D&H purchased Paul's, was transferred in 1977 to Ready Mixed Concrete in Cape Town. His position was filled by Ross Heron, who soon made a significant contribution to the rationalization of operations within the Group division.

Kya-MP also became part of D&H Quarries but was run independently by Rose Baiocchi in a highly service-orientated and personalized operation. She dealt mainly in the retail market for the smaller builders, leaving to D&H Quarries the larger bulk orders for the big customers, like Transitmix, Pioneer Ready Mixed Concrete and many of the road construction companies. It was an exciting day in 1978 when Rose was appointed a director of Kya-MP – the first woman director in D&H. This made no difference to her total involvement in everyday operations, however; her drivers all knew that nothing escaped Rose's attention and that she would readily even climb under their trucks to check that all was well.

LSM made good progress within the D&H Group and their products increasingly became an integral part of the construction industry. Their success was demonstrated in some prominent contracts – black coloured brick mortar was used in the SABC television complex at Auckland Park, and at the Military Hospital in Pretoria fourteen million bricks were laid using only LSM mortar without any cement. At Randfontein Estates Gold Mining Company a large amount of brick mortar was supplied to Roberts Construction for the 5,5 million bricks used in the new kitchen and hostels complex. The company continued to develop until the demand for its products warranted the establishment of another plant which, after two years of planning and construction, was finally commissioned in Chloorkop Quarry on the outskirts of Kempton Park in 1982. This was primarily to extend services to the East Rand and Pretoria markets, and the higher level of technical sophistication provided for the manufacture of coloured screeds and mortars. LSM also manufactured and delivered gunnites for the swimming pool industry. The company gradually entered into a closer working relationship with Ready Mixed Concrete, who were already marketing these products in the Cape and Natal, and at the end of 1983 the LSM vehicles were all changed to the RMC colours of green and yellow to enhance this image.

Any form of quarrying is inevitably a rape of the earth but the modern philosophy is one of restoring the land when the machines have stopped working and Darling and Hodgson wholeheartedly endorse this. In 1981 a rehabilitation programme for the Honeydew property was drawn up to be executed on completion of quarry activities in the future, demonstrating D&H's awareness of the environment and indicating their intention of developing the property as a profitable exercise in the long term. They have al-

View of Chloorkop Quarry with the LSM II plant in the foreground.

Above
Loading a D&H Quarries truck with sand at the Honeydew quarry.

Left
The planned reclamation scheme for the Honeydew property.

ready started planting trees in strategic areas in accordance with the plan.

In 1983, after further acquisitions and rationalization, D&H Quarries became the core of the northern region of the Group materials division under Ross Heron, who had been appointed general manager of the quarries division in 1980 when Peter Asher returned to Natal as regional director for the Group. Philip du Plessis, who had been transferred from Natal at the end of 1981 as production manager of quarries in the Transvaal, assumed responsibility for operations on the Reef. The northern region covers a range of quarrying and stone-crushing operations as well as LSM and Kya-MP, with head offices at Honeydew, where the sand reserves exploited first by Paul's Sand guarantee a working future of many years.

Natal Quarries

In the earlier part of this century the quarrying industry in the Durban area largely comprised family businesses, passing from father to son and often combined with small-scale contracting operations. The work was very labour intensive, at first done mostly by African and Indian women, and later by men, on a task-work basis. In recent years there has been a great reduction in labour numbers resulting from extensive mechanization. In 1932 the quarrying and stone-crushing industry in the area was rationalized through the formation of Associated Quarries, which most of the quarry owners joined. This organization introduced the quota system which has controlled the output of each quarry for many years.

D&H's first venture into quarrying in Natal took place in 1973 when they acquired Shire & Co, later known as Shires Quarry, a large hard-rock quarry situated north of Durban. This quarry had been in the hands of the Johnsen family since 1923, providing material for their small contracting business and becoming a proprietary company in 1957.

Originally all their transport was horse-drawn but steam wagons were later introduced and eventually motor vehicles. At first these seemed hardly an improvement – there was no shelter for the drivers, and the solid-tyred lorries lurched along in top gear at seven miles per hour, carrying seven cubic yards of stone. After the war Shires was awarded a big corporation contract for supplying and delivering sand on a yearly basis, and for this a small fleet of Albion trucks was purchased, which carried through until the Johnsen family decided to switch to Mercedes trucks.

There was always a problem with water seepage at Shires because the bottom of the quarry was lower than the surrounding water table. The original diesel pumps for removing the water used to break down frequently and the area was known as Jackson's Pool, because an unfortunate mechanic named Jackson used to strip and plunge in to effect repairs. The diesel pumps were eventually replaced by more efficient electric ones.

In the early seventies the two Johnsen brothers who were running the quarry decided to sell it in order to pursue other interests. D&H, who were looking for ways to provide

Shire & Co truck making a delivery to a D&H contract at Reservoir Hills, 1955.

the vital raw materials for their ready-mixed concrete operations, recognized the potential at Shires and made a favourable offer which was accepted. At first the quarry was run independently with the manager reporting directly to head office.

Operations were soon extended to the production of many grades of sand from waste stone products, and within a few years new offices had been built, plant improved and a new hostel constructed for black labourers. A liaison committee was set up to improve communications between labour and management which resulted, among other things, in a comprehensive training scheme for black workers. The overall result was a rewarding increase in production.

Adjoining land was purchased over the years to extend quarrying reserves, and in 1977 the Umgeni Quarries were purchased, primarily for their addition to the Associated Quarries' quota which had for some time been limiting production at Shires. The quarry itself was practically worked out and, having retained what was useful to them, D&H terminated the lease within a few months. In the same year Clairwood Quarry, covering a large area at Sea View just south of Durban, was acquired. This hard-rock quarry had been owned by the Mowatt family since the early 1920s.

The rock at Shires is dwyka-tillite, and Clairwood comprises two areas, the Blue Quarry which is also dwyka-tillite with dolomite, and the Quartzite Quarry with Table Mountain sandstone. The Umhlatuzana river running through Clairwood Quarry flooded its banks in 1933, doing considerable damage. Years later, at the end of the seventies, the river was canalized to prevent further flooding and at the same time extend the quarrying area. In the quarry's early days most of the work was done by hand. Rows of Indian women chipped away with hammers, making railway ballast, and the labour was paid each day either in cash or with special tokens. The latter were copper discs with Mowatt's Quarry stamped on one side and the value, from 6d to 10/–, on the other. For many years all the products were railed into Durban from the quarry and transported from there to clients by horse-drawn scotchcart.

Clairwood came into the Darling and Hodgson Group through their purchase of Construction Materials, an Australian company with ready-mixed concrete interests (Randmix) as well as quarries and crushers, which was holding an option on the quarry at the time. Of the seventy-nine people who were working for Clairwood in 1977 a large proportion had worked at the quarry for over ten years (nineteen of them over twenty years). When the Group materials division celebrated long service awards in 1979, those from Clairwood totalled five hundred and twenty-one years' service, with Emos Mzimande having completed an impressive forty-four year stint!

The manager of Clairwood at the time was Philip du Plessis, who had joined D&H in

Flood damage at Clairwood Quarry, 1933.

Shires Quarry.

Land reclamation scheme for Shires Quarry: proposed Reservoir Gardens township.

244

Clairwood Quarry

1977. Rowan Zoutendijk was appointed to this position in 1978 when Philip was given responsibility for all the Natal quarries. Rowan had been at Clairwood since 1966 when he joined on the maintenance side. He was given increasing responsibility over the years at both Clairwood and Shires until he was appointed manager of all the quarries in Natal in 1981 when Philip was transferred to the Transvaal. During this period the number of employees at Clairwood was considerably reduced and production streamlined.

In 1982 Darling and Hodgson purchased the Umzimkulu Quarry to provide material for the plant set up by Ready Mixed Concrete in Port Shepstone when they were awarded the concrete contract for the new Natal Portland Cement factory at Sumuma. The plant remained in operation after the factory was finished as the demand for concrete continued with the construction of the new casino hotel in Transkei just south of Port Edward and the rapid development on the south coast.

In 1983 the D&H materials division was divided into regional areas and the Natal quarries, stone-crushing and ready-mixed concrete operations constituted the eastern region. Within this, Shires, Clairwood and Umzimkulu quarries, under Rowan Zoutendijk, fulfilled their intended purpose of providing raw materials for the Group while extending their high quality D&H service to the commercial market.

Embecon

Concrete is made from four ingredients, sand, stone, cement and water, and for a very long time no one ever thought of adding anything more to it. However, it was the advantages and desirability of a fifth ingredient that Embecon set out to sell to its customers in 1966. Its first product was powder pozzolith which, when added to concrete, gave it a number of additional characteristics related to its workability and durability.

Pozzolith was brought to Darling and Hodgson by Ralph Youngworth, a young South African who had studied in America and then worked for Master Builders in Cleveland, Ohio which manufactured the concrete additive. Master Builders, a division of the Martin Marietta Corporation of America, one of the top hundred companies there, has its origins in the beginning of the century when the first concrete 'skyscraper' (all of sixteen storeys!) was built in Cincinnati, Ohio. A small group of men, inspired by the vision of concrete's great future as an important construction material, began to manufacture products which improved its quality. These developed along two paths, one for non-shrink grouts and floor hardners and the other for admixtures controlling the performance of concrete, including pozzolith.

Ralph was determined to introduce pozzolith to South Africa and, having checked its effectiveness under local conditions through the CSIR, he negotiated the distribution rights of all Master Builders' products in this country with Lane Knight, the vice president of Master Builders responsible for export sales. Amongst his earliest customers was Darling and Hodgson's Ready Mixed Concrete whose management readily appreciated the advantages of customizing concrete to the needs of a particular job.

Within a short time Ralph was no longer able to bring pozzolith into the country because of import restrictions. He turned to several companies for help in manufacturing the additive locally and the outcome was the establishment of Embecon, a 50/50 partnership between Darling and Hodgson and Master Builders. From the very beginning this was an immensely successful relationship, with Master Builders supplying the technical expertise and Darling and Hodgson the local management. Communication between the two has always been good, and the South African employees frequently attend training courses in America, as well as annual sales conferences where the latest information and developments are discussed. Master Builders run joint ventures throughout the world but the South African and Japanese operations are the only ones which they do not actively control.

The name Master Builders was not used in South Africa because there was already a Master Builders Association, and the name Embecon was chosen for the new company – 'Em' for Master, 'b' for Builders and 'con' for concrete. Master Builders' first representatives on the Embecon board were Steve Benedict, the president of Master Builders, and Bob Ahrens, the vice president international.

John Hodgson asked Ralph to start the new company for Darling and Hodgson and a pozzolith plant was set up on the Brailsford House property in Germiston, starting production in June 1966. Bob Ahrens visited South Africa to examine the locally engineered and manufactured installations and expressed complete satisfaction with the facilities. The product still had some imported content but this came into the country as raw materials which were not affected by import restrictions.

It was an exciting step for Darling and Hodgson; they were setting the pace in yet another sphere of development in South Africa and at the same time keeping to their policy of expanding their existing strengths through the beneficial use of admixtures in ready-mixed concrete. The first production manager was Steve Sandiford, who soon moved to the marketing side and Teddy Sykes was appointed in his place. The following year Trevor Stevens joined as production superintendent, a position he held until he was promoted to production manager in 1971 when Teddy was transferred to Purle Industrial Waste.

The use of concrete in the construction industry was increasing rapidly, providing many opportunities for promoting the use of pozzolith, and Ralph initiated seminars for instructing potential customers in the technical properties of pozzolith for improving concrete. In 1969 Walter Barker, a civil engineer by training, joined Embecon to take charge of the laboratory which was set up to develop admixtures specifically for South African conditions, and to train salesmen so that the company could provide a total service package, including the backup of a highly-trained field organization of concrete technologists. This has always been Embecon's main advantage over its competitors, and has fostered a remarkable atmosphere of camaraderie within its sales force and excellent customer relations.

The early days had an exciting pioneering atmosphere and there are many amusing stories told about trying to sell pozzolith in far-flung places. After a hazardous trip up to

Ponte, Johannesburg.

Cabora Bassa through Southern Rhodesia Walter Barker summed up the condition of the roads by saying, 'I don't know why the terrorists ever bothered to mine them!' A large amount of equipment had to be taken on a trip like that because there were no facilities on site, and a subsequent trip to Cabora Bassa, this time by charter flight – 'Air Taxi Portuguese' – because of the terrorist war on the ground, was nearly a disaster because of the weight of a huge test block of concrete. The block caused problems with security at the airport, too, and the irony of the situation was that when the cube eventually reached the laboratory it was too badly damaged to be used for testing!

The advantages of pozzolith gradually caught the imagination of contractors and it was used in a wide range of contracts. These included the Standard Bank Centre and Ponte in Johannesburg, the No 4 shaft of the President Steyn gold mine, the Hendrik Verwoerd dam wall and South Africa's first mechanically paved concrete road which was being constructed by Savage and Lovemore.

While working for Master Builders in America, Ralph had learnt that they made a higher percentage of their profits from their Masterplate industrial floor hardners and grouting products than from the admixtures. This was confirmed by George Tazzler of Master Builders on a visit to South Africa and Embecon soon extended their manufacturing operations. The factory at Brailsford House was enlarged in 1967 to accommodate the new plant and Dieter Wolff was employed to manage the new division. Its first contract was an acre of Masterplate commissioned by Consolidated Glass, and in 1969 and 1971 a white metallic Masterplate was used on the floor of the huge hangers built at Jan Smuts airport for South African Airways boeings. A non-shrink grout used in the installation of the scroll cases of the hydroelectric scheme contributed to Embecon's success at the Hendrik Verwoerd dam where record sales were achieved in both divisions. The new division also produced Anvil Top, which was used for flume linings and special floor protectors.

The demand for all Embecon products grew steadily and sales and distribution were facilitated by establishing offices in other key centres. Steve Sandiford was sent to Durban, where the office was based at first in the Jacobs depot and in 1972 moved to Pinetown. With Peter Steyn's assistance Steve gradually broke through the initial resistance in Natal and steadily built up a good reputation for the products. Craig Rowan opened an office in Cape Town, and sales representatives were soon appointed in Port Elizabeth to develop the area potential, especially in the motor industry. Pat McConnell was sent

Masterplate was used in the SAA jumbo jet hangars at Jan Smuts airport.

down from the Transvaal on the admixtures side and Ian Philp was appointed for the metals division. These two men were to stay with Embecon for many years, both achieving managerial status. Ian stayed on in Port Elizabeth while Pat was appointed Natal manager in February 1979. John Smetherham joined as sales representative in October 1972 and became Cape manager in March 1978.

Embecon's two divisions were run independently for nearly ten years. Dieter continued in the metals division, which was renamed the floor and grouting products division in 1971, and Ralph remained in admixtures until he was transferred to head office to be succeeded by Steve Sandiford. For several years the two divisional managers reported to John, but in mid 1971 Aidan Buccholz was appointed managing director of Embecon, and assumed responsibility for all company activities.

In 1975 the two sales divisions of Embecon were merged in order to minimize overlapping operations and Dieter was appointed company manager. Steve had decided to emigrate to England, and left Embecon. Under the new company structure salesmen promoted the complete range of Embecon products for the first time, which resulted in greater efficiency and more streamlined customer servicing. Unfortunately, however, a decision was made to increase prices and there was a dramatic drop in sales which affected Embecon's progress during the next few years.

Embecon products were used extensively in a scheme started in the mid seventies to produce hydroelectric power in the Drakensberg mountains with a pumped storage scheme involving the Sterkfontein dam. The company was represented by Bobby Goetsch, who maintained an excellent relationship with Escom during the contract. He had joined Embecon from another Group company, Vandex, as a salesman in the floor and grouting division in 1971 and was appointed salesman for special accounts in 1976. He controlled these accounts with Government departments with great enthusiasm and efficiency.

Aidan Buchholz was transferred to the United Kingdom in 1977 to take up a new challenge as managing director of Darling and Hodgson (Europe) and in early 1978 David Shephard was appointed company manager. A year later Embecon achieved record results once more and further expansion took place, with new offices established in East London and Kimberley. Chris White was appointed sales representative in the former area to serve the Border, Transkei and Ciskei markets, and Charlie Boucher in Kimberley with responsibility for the Orange Free State.

Embecon produces a rock support grout for use in mining.

Above left
The Drakensberg pumped storage scheme.

Above right
A 'Coca-Cola-red' floor at the Peninsula Beverages bottling plant in Athlone.

Right
Trevor Stevens in the Embecon laboratory.

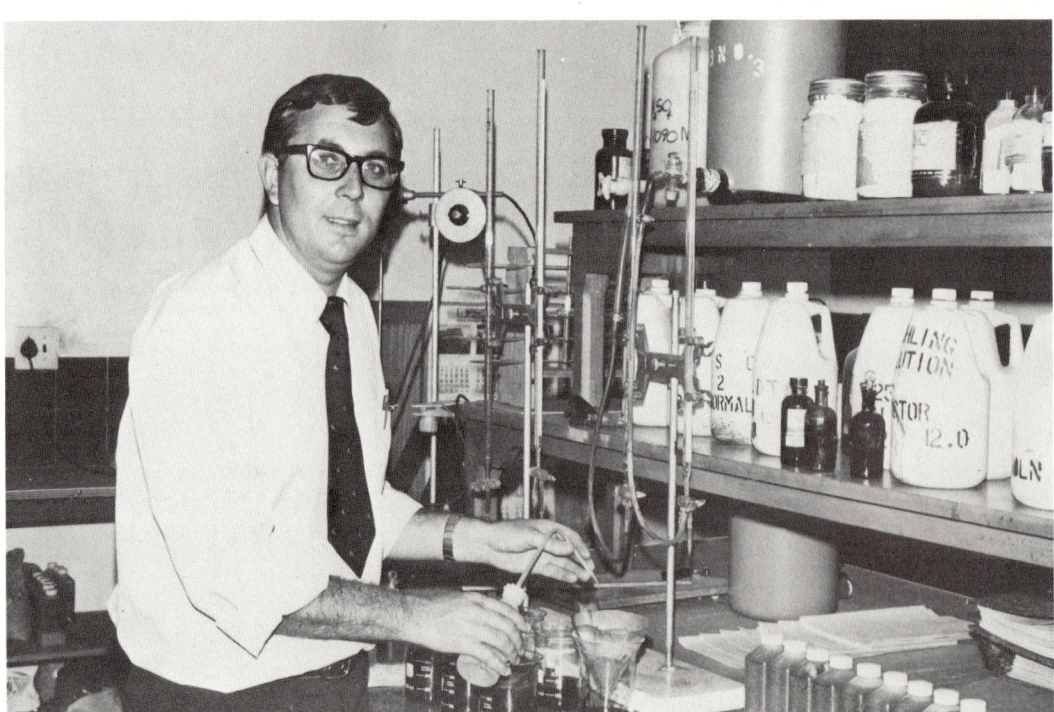

In 1980 David Shephard was transferred to Waste-tech and Trevor Stevens was appointed company manager. Trevor had been the backroom boffin for many years, keeping production going even in bad times, and he looked forward to broader horizons while maintaining a very active interest in technical developments. His long-standing experience and understanding of Embecon products stood him in good stead in his new position, and production and sales continued to increase steadily. The company built up an excellent reputation with various Government departments and Mervyn Stemmett,

Pozzolith was used in the Thabina dam project.

who had been based in Pretoria since 1972, worked closely with the Department of Water Affairs, Escom, South African Railways and others, including highly specialized work for the Defence Force. There was plenty of work for the private sector as well – Sun City in Bophutatswana provided a glamorous market, while more than 120 tons of Embecon products were used in the establishment of Ergo, Anglo American's ambitious gold reclamation scheme on the East Rand.

At intervals new products were introduced to the Embecon range. These included coloured Masterplate and an exceptionally quick setting and strong grout to hold roof bolts in mine tunnels, supporting the rock in place of the traditional props. There were also local technical innovations, including a superior resin (oil based) shutter release oil, which were offered to Master Builders in a reversal of the traditional situation. There have been significant advances in products for use in modern fast track building methods, such as a flowable concrete and a chloride-free admixture which accelerates setting time and produces early high strength, especially useful in the pre-stressing of concrete and in cold weather and maritime conditions.

Embecon has always been people rather than capital intensive, and its success has been more dependent than most companies on the quality of its sales staff. The year 1981 saw

Embecon admixtures facilitated fast track building methods at 11 Diagonal Street, Johannesburg.

the introduction of a successful centralized training scheme, both sales and technically orientated, based in Pretoria. This was initiated by Peter Steyn and taken over later by Mervyn Stemmett when Peter was transferred to RMC (Natal) as technical manager. Mervyn was appointed training manager in 1981 and the following year was promoted to personnel manager, while retaining his training responsibilities. Embecon has always maintained an exceptional team spirit and there are a remarkable number of employees of long standing with great dedication to their work. One of the old-timers is Peter Lotter, who has made a great contribution to Embecon through designing the right equipment for the right product in South Africa.

In 1983 Embecon moved to Electron where another Group company, Project Engineering, had been based. The new premises are spacious and the move took place with expansive sighs of relief after seventeen years at Brailsford House in quarters which became increasingly cramped as the company grew. Meshack May, who took charge of the larger factory, is an outstanding example of successful long service with Embecon. He joined the company as a driver in early 1966 and worked his way up to the position of production supervisor at the factory at Brailsford House.

Everything, including the training, was gradually moved to Electron. Among other activities in the new laboratory, under technical manager Ivor Boddington who worked closely with Trevor Stevens, Embecon technicians were testing local materials for the manufacture of products devised by 'Set Products', a company recently purchased in America by Master Builders. These are concrete-type products which have characteristics of rapid setting times and high early strengths, enabling critical repair jobs such as bridge decks to be carried out in minimal time. They are technically superior to anything available locally and are complementary to the Master Builders' range. They are opening up a new field for Embecon in that they will be released on the industrial retail market as well as being promoted and sold by the company's sales representatives in conjunction with their normal activities. Such innovative product lines combined with the traditional products, and the support of two exceptional parent companies, set the scene for Embecon's continued success in the future.

D&H Ash Resources

The promotion of a new product always needs something to catch the public eye, and when Darling and Hodgson started to market selected pulverized fuel ash (pfa) they chose to portray on their brochure the characteristic floating spheres of ash as seen under the electron microscope.

It is this spherical composition which gives pfa its unique property of acting as a lubricant when used as a substitute for a proportion of the cement in a concrete mix, improving its homogeneity and increasing its workability. It also creates increased strength and improved durability because it reacts with the free lime generated by the hydration of cement and the production of Portland cement bonded products which can cause weakening. Materials with these properties are called pozzolans, after the Roman *pozzuolano* which was volcanic lava of much the same chemical composition as fly ash, originating from a town called Pozzuoli, and which the Romans used in their concrete construction some two thousand years ago. The buildings still standing today prove the durability of the mixture.

The use of pfa in the production of grouts and mortars has a similar beneficial effect, and it also has tremendous potential in the field of stabilization and road construction, improving the properties of soils and aggregates used in base and sub-base courses in many ways, including the reduction of cracking and improved gradability. Its use reduces the cost of any cement-based product and is a contribution to energy conservation; every ton of cement replaced saves 7 000 megajoules.

Pfa is produced as a by-product of the generation of power from coal and, although it has been used overseas for many years, the considerable quantity produced in South Africa was washed out from the power-stations into slimes dams, losing most of its potential value as exposure caused chemical changes. Access to the pfa from all Escom power-stations came to the Group by chance through its acquisition of Randmix in 1977. The rights originally belonged to SAFIC Resources, a company which had been started by Paul Bates and Pierce Newton-King, and in which Randmix had taken a 60% shareholding. Darling and Hodgson recognized the potential of pfa as a raw material of the future and in 1978 bought out Pierce Newton-King's share in the company and changed its name to D&H Ash Resources. The Group acquired the total equity through the purchase of Paul Bates' shares in 1980, though he remained with the company until he retired in 1982, and in 1978 a plant was installed at Grootvlei power-station to remove the pfa directly from the power-station and store it in silos, ready for distribution by road and rail

Below left
The nature of pfa under a scanning electron microscope.

Below right
Pfa was used in the concrete mix for the Palmiet pumped storage scheme in the Cape.

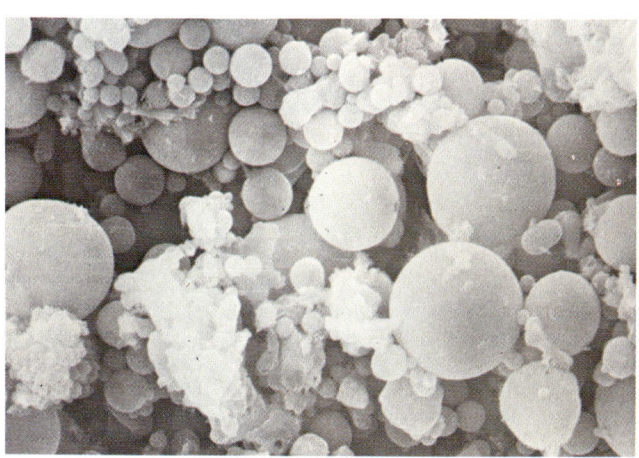

Tanker Services collecting pfa from Matla power-station.

tanker. The success of this pilot plant was followed by the installation of similar plants at two more power-stations – Matla and Taaibos/Highveld.

The effective use of pfa in the production of ready-mixed concrete has been clearly demonstrated in D&H materials' eastern and south-western regions and considerable research has been carried out to establish its best use. The companies in both regions act as agents for D&H Ash Resources and by 1983 the total sales were well in excess of 100 000 tons per annum.

In its early days D&H Ash Resources operated from the Group head offices in Hyde Park. Its subsequent growth warranted a move in 1983 to its own offices in Randburg, at Fernpark East, and a fully-equipped concrete laboratory was established at Honeydew. From September 1980 the company's development was guided by Jurgen Meyer who was constantly enthusiastic about an exciting and rewarding future for pfa. He worked with a good team, producing excellent technical work achievements, and the company continued to make a small but significant contribution to the Group by turning ashes into profits.

The Engineering Story

When Darling and Hodgson were preparing to go public in 1973 Union Corporation persuaded them to develop an engineering leg by purchasing Project Engineering. This was never part of John Hodgson's plan for his company, and at the time he was reluctant to agree, but Cyril Newnham and his colleagues at Union Corporation were convinced that it would be advantageous to the Group. Project Engineering was obtained at a very reasonable price and until 1980 was a highly successful member of the Group.

Project Engineering was started in 1962 by Dave Verhagen and three friends, Stan Patterson, Ivor Yeo and Barry Lowson, who had all decided to 'go it alone' after years of working for big corporations. Dave had previously formed Olympic Engineering, a small company which had been very successful. One of its first contracts had been the design and construction of the De Beers diamond pavilion at the Milner Park showgrounds in Johannesburg and another was for a crushing plant for Andrew Savage at the Savage and Woodward quarries in Port Elizabeth. As the demand for his services grew, Dave persuaded his partners in Project Engineering to purchase Olympic Engineering and use it as their operating company.

The company continued to operate in the Port Elizabeth area with a considerable amount of work for Savage and Lovemore. A subsidiary company, Project Services, was established there in the mid sixties. This started as a small drawing and consulting office under Peter Voisey, and a workshop was soon set up.

Olympic Engineering built a crushing plant at Cabora Bassa in the sixties, and designed, manufactured and built another at the Hendrik Verwoerd dam. While working on the latter such an excellent relationship was established with Union Corporation that Olympic Engineering was asked to participate in their platinum project in Bophutatswana. A workshop was set up in nearby Rustenburg and Olympic Engineering Rustenburg was established in the mid sixties, owned 60% by Project Engineering and 40% by Impala Platinum. It was a small but vigorous company which was involved in the construction programme that brought the Impala mine into production in record time, and it was also responsible for much of the mine's maintenance work.

During this period Ian Wilson of Union Corporation saw Project Engineering as a good industrial investment and suggested a closer link. Dave and his partners felt that they were in need of some sound financial backing and management support and gladly agreed, in 1967, to Union Corporation taking a 27% shareholding, with the option of extending this to 51% within a few years.

This enabled Project Engineering to widen its operating base. Treadlite Steel Flooring, which manufactured steel floor gratings, had already been acquired, and two structural engineering works, Neville Payne in Boksburg and Pan African Engineering, were absorbed into Olympic Engineering, although they retained their individual identities. In 1969 Savage and Lovemore took a one third interest in Project Engineering too, as a result of their close relationship in Port Elizabeth.

There was a heavy demand for the company's skills and expertise in the early seventies, with an exciting breakthrough into the big scene when it was awarded a major contract at Sishen near Saldanha Bay where Iscor was embarking on an ambitious scheme to export iron ore. This was an enormous project involving one of the biggest crushing plants in the world. At this stage Union Corporation began to feel that Project Engineering was perhaps too small to fit into their corporate scheme and could make a valuable contribution to another of their subsidiary companies. They offered it to D&H to help present an attractive image for going public in 1973. Structural engineering was comple-

Above
Impala Platinum.

Left
Castrol petro-chemical plant – designed, manufactured and erected by Project Engineering.

Flooring by Treadlite.

mentary to Darling and Hodgson's existing operations, and Project Engineering was forecast to contribute 15% of the Group's profits. James Draper, who had been seconded to Project Engineering from Union Corporation, helped to effect the transition and in spite of John Hodgson's personal reservations the deal went through in 1973 with Darling and Hodgson acquiring Union Corporation's 51% shareholding (they had exercised their option to increase their stake the previous year by purchasing the shares of one of the earlier shareholders, Ernie Acres) and a further percentage from Stan Patterson, giving 61% ownership. Stan soon retired but the other three partners retained their shareholding and remained with Project Engineering.

The company surged into a period of major growth and the future looked bright. Project Engineering had come into the Group with an order book of over R25 million and the big ore-handling contract at Sishen continued. Project Engineering purchased Cason Engineering Works in 1974 in order to manufacture idlers and pulleys for the contract. These needed to be of a quality which had never been produced in South Africa and were manufactured under licence to Fox of Australia. A further contract was awarded at Sishen in 1974 to erect the main workshops and stores.

Automatic welding of idlers – Cason Engineering.

The same year Project Engineering acquired a company which specialized in making shuttering for concrete work. This company, Stemco, came into the Group as Stelmo when Darling and Hodgson purchased Hume Prestressed Concrete (which became Hucrete) and was a useful extension of Project Engineering's capabilities. It was another step into manufacturing which lessened the company's reliance on project work and also helped to keep profits within the company. It was not successful, however, because the English staff returned to the United Kingdom, leaving the company with little expertise, and the work was gradually phased out.

Project Engineering became involved in an interesting contract at Richards Bay when they undertook to manufacture units for a project on the coast just north of the town, extracting the heavy minerals rutile, zircon and ilmenite from the sand through a dredging operation. In the same year they were commissioned to work on the new reduction plant at Union Corporation's Unisel Gold Mine near Welkom. These contracts suffered from delays and slow settlements which resulted in unexpectedly poor profits from 1976 onwards, and it was decided to decrease the company's dependence upon cyclical contractual work by further investment in manufacturing operations. D&H had by this time in-

Idlers and pulleys for conveyor belt systems – Cason Engineering.

creased their stake in Project Engineering to 79%.

In 1978 Rand Founders was purchased from John Daniels and his partners and became a wholly-owned subsidiary, adding a totally new dimension to Project Engineering in producing cast-iron and bronze castings for pump parts in the mining industry. The shadowy Dickensian atmosphere of the foundry in Stafford was a great contrast to the stark modern splendour of most of the engineering contracts. Rand Founders was a company some forty years old with a team of long-standing employees who continued operations under their new managing director Ivor Yeo. The works manager, Neville Egg, foreman patternmaker, Paolo Morara, and Tommy Bothwell, foundry foreman, between them clocked up nearly one hundred years with the company. The equally highly skilled machine-shop foreman, Peter Henning, was a newcomer by comparison. Paolo's Italian accent has always revealed his homeland, which he left during the last war. He came to South Africa on a free ticket, as a prisoner of war, never to return home.

Rand Founders settled into the Group and within a year Marlene Orlett was appointed accountant and company secretary, transferred from Project Engineering where she had been working for sixteen years. When she started with Project Engineering she admitted that she 'did not know a channel from a joist', but she learnt quickly, and this ready adaptability was just one of the qualities which led to her being appointed a director of Rand Founders in 1979. She joined Rose Baiocchi of Kya-MP as the only two company directors of the fairer sex within the D&H Group.

Ivor took charge of a new manufacturing leg of Project Engineering which comprised Rand Founders, Cason Engineering and Treadlite, while Dave Verhagen remained at

Above
Miscellaneous pump parts – Rand Founders.

Left
Pouring hot metal in the foundry.

the head of the structural engineering operations. Further expertise was developed in a third section of Project Engineering, under Barry Lowson, based at Brailsford House. Project Design and Management Services were made available to all Group companies, and the facilities offered by Barry's team were increased through extensive computerization. In 1979 a Project Engineering manufacturing facility was established near the industrial area of northern Natal with the acquisition of M&M Structural Engineering in Glencoe.

Meanwhile export opportunities in structural steel work were being investigated overseas, largely through Bill Metter whose company, Mettrex, had opened an exploratory office in Houston, Texas. For a couple of years there was no success, but then an opportunity beyond anyone's imagination appeared and suddenly Project Engineering was involved in building oil rigs, with two firm orders on their books. The concept caught everyone's imagination and enthusiasm ran high throughout the company as the first multi-million contract for Pool Rig 53 was signed, followed closely by a second for a BMC 250 hull. It seemed strange to many people that America should want to purchase oil rigs from South Africa but the enormous surge in demand for these units for the Mexican Gulf had outstripped the capacity of facilities in the USA. Also, financial backing from the South African Industrial Development Corporation at a very low rate of interest enabled Project Engineering to offer a most attractive price.

The initial expenses were formidable but the future looked good with promises of more contracts, and the fascinating potential was too great to relinquish. Darling and Hodgson turned to Murray and Roberts, old acquaintances with extensive structural engineering strength, and suggested the formation of a joint company for building rigs. The result in late 1980 was Amardah Shipyards, a name which was simply an acronym – A Murray And Roberts Darling And Hodgson company. Barry Lowson of Project Engineering and Syd Nicholls of Murray and Roberts began to co-ordinate the operations of the new company which were entirely separate from Project Engineering, and before long Allston Mitchell was appointed managing director.

The original dock site between the James Brown and Hamer and Sandock Austral Shipyards in Durban soon became inadequate and Amardah expanded onto a larger adjacent site leased from the South African Railways. Before the first two rigs were completed by Project Engineering, Amardah had embarked on the construction of two more, and there was a full order book for 1983. A euphoric atmosphere surrounded the whole project. Amardah had the necessary facilities for building four rigs a year, each to take fourteen to sixteen months, with a total value of R100 million which offered tremendous potential in foreign exchange. There was a licence agreement with the Baker Marine Corporation of Houston to supply back-up expertise and unit design, which could be modified to individual clients' requirements. The construction was carried out to a very high standard, constantly checked by representatives of the American Bureau of Shipping and the United States Coast Guard. Production was nearly 75% local content, and the project was a rousing stimulant to the Durban docks and local industry.

The first two rigs grew apace, the one eventually towering above the docks as high as a twenty-seven storey building, and became a major attraction. They were triumphantly launched in 1981, and in June they were towed by tug, lashed together on a barge, across the Atlantic to the Gulf of Mexico for final completion and delivery to their owners.

The third rig was launched in December 1981 and at the end of the year Allston returned to America. His place was taken by Cliff Mey from the Group coal division. By this time there was a dramatic decrease in the demand for oil rigs resulting from the sudden drop in oil prices and accompanying fall in exploratory work. It also became apparent that Amardah was making heavy losses. Everyone came down to earth with a bump.

Meanwhile Project Engineering continued its traditional operations, and had been awarded several multi-million rand contracts, the biggest worth R14 million for the main coal washing plant and conveyor systems at Iscor's Grootgeluk mine at Ellisras in the north-western Transvaal. This mine has one of the largest coal beneficiation plants in the world, and the contract was won in the face of strong competition. Smaller contracts

Amardah Shipyards, Durban, 1981.

were for Sasol II's ash-handling plant at Secunda, the primary uranium reduction plant at Union Corporation's Beisa mine near Welkom and the refractory specialities plant at Anglo American's Vereeniging Refractories.

In spite of these contracts 1980 was not a good year. Delays in completing jobs again proved very expensive and detrimental to profits. Secondment of senior men to Amardah left gaps on the engineering side and in January 1981 a new managing director was appointed when Dave Verhagen retired. Don Lanigan was brought in from the Group materials division with a vision of great scope for growth and improved profitability through more professional management. Through Don, based at Hyde Park and reporting to the industrial division's managing director Peter Loveday, engineering was brought into a closer association with the Group and all structural operations were rationalized within a new company, D&H Structural Engineering. In its first year this company was awarded a big contract for the construction of the Richards Bay coal export terminal with Swemsa Engineering, and a much smaller one comprising the components for a coal import terminal at Ghent in Belgium.

The engineering division continued to lose money, however, a situation aggravated by Amardah's heavy losses. In 1981 engineering losses caused Group profits to drop for the first time in fifteen years and it was decided to discontinue all unprofitable operations. Early in 1982 Darling and Hodgson sold their half share in Amardah to Murray and Roberts, and later in the year, disillusioned by the activities of the rest of the engineering division, they decided to terminate the entire engineering operation. They set about disposing of the various members of the division, and sold their disastrous

Conveyor systems under construction at Iscor's Grootgeluk mine at Ellisras.

Swemsa contract at Richards Bay to Group Five Engineering.

The remnants of the division, Cason Engineering and Rand Founders, were consolidated within a new Group manufacturing division, under the directorship of Lloyd Koch who also continued as managing director of D&H Coal. Cason Engineering was sold within a year, however, and Rand Founders was put under new management which modernized the foundry and set out to expand and diversify operations. Dave Bull, who was appointed managing director of Rand Founders, had been given the task of closing down the other companies of the D&H engineering division and setting Rand Founders on a more modern path. At the end of 1983 it was all that was left of the division, a reminder of D&H's ten years of agony and ecstasy in the field of engineering.

The Coal Story

A massive machine can be seen towering in the bushveld on an opencast coal mine near Piet Retief, mute evidence of Darling and Hodgson's entry into the coal industry. It is a huge electrically operated dragline, one of the latest forms of machinery for removing overburden and accelerating production. Its introduction to Savmore Colliery in 1982 confirmed Darling and Hodgson's commitment to coal, and today there are three active mines in operation with extensive reserves held by the company.

The Group entered the coal industry through its subsidiary Savage and Lovemore, whose senior management began to look for other ways of using their earth-moving equipment and expertise during the downturn in road construction in the mid seventies. Opencast mining offered a logical diversion and an investigating visit to America by Andrew Savage, David Lovemore and Gerry Schoonbee confirmed this. In 1977 Savage and Lovemore obtained a contract for stripping the overburden at Kanhym near Middelburg for BP, one of South Africa's major coal producers, and at first they had no intention of doing more than contracting work of this nature. Contracts were not easy to find, however, because most of the big mining houses did their own work or were already committed to subcontractors. Savage and Lovemore soon realized too that the big profits came from the mining itself, particularly as coal prices were rising rapidly, and in 1977 the company purchased a coal deposit at Rietvlei. The first marketing manager for coal was Ernest Gardner, who had been with Savage and Lovemore since the end of 1970 as company secretary, and had been made a director of the company. Although he had no experience of coal mining he was enthusiastic about the opportunities it offered and he readily accepted the challenge of the new venture.

The company then applied to the Anthracite Producers' Association for membership, assuming that it was a co-operative distributing body, only to find that it was a private organization holding a firm monopoly on local sales. Since this opening was closed to them, Savage and Lovemore were forced to look for an alternative market overseas. They discovered, however, that no coal could leave the country without an export permit, and that the Government kept very tight control over the allocation of permits. Not able to acquire one of their own, Savage and Lovemore came to an arrangement with the Makateeskop Coal Mining Company to work the Makateeskop coal dump jointly, and to use their permit to export anthracite from Rietvlei to France and Holland. The dump comprised fine material left after coal had been produced for ship bunkering, and there was a steady demand for this high quality material.

A virgin deposit at Pivaanspoort was purchased in 1977 from the Makateeskop Coal Mining Company and Savage and Lovemore's very first step into opencast mining was made there. Sadly it was a disaster. Although extensive drilling had indicated a satisfactory deposit, the coal seam proved to be of varying thickness, and the projected tonnage was never achieved. Another problem was that only the oldest equipment was sent to the mine, and nothing functioned very efficiently. The mine was closed after only six months, having lost a considerable amount of money.

The following year, 1978, Savage and Lovemore exercised their option to purchase a 90% interest in the Natal Iron Ore and Coal Mines, the holding company of the Makateeskop Coal Mining Company, which also owned an adit mine, Heritage Colliery, between Vryheid and Paulpietersburg in northern Natal. No longer new to the game, Savage and Lovemore proceeded to operate the colliery successfully, mining a low grade anthracite which was blended with similar coal from Rietvlei and exported, mainly to France.

Earthmoving equipment – Heritage Colliery.

The use of another export permit was acquired from Desert Spar, a company which had negotiated a sale contract into Korea. With the increased total exportable quota and a gradual entry into the local market, Savage and Lovemore Mining decided to upgrade their coal reserves by securing good quality bituminous coal deposits underlying the farms Anysspruit and Klipspruit near Piet Retief. Savmore Colliery was opened there. A blend of this bituminous coal and the Makateeskop dump coal was exported to Europe and supplied locally. Another dump, Inyati, was also acquired for blending purposes.

A dragline was purchased in 1982 at a cost of R4,5 million to increase production at Savmore Colliery. This is a Marion 7450 walking dragline with a sixty metre boom which strips the overburden in places where scrapers can not operate economically. It has a supporting Marion M2 drill for blasting. Working beside these brightly gleaming units the earth-moving machines look like dinkie toys. Savmore is mainly an opencast mine but in mid 1982 adit operations were also started.

A low grade bituminous coal deposit was acquired in 1979 with the purchase of Glisa Colliery, on the farm Paardeplaats west of Belfast in the Eastern Transvaal. It was an old mine which had supplied fuel for the Delagoa Railway in Portuguese East Africa in the last century and had been worked intermittently up until the sixties. This time it was opened by Savico Holdings, a partnership between Savage and Lovemore Mining (60%) and an Italian company, Icodev (40%), which guaranteed the purchase of the export production. Savage and Lovemore also purchased Sevmin Coal which gave them a permit to export coal through Maputo, 300 km away on the Moçambique coast. Improvements were made to the siding facilities at Glisa and an additional loading device was installed at Maputo harbour in conjunction with other coal exporters, but problems associated with

Dragline bucket – Savmore Colliery.

the railways and the harbour constantly hindered efficient export operations.

It was not easy to gain a firm foothold in the coal market which had been monopolized for many years by two organizations, the Transvaal Coal Owners' Association and the Natal Associated Collieries. In November 1979 Savage and Lovemore Mining was one of the founder members of the Independent Coal Producers' Association which was formed to help those companies excluded from these organizations. In the early days Savage and Lovemore Mining sold their coal on short-term contracts which capitalized on the often fluctuating prices, but they gradually developed a firmer local market. They consolidated their market penetration in Natal, hoping to expand into other provinces, through a lively company called Trans Tugela Coal. This had been started in 1976 by a group of men which included Barry Nel and Colin Jones, and had rapidly developed into a specialist coal marketing company in direct competition with the bigger coal companies. Savage and Lovemore first entered into a commission agreement with them in 1979 and in 1980 bought a 60% interest.

The growth of the embryonic coal subsidiary of Savage and Lovemore was dramatic and in 1980 its operations were promoted to Group divisional status, thereby facilitating further development. Cliff Mey was appointed managing director of D&H Coal under chairman John Hodgson and vice chairman Gerry Schoonbee. The offices remained in the Savage and Lovemore headquarters at Elandsfontein. Prospects for coal were riding high in South Africa and when Dr Neethling of the Minerals Bureau was quoted in 1980 as saying that 'coal could earn the same as gold by the year 2000' Darling and Hodgson felt their investment in coal was more than justified. John Hodgson had had complete faith in the venture from the beginning and there was a strong team spirit among the small group of people who were involved.

Production accelerated rapidly to satisfy increased demands from both local and the lucrative overseas markets, resulting in an exhilarating profit in 1981. The new coal division was contributing 15% of Group profits and had become one of South Africa's lead-

Screening coal – Glisa Colliery.

ing independent coal producers – no mean achievement in so few years. Aware that accessibility to the country's infrastructure was vitally important in the coal industry, Darling and Hodgson invested a great deal of money in improving railway siding facilities near their collieries.

The export of any commodity is always influenced by fluctuating shipping tariffs and in order to stabilize their freight costs, D&H Coal entered into a long-term contract of afreightment with a shipping company, Bulk Charters, which was operating bulk carrier ships around the world on time charter as 'hedge vessels'. Through their contract D&H Coal were able to secure a steady freight rate for a five year period and at the same time participate in the profits of the ships' operations. D&H formed a joint company, Savbulk, with Bulk Charters in order to acquire their own 'hedge vessel' in conjunction with Wah Kwong, a Hong Kong ship-owning group. The huge ship, a DW 41 000 MT type ore/bulk carrier, was built at Toyama in Japan and the months of construction culminated in a thrilling and memorable day in September 1982 when Ruth Hodgson christened the *Ruth Venture* at the Nipponkai Heavy Industries Shipyards. The ship was commissioned on 25 January 1983 for international trade, carrying mainly coal but also other commodities such as ferrochrome. With the drop in world freight rates the ship subsequently became an expensive asset, but in the long-term its potential should be realized.

At the beginning of 1982 Cliff Mey was transferred to Amardah, a subsidiary of the Group's engineering division, and Lloyd Koch was appointed managing director of D&H Coal in March that year. Lloyd, an accountant by training, joined the Group with a wide range of experience in the business world and a distinguished career in sport. Among his achievements he had captained the Rhodesian hockey team to the Tokyo Olympics in 1964. The rapidly growing coal division presented a stimulating challenge to Lloyd and his deputy managing director, Clive Straughan, who moved into new offices at Fernpark, Randburg in May. At the end of the year Gerry Schoonbee relinquished his responsibilities and soon thereafter retired from the Group. After the excite-

The Ruth Venture *on her sea trials.*

ment and action in early 1982 the end of the year brought disappointment when the coal prices fell and the export market collapsed, affected by the downturn in the world economy and reduction in energy consumption. All export to Korea ceased in February and most of Darling and Hodgson's forward coal contracts were cancelled. Profits dropped drastically. In step with many smaller coal mines which were ceasing operations, Heritage Colliery was closed down in 1982, leaving stockpiles of anthracite waiting for more favourable trading conditions.

D&H Coal has always exported through Maputo and Durban, neither of which has proved very satisfactory. Maputo suffers from the effects of Moçambique's independence and the port facilities for loading coal in Durban are inadequate even though the movement of coal through the docks was improved when a Durban Exporters Committee was formed to co-ordinate the efforts of the coal exporters and the South African Railways and Harbours' authorities in getting the coal from train to ship through Congella. There are coal facilities at Richards Bay, but the present terminal is not available to the independent producers.

At the time of writing, negotiations are underway for the establishment of a new coal-loading facility to provide for the Phase 4A additional permit allocations which were announced by the Department of Mineral and Energy Affairs in mid 1982. Its situation, either in Richards Bay or Durban, will have a significant effect on the fortunes of D&H Coal, since railage is the major factor influencing selling price and Richards Bay is much closer than Durban to the northern Natal coal fields.

The permit allocations are conditional upon the coal producer proving that it has sufficient reserves to sustain its quota for a thirty year term. D&H Coal's collieries are backed up at present by two unworked deposits at Spruitfontein and Sevmin, and there is an ongoing exploration programme for further reserves guided by D&H Coal's geologist Ron Robbins who joined the Group in 1979. Many of those investigated prove unsuitable but others are worthy of exploitation.

In 1982 there was a reorganization of the coal division into regional areas: north, under regional manager Gordon Hayward, comprising Glisa Colliery, and east under Ged

Coal en route to the coast.

Crawford, including Savmore, the dumps and Spruitfontein. When a new mine was opened in 1983 at Kromdraai near Witbank it was called Hayford Colliery, derived from the names of the two regional managers at the time. This colliery produces high and low grade bituminous coal, and is strategically placed to serve the industries of the PWV complex in the Transvaal. It is not expected to have a long life, however, as the deposit is small.

In May 1983 Darling and Hodgson's shareholding in Trans Tugela Coal was increased to 80%, and the total marketing of D&H Coal, both local and export, was consolidated under its name. Barry Nel had left the company by then, but Colin Jones continued as company secretary and retained a 20% interest in the company. The Savage family link was maintained with D&H Coal after it became a Group division through Andrew's eldest son Hugh, who, as marketing manager, moved to the Trans Tugela Coal office in Hillcrest, Natal. Hugh had been with D&H Coal for four and a half years, spending the first year on the mines gaining first-hand experience of the coal industry. He set about co-ordinating all the marketing operations, local and overseas, ably assisted by Dave Mitchell and Barry Farr. Management was streamlined throughout the division and Ged and Gordon were appointed managers of operations, and projects and development, respectively. That year D&H Coal moved its head office to the D&H headquarters at Hyde Park.

The year 1983 was a difficult one for D&H Coal. Most of the production was marketed locally against intense competition from all other coal producers, though some was exported to Taiwan (through Durban) and Malagasy (through Maputo). Glisa continued to supply the coal requirements of Maputo power-station, while most of its production was marketed in the Transvaal lowveld. The depressed market increased the demand for high quality coal and the decision was made to install a washing plant at Savmore Colliery to upgrade the market value.

From the beginning D&H Coal set out to be a low-cost producer and has continued with this philosophy. It gained a foothold in the coal business at first with the production of lower grade fuel for which there was a demand, and thereafter adapted to the changing market. In 1983 the future did not look very encouraging but D&H Coal was making the best of a difficult situation. Along with other coal producers it was looking forward to an upswing in the world economy when hopefully the challenge would again be to produce enough coal.

The People Story

For twenty-five years Darling and Hodgson was a small family business with a natural people orientation revolving around Bill Hodgson's charismatic personality. After Bill's death in 1959 his son John led the company through twenty-five years of escalating growth into a powerful group of companies. John consciously perpetuated the original family spirit characterized by a genuine concern for the well-being of all those who worked for D&H. He has always held the philosophy that people are the company's greatest asset and must be treated accordingly. As acquisitions were made over the years, John cultivated the image of a 'family of families', encouraging individuality and independence within operating companies and thereby gaining a special kind of loyalty and motivation throughout the Group which has given it a unique culture while not changing at heart. D&H has adapted to growth with increased professionalism which has equipped it well to meet challenges and exploit opportunities to their utmost.

In 1963, when the opportunity arose to link up with Union Corporation and gain significant financial backing, John and his fellow directors, Brian Malcomson and Jack Plane, had to consider the impact that such a move would have upon D&H and its people, and whether they would have to forfeit their independence and be absorbed into a more impersonal atmosphere. Having made the decision to join the Union Corporation group, however, they rapidly developed a sophisticated management philosophy which led to continued profit growth and ability to meet plans, satisfying the standards required by Union Corporation and allowing D&H to follow its own path of development and retain its family style.

The first step in this direction was taken in 1963 when John was sent on the Louis Allen management course along with other Union Corporation managers. He returned from the course revitalized. He had learnt nothing fundamentally new but it had shown him the value of a truly professional approach.

This was the turning-point in the management of D&H. Within a short time all the senior staff (there were not very many at that stage) had attended the course and a new discipline set the company on a determined path to success. John introduced a decentralized management philosophy which was to have a significant influence on future development. A policies and procedures manual was drawn up which spelt out clearly what was to be done in particular circumstances and contributed a great deal to the success of this philosophy. It rapidly became an invaluable handbook for all managers, allowing them freedom to operate in their own style on a daily basis within the parameters of company policy without reference to head office.

The Louis Allen course was established as a vital stage in every manager's training, initially conducted by Ralph Parrott but after some time run as an in-house programme laying the base for further managerial training. Ralph's association with the company continued, however, and he took a keen and helpful interest in its development. Seeing the need for further external management training, John in 1972 attended the executive programme at Stanford University in America. This added another dimension of sophistication and set the precedent for senior employees to attend similar courses at the University of the Witwatersrand, University of Cape Town, and overseas at Henley, Harvard, IMEDE and the London Business School. It also became company policy to send managers overseas to broaden their horizons through travel and exposure to businesses in other countries.

Meanwhile training was becoming increasingly important at other levels, and by the mid seventies it was an integral part of company policy. In 1975 John stated: 'Training is

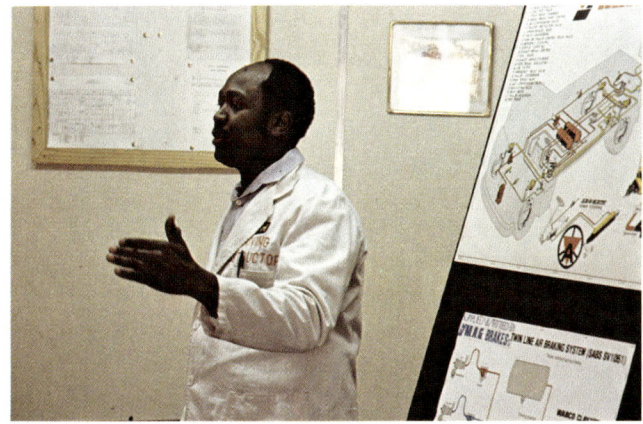

Training takes place at all levels and in all spheres of D&H.

learning and development, and it develops the Group as a whole by involving people in the learning process.' He also spoke of the Group's social commitment to extending leadership qualities and teaching skills.

D&H has developed a high standard of training throughout the Group at all levels, which has improved results and contributed most rewardingly to the growth of individuals both in their work and in themselves. It has also alleviated the ubiquitous shortage of skilled labour in South Africa. Training in basic construction skills was started in Savage and Lovemore in the Cape in the early seventies and was soon placed on a more formal basis. The programmes were gradually extended beyond basic skills and established at supervisor and management levels, the latter comparable with the Louis Allen course in the rest of D&H. Tanker Services and Ready Mixed Concrete initiated driver training in the early seventies.

John had always maintained that personnel staff as such were unnecessary if management operated satisfactorily but in 1980 the Group personnel policy began to change.

The annual executive planning conference, held that year at Mount Sheba, was a pivot-point in the history of D&H personnel matters. At that meeting Ralph Parrott, who had been invited to participate in the planning session, gave warning of the rumblings of a social industrial revolution in South Africa. His wide experience showed him that all the old conservative business methods were becoming increasingly challenged, labour unrest was rife, and labour relations were becoming of paramount importance. In future, he said, a lot more attention would have to be given to people at all levels, and to the employees' rights to negotiate. He recommended a greater emphasis on the training of management to work in harmony and understanding with labour and trade unions.

The directors of D&H took heed of these challenging words, which were a catalyst for the creation of a senior personnel appointment within the Group. When seemingly suitable outside candidates had been considered and rejected, Ralph suggested Aubrey Welsford for this crucial position. It was an inspiration. Aubrey had been a Group director for several years and had proved his authority and credibility to everyone. He was recognized as a man of ability and perception, with all the qualities necessary for personnel work enhanced by a warm and open personality.

Aubrey was appointed executive director of Group personnel and industrial relations in 1981 and began the mammoth task of equipping D&H to meet and to gain strength from the inevitable changes in the future. He instituted the policy of company handbooks which outlined the privileges, benefits and various company policies which affect employees. These relate to a specific company and are available in a range of appropriate languages. One of the benefits is the pension fund. The first D&H pension fund was started in 1959 and carried through until the company joined the Union Corporation fund on 1 January 1970. By 1982 the Group had grown to a size which warranted its own pension fund which is open to all employees after they have completed a probationary period.

In 1981 the Group established a code of employment practice following several other leading companies in the Republic. The code includes the principle of moving towards fully-integrated work areas, integration of other facilities and equal pay for equal work.

Aubrey Welsford.

Above left
Herbert Moloantoa conducts a training course.

Above right
The D&H Village.

It had been company policy for some time to select transport drivers only on merit, long before job reservation was legally relaxed, and the directors were wholehearted in their support of the extension of equal opportunity. John spoke eloquently in his launching of the code, recognizing the inevitable difficulties but positive that this was the way to turn the problems of tomorrow to advantage. The strength created from the combination of individuals of different race, sex, creed and colour must lead to a harmonious work atmosphere and a more stable South Africa.

Industrial relations rapidly became an integral part of Group business strategy, setting a firm base on which to ride any storms of unrest. Initially each division set up an industrial relations section within the personnel department, but, as progress and acceptance at operating level was slow, a Group industrial relations department was created in October 1981, headed by Johan Burger from Savage and Lovemore. The first members of the department were Herman Knoethe and Herbert Moloantoa, D&H's first black manager, from the industrial division, and Marianna Coetzee from the construction division. The department was given the mandate to develop common industrial relations structures and introduce them into the operating companies. Strong emphasis was laid on the establishment of extensive training programmes to ensure effective and knowledgeable action, and works committees and councils were established to provide communication channels and forums for discussion, building bridges of trust and co-operation in all directions. The introduction of a disciplinary code, grievance procedure and system of worker representatives established specific patterns of procedure for handling staff.

After fifteen months the central department, having completed its mandate, was disbanded and the action moved closer to operations. The construction and industrial divisions again set up their own departments in the divisional headquarters at Kempton Park and Hyde Park respectively. Aubrey continued to co-ordinate the overall scene, picking up problems quickly from monthly meetings with industrial relations representatives from each division and regular audits at operating company level of the code of employment practice, and ensuring that they were never ignored.

By the early eighties the comprehensive training programme developed in construction was being followed in materials and services and adapted to their particular needs. The construction division developed significantly through acquisitions which introduced different training methods at varying levels of advancement and in 1983 Tony Hibbert was transferred to the Reef to co-ordinate and standardize training. By this time the materials and services divisions had grown large enough for each to establish its own

Above left
Ruth Hodgson congratulates one of Germiston's best young drivers on winning a gold award.

Above right
Happy smiles from a proud award winner and John and Ruth Hodgson.

training section under Roy Teall and John Press respectively. The introduction of the concept of industrial relations accentuated the importance and value of training and each contributed to the success of the other within the personnel division of the Group.

The training programmes are supported by rewards and incentives in the form of various annual awards. These apply to individual companies and the yearly presentation parties are an eagerly anticipated highlight of the year, when everyone gathers together with their wives or husbands for an enjoyable evening. John and his wife Ruth attend all these gatherings, appreciative of the opportunity to be with so many D&H people. The warmth of Ruth's smile and handshake makes each award special and her genuine interest is revealed in her thoughtful concern for all who are present. John's congratulatory speeches always encompass everyone, especially emphasizing that no one can achieve great things without the support and encouragement of those around him at work and at home. There is no doubt that his words inspire all present to new pride and dedication in their work.

The greatest achievement of the personel department has been the recognition of each person in the Group as an individual and Aubrey introduced the phrase 'D&H Cares' which has become a watchword throughout the Group. D&H does care, for the welfare, the security and the future of everybody within the Group, not just the employees but their families as well.

In recent years there has been a significant upgrading in accommodation for Group black workers both on site and in the urban situation. The latter is particularly fraught with difficulties and in the early eighties D&H determined to ease these problems for their black staff in the Johannesburg/Kempton Park area and the company embarked on an ambitious project which proved to be a striking example of how the private sector can help to alleviate the black housing shortage and, in particular, improve the quality of life for migrant labour. In George Goch, near Benrose, on the outskirts of Johannesburg, Combrink Construction completed the first phase of the D&H Village, providing comfortable hostel accommodation with a homely atmosphere in an attractive garden setting. It was officially opened by the Minister of Co-operation and Development, Dr P G J Koornhof, on 23 November 1983. The complex was designed in close collaboration with the people who were to live there in order to satisfy their requirements and it stands as a practical indication of D&H's concern for all their employees.

Over the years D&H have established educational benefits. Since the mid sixties employees have been able to attend diploma courses at technicons while working for the company, and a significant number of graduates have stayed within the Group. Perhaps the most obviously successful participant has been Mike Lawson who joined Savage and Lovemore in 1963, and in 1983, after twenty years with the company, was appointed

Long service awards:

Nine Paul's Sand employees (with John Hodgson and Paul Nucci) who achieved a combined length of service of 223 years in 1976.

Far left
Bryan Johnson – 20 years in 1981.

Left
Bill Rowlings – 21 years in 1975.

Below left
Jim Mabasa and Mack Mashigo – 33 and 22 years respectively in 1971.

Below right
June Klynhans – 20 years in 1981.

area director for the company in the Western Cape. D&H have also introduced a bursary scheme for university studies in engineering, accountancy and science, and tuition reimbursement, available to all employees within the Group, for approved courses is a great stimulant to further education.

In recent years a sum of money directly related to the dividends paid has been set aside each year for allocation to outside causes. These cover diverse needs and include universities and technicons, the upgrading of teachers of mathematics in Soweto, leadership training of prefects at black high schools in Soweto, welfare organizations and nature conservation projects.

The philosophy that D&H cares, and always has cared, is clearly reflected in the number of the Group's long term employees. When Bill presented his loyal foreman Dutton with a gold watch after twenty-one years' service he set a lasting precedent. Since then twenty years' service has been recognized with an appropriate presentation. Brian Malcomson has been with the Group for thirty-one years, not far behind John himself who joined his father in 1947, and in 1984, D&H's jubilee year, there are other stalwarts still with the Group after twenty years or more of dedicated contribution to its development. These include Edward Sunde (1960), Bryan Johnson (1961), Peter Asher (1963), Roger Cuningham (1963). Two splendid examples of young men who grew up in all respects with D&H are Phil Erasmus (1961) and David Bath (1964) who rose through the ranks of their divisions to become managing directors and in 1983 were appointed to the Group board.

These men have all been supported and encouraged by many others, both men and women of all races who have devoted a similar number of years to D&H. Some have already retired after many years of Group service, amongst them Andrew Savage, David Lovemore and Gerry Schoonbee, while others have joined the Group with later acquisitions and chosen to stay.

Another D&H tradition was established with the first Wives' Day in 1976 when wives of senior management were gathered together, primarily to be given some understanding of what their husbands do when they leave home early in the morning and come home late at night – and often work over the weekends and go away on business trips. This has become a yearly event, a day when the wives have the opportunity to meet each other, listen to interesting and informative talks and visit some group associated operations. It is in many ways Ruth's day and she enjoys sharing her pride in the Group and her enthusiasm for all its activities.

D&H people not only work hard for the Group, they play hard for it as well. There is a long-standing tradition of extra-mural activities in the sporting field and a strong em-

Below left
Marathon runners receiving encouragement at the Waste-tech waterhole.

Below right
Enjoying a D&H golf society meeting.

phasis on health and fitness. Within the Group there are many cricket and football teams, which challenge each other as well as companies outside the Group. The often relaxed approach to their game was once aptly described as having 'enthusiasm way out in front, fitness and talent a little further behind'! In 1976 a golf society was formed and this meets throughout the year, culminating in a grand annual Swazi golfing safari, a family weekend much enjoyed by all those who participate. There are individuals within the Group who accept greater challenges as well. There has been a steady increase over the years in the number of D&H employees who run in the famous Comrades Marathon between Durban and Pietermaritzburg, and the discipline of running develops an indefinable bond among those who participate. Others train ardently for the strenuous Duzi Canoe Marathon each year and for the Iron Man Triathlon contest. Some people have reached provincial level in sports which include rugby, soccer and water polo and there have been at least two Springboks (skiboat fishing and parachuting) in the Group.

The encouragement and recognition of achievements like these are an indication of what makes D&H different from most big companies. It offers an environment where

Waste-tech soccer team.

D&H Transport (Transvaal) cricket team.

John and Ruth Hodgson in the tranquil surroundings of their home, Sunbury.

the individual is encouraged to achieve his personal goal, aware that he (or she) is more than a cog in the profit-making machine and that D&H cares about him and his family. The result is a structure of personal relationships which give tremendous strength to D&H. The quality, loyalty and camaraderie which characterize its people have created the Group's greatest asset which is spearheading its confident thrust into the future.

At the business planning conference held in December 1983 David Bath quoted John Steinbeck with words which say it all:

> Man, unlike any other thing organic or inorganic in the universe,
> grows beyond his work, walks up the stairs of his concepts,
> emerges ahead of his accomplishments.

The Finance Story

Introduction by Brian Malcomson

The finance and accounting aspects of D&H have been my responsibility for over thirty years. This could have been a routine and undemanding task – but nothing in D&H stays routine for long and there has always been lots of change and challenge. It has, in fact, been an endless chase to keep up with events and in particular with John Hodgson (rather like chasing a comet). The excitement and challenge available in the contracting world provides a wonderful opportunity for anyone prepared to get involved (and to look for involvement when not totally necessary). I have been extremely lucky to have become involved long ago when things, in retrospect, were much more simple and uncomplicated.

To be in at the beginning of all major developments in D&H was a privilege granted to no one else but John. This aspect helped to make it 'our company', together with anyone who wanted to stay the pace and join the fun. In spite of many hurdles, dramas, extreme pressure and near disasters, it has always been fun. In the 'olden days' it was easy and required only an afternoon twice a week to keep up to date, and even as late as 1959 it was possible to deal with all financial aspects alone with the help of a wages clerk. At that stage it became obvious that assistance was essential and I was joined by Trevor Snell as accountant and Louise Joubert as typist in 1964. Louise is still with the Group and Trevor has recently re-joined a Group much changed in the interim. Over the years the assistance has grown as D&H has grown – starting at home where Pam my wife, and my children David and Susan, learnt to accept, not always willingly, that D&H was a major factor in my life and gave me the support that was necessary.

In time, when the operating companies each grew to a bigger size, accountants were appointed who became directly involved at the coal face. Back at head office there was a small number of supporting accountants who stayed for a while, then moved into the operations or left the group for other opportunities. Among these were Bill Adams, Roy Morris, John Kerr, Bill Robinson, Roy Gillette and John Parrott, all of whom were part of D&H growing up. In 1975 Terry Stone joined head office and soon became involved with Peter Loveday in keeping an eye on the growing materials, services and engineering divisions. Terry has since taken over the Group treasury and comptroller's function and still battles with the near impossible task of consolidating 150 to 200 subsidiaries which, like Topsy, just keep on growing.

When D&H head office moved to Hyde Park Louise Joubert was transferred to Savage and Lovemore so that she could stay in the Germiston area and Joan Plumb took over as finance secretary until she succumbed to the challenge of secretary to John. Jill Thackwray took over in 1976 and has coped wonderfully with financial language and figures ever since.

Although profits and cash flow were usually strong in D&H there was always the hungry urge for growth and grasp of new opportunities. We have always carefully planned this drive so as to use facilities to the full and keep financial administration stretched to its optimum. This technique has not changed one single bit over the last thirty years and the brightest and most enthusiastic new schemes have always been greeted by my query as to where the funds were supposed to be obtained. John's stock reply has always been to ensure that the 'right' decision was made and every opportunity seized, followed by an equally stock afterthought – 'I am sure that you will resolve the financial problem somehow.'

D&H over the years has learned to use fully the maximum gearing possible and we es-

Brian Robert Malcomson (executive director, finance).

tablished in the early days that high borrowings were not a problem provided that cash flow was very carefully controlled. The Tanker Services operation, for example, was established in 1959 within a share capital of R40 and an overdraft of R10 000. The oil companies were happy to provide credit facilities of 120/180 days and customers were pressed to pay within 30 days. This gap allowed us to purchase tar sprayers and bitumen tankers on hire purchase and meet the monthly payments with ease, contrary to the fears of conventional financiers who looked only at total debits and credits without taking into account the timing advantage of careful cash flow control.

As D&H grew in size and more and more people got into the act, the head office function changed. When divisional managers were appointed their staff took over the detailed running and John and I would travel around the country visiting all divisions once a quarter in Durban, Port Elizabeth and Cape Town and so were still able to keep close contact. Later, when there was too much on the go, divisions started coming to Sandton for quarterly board meetings.

John moved away from direct control at this stage and concentrated on expanding and finding new outlets and challenges for the ever growing group of managers. He found that negotiations, disposals and settling in of new operations took a great deal of time. The establishment of Wimpey Waste Management in the United Kingdom and D&H Canada provided exciting opportunities but sadly little profit and our overseas venture was brief. We have taken many opportunities over the years and I have learnt by experience that John's greatest skills emerge in the conceptual development and the strong negotiation to completion. Once the broad concept has been achieved he loses the challenge, leaving the details to others to tidy up. The pressures are there as we all do this, but fortunately so is the fun, which gives D&H its special atmosphere.

B R Malcomson
March 1984

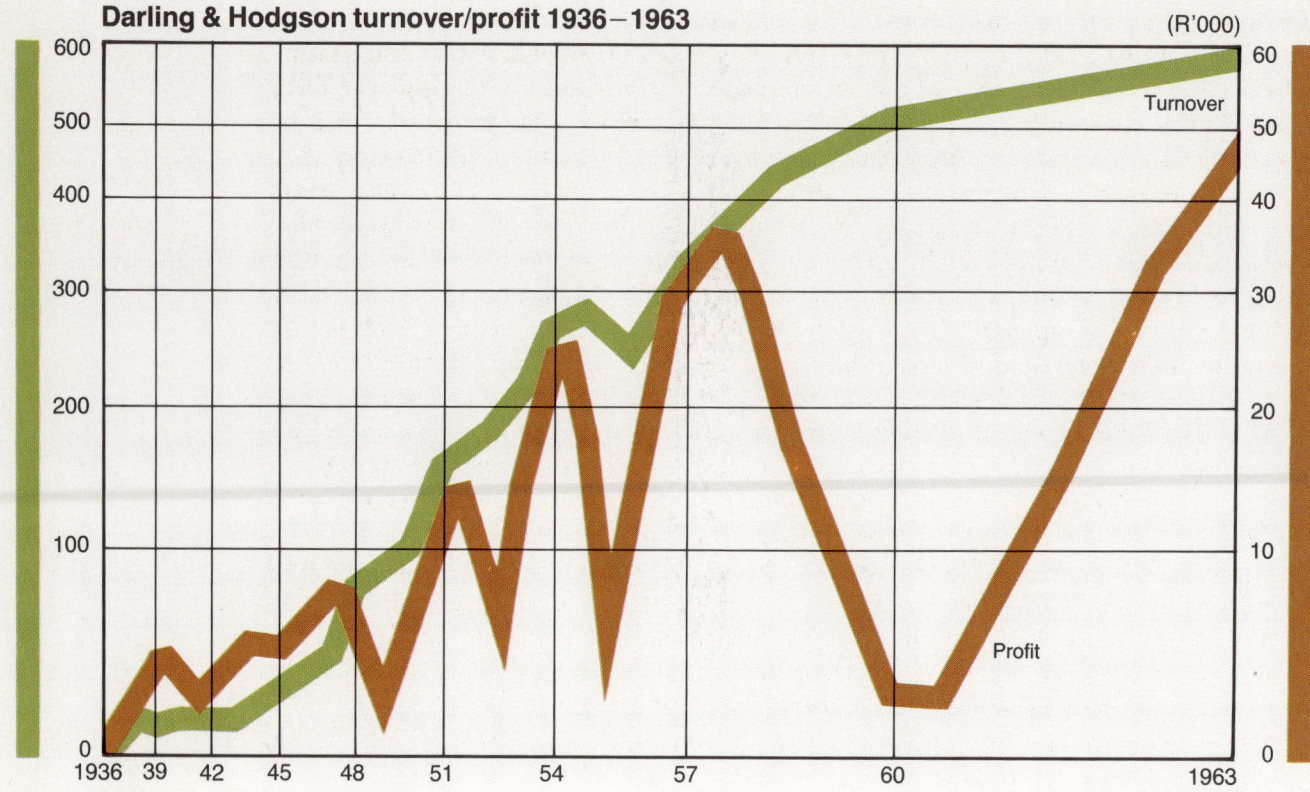

This graph reflects the steady growth of Darling and Hodgson's turnover over the period 1936 to 1963. Profit tended to follow at a 10% per annum rate but there were a few years when there were set-backs and profits nearly disappeared. This was not significant at the time but in the overall picture profit clearly lagged behind turnover.

The financial history of Darling and Hodgson reveals high priority given to the careful and expert control of cash flow, and this must have been a major factor from day one as early financial records show amounts of low value passing through Bill Hodgson's one-man business operation.

In 1936, the first financial year for which records are still available, Bill's business reflected an annual turnover of £2 602 (R5 000). This grew quite steadily even during the war years until 1944 when it reached £13 364 (R26 000) and by 1947 it had progressed to £21 166 (R42 000). During this period profits remained at a relatively constant rate and represented Bill's labours before charging any salary. With inflation not a factor in those days the rewards of his effort were sufficient to provide well for his family and also to enable his children to enjoy a high level of education at private schools. Bill had no wish to expand his business and was satisfied with the returns it gave. When John joined his father in 1947 he had a very different approach and his enthusiasm was fired by ambition. There was a noticeable improvement in turnover but it was some time before this extra effort was reflected in the level of profits.

Very little capital was introduced into the business at any stage and growth was dependent on retained earnings and bank overdrafts. In 1948, when Darling and Hodgson became a limited company, it was registered with a capital of £5 000. This was, however, merely a bookkeeping entry as it was represented only by a value placed on goodwill. That goodwill has continued to grow rapidly over the last fifty years and remains a very strong factor in the present market capitalization of Darling and Hodgson at R170 million. How correct the original assessment has turned out to be!

Only after the company was registered in 1948 was it possible to justify external loans, and useful funding was provided in 1949 and 1950 by loans from the Robson and Gulliver Trusts. Bank overdraft facilities rose in that year to £3 000, with personal guarantees from Bill Hodgson and his close friend Wolton Gray. Further loans came from Tom Robson and Jack Plane in 1952. These were converted into preference shares the following year and subsequently acquired directly by the Hodgson family.

Overdraft finance during this period was a constant worry for Bill and John, with an anxious bank manager frequently on the telephone as soon as drawings approached the limit. At this stage the close association with Harry Eastwood was responsible for an offer of overdraft facilities by Netherlands Bank in 1953. The size of the facility and the more relaxed approach of this bank had an enormous impact on the development of Darling and Hodgson. From that date on the banks have become increasingly involved partners in the growth of the Group, creating a friendly association which has been the cornerstone of development over subsequent years. Ironically, as new associates became involved in the Group and other activities were developed, Netherlands Bank participation became increasingly less significant and although many banks are now fully involved, the real support has come from Barclays and also from Standard Bank.

After 1953 profits started to climb quite dramatically, with Tarmac Industries developing rapidly and additional contracting work undertaken by Darling and Hodgson in the Cape, Natal and in Rhodesia. These all made useful contributions and profits grew steadily (except for a sharp dip in 1956 which looks dramatic but involved only R20 000) until the late fifties, at which stage turnover had reached nearly half a million rand with profits in excess of R30 000 per annum. Sadly Bill died in 1959. Although grieved by his father's death, John rapidly began to pursue his ambitions for expansion, which he had held in check in respect of his father's wishes to keep the company small. Tanker Services and RMC (SA) were established in 1959 and 1960 respectively.

In the early sixties profits began to fluctuate considerably, affected significantly by the demands of Darling and Hodgson's first really big contract, Collondale airport in East London. The increasing pressure of funding turnover that had climbed to almost R500 000 per annum placed a great strain on the shareholders who had guaranteed the company's overdraft and hire purchase agreements with all their worldly possessions. When an opportunity arose in 1963 to take in Union Corporation as a majority partner it was a very welcome relief to shed the guarantees and look to 'big daddy' to stand behind all future developments. A pattern of steady growth was established and Darling and Hodgson were able to succeed on their own with the underlying support of Union Corporation.

The association with Union Corporation also provided shareholders with an opportunity for the first time to take out in cash some of the profits that had been ploughed back year after year for thirty years.

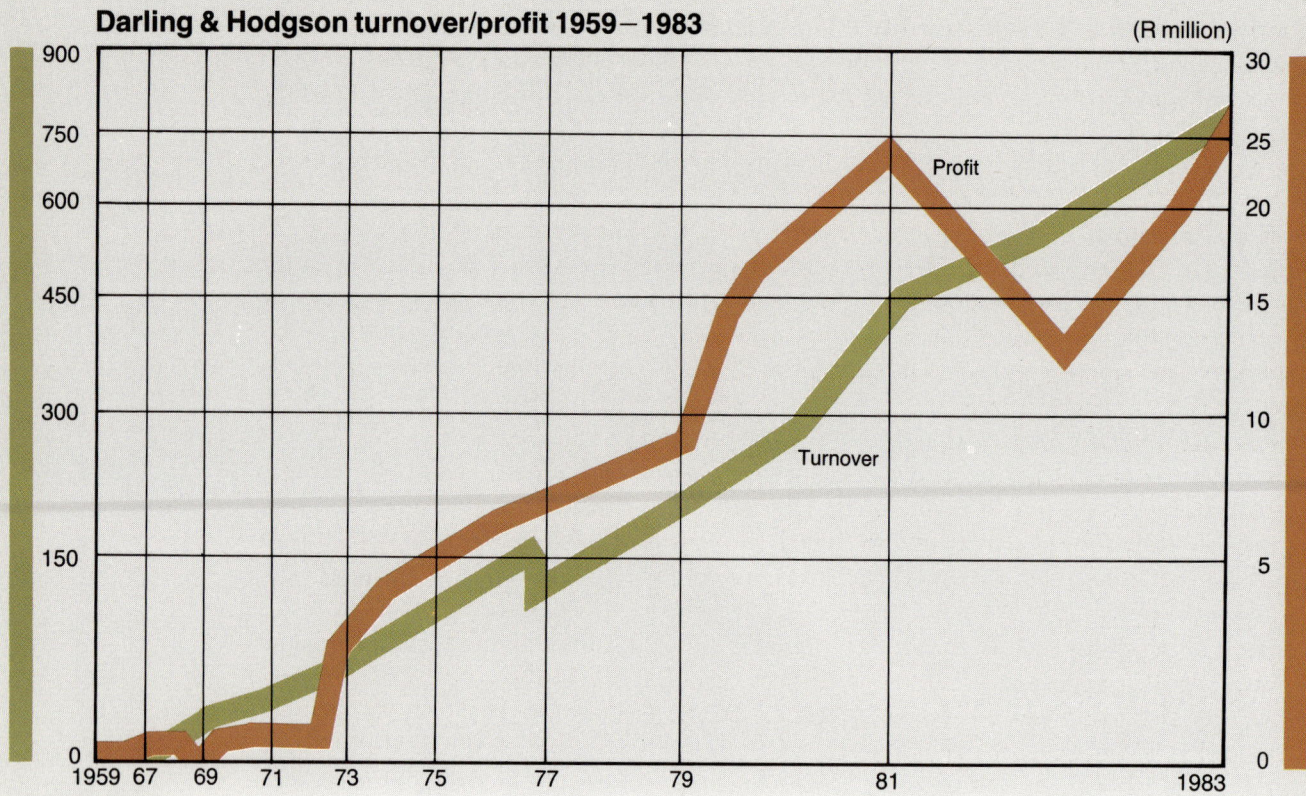

This graph reflects the change that took place after Union Corporation became a shareholder. It indicates the relative insignificance of all that had happened up to that stage and the benefits that were achieved through the larger, well-funded organization. The rapid increase in turnover produced an equally rapid increase in profits with less fluctuation, except in 1982. The company clearly became more efficient and managed to extract more profit in proportion to turnover than in the previous period.

The partnership with Union Corporation had a dramatic impact and the extra available finance facilitated rapid development and the exploration of many opportunities.

After 1963 turnover climbed to R2,3 million and escalated rapidly up to R75 million in 1973 as a result of vigorous organic expansion accompanied by the acquisition of new subsidiaries and associated companies. The first of these were 51% of A G Burton (100% within two years) and a minority interest in Savage and Lovemore, both acquired in 1963. The following year the joint association with Tarmac UK through V F J Hall had a significant impact on turnover but little joy in profits and the next year this partnership was dissolved. However, the partnership with United Bulk Transport, established in 1967, increased the bulk transport operations very rapidly. There again, however, the 50/50 arrangement did not prove satisfactory and profits in 1969 reflected a loss of R123 000 even though turnover had risen at this stage to R39 million. A considerable portion of this loss came from road construction operations which had recently all been rationalized under Savage and Lovemore, with accompanying problems of merging and tidying up the past.

The company reflected a debt equity ratio ranging between 75% and 100% during this period which would have been cause for concern in the earlier days but was accepted by the bankers in the light of the Union Corporation shareholding. This high level of borrowings remained right through to 1973, when it reached R13,7 million. This did not reflect the total funds available for growth, however, as there had been several changes in the share capital, commencing in 1964 when funds advanced by Union Corporation were converted into 1,1 million convertible redeemable preference shares.

Further capital was introduced in 1968 when Union Corporation took up the total rights issue of 200 000 ordinary shares at R5, and an additional R2 million new preference shares which were needed to fund the increased stake in Savage and Lovemore and another subsidiary, Ready Mixed Concrete, both to 51%. This was followed by a further issue of ordinary shares in 1969. The willingness of Union Corporation to pay a four times premium indicated their confidence in the future prospects of the Group which was confirmed when profits after tax increased from R100 000 in 1968 to R881 000 in 1972.

D&H's first ordinary dividend in thirty-two years was declared in 1966, at 5c per share. The following year saw a dividend of 10c and 1968 one of 15c. Since then shareholders have been assured of an increasing return on their investment.

The impact of tax became a significant factor in 1970 but the special allowances which were available in manufacturing operations and initially in the contracting field enabled the Group to keep its average tax rate well down from 1973 onwards. From time to time acquisitions made within the Group have also brought their own assessed losses which have contributed to the low average tax rate.

In 1973 the whole Group structure was carefully examined. Probably influenced by the conversion date of the preference shares issued in 1968 which could not be converted to ordinary shares after 1973, Union Corporation recommended that the time had arrived for Darling and Hodgson to become a public listed company. This decision opened many new opportunities for development and also provided some of the original shareholders with an opportunity to realize part of their locked-in investment. With the inflow of public money it was possible to terminate the partnership with United Bulk Transport, to make Ready Mixed Concrete a wholly-owned subsidiary, to increase the stake in Savage and Lovemore to 75%, to take over a majority shareholding in Project Engineering, to purchase Mazista and to make the first move into commercial quarries through Shires. In spite of the very successful share issue, the borrowings at the end of 1974 reached R27 million and a debt-equity ratio of 124% which was a little alarming. In order to ease this situation and also provide further funds for yet another development, a rights issue of 3,5 million shares was arranged in 1975 which brought in significant capital and also increased the borrowings potential.

The phenomenal growth in turnover from R75 million in 1973 to R763 million by the end of 1983 also brought a very rapid improvement in earnings which grew from R2,6 million at flotation up to R27 million within ten years. A significant contribution to profits was made by the purchase of the Fowler Holdings group in 1981, and the acquisition of a majority shareholding in Group Five Engineering in 1983 boosted the contribution from construction operations to R17 million. The total borrowings continued to climb, reaching R123 million at the end of 1983, reflecting a debt–equity ratio again up to 90%. This was largely due to the disastrous results in the engineering division from 1981 which caused Group profits to fall in 1982 for the first time in fifteen years. The total cost of funding this division and the abortive move into oil rig construction cost the Group approximately R45 million and severely impacted future profitability.

The results of 1983 proved that D&H was back on course with a firm foundation for future growth. Not only were they better than 1982, they were 10% ahead of 1981 which had been a boom year. The acquisition of a significant shareholding in Blue Circle Cement at the beginning of 1984 further ensured success in the future.

The very close and harmonious relationship that the Group has had with its bankers since 1963 has enabled it to manage its finances using short-term borrowings only and it has avoided the restrictions which long-term funding can produce. Overall the cost of this form of finance has been favourable but it inflicts a heavy burden when interest rates are very high.

The Group has also maintained excellent relations with its auditors and legal advisers, Goldby, Panchaud and Webber, who were appointed Group auditors in 1963 as a result of Darling and Hodgson's new association with Union Corporation. They found it necessary in 1964 to include a mild qualification in their auditors' report, arising out of Darling and Hodgson's unwillingness to provide for losses in certain contracting subsidiaries which they believed would soon rectify themselves. This qualification proceeded into 1965 and appeared again in 1967, after which no further problems were experienced. The relationship with Goldbys, and especially Roderick Macintosh, has grown strongly since then and the auditing relationship of the Group as a whole has been considerably enhanced by the contribution of Strelitz and Mitchell in the Savage and Lovemore group, and subsequently of Cooper Bros who were involved in Fowler Holdings and in Group Five Engineering. In 1959 an association was developed with the legal firm of Bowman, Gilfillan and Blacklock when Standish O'Grady became involved in all the problem areas. This association has lasted ever since and has proved extremely valuable. Standish's guidance has saved many disasters, and close personal relationships have developed. These relationships echo in many ways those that Bill Hodgson established in the early days of Darling and Hodgson, and they have all had a significant influence on the successful development of the Group to the position it holds in 1984.

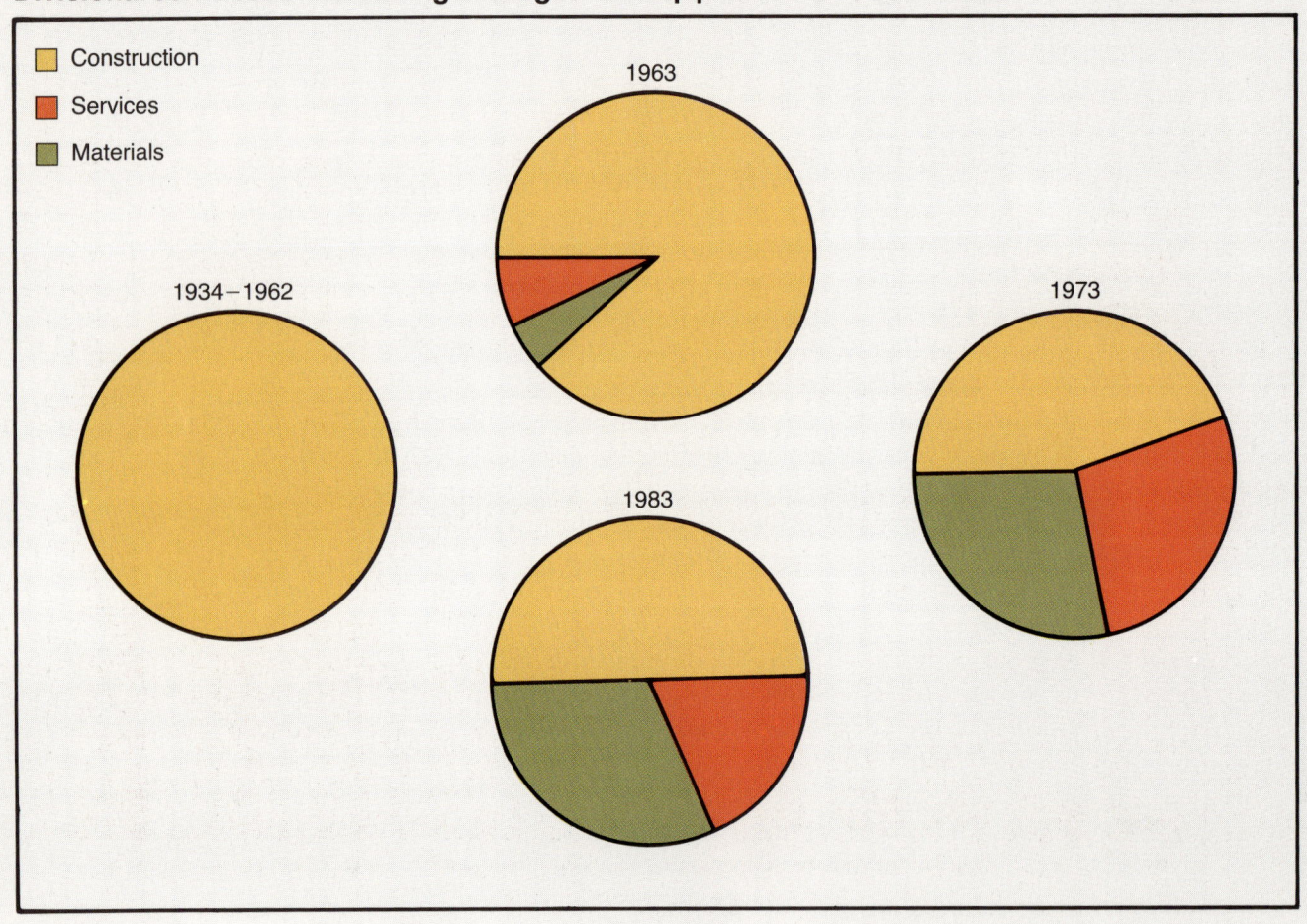

Divisional contribution to Darling & Hodgson Group profits from 1934–1983

The pie diagrams show the relative contributions of the three main operating divisions of the Group at various stages in the history of D&H. Up to 1962 all profit contribution came from the construction division. In that year small profits were made by the transport and ready-mixed concrete operations for the first time. In 1973, however, the picture changed when minority shareholdings were purchased in all companies and development escalated. Although the construction division maintained its position as the major contributor until 1982, the materials division has shown the most dramatic and steady improvement to date. The engineering division is not included as it was never really part of the Group and its closing down in 1983 brought to an end an unfortunate period when the last three years' losses totally wiped out the earlier profits. Coal produced profits from 1980 to 1982 but fell away in 1983 when prices for export dropped disastrously.

The year 1984 will reflect an even stronger construction contribution when the greater stake in Group Five Engineering merged with the D&H construction interests will constitute one of the largest civil engineering units in the country. The association with Blue Circle will help to restore the balance with materials only in 1985 when a major upturn is expected. Services is in a difficult position to keep up with the other divisions as it already has a very high share of the market and will need to search vigorously to find new opportunities.

The bar chart reveals the relative contributions of the main operating divisions of the Group between 1973 and 1983. Engineering is not included, but the fluctuations of the coal division are clearly indicated.

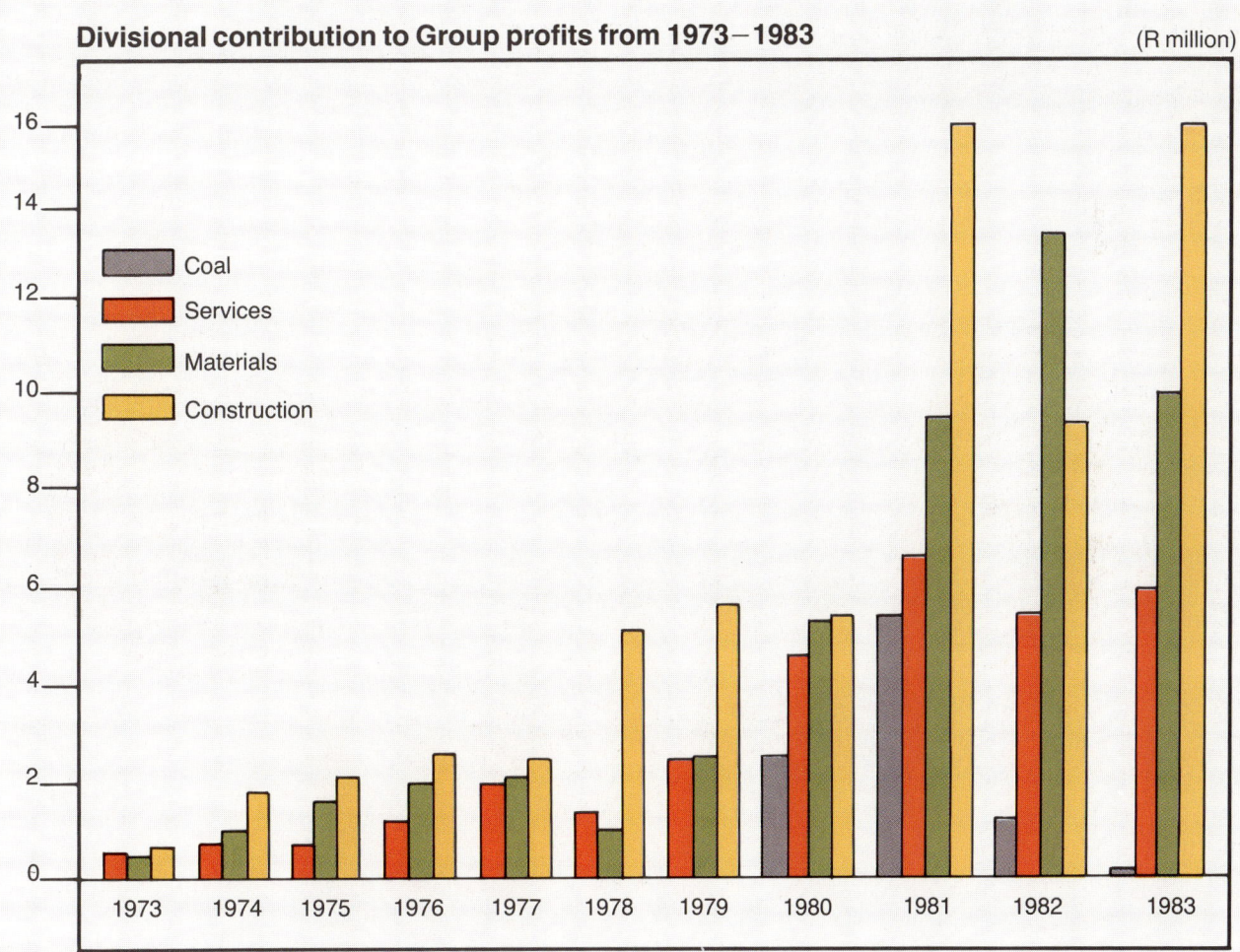

D&H at a glance

Darling and Hodgson established as a partnership	1934	
Offices in Cullinan Building, Johannesburg		
Sandy Darling bought out	1935	
Yard established at Heriotdale	1947	
John Hodgson joins the family business		
	1948	Tarmac Industries
Darling and Hodgson (Pty) Ltd incorporated		
Bill Hodgson chairman and managing director		
John Hodgson managing director	1951	
	1952	Tarmac Industries a wholly-owned subsidiary
Brian Malcomson joins Darling and Hodgson	1953	
First spray tanker purchased		
Komga – first road contract outside Transvaal		
	1954	Darling and Hodgson (Rhodesia)
		Darling and Hodgson (Natal)
		Darling and Hodgson (Cape)
Offices and yard established at Brailsford House	1955	
Brian Malcomson financial director		
	1958	Collondale airport – first contract over a million rand
Bill Hodgson dies	1959	
Jack Plane chairman		
		Tanker Services
		Darling and Hodgson (South West)
	1960	Windhoek Crushers
		Ready Mixed Concrete (SA)
	1961	Ready Mixed Concrete (PE)
		Ready Mixed Concrete (Cape)
		Ready Mixed Concrete (Reef)
	1962	Ready Mixed Concrete (East Rand)
Union Corporation acquires 51% of Darling and Hodgson	1963	
Darling and Hodgson Holdings formed		
		Savage and Lovemore – 25%
		A G Burton – 51%
Rights issue	1964	
		Ready Mixed Concrete (Natal)
		A G Burton – 100%
	1965	Ready Mixed Concrete (SA) 50% partnership with Pioneer Ready Mixed Concrete
	1966	Embecon
	1968	Tanker Services 50% partnership with United Bulk Transport to form United Tanker Services
D&H's name leaves the construction industry		All construction interests merged into Savage and Lovemore
		Savage and Lovemore – 51%
Rights issue		
		Vandex
	1969	Purle Industrial Waste
Corporate head office moves to Hyde Park Corner	1970	
D&H logo registered	1971	
		Vandex sold
	1973	Project Engineering – 61%
		50% in United Tanker Services sold – Tanker Services wholly-owned except in the Cape
		Ready Mixed Concrete wholly-owned
		Savage and Lovemore – 75%
		Mazista – 65%
John Henderson chairman		
Darling and Hodgson goes public		
		Shires Quarry – 100%
	1974	Hume Prestressed Concrete – 100% name changed to Hucrete
		Paul's Industrial Investments acquired
		Dunn's Blue Rock Quarry purchased by Savage and Lovemore – name changed to Cape Blue Rock Quarry
		Cason Engineering – 100%
	1975	Project Engineering – 79%
		Mazista – 100%
		Purle changed to Waste-tech
		Omnibus – 60%
Rights issue		
	1976	Evander Crushers
		Zweiamic Transport – 100% name changed to Refrigerated Transport
John Hodgson chairman and chief executive		

	1977	Underwater Construction – 51%
		W J Bulk Transport – 100%
		Construction Materials (Randmix) – 100%
		Option exercised on Clairwood Quarries
		SAFIC Resources – 60%
		50% sold in Pioneer Ready Mixed Concrete
		Ready Mixed Concrete (East Rand) sold
		Ready Mixed Concrete (Natal) wholly-owned
	1978	Savage and Lovemore – 96%
		Savage and Lovemore Mining
D&H (Europe) BV formed		Wimpey Waste Management in the United Kingdom
D&H extends operations into Canada		
		Shareholding in United Tanker Services (Cape) sold
		D&H Flora
		D&H Automotive Services
		Rand Founders – 100%
		Omnibus – 100%
		SAFIC Resources – 80%
		name changed to D&H Ash Resources
	1979	Monahan and Frost – 100%
		Refrigerated Transport –
		name changed to D&H Freight Lines
		Hucrete sold
		Hydrochem – 51%
	1980	Savage and Lovemore – 100%
		Containerisation Africa – 60%
		name changed to D&H Semi-Bulk Systems
		D&H Flora sold
		D&H Ash Resources – 100%
		Amardah Shipyards – 50%
		D&H Coal
		Shareholding in Wimpey Waste Management sold
	1981	Fowler Holdings – 100%
		includes Fowler Construction
		Combrink Construction
		R H Morris
		Felbitem
Code of employment practice adopted		
		Pine Smyth – 50%
		D&H Semi-Bulk – 100%
		Chemintal – 100%
		D&H Industrial Services
		D&H Structural Engineering
Canadian interests sold		
D&H's name returns to the construction industry	1982	D&H Construction
		D&H Civils
		Hydrochem – 100%
		Stevenson Construction – 100%
		Roadmix – 100%
		Omnibus sold
		Keir and Cawder – 66%
		Brits Crushers – 100%
		Mooinooi Crushers – 100%
		Umzimkulu Quarry – 100%
		Shareholding in Amardah Shipyards sold
		Majority of engineering operations closed
		Rooikraal Quarry
		Group Five Engineering – 20%
	1983	Keir and Cawder – 100%
		Ready Mixed Concrete opens in Bloemfontein
		D&H Freight Lines closed
		Cason Engineering sold
		Mazista sold
		Group Five Engineering – 50,7%
		M&S Crushers – 100%
	1984	D&H's construction division merges with
		Group Five Engineering
		Group Five Engineering – 65,5%
		Blue Circle – 30%
		45% of D&H materials division sold to Blue Circle
		Garocade and Harvester timber transport companies – 100%
Rights issue		
D&H's 50th anniversary		

Long Service Employees – over twenty-five years in December 1983

		Date of Joining
CORPORATE HEADQUARTERS		
	John Brailsford Hodgson	4.08.1947
	Mack Mashigo	11.11.1949
	Brian Robert Malcomson	1.05.1953
	James Magagula	15.04.1956
CONSTRUCTION		
Savage and Lovemore	A G Velthuysen	4.01.1953
	Jaki George	7.06.1953
	G C Bakkes	1.10.1954
	G C Kettlewell	1.11.1955
	Willie Payi	1.03.1956
Fowlers	Johan Prinsloo	18.02.1947
R H Morris	W O Ngoqi	9.05.1952
	W Louw	20.02.1958
Roadmix	Jack Mpondo	8.08.1953
	Christopher Appelgryn	30.08.1955
	Mias Ntsomi	12.02.1957
Stevenson Construction	Raphael Nqwabi	14.01.1949
	Zebvon Buthelezi	± 1959
SERVICES		
Tanker Services (Natal)	Johannes Jacobus Engelbrecht	8.03.1955
W J Bulk Transport	Gladys Charlotte Thorpe	1.11.1957
MATERIALS		
D&H Quarries	Samuel Mabasa	8.09.1951
	Aaron Chimfumbo	6.11.1953
	George Ngwenya	5.08.1954
	Harry Madonsela	1.06.1955
	Samuel Kekana	1956
D&H Materials – south western	Joseph Mayinji	5.01.1958
	Setembiso Mafusini	24.07.1958
D&H Materials – central	Pieter Eliza Kleynhans	10.03.1944
	Hendrik Christiaan Lindeque	1.06.1948
	Mokasie Piet Matsuimane	30.10.1952
	Rudolf Gerbrand Pieterse	28.04.1953
	Jacobus Hendrik Wiese	20.01.1955
	Wilson Mangope	5.04.1955
	Henry Lerole Makgahlela	10.10.1955

D&H Materials – central	Mokula Paul Tlhalogang	21.01.1957
	Alphonse Lefela	26.06.1957
	Jonas Moduka	3.02.1958
	Willem Haltile	1.07.1958
D&H Materials – eastern	William John Watson	1.06.1936
	Naddragen Maurice Moodley	13.11.1952
	Paulos Mafisa	11.12.1954
	Manamolela Nhlapo	11.01.1955
	Mabusa Shabalala	1.09.1955
	Pupu Steven Sithole	26.02.1957
	Mbungwa Mketwa	3.12.1957
	Letuka Qupete	8.04.1958

MANUFACTURING

Rand Founders	William Wallace	20.01.1946
	Thomas Bothwell	11.05.1948
	Poala Morara	8.03.1948
	December Magwaza	20.05.1954
	Zaccheus Nyondeni	26.01.1956

GROUP FIVE ENGINEERING

Basil Read	D Ntuli	1.07.1950
	W L Schott	9.08.1951
	Johannes Sekgobela	5.01.1952
	James Sambo	26.08.1952
	Piet Thokwana	9.09.1952
	July Ndhlovu	15.11.1952
	Jan Ngozo	15.11.1952
	Fannie Skosana	13.02.1953
	Klaas Mokgesi	6.05.1953
	H A Manders (Senior)	3.01.1955
	Phineas Kobe	4.01.1955
	J J Manders (Senior)	11.05.1955
	T M Makoena	1.07.1955
	Daniel Mahlayela	1.08.1955
	C S van Hees	17.08.1955
	Jan Boshomane	12.10.1955
	Lucas Nkobe	6.02.1956
	D Moutaung	1.07.1956
	Phillemon Molokomme	2.11.1956
	P F Cranco	1.01.1957
	Titus Marakalala	1.02.1957
	M W Moremi	28.02.1957
	Alfred Jwara	9.07.1957
	H A Manders (Junior)	22.01.1958
	P J Pienaar	1.02.1958
	Joseph Sethosa	25.05.1958
	L V Mosala	9.09.1958
	P Cairns	1.10.1958
	M P Mosala	13.10.1958
	Daniel Magane	1950
	Titus Mokoena	1955
	January Sikuni	1957
	Samson Mohlomi	1957

Basil Read	Nelson Mlangeni	1957
	Solomon Monyai	1957
	Jim Silwane	1958
McLaren and Eger	J F van der Berg	1.04.1943
	W Mokone	1.01.1949
	P E Leteane	1.02.1951
	R C Heddon	1.03.1951
	D K Brooks	1.06.1952
	M Nxumalo	28.05.1952
	J P Wilken	6.07.1953
	R Shemba	4.10.1954
CMGM	Aaron Khumalo	1949
	Job Siphiwe Cele	1949
	Petros Zwane	1950
	Piet	1952
	Jonas Kwale	1952
	Rex Mangale	1952
	Andries Mashele	1953
	Johnson Mhlungu	1953
	Two Boy Motloung	1954
	Jack Matlokotsi	1954
	Enos Dlamini	1955
	Botile Tatolo	1955
	Absalom Maseko	1956
	Johan Ngwenya	1957
	Piet Zulu	1957
	Hezekia Buthelezi	1957
	Timothy Nkosi	1958
	Lyn Eustace	1958
	Thomas Buthelezi	1958
	Jim Makohabu Vilahazi	1958
	Elliot Sithole	1958
	Griffith Sikani	
	Sibonona Simelane	
	Albert Langa	
	Bible Khumalo	
	Lucas Mabema	
	Elmon Nkuna	
	Alfred Sibiya	
	Koos Meintjies	
	Martin Muller	

Acknowledgements

It was only when we had finished writing and contemplated the three years that were spent preparing this jubilee book that we realized how many people had helped us in putting together the history of D&H. It is impossible to mention everyone, but we hope that each person who spared time and thought for our project will see evidence of his or her contribution in the book and know that we appreciated it.

Most particularly we thank John Hodgson and Brian Malcomson who helped and encouraged us beyond all expectations, making time for regular meetings and discussions, each time inspiring us with greater enthusiasm. They read and checked everything that we wrote with infinite patience. From Ruth Hodgson we gained special support and a warm understanding of the company.

The initial research was undertaken by Rosemary with Cathy Bath who approached the project with an enthusiasm born from her husband David's involvement in D&H. She was constantly cheerful and efficient – thank you, Cathy!

We are grateful to many people who worked for the company in the past, some who still do and others who have had a close association with Darling and Hodgson, all of whom helped in particular to build up a picture of the early days. Hubert and Diana Goetsch shared their memories of Bill and Mabel and the small family business. Bill's good friends and business associates looked back over the years for us – Ernest and Helene Newbury, Philip Lowman, Viv Lyons, Harry Eastwood and Switch Cuningham. Ian Glauber gave us a vivid picture of Darling and Hodgson in the developing field of ready-mixed concrete. The early period of association with Union Corporation was described by Ian Wilson, John Henderson, Cyril Newnham and Aidan Buchholz.

When we turned to individual companies the people who had been with them for many years shared their experiences and their photographs, as well as providing other sources of information. We thank them all, especially Andrew Savage and David Lovemore, Howard Johnsen, Charlie Mowatt, Wally Rodd, Ian McLaren, and Fanie Gouws, who rescued a very old Fowler's minute book and gave it to the D&H archives.

Those who were interviewed provided us with the backbone of the book. Then we began to delve into minute books and records to confirm dates and expand the story. Again we met with willing assistance wherever we went, from the Johannesburg Reference and Africana libraries to D&H's operating companies. We are grateful to Mr Vos of Escom who shared with us some of the information that he is gathering together for that company's archives; also to Mrs Linaker at Lonrho who made it possible for us to examine the early minute books of Tweefontein Colliery, and to Mrs den Bakker whose father worked at the colliery with Bill. We appreciated guidance from Dolores Fleischer who set us on the right path in the beginning and continued to advise us during the writing of the book.

We thank the numerous secretaries in the Group who willingly and promptly produced information for us, especially in the few weeks before the book went to the publishers when our time was running out! We also thank all those senior managers and directors who checked specific sections of the book. We made extensive use of the in-house magazines and appreciate the work that the editors have done over the years!

When it came to illustrating the book we turned to Eddie Barton in the public relations department, who gave us inestimable assistance and found fascinating photographs which complemented those so kindly lent to us by other people. He also turned his inimitable artistic talent to producing the book's cover picture. We thank him, and also Caroline Hendrickse who joined D&H to create a library soon after our project started and brought order to a wealth of information.

Writing the D&H history has been a happy and rewarding time for us both. It has also been an all-absorbing task, and our last and far from least thanks go to our immediate families who have shown infinite patience and understanding. They have constantly supported and encouraged us, even answering the oddest questions with equanimity!

Rosemary Hayward
Nancy Stratten
April 1984

Selected Index

Illustrations indicated in **bold**

AE&CI, 151, 198, 199, 218
A G Burton, 52, 54, 59, 62, 63, 66, 86, 90–95, 106, 107, 288
Acres, Ernie, 258
Adams, Bill, 283
Adams, Buck, 46, 54, 55, 57, 58, 65, 168
Adamson, Bill, 59
African Products Manufacturing Company, 180, **180**
Ahrens, Bob, 246
Alty, Tony, 171, 173
Amardah Shipyards, 79, 82, 262, 263, **263**, 269, 289
Anderson, Colin, 59
Anderson, Ken, 24
Anglo Alpha Cement, 175, 217, 220
Anglo American Corporation, 26, 170, 184, 251, 263
Ansermino, Adelmo, 236
Arnot, Tony, 190
Asher, Peter, 76, 79, 206, 207, 220, 221, 223, 239, 241, 280
Ashmore, Benson and Peas, 16, 18
Associated Quarries, 242, 243
Austin, Ed, 46

Bacon, Francis, 52
Baiocchi, Rose, 236, 237, **237**, 240, 260
Baker, Sir Herbert, 133
Baker Marine Corporation, 262
Barclays Bank, 21, 30, 37, 61, 287
Barker, Walter, 205, 247, 248
Barlow, Trevor, 188
Barlow Rand Group, 138, **138**, 139
Barton, Eddie, 79, 80, 197, 297
Basil Read, **7**, **8**, **9**, 10, 86, 89, 131, 147, 148, 149, 151, **151**, 152
Bates, Paul, 253
Bath, David, 5, **5**, 79, 82, 84, **84**, 207, 209, 210, **210**, 216, 223, 225, 226, 227, 230, 231, 280, 282
Bauer, Herman, 114
Bayley, Sally, 189
Bayliss, Bill, 92
Beaumont, Jim, 170, 171, 173
Beets, 'Mannetjies', **186**
Bell, H E, 30
Bell, Des, 170, 188
Belmont Tiles, 237, 239
Benedict, Steve, 246
Beveridge, J M, 212
Bewick, Ian, 199
Bianco, Papa, 47
Bildt, 26, 27
Blackwood-Murray, Rob, 191
Blakeway, Ralph, 212

Blakey and Hope, 143
Blue Circle, 4, **7**, 11, **12**, 217, 289, 291
Blumenthal, Mr, 29
Blundell, Lawrence, 186
Boddington, Ivor, 252
Booth, Stan, 167, 172, 173
Botha, Hennie, 119
Botha, Paul, 186
Bothwell, Tommy, 260
Boucher, Charlie, 249
Bowman, Gilfillan and Blacklock, 290
Boyd-White, Charles, 170
Brailscar, 75
Brailsford House, 40, 42, 43, 44, **44**, **45**, 46, 47, **48**, 49, 54, 55, 56, 57, 62, 66, 70, 81, 92, 93, 107, 161, 164, 165, 166, 167, 171, 176, 178, 179, 184, 186, 191, 212, 215, 246, 248, 252, 262
Brailsford Investments, 43
Breedt, Jack, 102, 114
Brickor, 194
British Petroleum, **6**, 156, 266
Brits Crushers, 208
Brockley Quarry, 209
Brooks, Hugh, **186**
Broude, Solomon, 212
Buchholz, Aidan, 58, 59, 70, 76, 78, 92, 194, 197, 198, 249
Buckingham, Joe, 170
Bulk Charters, 269
Bulk Concrete, 212
Bull, Dave, 264
Burger, Johan, 277
Burger, Maurice, 42, 52, 54, 63, 65
Burger, Shirley, 36, 52
Burton, Ben, 90, 91

C and J Reid, 145, 151
CMGM, **7**, 10, 126, 147, 148, **148**, 150, 151
CMGM Building, 151
CMGM Glybeton, **9**, 151
Cabora Bassa, 175, 248, 256
Cade, Eric, 25, 35
Callegari, Vic, 176, **186**
Caltex, 167
Cameron, Steve, 102
Campbell, Edith, 195, 200
Cape Blue Rock Quarry, 113, 208, **208**
Cape Portland Cement, 172
Cape Provincial Administration, 98, 99, 104, 134
Carmont, Mildred, 29
Cason Engineering Works, 258, **259**, 260, **260**, 264
Cement Marketing Organization, 175
Cement Producers Association, 173
Central Services, 187

Chanderpol, Robin, **178**
Chemintal, 199
Chloorkop Quarries, 237, 240, **240**
Christiani and Nielsen, 218, 219
Clairwood Quarry, **10**, **203**, 206, **207**, **226**, 227, 243, **243**, 245, **245**
Clark, George, **5**, **82**
Clayville Quarry, **209**
Clifford Harris, 86, 98, 167, 168
Clinch, Brendan, 26
Clogg, Peter, 147, 150, 153, **153**
Coetzee, Marianna, 277
Cole, Des, 226
Collondale airport, 45–47, 49, 50, **51**, 54, 56, 57, 86, 101, 219, 287
Combrink, Alex, **5**, 79, **82**, 83, **84**, 88, 89, **89**, 118, 119, 129, 131, 132, 134, 137, 138, 139, 140, 144, 147, 154
Combrink, Fay, 137, 138
Combrink Construction, **6**, **7**, 10, 79, 88, 89, 127, 129, 131, 137–140, 150, 278
Concor, 86
Concrete roads, 104–106, 113, 116, 129
Consolidated Commercial Company, 92
Consolidated Crusher Holdings, 67, 212, 217
Consolidated Stone Crushers, 211
Construction Materials, 243
Containerisation Africa, 82, 160, 189
Continental Sleepers, 78, 205
Cook, Jimmy, 44, 116
Cookeshaft Crushers, **11**, 206
Cooper Bros, 290
Corner House Investments, 212
Cramond Earth Movers, 40, 45, 46, 47, 54
Cranemix Plant Hire, 222
Crawford, Ged, 270, 271
Crawley Motors, 170
Croad, Tony, 74
Crofthead Quarry, 209
Cronje, Don, 233
Cross, Rod, 35, 36, 83
Crow, John, 215
Crown Crushers, 212
Crown Mines property, 173, 175, 178, 200, 212, **213**, 214, 215, 216, 217, 221, 223, 236
Cullinan Building, 24, **24**, 29, 30, 35, 36, 83
Cuningham, Roger, 92, 113, 114, 115, 119, 280
Cuningham, Switch, 45, 92, 163

D&H Ash Resources, **7**, 11, 75, 206, 207, 209, 253–254
D&H Automotive Services, **7**, 13, 159, 187–188
D&H Canada, 78, 79, 207, 285
D&H Civils, 88, 89, 119, 126, 151
D&H Coal, 15, 79, 82, 264, 268–272
D&H Construction, **7**, 10, 84, **87**, 88, 89, 119, 131
D&H Enterprise, 161, **161**
D&H (Europe), 77, 78, 249
D&H Explorer, 160, 161
D&H Flora, 77, 79, 159, 196
D&H Freight Lines, 82, 158, **158**, 177
D&H Industrial Services, 199
D&H Lime, **7**, 11, 209
D&H News, 71, 79, **80**
D&H Quarries, 11, 209, **239**, 240, 241, **241** (*see also* Paul's Sand)
D&H Semi-Bulk, **7**, 13, 82, 160, 189–190
D&H Structural Engineering, 190, 263
D&H Village, **277**, 278
D B Lovemore Earthmoving Contractor, 97
D F Malan airport, 108
Daniels, John, 260
Darling, Sandy, 21
Darling and Hodgson (Cape), 42, 44, 49, 168, 287
Darling and Hodgson (Natal), 42, 44, 45, 50, 163, 166, 287
Darling and Hodgson (Pty) Ltd, 28, 30–59, 62, 65, 66, 71, 86, 91, 92, 93, 95, 99, 100, 101, 102, 103, 106, 107, 116, 128, 145, 163, 165, 166, 286, 290
Darling and Hodgson (Rhodesia), 40, **42**, 44, 52, 287
Darling and Hodgson (South West), 54, 58
Davidson, Les, 146
Dawson, Stuart, 147, 150
Dawson-Squibb, Mrs, 24
De Beer, Harold, 195
De Beer, Peter, 159, 162, 187, 188
De Beer, Tom, **5**, 6
De Luca, Aldo, 236, 237, 239
De Neef, Peter, 42, 50, 52, 65, 166
De Wet, John, 118
Department of Water Affairs, 65, 68, 113, 194, 251
Desert Spar, 267
Dick, Graham, 176
Dividag, 205
Douglas, Neil, **153**, 154
Draper, James, 258
Du Plessis, Philip, 241, 243, 245
Dunlop Heywood, 59
Dunn's Blue Rock Quarry (*see* Cape Blue Rock Quarry)
Dura Foundation, 150
Durandt, Laurie, 78, 79, 206, 207
Durban Cement Company, 175, 188, 220
Durban Exporters Committee, 270
Dutton, 26, **26**, 32, 56, 280
Dyckerhoff, Widmann and Thompson, 102
Dyckerhoff and Widmann, 204

East Rand Crushers, 206
Eastern Province Cement Company, 217
Eastwood, Harry, 37, 287
Edward, Teddy, 37
Edwards, Tommy, 228
Edwards, Willie, 228
Eger, Fred, 149
Egg, Neville, 260
Electricity Supply Commission (*see* Escom)
Embecon, **7**, 11, 68, 70, 71, **72**, 73, 75, 77, 106, 193, 202, 204, 205, 207, 209, 228, 246–252
Engelbrecht, Hannes, 175
Erasmus, Phil, 5, **5**, 55, 62, 67, 76, 84, **84**, 156, 159, **161**, 162, 166, 167, 170, 171, 173, 174, 175, 176, 177, 178, 179, 198, 280
Erikson, Des, 228
Escom, **8**, 37, 42, 97, 109, 113, 122, 124, 125, 136, 150, 151, 199, 206, 249, 251, 253

Evander Crushers, 205, 206, **206**, 239, **255**
Everitt, Tony, 170

Falkson, Aubrey, 31
Farr, Barry, 271
Felbitem, **7**, 10, 88, 89, 127, 129, 131, **131**, 132
Figula, 237, **238**, 239
Fisheries Development Corporation of South Africa, 121
Fishwick, Thomas, 127, 128
Fletcher, Ben, 24
Forbes, Joe, 22, 37
Fowler, John, 127
Fowler Construction, 79, 88, 89, 116, 127, 129, 131, 139, 145, 146
Fowler Holdings, 79, 88, 118, 127–132, 133, 134, 135, 138, 139, 289, 290
Fowler Tarspraying Company, 24, 33, 34, 37, 127, 128, 129, 170
Fox, 258
Fox, Steve, 196
Foyn, Peter, 191
Fraser, Vic, 117, 118
Fraser Quarries, 217
Frederickson, Ginger, 181, 182
Frew, Gordon, 236, 237, 239
Frith, T H, 165
Frost, Arthur (Jack), 124, 125
Fuchs, Harry, 87, 119, 120, 122, **122**, 123
Fulton, Dr Sandy, 216

G&W Base Minerals, 57
Garcia, Eduardo, 173
Gardner, Ernest, 266
Garocade, 4
Gassecure, 153
Gay, Shirley (*see* Burger, Shirley)
Gencor, 5, 6, 82
George Wimpey Ltd (*see* Wimpey)
Gillette, Roy, 283
Gillis-Mason, 148, 151
Glauber, Ian, 217, 224
Glisa Colliery, **7**, 15, 267, **269**, 270, 271
Goetsch, Bobby, 249
Goetsch, Diana, 18, 25, 26, **27**, 40, 44, 165
Goetsch, Hubert, 40, 43, 47, 54, 55, 62, 67, 165, 166, 167, 168, 191
Goldby, Panchaud and Webber, 289, 290
Gonome, Alex, 114
Govender, Theogarajan, 176, **178**
Grady, Jack, 35, 36
Gray, Wolton, 127, 128, 149, 286
Greenberg, Mark, 211, 212
Greville, Tony, 57, 58
Griffiths and Inglis, **7**, 10, 146
Grinaker, Ole, 24
Grinakers, 46, 54, 78, 79, 205
Grindrods, 170
Grobbelaar, Pieter, 237, **238**
Groth, Peter, 38, 40, 42
Group Five Engineering, 4, 6, 84, 89, 119, 126, 131, 139, 140, 147–154, 264, 289, 290, 291
Group Five Projects, **7**, **9**, 10, 152, **152**, 153
Guntert, Ron, 104

H&W Properties, 58
Hall, Johnny, 32
Hall, Len, 159
Hammon's Transport, 35
Hancock, Basil, 104, 113, 114, 119
Hansen, Frank, 219
Harbour Carriers Association, 170
Hardy, Graham, 209, 227, 228
Hardy, Terry, 90, 91
Harvester Timbers, 4, **14**
Hattingh, 32
Hattingh, Ian, 193, 194, 196, 197, 198, 201
Hattingh, Wally, 32
Hawkins, Hawkins and Osborn, 46, 56, 91
Hayford Colliery, **7**, 15, 271
Hayward, Gordon, 270, 271
Heddon, Roy, 151
Henderson, John, 71, 72, 74, **74**, 76
Henderson's Transvaal Estates, 16
Hendrik Verwoerd dam, 65, 93, 104, 248, 256
Henning, Peter, 260
Heriotdale yard, 27, 29, **30**, 32, 35, **36**, 43
Heritage Colliery, 266, **267**, 270
Heron, Ross, 209, 239, 241
Hibbert, Tony, 117, 118, 119, 277
High Structures, **150**, 151
Higham, Stan, 193
Hill, Pat, 56, 62, 65
Hills, Arthur, 125
Hirst, Steve, **178**
Hodgson, Bill, 1, 16, 17, **17**, 18, **18**, **19**, 20, 21, 22, 23, 24, 25, 26, 27, **27**, 28, 29, **29**, 30, 31, **33**, 35, 36, 37, 40, 42, 43, 44, 45, 46, 47, 48, 49, 84, 86, 92, 128, 156, 163, 165, 274, 280, 286, 287, 290
Hodgson, Diana Mary (*see* Goetsch, Diana)
Hodgson, John Brailsford, 1–3, **5**, 15, 18, 22, 25, 26, 27, **27**, 28, 29, **29**, 30, 31, 32, **33**, 34, 35, 36, 37, 43, 44, 45, 46, 47, 48, 49, 50, **50**, 54, 55, 56, 57, 58, 59, 60, 61, 62, 66, 68, 69, 70, 71, 72, 74, 76, 77, **77**, 79, 81, 82, **82**, 84, **84**, 86, 91, 92, 100, 103, 106, 117, 118, 122, 128, 131, 132, 137, 147, **153**, 156, 158, 162, 163, 166, 169, 170, 173, 174, 179, 183, **186**, 187, 191, 194, 204, 209, 211, 212, 214, 215, 216, 217, 218, 220, 221, 222, **222**, 224, 233, 246, 249, 256, 258, 268, 274, 275, 277, 278, **278**, **279**, 280, **282**, 283, 284, 285, 286, 287
Hodgson, Mabel, 16, 17, 18, **19**, 20, 25, **27**, 35, 43, 44, 128
Hodgson, Margaret, 31, 81
Hodgson, Robert, 31, 173
Hodgson, Rosemary, 31
Hodgson, Ruth, 30, 31, 34, 35, 44, 49, 55, 81, 269, 278, **278**, 280, **282**
Hodgson, William Alfred (*see* Hodgson, Bill)
Holness, Tony, 198
Holtman, Len, 221, 228
Honeydew Motors, 237, 239
Hooper, Bill, 225, 226, 228, 237, 239
Horn, Robbie, 181
Horowitz, Isaac, 212
Horowitz, Robert, 59, 211, 212, 214, 217
Howard College project, 195, **195**, 198, 200
Hucrete, 75, 76, 78, 204, 205, **205**, 206, 227, 239, 259
Hulley, David, 42

Hume Pipe Company, 212, 217
Hume Prestressed Concrete Products (*see* Hucrete)
Hunasgeria Tea Company, 62, 91, 92
Hut Club, 195, 200
Hyde Park Corner, 5, **7**, 70, **70**, 81, 137, 158, 205, 209, 234, 254, 263, 271, 277, 283
Hydrochem, 198, 199, **199**

Icodev, 267
Immerpan Quarry, 209 (*see also* D&H Lime)
Impala Platinum, 72, 95, 256, **257**
Independent Coal Producers' Association, 268
Industrial relations, 80, 118, 119, 276, 277, 278
Irlam, Derek, 194
Iscor, 5, 18, 34, 128, 129, 147, 148, **148**, 150, 179, 199, 223, 256, 262, **264**

J&J Smith, 143
J B Hodgson Recreation Centre, 162
J B M Hertzog airport, 149
J H Plane and Company, 31, 37, 45, 48, 163, 164, 211, 212
James Thompson, 44, 141, 149
Jamieson, Sandy, 89, **89**, 140, 147, 149, 150, 153, **153**, 154
Jan Smuts airport, 44, 56, **56**, 113, **113**, 129, 159, 248, **248**
Jean Levebre, 129, 131
Jelley, Bernard, 229
Jennings, Digby, 198
Johannesburg Hospital, **137**, 138
Johannesburg Stock Exchange, 4, 29, 67, 72, 73, 74, 75, 129, 147, 201, 233
Johannsen, Des, 179
Johanson, Gus, 147
John Laing and Son, 50, 86
Johnsen family, 242
Johnson, Bryan, 206, 209, 218, 219, 223, 225, 229, **279**, 280
Jones, Colin, 268, 271
Jones, Mike, 194, 197
Jordaan, Geoff, 229
Joubert, Louise, 283
Jowell's Transport, 156, 170, 172, 174

Kariba dam, 90, 104
Keegan, Edwin, 218
Keir and Cawder, 83, 208, 209, 230, 231
Kelly, Garth, 129
Kernick, Peter, 208
Kerr, John, 283
Kettlewell, Glen, 97, 101, 107
Kimberley airport, 63
Kirsten, Noel, 49, 101
Klynhans, June, **279**
Knight, Lane, 246
Knoethe, Herman, 277
Koch, Lloyd, 84, **84**, 147, **153**, 264, 269
Koeberg Nuclear Power Station, 5, **120**, **121**, 122
Koen, Gert, 56, 145, 146
Komga contract, 40, **40**, 42
Kotzee, Theunis, **84**, 129, 137
Kreeve, Mannie, 22, 27
Kya-MP, **7**, 11, 237, **237**, 240, 241, 260

L&F Metter, 113, 222
LSM (Lime, Sand, Mortar), **7**, 11, 204, 237, 238, **238**, 240, **240**, 241
LTA, 54, 219
La Grange, Denys, **82**, 83, **84**, 102, 118, 119
Laburne, R J, 194
Labuschagne, Gerry, 214, 217, 221
Lane, Hugh, 80
Langerman, Peter, 66, 70, 212, 214, 215, 216, 218, 220, 221, 222, 223, 236
Lanigan, Don, 79, 84, 207, 225, 230, 263
Lardner, Frank William, 133
Lattaney, Dick, 47, 219
Law, Fred, 147, 148, 150
Lawson, Mike, 118, 278
Lehlabi, Joseph, 214
Leo, Elmor, 209
Les Entreprises de Travaux Publics André Borie, 65
Lever, Frank, 70, 173
Limmer Asphalt, 66, 107
Little, John, 163
Lloyd, Bunny, 101, 111
Loc-pipe, 78
Lombard, Ray, 200
London Assurance Company, 37
Lotter, Peter, 252
Louis Allen Management Course, 69, 274, 275
Lourens, Daan, 32
Loveday, Peter, 76, 77, **77**, 79, **82**, 83, 84, 159, 162, 206, 207, 209, 263, 283
Lovemore, David, 55, 57, 62, 79, 86, 87, 95, 97, **97**, 98, 99, 100, 102, 104, 105, 106, 107, 116, **116**, 117, 266, 280
Lovemore, Enid, 98
Lowman, Hilda, 18, 128
Lowman, Philip, 18, 127, 128
Lowson, Barry, 72, 256, 262
Lundie, Ian, 137
Lupton-Smith, Mike, 147
Lyons, Viv, 22
Lyons Transport, 22, **23**

M&M Structural Engineering, 262
M&S Crushers, 208
MGC Engineering, 147, 148
MGM, 137, 147, 148
MGM, Gillis-Mason and Clogg, 148
Mabasa, Jim, 21, 22, 26, 27, 35, **279**
Mabasa, Samuel, 44
Macintosh, Roderick, 290
MacNicol Construction Company, 52
Mafusini, Setembiso, 219
Magnusson, Ollie, 195
Maguire, Jim, 62, 91, 113
Makateeskop Coal Mining Company, 266, 267
Malcomson, Brian, **5**, 36, 37, 42, 43, 44, 48, 55, 59, 61, 62, 70, 72, 75, 76, 81, **82**, 84, **84**, 92, 100, 106, 147, **153**, 163, 173, 212, 274, 280, 283–285
Mann and Garstang, 142
Markow, Pat, 114
Martin Marietta Corporation, 68, 204, 246
Mashigo, Mack, 44, **279**
Mason, Tony, 68
Master Builders, 68, 204, 246, 248, 251, 252

May, Meshack, 252
Maynard, Geoff, 221
Mazista, 73, 74, 75, 77, 82, 204, 205, 206, 209, 233–235, 239, 289
McConnell, Pat, 248, 249
McCue, Bob, **153**
McIntosh, David, **119**
McLaren, Ian, 150, 151
McLaren, J W, 149, 150
McLaren and Eger, **7**, 10, 147, 148, 149, **149**, 150, 151
Merrol Fire Protection Engineering, 153
Meteor Motors, 237, 238
Metkor Holdings, 129, 134, 138
Metter, Bill, 222, 262
Mettrex, 262
Mey, Cliff, 262, 268, 269
Meyer, Eddie, 225, 237, 238
Meyer, Jurgen, 254
Mineral Surveys, 58
Mitchell, Allston, 262
Mitchell, Dave, 271
Mitchley, Paula, **49**
Mmabatho international airport, **151**, 152
Mobil, 45, 128, 163, 168, 219
Modder River contract, 98, 99
Model Development, 135
Model Morris, 135
Moleta, Albert, **238**
Moloantoa, Herbert, 80, 277, **277**
Monahan, Peter, 124, 125, 126
Monahan and Frost, 76, 88, 89, 118, 124–126
Monro, Hugh, 71
Montalev (SA), 129
Moodley, Sydney, 193
Mooinooi Crushers, 208
Mooiplaas Crushers, 206
Morara, Paolo, 260
Morgan, Tony, 77, 78, 191, 193
Morris, Richard Henry, 133
Morris, Roy, 283
Mowatt family, 243
Mundell, Jock, 175
Munnik, Enard, 81
Munro, Roy, 65, 145
Murray and Roberts, 79, 109, 176, 209, 230, 262, 263
Murray and Stewart, 196, 217, 218, 228
Murray Transport Services, 68, 72, **72**, 76, 191, 194, 195, 196, 197
Mzimande, Emos, 243

Natal Iron Ore and Coal Mines, 266
Natal Portland Cement, 245
Natal Provincial Administration, 63, **64**, 104, 163
Natal Quarries, 242–245
National Acceptances Limited, 235
National Portland Cement Company, 218
Natref Oil Refinery, 129, 148, 179
Nel, Barry, 268, 271
Nel, Manie, 146
Netherlands Bank, 37, 287
Netherlands Insurance, 37
Nevill, Ric, 195, 200
Neville Payne, 256

Newbury, Ernest, 20, 23, 24, 37
Newbury, Helene, 20
Newman, Peter, 193
Newnham, Cyril, 71, 72, 256
Nicholls, Syd, 262
Nkutha, Joseph, 38
Normac Building Systems, **9**, 151
Norris, Paul, 158, 175, 178, 179
Nucci, Otello, 236
Nucci, Paul, 239, **279**

Odendaal, Winston, 196
O'Grady, Standish, 290
Olive Hill Quarry, 209, 231
Olympic Engineering, 256
Olympic Engineering Rustenburg, 256
Omnibus, 76, 82, 157, **157**, 158, 177
Orange Free State Provincial Administration, 170, 175
Orlett, Marlene, 260

P E Contracts, 102, 107
P E Holdings, **72**, 103, 156, 168, 175, 196, 217, 230
Pakes, Bernard, 230
Palframans, 170
Pan African Engineering, 256
Parem Enterprises, 223
Park Station, 29, 38, **39**
Parrott, John, 283
Parrott, Ralph, 69, 71, 80, 274, 276
Partridge, Bill, 60, 62, 71, 100, 166, 168
Patterson, Stan, 72, 256, 258
Paul's Sand, 75, 204, 205, 206, 207, 210, 225, 233, 234, 236–241
Pavitt, Ted, **5**, 77, **82**
Pelser, Piet, 32
Perma-pipe, 78
Perry, Jock, 107
Peter Clogg Construction, 147, 148
Phillipson, Rod, 222, 228
Philp, Ian, 249
Pickering, Mrs, 68
Pieters, Dave, 173
Pieterse, Dudley, 79, 175
Pine Smyth, **7**, 11, 208
Pioneer Crushers, 22, 27, 37, 217, 223
Pioneer Ready Mixed Concrete, 67, 68, **72**, 75, 176, 204, 217, 223, 224, 240
Plane, Jack, 31, 37, 44, 45, 48, 49, **50**, 59, 60, 74, 156, 163, 168, 204, 211, 212, 222, **222**, 274, 287
Plint, Arthur, 133
Pluck, Alan, 208
Plumb, Joan, 81, 82, 283
Pollution abatement centres, **14**, 194, 196, 197, **197**, 198, **198**, 200
Portland Cement Institute, 104, 212, 214, 216, 217, 220
Post Office Department, 102, 153
Potgieter, Paul, 198
Potgieter, 'Pottie', 219
Powell Duffryn Pollution Control, 78
Press, John, 278
Pretoria Portland Cement, 139, **139**, 140, 150, 217, 218

Prinsloo, Dries, 147
Professional Hauliers Association, 162
Project Design and Management Services, 262
Project Engineering, 72, **72**, 76, 252, 256, **257**, 258, 259, 260, 262, 289
Project Services, 256
Proudfoot, Mike, 189, 190
Proudfoot's Transport, 21
Public Works Department, 26
Pumpmix, 219, 220
Purle Brothers (*see* Purle UK)
Purle Industrial Waste Disposal, 68, 70, **72**, 75, 76, 77, 80, 159, 191–197, 247
Purle Landfill, 194
Purle UK, 68, 77, 191, 193, 194, 197

Quarryman, 175, 209, 230, **232**

R B Taylor and Hoar, 30, 35
R H Morris, **7**, **8**, 10, 88, 89, 127, 129, 131, 133–136, 139, 219
Racec Construction, 129
Rademeyer, Caspar, 193
Ranch Building Materials, 237
Rand Founders, **7**, 15, 260, **261**, 264
Rand Mines, 67, 193, 204, 212, 216, 218, 223
Randles, Peter, 223, 227
Randmix, 75, 202, 206, 207, 224, 225, 243, 253
Ransdayal, Vinod, 118
Rapidmix, 223
Read, Basil, 86, 149, 150
Read, Peter, 135, 136
Ready Mixed Concrete, **7**, 11, **11**, 59, 66, 67, 68, 70, 72, **72**, 73, 75, 141, 173, 175, 200, 204, 206, 207, 209, 211–232, 236, 238, 239, 240, 245, 246, 252, 275, 287, 289
Reef Levebre, 151
Refrigerated Transport, 76, 158, 177
Reliable Production Company, 153
Reoch, Jim, 68, 215, 223
Reservoir Hills contract, 42, 50, **51**, 56
Richards, Grace, 43
Richards, Whitmore, 59
Richards Bay, 5, 86, 113, 114, 115, 116, 153, **225**, 226, 259, 263, 264, 270
Richardson, Ken, 92
Rifkind, Cecil, 113
Rights issue, 5, 67, 75, 288, 289
Ritemix, 228
Roadmix, **7**, 10, 88, 89, 132, 145–146
Robbins, Ron, 270
Roberts Construction, 70, 137, 147, 148, 152, 215, 216, 218, 240
Robertson, Keith, 217
Robinson, Bill, 283
Robson, Ruth Reid (*see* Hodgson, Ruth)
Robson, Tom, 37, 44, 45, 287
Rodd, Wally, 115
Rolfe, Terry, 76, 205, 237, 239
Rooikraal Quarry, **12**, 208, **210**
Roscoe, Rodney, 193
Rossiter, O B, 113
Roux, Con, 46, 47, 49, 55, 62, 65, 93, 212
Rowan, Craig, 248
Rowe, Dennis, 188

Rowlings, Bill, 40, 44, **279**
Rubbish Removers, 196
Ruth Venture, 269, **270**

SA Townships Mining and Finance Corporation, 23
SAFIC Resources, 207, 253
SAPPI, 56, 58, 71, 82, 126, **149**, 150, 151
SWA Road Construction, 55, 58
Sable Construction, 104
Saldanha Bay, 5, 110, 122, 152, 228, 256
Sandiford, Steve, 77, 246, 248, 249
Sasol, 129, 131, 198, 199
Sasol II, 5, 125, 150, 157, 205, 263
Sasol III, 5, 125, 150, 157
Satmar, 40, 164, 169
Savage, Andrew, 2, 6, 57, 62, 79, 86, 87, 96, 97, 98, 100, 101, 102, 103, 106, 107, 116, **116**, 117, 217, 256, 266, 280
Savage, Hugh, 98, 271
Savage, Twinks, 98
Savage and Hill, 96
Savage and Lovemore, **7**, 10, 55, 57, 59, 62, 63, 66, 70, 71, 72, **72**, 76, 79, 83, 86, 87, 88, 89, 91, 95, 96–119, 122, 125, 126, 132, 139, 208, **220**, **225**, 248, 256, 266, 267, 268, 275, 277, 278, 283, 288, 289, 290
Savage and Lovemore Mining, 76, 117, 266–272
Savage and Son, 96, **96**, 97, 98, 100, 102, 217
Savage and Woodward Quarries, 218, 256
Savbulk, 269
Savico Holdings, 267
Savmore Colliery, **7**, 15, **15**, **265**, 266, 267, **268**, 271
Scheepers, Jannie, 140
Schonken, Johan, 66, 94, 106, 113
Schoonbee, Gerry, 52, 62, 66, 79, **82**, 88, 91, 92, 95, 100, 101, 104, 106, 107, 113, 118, **119**, 125, 132, 266, 268, 269, 280
Scott, Peter, 197, 199
Scott and De Waal, 38
Serrano, Tony, 173
Servitek, 153
Seven T Construction, 86, 114, 115
Sevmin Coal, 267
Sharland, Mabel Victoria (*see* Hodgson, Mabel)
Sharpe, Beattie, 233
Shell, 156, 163, 164, 168, 198
Shemer, Lionel, 107
Shephard, David, 202, 249, 250
Shire & Co, 242, **242**
Shires Quarry, 75, 204, 205, 210, 239, 242, 243, **244**, 245, 289
Sibson, Ken, 190
Skolz, Gert, 140
Slabbert, Peter, 137
Smetherham, John, 249
Smith, David, 202
Smith, Hugh, **5**, 71, **82**
Smith, Peter, 206
Snell, Trevor, 55, 56, 283
Société Dumez, 65
Socony, 45, 156, 163, 164, 165, **165**
Sofam, 129
Sokolic, Frank, 219, 229

South African Industrial Development Corporation, 214, 262
South African Iron and Steel Corporation (see Iscor)
South African Railways, 57, 98, 102, 114, 116, 125, 149, 157, 158, 170, 198, 205, 219, 251, 262, 270
South West Africa Administration, 54
Southern Waste, 196
Southey, Joe, 191, 193
Spiers, Brian, 209, 217, 218, 230
Spring, Ronnie, 141
Springbok contract, 55, 99
Stag Bulk Transports, 156, 170, 171, 173
Standard Bank, 133, **133**, 135, 248, 287
Standard Merchant Bank, 73
Standard Oil Company of South Africa (see Socony)
Stein, Jack, 32
Stelmo, 259
Stemco (see Stelmo)
Stemmett, Mervyn, 250, 252
Sterkfontein Hospital, 31
Stevens, Trevor, 247, 250, **250**, 252
Stevenson, Bob, 141, **141**, 142, 143, 144, 221
Stevenson Construction, **7**, 10, 88, 89, 141–144
Steyn, Peter, 228, 248, 252
Stone, Terry, **84**, 283
Stratten, Tommy, 59
Straughan, Clive, 269
Strelitz and Mitchell, 290
Strydom, Dirkie, 178, 179
Strydom, Fatty, 40, 56, 57, **164**
Strydom, Koen, 57
Sunde, Edward, 49, 55, 62, 66, 92, 93, 94, 95, 99, 100, 106, 107, 117, 119, **119**, 280
Supermix, 223
Swait, John, 170
Swemsa Engineering, 263, 264
Swerdlow, Alf, 45, 50, 163, 164, 166
Sykes, Teddy, 193, 194, 195, 199, 247

T G Vorster, 86, 104
Taal, Maarten, 107, 111
Tanker Services, **7**, 13, **13**, 45, 50, 55, 57, 59, 67, 68, 75, 76, **155**, 156, 158, 159, 160, 161, 162, 163–179, 183, 184, 188, 193, 195, 200, 234, **254**, 275, 284, 287
Tarmac Industries, 30, **31**, 32, 34, 35, 36, 40, 44, 56, 62, 66, 86, 106, 107, 145, 211, 236, 287
Tate, 40
Taylor, R B, 35
Tazzler, George, 248
Teall, Roy, 278
Thackwray, Jill, 283
Theobold, Peter, 71, 212
Thöle, Lyle, 91
Thomas, Pat, 111
Thornton's Bulk Transport, 156, 170, 175
Till, Lawrence, 173
Todd, John, 162, 183, 186, **186**
Tosas, 131
Total, 129, 131, 219
Trailer Manufacturing Company, 163, 168

Training, 69, 81, 84, 114, 117, 118, 119, **162**, 176, 200, 232, 243, 246, 252, 274, 275, **275**, 276, 277, **277**, 278
Trans Atlas Holdings, 67
Trans Tugela Coal, 268, 271
Treadlite Steel Flooring, 256, **258**, 260
Trencor, 196
Triamic, 149, 151
Trickett, Dick, 102
Tucker, Peter, 150
Tulloch, Lyn, 137
Tweefontein Colliery, 16, 17, 18, 37, 127

Umgeni power-station, 42
Umgeni Quarries, 243
Umzimkulu Quarry, 208, 245
Underwater Construction, **7**, 10, 76, 87, 88, 89, 118, 119, 120–123, 136
Unidrilling, 59
Union Corporation, 58, 59, 60, 61, 62, 65, 66, 67, 69, 70, 71, 72, 74, 77, 82, 86, 91, 92, 95, 100, 103, 106, 122, 156, 166, 204, 205, 222, 256, 258, 259, 263, 274, 276, 287, 288, 289
Union Corporation Public Works, 65
United Bulk Transport, 67, 68, 156, 170, 171, 288, 289
United Tanker Holdings, 170, 191
United Tanker Services, 67, 70, 72, **72**, 156, 170–174, 175, 191
United Tanker Services (Cape), 170, 172, 173, 174
United Transport, 67, 156, 170, 173
Upington airport, 93

V F J Hall, 66, 288
Van Aswegan, Neville, 161, **161**
Van der Spek, Wilhelm, 180, 181, 182, 183
Van der Walt, Syd, 152, 153, **153**
Van Eck, Dr H J, 214
Van Niekerk, Dennis, 99
Van Niekerk, Mrs, 29
Van Nus, John, 104
Van Rhyn, Elias, 219
Van Vuuren, Jans, 159, 160, 161, 162, 178, 179, 180, 183, 184, 186, **186**
Van Wyk, Abie, 175
Vandex, 68, **69**, 249
Venter, Arnoldus, 32
Venter, Bill, 129
Verhagen, Dave, 72, 79, 256, 260, 263
Viljoen, 32
Victoria Falls road contract, 52, 90
Vogt, Jimmy, 37
Voisey, Peter, 256
Vorster, Alan, 114
Vorster, Theunis, 104
Voss, Gerard, 62, 65

W A Morrison, Abel and Somersvine, 30
W and C French, 149
W J M Construction, 105
W J Bulk Transport, **7**, **13**, 76, 159, 160, 161, 162, 177, 178, 179, 180–186, 195
W T Rodd Construction, 86, 115
Wah Kwong, 269

Wakelin, D H, 166
Wakkerstroom Construction, 116
Walter Kirby, 71, 212
Wasteaway, 196, 199
Waste-tech, **7**, **14**, 15, 76, 80, 159, 176, 191–202, 250
Waste-tech Recycling, **7**, 15, 199, **200**
Waterkloof Air Station, 25, 26
Watermeyer, C de G, 212
Watson, Mike, 129, 146
Webster, Arthur, 157, 158
Weedon, Des, 57, 58
Welsford, Aubrey, **5**, 76, 78, 80, **82**, **84**, 276, **276**, 277, 278
Welsh, Iain, 80, 197
Wesco Group, 139
Wessels, Philip, 62, 91
West, Derrick, 175, 178
Wheeler, Hugh, 71
White, Chris, 249
Whites Cement, 175, 217
Wiese, Manie, 173
William Savage and Son, 96
Willowmore contract, 52, 54, 90, 91

Wilson, Boyd, 98
Wilson, Ian, 59, 60, 61, 62, 71, 91, 92, 103, 106, 166, 256
Wimpey, 78, 79
Wimpey Waste Management, 78, **78**, 79, 198, 285
Windhoek Crushers, 54, **54**, 55, 57, 58, 165
Winter, Mike, 200
Wirth, Elize, 109
Wolff, Dieter, 248, 249
Wolton Gray, 128, 149
Wonderboom airport, 63
Wood, Geoff, 200
Woodland, Geoff, 99, 101, 102, 104, 107, 108, 118
Woodland, Gloria, 99

Yeo, Ivor, 72, 256, 260
Young, Noel, 221, 228
Youngworth, Ralph, 71, 246, 247, 249

Zanen Contractors, 50, 86, 91
Zoutendijk, Rowan, 245
Zweiamic Transport, 158, 177